BIRD OF PARADISE

The Blog

Part 2

September 15, 2005-April 22, 2006

A Compilation by

James A. Tweedie

Duncrest Press

Credits

Cover Design © by James Tweedie

Printed in USA by Dunecrest Press, Long Beach, WA 98631

ISBN: 978-1-945539-17-6

Preface

Bird of Paradise (the blog) was inspired by talk radio host Hugh Hewitt, who urged his listeners to enter the emerging world of blogging and engage the internet community in whatever topics they were passionate about. As one of Hugh's fans, I took the bait and opened up a free site hosted by blogspot.com. I chose the name "Bird of Paradise" because at the time I was a "Tweedie-bird in paradise" (i.e. Hawaii). My email address at the time was "tbirdofparadise" for the same reason.

I used the blog as a venue for expressing my feelings and opinions on a wide variety of subjects with special attention to politics (strongly supportive of Republican/conservative views), the war on terror (of personal interest since I was serving a congregation—Mililani Presbyterian Church—with a strong military membership including a significant number of men and women deployed to Afghanistan and Iraq), and theology (especially in regards to reflections on my own ministry as well as Islam in general and radical Islam in particular). As pastor to a politically diverse congregation I felt constrained to keep many of my personal opinions to myself. My blog gave me a semi-anonymous venue to speak my mind more openly than I could otherwise

My blogsite masthead described my intentions as follows

> WHEN I HAVE THOUGHTS ON MATTERS OF FAITH, NEWS, PERSONAL ENCOUNTERS, OR...SIMPLY THOUGHTS BY THEMSELVES, I WRITE THEM DOWN AND GET THEM OFF OF MY CHEST AND ONTO SOMEONE ELSE'S

My first blog entry was dated Saturday, November 20, 2004 and—although there were a few scattered posts later—my final posts were written in May, 2007. My earliest blogs were not illustrated, mostly because I had not yet mastered the HTML coding and use of URLs necessary to make my site more attractive.

As time went by, my readership grew to 400 to 600 hits each week. I networked and posted on other sites on the web and grew a following of folks who read my postings each day and occasionally linked back to them. Recently, as I compiled my posts for publication, I was surprised to discover how much I had written for the blog.

Highlights of my shortlived blogging career included being quoted by and linked to such major national sites as *Hugh Hewitt*, *Rush Limbaugh*, and *Powerline*. My article on the passing of Coretta Scott King was honored as "Culture Pick of the Week" by a major blogging aggregate. One picture I posted in reference to a major international event went viral; ranking third highest on Google search and getting so many hits that it shut down my Photobucket account. My article honoring a firefighter who died in the collapse of the World Trade Center towers received comments from members of his family who expressed gratitude for my kind words. My postings on matters related to Islam generated many comments from Muslims eager to criticize and challenge my views. I entered into these dialogues with enthusiasm, insofar as they gave me an opportunity to defend the Christian faith, raise questions concerning Islam, and articulate the Gospel to those who were standing in opposition to it.

Now, ten years later, I find myself more or less disenfranchised by both of our nation's major political parties. While I may still be inclined to be more "conservative" than "progressive," I am now less conservative than I was when I was blogging. This three-volume collection of my blog posts represents a snapshot of my thoughts at a particular time of my life. Even so, I still "own" what I wrote back then, even though any given post may or may not represent my thoughts and opinions today.

Back in the first decade of the 21st century blogging was still in its "Wild West" stage of development, inventing itself as it went along while going through the the process of figuring out its ethics and protocols. "Hat tips" or "HTs" were a way of acknowledging the original source of information culled from other bloggers. I, along with everyone else, infringed on copyright in my use of other people's photographs and I would now have second thoughts about posting so many photographs of adults and children in my congregation without their permission. I did, however, consciously make an effort to never mention the name of my congregation by name, or to mention the name "Tweedie" or the names of my wife or three daughters in the text of my posts. This was done to prevent anyone searching for these names on the internet to link them with my blog.

I did most of my writing in the evenings after my wife had gone to bed for the night and my attempts to create articulate postings on the fly improved my writing skills immensely. For better or worse I have preserved every blog I posted, along with every error in spelling and grammar. Unfortunately, some of the photographs that once adorned these posts disappeared over time as html links were broken. Other photos were censored by Photobucket (such as my posting of the infamous Danish Mohammed cartoons) and still others evaporated after apparently offending somebody with enough clout to delete them (or have others delete them) from my Blogspot or Photobucket accounts. For the life of me, I do not understand the logic behind these deletions—such is the world in which we now live.

I have taken the time and effort to preserve my ***Bird of Paradise*** blog postings for the same reason that people create photo albums: To preserve a memory of the past and create a historical record of who we once were and the way things used to be. The entire blog is, of course, still available on-line at **www.tbirdofparadise.blogspot.com**.

I do not expect anyone to ever read these three volumes of blog postings, but I would be pleased if someone did. If you happen to be that brave person, I hereby welcome you to ***Bird of Paradise*** and invite you to enter the world of my thoughts, such as they were from 2004-2007.

James A. Tweedie
Long Beach, Washington
December 2017

BIRD OF PARADISE

WHEN I HAVE THOUGHTS ON MATTERS OF FAITH, NEWS, PERSONAL ENCOUNTERS, OR...SIMPLY THOUGHTS BY THEMSELVES, I WRITE THEM DOWN AND GET THEM OFF OF MY CHEST AND ONTO SOMEONE ELSE'S

About me

Gender	MALE
Industry	Religion
Occupation	Pastor
Location	Hawaii, United States
Introduction	I'm a Christian Pastor in Hawaii. Married with three daughters who are either in high school (1) or college (2). I do not know how to surf except on the internet. Like most Christians I am an optimist and have a sense of humor. My wife is wonderful.
Interests	philosphy, religion, Jesus, Christianity, science, music, literature, sports, world events
Favorite Movies	Lawrence of Arabia, Gandhi, Patton, Star Wars (episodes 4 & 5...the first two), LOTR, most of Monty Python and the Holy Grail, Princess Bride, most of Mel Brooks, Secondhand Lions, most of the "classics" such as W of Oz, Casablanca, etc.
Favorite Music	Anything by J.S. Bach, most other pre-20th century renaissance/baroque/classical composers, Manhattan Transfer, Beatles, and favorite selections from many other groups, including rock, jazz, country, big band...any music that is good!
Favorite Books	The Bible, Lord of the Rings, anything by CS Lewis, all four of the Hitchiker's Guide to the Universe trilogy, and most, but not all, of what are considered to be, "classic" works of literature, I have discovered that they are, considered "classics" because they are really, truly good, (except for Jane Austin who's humor escapes me entirely)

BIRD OF PARADISE

Part 2

THE MIDDLE

November 20, 2004-September 11, 2005

THURSDAY, SEPTEMBER 15, 2005

My Trip to LA

I just returned from a three-day trip to Los Angeles. The main reason for the visit was to attend a meeting of the Presbytery of the Pacific, of which I am a member.

Before the meeting I spent some time with Daughter #1 who moved to LA to pursue graduate studies in August. To her amusement I slept on the new sofa she purchased for her apartment. I remember sleeping on my future wife's sofa when I would visit her at her mother's apartment years ago. I remember Daughter #1 sleeping on our sofa when she has visited us from her own apartment from time to time over the past two years. Now it was my turn to sleep on her sofa! Just knowing that it was my own daughter's sofa turned it into the most comfortable and satisfying "bed" that I have slept in for a long time!

The Sofa

Presbytery met at Immanuel Presbyterian Church near downtown LA. It is a gothic marvel....nearly sublime in its exhuberant excess....what some architectural history writers often refer to as a "gothic pile."

Even so, it has been magnificently maintained and proved to be an inspiring venue for our presytery business on Tuesday night.

Wednesday I spent at the Presbytery's annual Pastor's retreat, held (of course) at a Roman Catholic inter-faith retreat center (Mary & Joseph Retreat Center).

The site offers a spectacular view of the city of Los Angeles from the top of Rolling Hills as it blurs into Rancho Palos Verdes above Torrance. The day was billed as a "spiritual retreat" and there was time set aside for personal reflection and meditation. A lovely, landscaped garden area enhanced this aspect of the retreat.

I connected with some new friends and collegues in ministry and strengthened the ties that have bound me with friends that I have known since my seminary days back in the late 1970s.

All in all it was a good trip. I moved from family (Daughter #1) to family (Presbyery) without missing a beat. "We are all one in Christ Jesus."

As a bonus I enjoyed the pleasure of interesting airplane companions including the Principal of Waianae Elementary School and a rock musician (born the same year as me) from Palm Springs now living in Lahaina!

I also came home with some good ideas stolen from West Hollywood Presbyterian Church and a fresh look at some very familiar and meaningful passages of scripture.

There are good people in LA and I was privileged to have spent several days with some of them.

View of LA at night

Sea Lions Sink 37-Foot Sailboat

Move over Moby Dick. It's not enough now to simply ram the Pequod with your forehead. California Sea Lions have found a new way to sink a boat.

This past week, 18 Sea Lions climbed onto a 37-foot sailboat in a Newport Beach marina in Southern California. Their combined weight effectively scuttled the sailboat, sending her to the bottom faster than you can say "Capt'n Ahab."

According to the LA Times, boaters are being deafened by the barking of hundreds of swarming Sea Lions, people are being attacked, ocean fisheries are being depleted by their voracious appetites and, most frustrating of all, they have decided that they prefer to sun themselves on peoples boats.

Many inspired attempts have been made to defeat this mammalian invasion from the sea, including fiberglass whales, rubber bullets, plastic chairs tied to the side of boats. Some have even given up and resorted to sleeping pills.

The most effective repellent discovered so far is......the squirt gun, or simply splashing water on the Sea Lion's faces. *"These animals hate to get wet," said marine mammal biologist Monica DeAngelis of the National Marine Fisheries Service. "It's kind of funny."*

Several years ago in Monterey, 1,500 sea lions attacked the coast, damaging or sinking over 40 boats and leaving a stench of poop on the deck, so to speak. Not to mention, apparently, a peculiar propensity to vomit.

A 24-7 coast patrol equipped with....yep....squirt guns, finally convinced the sea lions to look elsewhere for fun and entertainment to wile away those leisure hours.

According to maritime estimates, there are now over 400,000 sea lions along the California coast with an additional 100,000-200,000 more in reserve, hiding off the coast of Baja California.

If Alfred Hitchcock were alive today I have no doubt that he would happily turn this entire matter into a lucrative summer movie blockbuster.

Just when you thought it was safe to go back in the water...

FRIDAY, SEPTEMBER 16, 2005

The Readers' Digest 1-Minute Condensed Version of Senator Joe Biden's Stammering

My post title is intentionally long to make up for the interminable brevity (one minute) of Radioblogger's latest *tour de force*. He has strung together little clips of Senator Joe Biden's stammering during the Judge Roberts confirmation hearing this past week. If you missed the world premier of this little gem on the Hugh Hewitt show yesterday you can listen to it by clicking here.

I must confess that it makes the senior (Democratic) Senator from the state of Delaware sound like a complete idiot. That was, of course, the whole point. But the flip side of the story is that it could be done to anyone.

Back in my high school Speech & Debate class we all held a coin in our hands whenever someone would make a class presentation. If we said, "uh" or "um" or "you know" or stammered everyone would start tapping the coins on the desk. People are genuinely surprised when the coins started clicking. Why? Because we honestly do not realize our poor speech habits unless someone else points them out to us.

I learned a great deal from that class. Apparently Joe Biden never had the opportunity to take one like it.

C-Span would be far more interesting and our Congressional orations would certainly be far more interesting if we could issue coins to everyone sitting in the Capitol's public galleries (including public seating in the hearing rooms) and let them start clicking.

Joke Of the Day

My wonderful wife just walked in and shared a question she had just heard on "Regis & Kelly."
If a man speaks out loud in a forest and there is no one to hear him is he still wrong?
Kelly's answer was, "Yes, of course."

My Wonderful Wife says that it was the correct answer.

What can I say?

A Palestinian Needs a Bulldozer

Yesterday somewhere I read about a Palestinian man who returned to his olive orchard in Gaza after the Israeli pullout only to find that all of his trees had been knocked over and buried. He was trying to find a bulldozer so he could dig up and remove the buried trees.

This is ironic insofar as the Presbyterian Church USA (of which I am a member) is proposing to divest itself of its holdings in Caterpillar because Israel uses Caterpillar bulldozers to knock down the homes of suicide bombers and to build their "security wall."

But doesn't the attempt to hurt Caterpillar's finances affect its ability to market its product to places like "Palestine" as well as Israel? If the cost of a Caterpillar tractor or bulldozer goes up, who will it hurt more? An Israeli? or a Palestinian?

The whole point of this "divestment" concept escapes me entirely.

Then again, foolishness needs no justification.

Hamas Blows Up Section of Gaza-Egypt Border Wall

Hamas members cleared an area along the Gaza-Egypt border Wednesday and blew a massive hole through the wall.

According to BBC, thousands of Palestinians swarmed through the breech into Egypt. Some sought to visit relatives, others to buy food and other items.

While Egypt condemned the action it did nothing to prevent it.

Palestinian President Mahmoud Abbas declared yesterday that the Palestinian Authority had regained control over the border.

The downside of all this was brought to light on the Hugh Hewitt show today when Hugh, curious about this incident, called up his (very Conservative) American-Israeli friend, Yoni Tidi, for some insight.

Yoni claims that Hamas and al Qaeda operatives had breeched the wall to facilitate the movement of arms and explosives into Gaza from Egypt.

According to Yoni, the cost of an AK-47 rifle had dropped more than 50% in the past two days and the price of ammunition had dropped even more than that. This, he said, was clear evidence that there had been a significant influx of weapons.

I suspect that Yoni is unfortunately correct in his assessment of the motives of Hamas in this matter. I also strongly suspect that neither Abbas nor Egypt are really telling the truth when they say that they have regained control of the border.

It is in both of their interests to keep Israel distracted and destablized.

If I were a resident of Gaza I think that before too long, I would be looking back at the years of Israeli occupation and remembering them as the "good old days."

Quote Of the Day: Hugo Chavez

Venezuelan President Hugo Chavez has been telling everyone he can grab by the lapels at the UN, that **the United States is planning a military invasion** of his country. He says that he has the maps, etc. to prove it, too.

In a demonsration of either his lack of wit or his lack of touch with reality, Chavez offered this *bon mot*:

In the event of a U.S. invasion, Chavez said the United States can "just forget" about receiving any more oil from his country.

I don't know about you, but I, for one, will find it difficult to sleep tonight with that threat hanging over my head.

PS: Memo to Hugo: If the United States invades Venezuela, we will control the oil...and you won't.

Niger's Prime Minister Tells the World: "Stop Sending Food To Niger"

Niger is the poorest country in the world. According to the aid group MSF, however, over 1 million people have not received any food at all in the past six weeks.

But Niger's Prime Minister, Hama Amadou, knows that national pride is far more important to preserve than a million people or so. Accordingly, he has called for an end to the large-scale food distribution program initiated by the United Nations and other relief agencies.

A large part of the country has already harvested its crops and is already eating them, he said....Between now and the end of September the harvest will be completed. We're happy that these crops are of good quality and that the people of Niger will no longer need any food aid.

He lashed out at donor nations that had exploited the situation to make great promises of aid but had, in reality, done little and sent nothing.
Our dignity suffered. And we've seen how people exploit images to pledge aid that never arrives to those who really need it.

At least 40 people a day were dying of hunger and related diseases in just one surveyed area alone.

No doubt those dying folks are feeling much better now, knowing that their country is suddenly (& miraculously) self-sustaining, that large harvests will eliminate their hunger and that the pride and honor of their nation has been restored.

No doubt they will also return to playing polo, lounging by the pool and debating the relative merits of beluga caviar as opposed to those inferior imitations. *Bon appetite!*

Odd thought: I wonder what Prime Minister Amadou is having for dinner tonight?

Judge Roberts Out of the Frying Pan

US Supreme Court Chief Justice nominee John Roberts completed his pre-confirmation Senate Judiciary Committee grilling today.

To no one's surprise, Judge Roberts did not choke, faint, scream, swear, vow to overturn *Roe v. Wade*, kick a dog or strangle a single Senator.

In short, Committee Democrats were reduced to misrepresenting Major League Baseball's strike zone, croaking over "hapless toads," mispronouncing the word "Viejo" as "Viheo" and finding 1001 ways to slip the word "*amigos*" into a sentence.

For their part, on the other side of the aisle, Republican Senators and conservative pundits spent today biting their tongues and striving mightily to avoid using the phrase "slam dunk" in any of their public comments and interview statements.

By all accounts, including those printed in the New York Times and the Washington Post, Judge Roberts did done real good and is almost certain to be a "shoe in" when the entire Senate votes on his confirmation next week.

President Bush's next nominee, the one who will replace Sandra Day O'Conner on the High Court, will probably not have the luxury of sitting in the frying pan as Roberts did this past week.

It is absolutely, incontrovertibly, without any doubt whatsoever certain, that Democrats will throw the next nominee directly into the fire.

Then again, I could be wrong,

SATURDAY, SEPTEMBER 17, 2005

Hurricane Season in Hawaii

The Atlantic and Gulf of Mexico have captured all the hurricane coverage this year and for good reason. But don't forget Hawaii! We are in a hurricane zone, too.

At the moment there are two hurricanes (Jova & Kenneth) and a tropical depression (Lidia) headed in our direction from the east.

In five or six days there is an 8% chance that Jova could come within 250 miles of Honolulu. At this point there is even less chance of being threatened by Kenneth or Lyda.

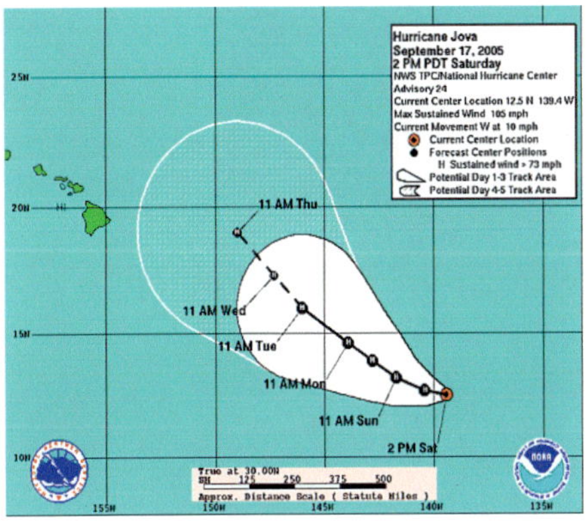

Hurricane Jova On the Move

But....the Civil Defense is already setting up information tables at WalMarts etc. to make sure the people know what is happening and what to do to prepare for a disaster (whether natural or un-natural!).

As I mentioned in an earlier post, Hawaii really does have its act together (in contrast to Louisiana/New Orleans where we now discover there are 4 Louisiana Homeland Security officials under indictment .... LA Times story here... for the disappearance of over $60 million in disaster preparation funds, etc. and the indictments were handed down before hurricane Katrina!).

We will be sharing some information with the congregation during worship on Sunday, including handing out a brochure called "Emergency Checklist" distributed by Civil Defense with the cooperation of FEMA and the State of Hawaii. (Just a thought, why have we heard nothing of the Civil Defense presence in Louisiana/New Orleans?). We will also distribute a list of designated hurricane shelters on Oahu.

Thanks to my good friend and church Elder John, I have the entire 10+ page document for Hawaii Civil Defense re Hurricanes, etc. available for you to see **here**.

Also from John, here is a list of on-line sites the specialize in hurrican/storm/weather related matters:

http://hurricane.terrapin.com/ https://metoc.npmoc.navy.mil/cgi-bin/abpwcreate.cgi
http://www.solar.ifa.hawaii.edu/Tropical/tropical.html http://www.prh.noaa.gov/
http://www.solar.ifa.hawaii.edu/Tropical/PS/nep.latest.pdf
http://williams.best.vwh.net/gccalc.htm http://www.pdc.org/iweb3/index.jsp

We have not had a hurricane hit the islands since Hurricane Ikiki hit on September 11, 1992. Kauai was hit straight on with major damage sustained. Ten years later there is still plenty of evidence of damage from that storm. If one should hit Honolulu and Oahu, the entire economy of the state could easily shut down. Fortunately, we are not below sea level like New Orleans!

May God have mercy on us all.

A Donation to the Blood Bank of Hawaii

Today I donated blood. I do this every so often....not as often as I used to....but once or twice or sometimes three times each year. My blood type is o+.

Lots of aloha from the Blood Bank staff

I made my donation at the roving Blood-Mobile that was visiting here in Mililani today.

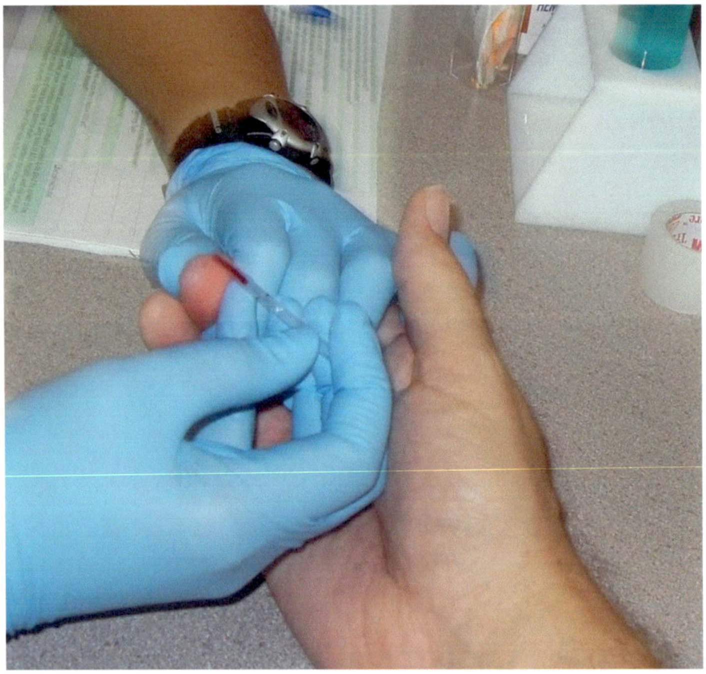

Just a little finger poke

After signing in and filling out all the forms I was ushered into a little room, asked some more questions and then checked to see how my hemoglobin (Iron) was doing. This meant a little finger poke and taking a drop of blood. This is then dropped into a liquid solution. If the blood clots and drops to the bottom your hemoglobin is sufficient and safe to donate. If it does not (and this happened to me once) then you are asked to go home for 4-8 weeks and increase your iron intake before coming back.

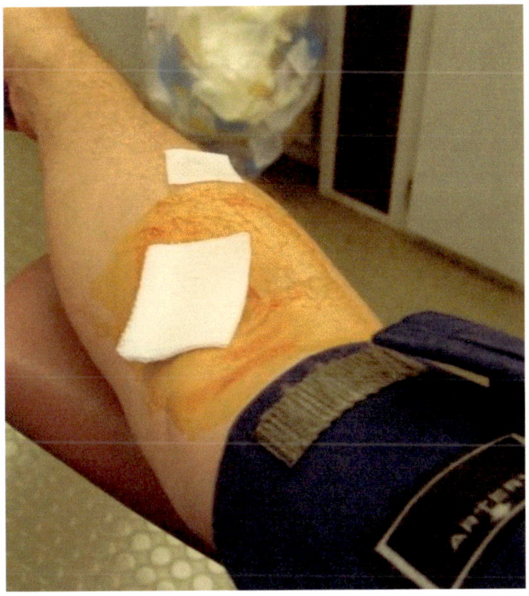

All sterile and ready to go

Next, you get to lie down on a comfy couch where they prep your arm with an antiseptic solution (this is washed off later, before you leave).

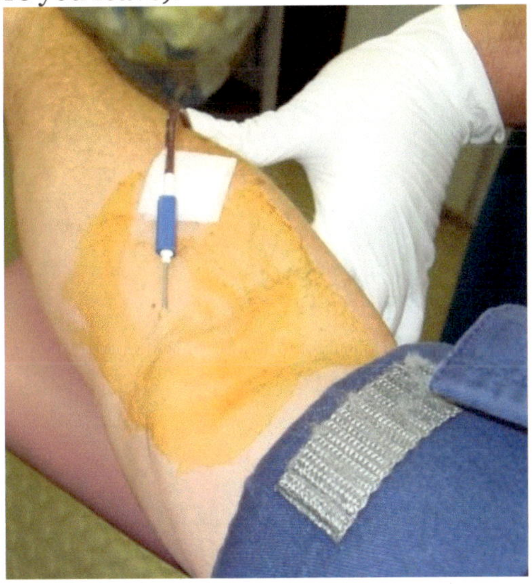

A bull's eye!

Then comes the needle poke. My nurse did a grand job. It slipped in painlessly, right in the vein the first try.

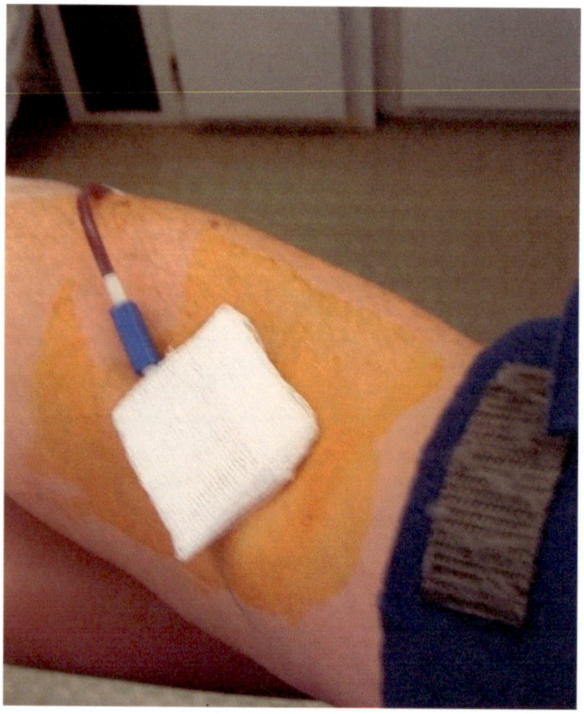

Love and life to share

The blood then moves down a plastic tube into a plastic bag. This takes 5 to 15 minutes depending on how fast your blood flows! I was one of the faster ones today, draining out my pint in 5 minutes.

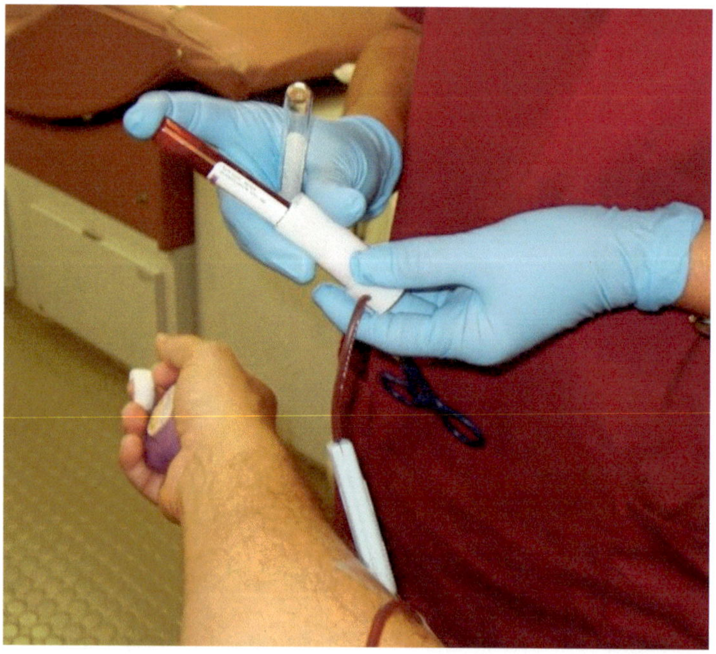

Yep, it looks red to me!

After the bag is filled, five small test tubes are filled up with blood for testing. They check for SARS, AIDS, Syphillus and many other blood-transmitible organisms and conditions. By the time your blood is used to help someone else, it has been rigorously tested and declared to be very, very safe.

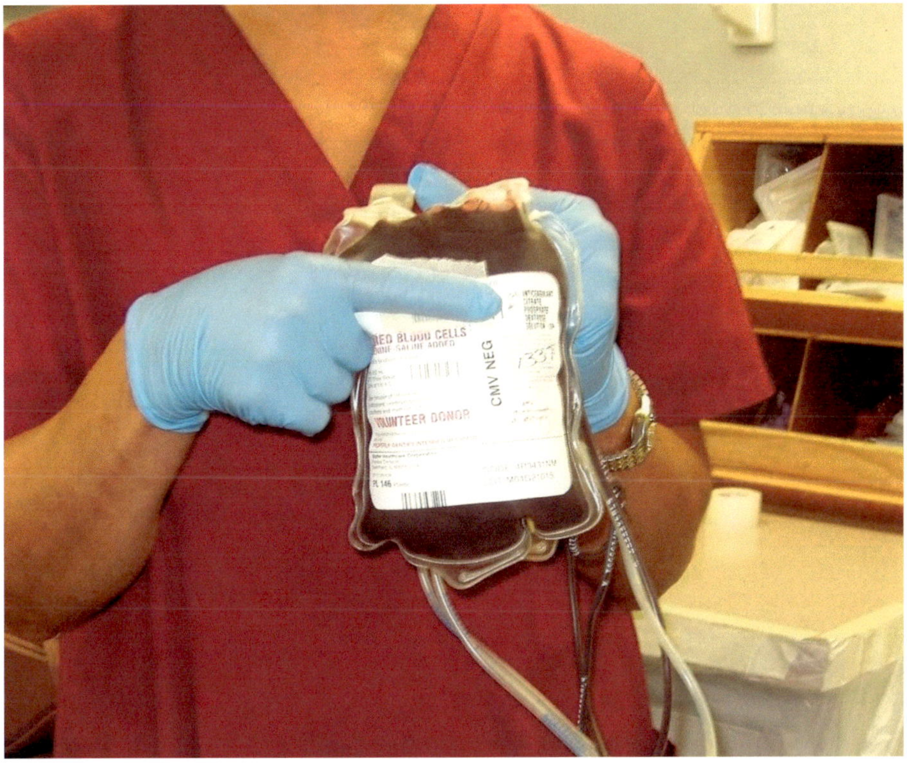

What I have, I give to you

After this, they make you stay put for a short while, reclining on the "couch" and drinking water or juice to re-hydrate.

When it's time to leave you are offered a snack/treat (I took a couple of cookies) and another drink.

Two months later, you can come back and do it again!

Blood Bank of Hawaii

You can read more about the Blood Bank of Hawaii at its web page www.bbh.org.

If you have never given blood before, do so. I have never had any after-effects and you probably won't either!

If you have not donated blood in a long time, set up an appointment with your local blood bank.

Someone you may or may not know will be very glad you did.

HT to the Blood-Mobile staff and for their cooperation in granting me permission to take the photos today.

The "Other" Israeli Security Wall at Rafah, Gaza

As I posted yesterday, Hamas has breached the wall between Gaza and Egypt, allowing a massive surge of Palestinians to cross back and forth along the border area near the town of Rafah.

This wall has an interesting history.

Israel began building it in 2002 to prevent exactly the sort of thing that happened this week....the cross-border transfer of weapons and munitions.

In 2003, supposedly to increase security and establish a clear line of sight, Israel began demolishing over 940 homes (leaving an estimated 13,000 Palestinians homeless) in order to widen the open area between the border and the homes. It was during this demolition that the American activist Rachel Corrie was killed when she laid down in front of bulldozer and was crushed.

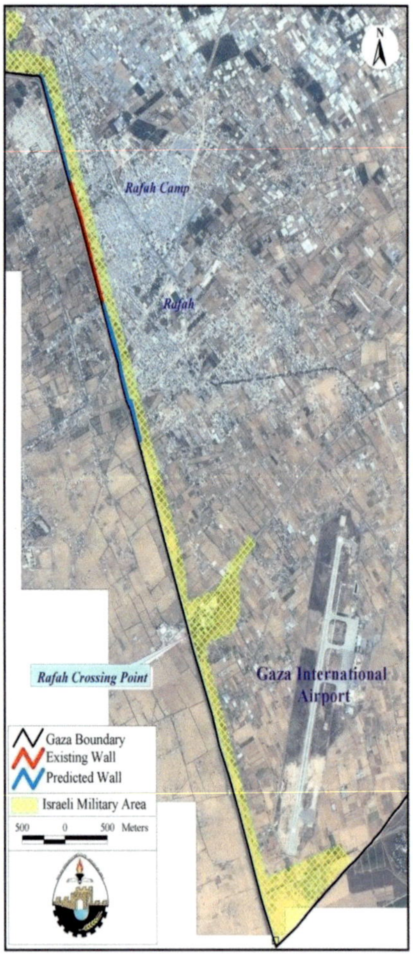

The map shows the extant of the wall and its proposed expansion. Note that the border between Egypt and Gaza is only 7 miles in length.

The irony of the wall is that, although it was built by Israel and has been christened "The Apartheid Wall" by pro-Palestinian supporters, now that Israel has left Gaza, both Egypt and the Palestinian Authority are trying to preserve it!

Hamas, of course, and al-Qaeda, al Aqsa Martyr's Brigade, etc, would like to see it torn down but, the wall that once provided security for Israel is now viewed by President Abbas as a useful control for keeping the integrity of the border intact.

Is it possible that, someday, the "other" security wall that Israel is building along the West Bank border will be viewed by a Palestinian Authority as something worth preserving as well?

For all the international huffing and puffing and indignation over the building of the Gaza wall it seems that, when it comes right down to it, if Israel had not built it, the Palestinian Authority might eventually have been forced to build it itself!

What follows are a few photos of the Gaza/Egypt/Rafah Wall (which is made of steel) and the cement/chain-link wall being built along the West Bank/Israel border.

The West Bank Wall

Sniper tower

The Gaza/Egyptian Wall at Rafah

Part of the cleared "security zone" at Rafah

An Israeli tank takes a peek with the Gaza Wall behind it

Palestinians pass through a breach in the wall last week

Egyptian troops reinforcing the wall

It's been said that "good fences make good neighbors." One can only hope that, in this case at least, it might be true.

SUNDAY, SEPTEMBER 18, 2005

Joke of the Day

Following worship and Sunday School today, Charlie told me this.....As the pastor began her sermon, she looked out at the congregation and asked, "Why are we here today?" Getting no answer she asked again, "Why are we ***here*** today?" A woman in the back stood up and said, "Because we aren't all *there*?"

Qur'an--Sura 42:25 & 40 vs. Ayatollah Khomeini

Ayatollah Khomeini:

Even if Salmon Rushdie repents and becomes the most pious man of all time, it is incumbant upon every Muslim to employ everything he has, his life and his wealth, to send him to hell.
Contrast this with the Qur'an--Sura 42:25 & 40:

And He (Allah) it is Who accepts repentance from His servants and pardons the evil deeds and He knows what you do

He who forgiveth, and is reconciled unto his enemy, shall receive his reward from God; for he loveth not the unjust doers.

Hmmm..... Maybe I took something out of context here......

North Korea Agrees to Give Up Nuclear Weapons Program

A joint statement from the six-nation multi-national negotiation team has announced an agreement in which North Korea will abandon its nuclear weapons program. In exchange, the United States has promised that it has no nuclear weapons in South Korea and does not intend to invade North Korea. According to the agreement North Korea's energy needs would be suplimented by electrical power from South Korea and further discussions will include the possibility of the procurement of a light-water nuclear reactor.

I am absolutely amazed by this announcement which seems to come almost out of nowhere. The past months have seen virtually no movement and no meetings taking place at all. It is only in the past month that formal contacts had been renewed.

In any case, the agreement is a stunning victory for President Bush, who has consistently stood by his demand for multi-national rather than bi-lateral negotiations as had been demaded by North Korea.

The world is slowly, slowly realizing that George W. Bush is the real deal. What you see is what you get. When he says something, he means it. No double talk. No prevarications. No, "It depends upon what the meaning of the word 'is' means."

When a country, like the United States, can negotiate from a position of strength, it can, and should, set the perameters for the negotiations. President Bush has done this and has done it very effectively.

People have criticized him for being "stubborn" or "inflexible" or even "naive" because of this habit of saying what he means and meaning what he says. Other nations, who are used to saying much without meaning anything at all, or saying one thing while meaning another, have been baffled, bewildered and threatened by Bush's lack of international sophistication in this subject. For them, Bush is completely unintelligible.

Now, however, both the President's domestic international critics will have to take notice and accept the cold reality that George W. Bush does really "carry a big stick" and knows how to use it.

With North Korea out of the nuclear arms race, the eyes of the world will no focus even more on the brazen and undisguised efforts of Iran to develope its own nuclear weapons program.

Until now, the possibility of strangling that program short of a military attack seemed highly doubtful. But the position on the field has changed dramatically today and Iran is in a much weaker position that it was before. Bush's success with North Korea, and his success in working with six nations to close the deal will most certainly put pressure on Iran's European "allies" to rethink the appeasement strategy.

I have no doubt that soon, the United Nations will be confronted by a formal proposal to impose international economic and diplomatic sanctions on Iran. It is unlikely that, even if such a proposal should be passed, that Iran would call it quits. Unless there are some impressive diplomatic moves by other Muslim nations to "persuade" Iran to change its mind, I fear that the military option will loom larger in the coming months.

Iran will become increasingly isolated during this period and, with its back against the wall, will have to decide whether, in the long term, the possibility of possessing nuclear weapons outweighs the possibility of the total breakdown of its political structure as a result of a strangled economy.

These are dangerous times. But, by God's grace, less so today than yesterday.

ht: Captain Ed

MONDAY, SEPTEMBER 19, 2005

NY Times Skewers Media Inaccuracies In Katrina Coverage

Tomorrow's New York Times will carry an article by David Carr entitled, "More Horrible Than Truth: News Reports."

The article concerns the rumors, hearsay and urban legends that grew out of the post-Katrina chaos in New Orleans and found their way, often with "attribution," into radio, television, print and internet media.

The central point of Carr's article is this:
Victims, officials and reporters all took one of the most horrific events in American history and made it worse than it actually was.
Where were all the rapes? None have yet been substantiated (although two attempted rapes have been documented). Where is the 7 year old girl who was raped and had her throat slit? Where are all of the murders in the Convention Center (none) and the Super Dome (one)?

Yes, a police officer was shot. Yes, a National Guard soldier was shot in the leg. Yes, some idiot did take a shot at a rescue helicopter and, yes, police from Gretna, La., did in fact turn back hundreds of fleeing refugees.

The situation was not helped by outbursts such as these from New Orleans Police Chief Eddie Compass and Mayor C. Ray Nagin on the September 6 "Oprah." Compass on the Super Dome: "We had little babies in there, some of the little babies getting raped." Mayor C. Ray Nagin concurred: "They have people standing out there, have been in that frickin' Superdome for five days watching dead bodies, watching hooligans killing people, raping people."

Fox News and MSNBC are also cited for allowing on-site reporters to broadcast unconfirmed reports live on national broadcasts. After one outburst, Fox News' John Gibson was honest enough to concede, "we have yet to confirm a lot of that."

Even bloggers are cited as spreading false reports and giving them legitimacy.

It is hard, however, to find fault with any news source that uses direct quotes from Police Chiefs, Mayors and National Guard troops as story material. If media cannot assume that these folks know what they are talking about, who *should* they consider to be a reliable source?

In any case, there were, throughout the entire ordeal, places where folks could go to get the unadulterated facts. In the on-line world, bloggers such as Michelle Malkin, Irish Trojan Blog, Right Wing Nut House, etc., provided detailed and breaking news direct from a variety of sources, leaving it up to the discerning reader to determine what was wheat and what was chaff.

Carr's closing words express the feelings of many of us who were both tantalized and frustrated by the media's hyperbole:
Even now, the real, actual events in New Orleans in the past three weeks surpass the imagination. Who needs urban myths when the reality was so brutal?
Amen.

Being Thankful Is Good For You--But Who Do You Say "Thanks" to?

The good news, being grateful is good for you.

The bad news, USA Weekend doesn't get it.

Here is the little "blurb" in yesterdays national Sunday paper magazine:

Say Thanks. Research shows that people who remind themselves every day of the things they're grateful for are happier, sleep better and exercise more than those who don't.

What's missing? Who are you supposed to say "Thanks" to?

I would wager that virtually everyone who reminds themselves "every day of the things they're grateful for" say "thank you" to God.

Without someone to say "thanks" to, gratitude simply degenerates into an attitude of "I sure feel lucky!"

USA Weekend reminds me of the old saying by G.K. Chesterton:

The worst moment for the atheist is when he realizes he's thankful and has no one to thank.

Click here if you want to read an old Christian comment on the subject.

Patriotic Iraqi Cow Takes on Al Qaeda Single-Handed

A post by Phil & Becky forwards the story of an Iraqi cow found chewing on PE-4 (plastic explosives) with blasting caps stuck into it.

The speculation on whether the cow was a hero or a co-conspirator proves that there is still a sense of humor among our troops serving over there. Read the story and smile.

ht: Mudville Gazette

Political Cartoon Captures Roberts Hearing Perfectly

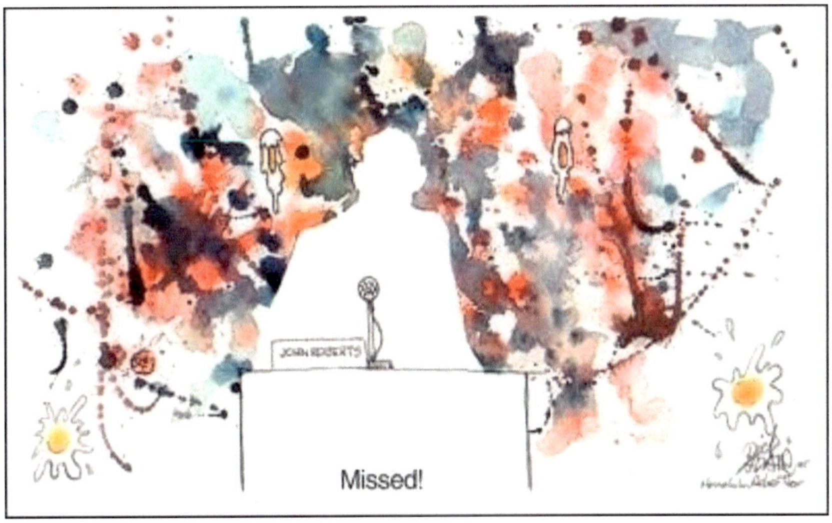

I'm not normally a big fan of Honolulu Advertiser's political cartoonist Dick Adair. I have on several occasions threatened to drop my subscription in response to some of his mean and partisan attacks on President Bush and the war in Iraq.

Even so, he is a good cartoonist and, more often than I would like to give him credit for, comes up with a winning visual encapsulation of a news story.

Today was one of his good days. This cartoon captures the essence of the Senate Judicial Committee hearing on his appointment to the US Supreme Court as Chief Justice. As the cartoon shows, the Democrats keep throwing but they rarely, if ever, hit anything.

TUESDAY, SEPTEMBER 20, 2005

Aussie Alchoholic Acronym Angers Aborigines

Can you tell the difference between "ALCO" and "ACLO"? Perhaps you can, but a police vest manufacturer in Australia and the Aboriginal Community Liaison Officers they were made for apparently can't! At least that's the news from "Down Under" via BBC. Read it here and then double-check check what's on that sweat shirt you've been wearing.

Why Idiots Leave So Few Offspring

This photo, courtesy of CNN and taken in the Florida Keys as Hurricane Rita passed by today, tells you everything you need to know.

Simon Wiesenthal--Rest In Peace

For many, he was an avenging angel, relentlessly tracking down Nazis and others who collaborated in attempting to turn the "final solution" into a reality during WW II. For others he was a fraudulent charlatan, forging drawings, concocting "sightings" of Nazi fugitives and claiming credit for successes achieved by others.

The man was Simon Wiesenthal who died today in Vienna, Austria, at the age of 98.

Far beyond any of his own achievements, Wiesenthal became the international symbol of conscience seeking justice in the wake of the war crimes committed against Jews during the Third Reich.

Besides his renown for tracking down individual Nazi criminals around the world, Wiesenthal's greatest success may have been the massive documentation of Nazi crimes and the men who committed them that he compiled after the War.

Wiesenthal's obituary in today's New York Times is both a cogent and concise compilation of his life, his achievements, his disappointments, his renown and the complexity of his character.

For the Nazi apologists who deny that the holocaust actually took place, Wiesenthal became the symbol of what they considered to be Jewish deception and lies.

"Simon Weisenthal accuses the 'bad' Nazis" (note swastika in corner)

He was both hated and feared, as well as respected and honored. It is said that he even took a bit of pride in hearing how former Nazi fugitives would threaten one another by saying that they might tip Wiesenthal off as to someone's whereabouts.

To his eternal credit, Weisenthal collected criminal evidence while it still was there to be collected and virtually created an international demand for justice following the defeat of Nazi Germany in 1945. He was a lone and controversial voice throughout his life. It is beyond any doubt whatsoever that, without the efforts of Simon Weisenthal, a good many men who had collaborated with evil would have lived out their lives in peace when, in fact, they had no right to do so.

The NY Times obituary ends with this wonderful paragraph:

> *He was often asked why he had become a searcher of Nazi criminals instead of resuming a profitable career in architecture. He gave one questioner this response: "You're a religious man. You believe in God and life after death. I also believe. When we come to the other world and meet the millions of Jews who died in the camps and they ask us, 'What have you done?' there will be many answers. You will say, 'I became a jeweler.' Another will say, 'I smuggled coffee and American cigarettes.' Still another will say, 'I built houses,' but I will say, 'I didn't forget you.' "*

I trust that many will join with me is promising that, in a similar way, we will not forget Simon Weisenthal.

WEDNESDAY, SEPTEMBER 21, 2005

Beachcombing Mystery

While collecting puka shells ("puka" is the Hawaiian word for "hole" hence a piece of shell with a natural hole in it used for stringing necklaces, bracelets, etc.) on Sunset Beach (North Shore Oahu) I came across these little pieces of battered aluminum. I have speculated that they are the remains of aluminum cans, beach chair frames, etc. If you have ever found stuff like it please let me know. If you have a theory of your own as to where it comes from, let me know that, too.

In any case, they look almost exactly like gold nuggest....minus the gold!

Sad Story--Strange Link

The story is a sad one. But, when I saw the link, my first thought was that it referred to something that could be displayed at Ripley's Believe It or Not!

""Rescuers find man with wife's body

Why I Read the News

I love a good story. I like surprise twists in a plot. I like new and colorful characters. I like not knowing what happens next and then watching things reveal themselves piece by piece like tesserae in an archaeological dig.

Great literature does this very well and, as a creation of the human imagination, it captures the essence of life as we experience it every day, with all of its comedy and tragedy.

But literature is simply a recreation of the real thing, which is the daily reality of the history of our life and of the history of our world being created each day before our eyes.

For many people, the daily drama of their own lives provides more than enough to satisfy their need for excitement. Television shows, movies and books fill in most of the rest.

For myself, the news of the world provides a large-scale drama that far exceeds the finest product of the most creative expression of human imagination.

History, both human and cosmic, fascinates me because it transcends me. It is the context in which I live and move and have my being. Personally, I am little more than a very minor sub-plot in the story line. Sometimes a minor sub-plot, like Rosencranz & Guildenstern in Hamlet, can become somewhat interesting in their own right. But the greater story in which they exist is what ultimately gives them meaning and purpose.

The daily news of my life, on every scale, gives meaning and purpose to my life as well.

Keeping up with the news enlarges my world and, in a mysterious sort of way, enlarges me as a result.

The accuracy of the news that I read or watch each day is also very important, for I want my reality to be grounded in....well....reality!...and reality is nothing less than truth itself. If my understanding of the world around me is based on lies and half-truths then the context of my life and the meaning and purpose I derive from it will be false as well.

Deep down inside of me is a place, or a voice, or a hunger that compels me to believe that the news of the day, even that on a cosmic scale, is still too small to satisfy. There is, there must be a reality, a truth, that transcends time and space and, in its turn, gives meaning and purpose to it all.

This I believe to be a transcendent or super"natural" world....what is often called the "spiritual" world. As a Christian I believe that "God" (who transcends even the "spiritual") has revealed a few key pieces of this otherwise hidden reality to me.

The most important piece of this reality that God has revealed (meaning it came to us, we didn't "figure it out" or "make it up") is the person of Jesus Christ. This is the man who said, "I and the Father are one." "He who has seen me has seen the Father." "I am the way, the truth and the life." "You shall know the truth and the truth shall set you free." This is the man who died on a cross, but transcended death.

Because I believe and trust in Jesus Christ, I am compelled to believe that God is good, loving, just, merciful and sovereign (meaning having final authority over all things). I believe that I live and move and have my being ultimately in God, and not just in this world.

The meaning and purpose of my life, although obscured by the complexities and confusions of the created world, are revealed, clarified and validated only in a true knowledge of God.

This is why I find the Bible to be so compelling. For the Bible is, indeed, "The Greatest Story Ever Told." It provides the larger context for the news of the day. It provides the larger context for the daily unfolding of my own life. It does, in fact, allow me to "read the signs of the times" in a way that is consistent and satisfying....as well as motivating.

The drama of my personal life is grounded in: 1. Loving God with all my heart, with all my soul, with all my mind and with all my strength; and, 2. Loving my neighbor as myself.

The fact that the world is a place of violent conflict and a place where love of God and love of neighbor is rarely encouraged makes living this sort of life a difficult and challenging one. But I have learned to take the good with the bad. I accept the presence of evil and of good. And I have learned to stand firm on the side of God's goodness, love, mercy, justice and power.

I know my place in the world.

I may not know what will come next in the story, but, because God has given us a "sneak preview," I do know how the story will end: Those who seek to live out God's purpose in their lives in the manner revealed to us by Jesus will, in the end, receive what they seek. On that day I will at last be satisfied.

And that is why I read the news.

Good News Drama As Crippled Airliner Makes Spectacular Landing In Los Angeles

A JetBlue passenger jet heading from Burbank to New York City suffered a jammed front landing gear immediately after take-off today. After three hours of burning off fuel (both for safety and to lighten the airplane) the pilot made a textbook landing. The nose gear did not straighten out but remained in place even after the tires had disintegrated. Sparks flew and flamed but the plane came to a safe stop and all passengers were removed without incident.
You can watch the video of the landing (and I think you should) by clicking on the (FoxNews) link above and then clicking where it says, "video."

One odd note is that JetBlue carries live television feeds on its on-board screens. The passengers were able to watch the local news coverage of their situation as they circled. I do not yet know if the screens were turned off during the actual landing or not. Given the fact that the oxygen masked dropped down and the passengers were ordered to enter the "braced" position, I should doubt that anyone on that plane was considering the possibility of channel surfing at that moment.

Praise and glory to the pilots on that plane who clearly knew what needed to be done and, more importantly, knew how to do it successfully!

No Real Story Except Hurricane Rita

If there is another story that takes a headline away from Hurricane Rita during the next week it will probably need to be something close to being as important as the Second Coming of Jesus!

Today, Rita became the 3rd most powerful Atlantic hurricane on record...a Category 5 with sustained winds of 175 miles per hour.

If I were on the Central Gulf Coast of Texas or even in Houston today, I would be packing my bags and heading for New Mexico, Oklahoma or even Louisiana as quickly as possible.

According to one story, scientific weather watchers on the barrier islands near Padre Island, who had settled into observation areas especially built to house them during hurricane observations, have already abandoned their positions and fled inland to places very far away.

Modern North American civilization has had very little experience with storms of this magnitude. It is uncertain what will actually happen should it remain a category 5 hurricane when it whips through or near Galveston late Friday night. One speculation is that the mighty Galveston seawall will successfully defend against the initial storm surge (although vast amounts of water will spill over the top) but a "back-side" storm surge from the unprotected back of

Galveston Island could probably result in great damage and massive flooding.

Houston is also a mystery. Much, if not most of the central city is at virtual sea level, linked to the Gulf of Mexico by a shipping channel. Heavy rains several years ago flooded much of the city and the coming rain, channel surge, hurricane winds and miscellaneous tornados could render the city almost as uninhabitable as New Orleans in the next several days.

It is hard to imagine that the costliest natural disaster in United States history could be followed by an even costlier one within a matter of weeks.

The oil industry is also at great risk. The number of oil refineries in the Galveston/Houston area is three times greater that in the areas impacted by Hurricane Katrina. Approximately 1/4 of our nation's refining capabilities are located in the projected path of Rita.

It is ironic that the state (Texas) and the city (Houston) that extended the warmest and most gracious hospitality to tens of thousands of evacuees from New Orleans may now find themselves in the position of seeking aid, comfort and refuge from others.

If Jesus' Golden Rule has any true reciprocity built into it, then the generosity that Texas has shown to its neighbors ought to be repaid many times over by us all.

One can only pray that God, in his mercy, will see fit to spare these folks and our nation the awful tragedy that now looms so darkly, moving inexorably forward upon the face of the deep.

Perhaps, in our pride and our arrogance, we, as a nation, need to be knocked to our knees at least this one time more before we actually "get it"......by which I mean that we understand that the technologically sophisticated "Tower of Babel" which we have built in our attempt to be like God is as vulnerable as the Empire's "Death Star" and as fragile as the "Titanic."

America, despite its greatness, is not the measure of the world.

Apart from God himself, the measure of the world for at least the next few days will be a hurricane named Rita.

Lord have mercy. Christ have mercy. Lord have mercy.

THURSDAY, SEPTEMBER 22, 2005

Re Tyra Banks' BIG, BORING BOSOM

It's on the radio. It's on the TV. It's in the newpapers. It's on the internet. It will be in national magazines. For all I know, it's already reached the Moon and Mars!

TYRA BANKS' BREASTS ARE REAL--THERE ARE NO IMPLANTS IN THEM--SHE HAS PROVEN THIS BY HAVING A BREAST SONOGRAM LIVE IN FRONT OF A TV SHOW AUDIENCE (AFTER HAVING ALL THE MEN LEAVE FIRST)--BECAUSE SHE IS A "SUPERMODEL" SHE SEEMS TO BELIEVE THAT PEOPLE REALLY CARE WHETHER HER BREASTS ARE REAL OR NOT

Point 1: Tyra Banks needs to get a life.

Point 2: Who cares?

Point 3: People who care about this need to get a life.

Point 4: Who is Tyra Banks?

Point 5: See Point 2.

Belated Note On Bob Denver aka Maynard G. Krebs

As some know, television legend Bob Denver died September 6 after a struggle with cancer. His death was obscured by the necessary coverage of the post-Katrina disaster.

Denver was famous for his role as Gilligan, the hapless, bumbling but sincere crew member of the doomed sailboat, "Minnow." Gilligan, along with six other shpwrecked shipmates, spent several years on "Gilligan's Isle," somehow able to be marooned and yet watched by millions of TV fans at the same time.

For me, however, Denver was never really Gilligan (who apparently did not have a first name....unless Gilligan *was* his first name....then again, he *might* have had a first name....). No, for me Bob Denver was and will always be Maynard G. Krebs, beatnik sidekick and friend to Dobie Gillis.

Maynard's empty-headed, drop-out incarnation of 'cool' left an indelible impression on me.

From Maynard I learned the art of satire.

From Maynard I learned that even nice guys can be complete idiots and that complete idiots can be nice guys.

From Maynard I was later able to understand that hippies were more often than not, simply empty-headed, drop-out beatniks on drugs but without the 'cool.'

From Maynard I learned that, in contrast to Dobie, there is more to life than girls.

From Maynard I learned that trying to grow a beard without good facial hair was something that belonged only on a TV comedy series.

From Maynard I learned that going to school, studying hard and continuing on through college was the best possible way of avoiding turning out like Maynard.

From Maynard I learned that, if Dobie and Maynard could be friends, then I could be friends with just about anybody!

From Maynard I learned that, if I ever had a son, I would never name him Maynard.

Bob Denver.....you made me smile. You helped me to "grow up" and gave me genuine insight into the adolescent and adult world I was preparing to enter.

Bob Denver.....all evidence to the contrary, you never set sail on the "Minnow;" you never were stranded on a desert island; you were never rescued and returned to the civilized world; you were never Gilligan.

Bob Denver.....you were Maynard G. Krebs. You are Maynard G. Krebs. You will always be Maynard G. Krebs. You will always wear the baggy torn sweatshirt; you will always carry your bongos; and you will always, eternally shriek whenever you hear the word, "work."

I have no need to say "farewell".....because you have never left.

Hamas Turns Gaza Synogogue Into Weapons Museum

Despots and slimeballs love to take other folks' religious shrines and defile them. The Romans, after capturing Jerusalem in 70 AD sacrificed a pig in the Jewish Temple before dismantling it stone by stone. In Africa and the Middle East, thousands of Christian churches have been converted into mosques. When I was in the old USSR, Kazan Cathedral in Leningrad (a city now called by its historic name, St. Petersburg) had been transformed into a Museum of Atheism. Another former church was being used as a sports and recreation facility.

Now that the Palestinian Authority has taken charge of Gaza (sure they have) Hamas has apparently decided that blowing up abandoned synagogues is not enough and a waste of good buildings besides. Today they announced that they were going to convert a synagogue into a........well, read the story for yourself:
WASHINGTON - Emboldened by Israel's withdrawal from Gaza and part of the West Bank, Hamas yesterday announced its plan to turn a synagogue in Netzarim into a museum that would display weapons employed by the terrorist group's members against Israeli civilians.
Oh, sure these folks want peace. Where in Israel do we find a museum dedicated to displaying the weapons that kill Palestinians? Where, even once, have we seen the Israeli occupying army defile a single Muslim mosque in the West Bank or Gaza?

Armed Palestinians, on the other hand, thought nothing of seizing the Church of the Nativity in Bethlelem some years ago, holding the Christian leadership hostage, peeing and deficating inside the church and using pages torn from Bibles as toilet paper.

Hamas again and again has demonstrated that it is a vile, hateful and evil organization that views the death of Jewish women and children as something to celebrate. It is fascist in its intolerance of others and offers nothing but death and destruction for those who follow its path to hell.

It does not matter in the least what Hamas members have suffered in the past. Nothing.....I mean absolutely nothing, nothing, nothing, can justify their consuming, murderous, hate-driven, genocidal behavior towards the Jewish people.

"Oh," say their apologists, "but look at all the good they are doing to provide supplemental financial support for the poor, the educational programs they support, the medical clinics, the social organization of the oppressed. The people love them and follow them because Hamas alone supports them in their misery."

Bunk! Hamas cares about the "refugees" and other Palestinians in Gaza and the West Bank only insofar as they can be used and manipulated to further Hamas' plans to destroy Israel and kill every Jew they can find.

Any Palestinian who does not support Hamas or, even worse, publically questions their influence, power, presence and behavior, is in danger of being accused of being a Jewish sympathizer and then murdered or executed.

The Palestinian people are cowed in the same way that the German people were cowed under the iron boots of the Nazi SS.

One can only wonder what Hamas would do if it gained full access to East Jerusalem as the Palestinian Authority continues to demand.

Faith is certainly not a central factor in their philosophy. They will kill a fellow Muslim without a thought and blow them up on Israeli buses along with Jewish children.

The Bible tells us that "Pride goeth before a fall." Pride will prevent Hamas and its supporters from ever accepting anything less than the total and complete elimination of the nation of Israel from the face of the earth. Pride will prevent Hamas from ever accepting or agreeing to any compromise "peace settlement."

Pride has already brought about the demise and fall of the once proud, productive and peaceful people of Palestine. Wherever they have gone, to the West Bank (then Western Jordan) after the newly established nation of Israel defeated their resistance, to Jordan itself after the 1972 Yom Kippur War, into southern Lebanon following the disaster known as Black September, and now, once again, back to the West Bank and Gaza, the so-called Palestinian "leaders" of every stripe and color have brought nothing but death, despair and destruction to their people.

Even if Israel should call it quits, forsake the "land of promise" and move every Jew in the Middle East to South America, does anyone really think that Hamas or the Palestinian Authority or al Aqsa Martyrs Brigade or al Qaeda or Fatah would ever improve on what Israel has done with the land it has nurtured and developed over the past 75 years or so? Does anyone truly believe that the foundational values, vision and ethics of these people could bring anything but a total breakdown of everything good and beautiful that Israel has planted in the Middle East?

Hamas and its kind offer the world and their own people nothing.

Except, perhaps, the awe-inspiring achievement of converting a Jewish house of worship into a weapons museum.

Wow.

Palestinian Authority Issues "Peace" Stamp Featuring "Guess-Who?"

Yep, folks, the Palestinian Authority has done it again. In its inexorable and insatiable search for peace in the Middle East it has issued a set of postage stamps bearing two of the most celebrated peacemakers of our time: Yasser Arafat and French President Jacques Chirac.

Freedom-loving people throughout the world will want to snap up these collector's items right away. No doubt the people of Iraq, about to vote on a national constitution written and endorsed by a freely elected, representative Parliament, will be especially exited to see Chirac honored in this manner.

Surely, there must be somewhere, someplace, some home or hovel in Iraq that proudly displays a photo of Jacques Chirac on the wall.

Other than the French consulate, I mean.

Loopy Afghan Election Clause Just Might Give the Wrong Idea......

It's called simply, "The Assassination Clause."

As Afghanistan prepares to hold its first free parliamentary elections in thirty years this coming weekend it remains a complete mystery as to who will win and who will lose the hundreds of contested seats.

One thing, however, is clear. If the winner of an election has the bad luck to find themselves assassinated they needn't worry about how their replacement will be chosen or even who it would be.

A BBC report tells us that some concern has been expressed
.....about what has come to be known here as the assassination clause - it allows losing candidates to take the place of the winners if they happen to be killed.
Yep. Sounds good on paper, doesn't it. If the person the people choose to lead them is killed just go ahead and replace him with the person the people voted to reject.

You don't suppose the losers will be tempted to give this clause a shot, do you? (Oops, bad choice of word).

Somehow, when Jesus said that "the last will be first and the first will be last" I do not think he had the parliamentary elections in Afghanistan in mind.

FRIDAY, SEPTEMBER 23, 2005

Two Separate Deaths--God's Will? A Christian Reflection

Two stories in today's news:

Boxer Leavander Johnson died today of complications resulting from a brain hemorrage. The boxer was injured during a featured fight at the MGM-Grand Hotel in Las Vegas last Saturday night. His promoter, Lou Dibella, was quoted as saying, "...this was not a situation where anyone failed Leavander Johnson. ***It was just God's will****. It's a sport that's inherently dangerous."*

And then this story:

> *Don Maurice Airline, 24, of Metairie, Louisiana, who evacuated to Texas and then to Tennessee to escape hurricane Katrina, was found dead in Chattanooga, less than a mile from the Red Cross shelter he had been staying at. He had been shot in the head five times. The motive may have been to rob him of his relief money. At the time of his death he was preparing to move to a motel. He was also scheduled to begin work at a new job tomorrow. His mother, Sheila Airline said, "**This is how God had it planned.** He was evacuated out of the storm and out of the storm he gets killed."*

Tragedy brings emotional trauma and confusion to those effected by it. Always. Every time. It is our natural inclination to seek meaning in such events, to find a purpose that can give some measure of value to the loss.

It is sad, indeed, to be in a position to say, as anti-Iraq war mother Cindy Shehan asserts, that her son "died for nothing."

When the tragedy involves death, something deep within us desparately cries out, "No! He must have died for *something*!" But what is that "something?"

One of the two people quoted at the beginning of this post lost a client/friend/business partner. The other lost a son. Both, almost instinctively, turned to God for the anwer to the question, "Why?"

"It happened," they seem to say. "Therefore it must have been God's will."

This sentiment seems to bring a sort of comfort to many people during such an ordeal. But the idea is not a very deep one and begins to unravel rather quickly if it is looked at very closely.

Could it be that the death of Leavander Johnson or that of Don Maurice Airline was the unalterable result of God's eternal edict? Was it etched in stone that each of these men should die in this manner from the day that they were conceived?

If this is what Leavander's promoter means; or if this is what Don Maurice's mother means; then what does this mean?

A quick glance at he Bible will show us that this cannot be the case. This form of "predestination" or "fatalism" is not supported by the words, the teachings, the history that forms the foundation of the Christian faith.

The very nature of (*agape*) love, central to our faith, requires that human beings be free to act independently of God. Love cannot be "predestined." Love must always be freely chosen and freely given or else it is not love at all. Genuine love of the kind revealed to us in the Bible cannot be artificially induced. Nor can a God of love be the prime mover in an act of evil (such as the murder of Maurice Airline...more on this later).

From a Reformed Protestant perspective we assert that God (Father, Son & Holy Spirit) is Sovereign. This means that God possesses full and complete authority over all things.

This does not mean, however, that everything that happens is a reflection of "God's will" or has been predetermined by God and is unalterable by our freedom (which is only illusory, at best).

On the other hand, the Bible does record many events that took place in response to God's direct intervention...things that happened because God explicitly desired that they occur...things that happened because God personally caused them them occur.

Examples might include the "hardening of Pharaoh's heart," the creation of the universe and "all that dwells therein," the birth of Jesus and the death of King Herod Agrippa.

Could it be that the death of Leavander Johnson or that of Don Maurice Airline was the result of God's direct intervention? Did God not only will but personally plan out and personally cause the death of each of these men?

If this is what Leavander's promoter means; or if this is what Maurice's mother means; then what does this mean?

Does it mean that what the Bible calls evil (and the murder of a man is certainly evil according to the Bible) is, at least in some instances, brought about by the will of God?

This cannot be! If this is even a remote possibility then the Bible is a crock and a lie. For the Bible assures us that "**God is love**." The Bible assures us that God is the creator only of "good things" and "very good things."

Evil, the Bible tells us, is the result of sin...rebellion against God. Is God in rebellion against himself? Jesus mocked this idea, **saying**, "A house divided against itself cannot stand." Words that Abraham Lincoln later used to describe the division of our nation during the Civil War.

But direct intervention is not the only way that God can assert his sovereignty. God is also free to stand back and let the natural "cause and effect" course of events unfold on their own.

In this sense, God either wills or permits things to happen. There are times where God permits things to happen because they are according to his will. The death of Jesus on the cross is perhaps the greatest example of this that we have. God did not cause Jesus' death. But it was of eternal importance that Jesus die at that particular time and in that particular way.

God was not responsible for Jesus' death (although God could have prevented it from happening if that had been God's will). Jesus' death was the result of the sinful, rebellious and misplaced zeal and passion of a majority of the Jewish ("*Sanhedrin*") Council in Jerusalem reluctantly, but unjustly, empowered by the order of the Roman Governor of Judea, Pontius Pilate. The responsibility for Jesus' death is shared as well with all who stood by, either consenting or remaining silent....including Jesus' own followers.

Could it be that the death of Leavander Johnson or that of Don Maurice Airline was permitted by God because it was an important or necessary part of God's eternal plan? Although not directly caused by God was the death of each of these men a reflection of God's will?

If this is what Leavander's promoter means; or if this is what Don Maurice's mother means; then what does this mean?

Well, first of all, it would mean that there is Divine meaning and purpose in their deaths. It means that, somehow, known only to God, some greater good will come as a direct result of their deaths. It means that the fulfillment of God's eternal plan for his creation required that these men die at the time and in the manner that they died.

This, I believe, is most likely what Lou Dibella and Sheila Airline were thinking when they made their comments to the press.

It is possible to see a connection of this sort, perhaps, in the death of so many firefighters and police officers at the World Trade Center on September 11, 2001. "They died so that others might live," we say.

But the connection is not as clear in the case of Leavander and Don Maurice. It is hard to see a direct relation between being murdered or being legally beaten to death and any kind of moral or spiritual benefit to the world.

It is, I suppose, possible that their deaths were willfully permitted by God in order to prevent some greater harm happening at some future time. But it is difficult to see how the progress of God's Kingdom was somehow furthered by these tragedies.

It is true, however, that good can come in response to these deaths. After all, the **Bible affirms** that, "we know that in all things God works for the good of those who love him, who have been called according to his purpose."

In response to this, Christians will always be seeking ways to bring good out of everything that happens in life....especially when bad things happen, or even tragic things like an hurricane or a murder or war or famine or a death caused by repeated poundings to the head in a boxing ring.

For Christians, such events offer an opportunity to put their faith to the test. To trust in God. To persevere in good works. To stand for justice and to offer comfort and relief. Perhaps some new and beneficial safety rule will be adopted by professional boxing organizations as a result of Leavander's death. Perhaps some new method of providing financial assistance to evacuees will be created to reduce the likelihood of someone being suspected of having cash/valuables in there possession such as may have been the case with Maurice Airline.

But this is still a far cry from asserting that God permitted these deaths so that some greater good would result. Some greater good may, of course, result. but that would be determined by how we choose to respond to these tragedies. Not as a direct consequence of there.

There is, of course, yet another way of understanding these tragic deaths. It is relatively simple concept but, perhaps, even more profoud than the others we have considered.

Could it be that the death of Leavander Johnson or Don Maurice Airline was no more than a result of mere circumstance? That Leavander might still be alive and well today if he had only ducked, bobbed or weaved more successfully during his fight? Or if his opponent had chosen to throw a right jab instead of a left hook? Or if Maurice might still be alive if he had chosen to stay in Texas or had decided to turn left instead of keeping straight ahead down another when he went walking on that fatal night?

If this is what Leavander's promoter means; or if this is what Don Maurice's mother means; then what does this mean?

Well, to be honest, I do not believe that either of these people had this in mind when they said words to the effect that the deaths of these men was "God's will."

Sometimes, I'm afraid, things just happen by random accident. Things happen as a result of a culmination of a multitude of individual choices and decisions over many years that converge at a particular moment of time, resulting in what we can only describe as a tragedy.

Those tragedies caused by human choices always carry some measure of moral responsibility by those who were affected by those choices.

Someone chooses to have one too many drinks before driving home in the evening.

Someone doesn't notice the small kink in the parachute line that will become a tangled knot then the chute tries to open.

Someone doesn't make sure that their handgun is securely locked in their home with the chamber empty and the ammunition locked safely away in a separate place.

Someone for some reason lacking a normal human conscience or moral compass believes that his need for $25 is more important that another person's life.

Those tragedies caused by natural forces such as hurricanes, tornados, earthquakes, tsunamis, volcanic eruptions, flooding, famine, disease and plague may well be either ameliorated or magnified as a result of human choices. In the end, however, they transcend the realm of human morality and reflect the risks and dangers inherent in living in a world where such events are necessary in order to provide an environment where human life can exist at all.

Tragedies sometimes simply happen in complete defiance of God's own will or desire. There are times when we must conclude, as the late Bible scholar William Barclay said when his only child and her finace drowned in a boating accident, that "God wept."

While God may extend supernatural protection to us for a particular reason at particular times in our lives (as God clearly did with the young and future king David) there will come a time when God will leave us to fend for our own and bear the sinful consequences of our own actions, the actions of others or a combination of both.

Yet, for a Christian, there is consolation in even this. The Bible makes it clear that the fullfullment of God's plans, purposes and promises will not and cannot be denied. They will come to pass in the time of God's own choosing. We can find comfort in knowing that the coming Kingdom of God has in no way been beaten back or cast in doubt by the deaths of Leavander and Maurice.

In the end, our lives only have meaning and purpose within the larger picture of God's plan for human history. For a believer, there is the comfort in knowing that, in death by whatever means and at whatever age, our purpose in life has been fulfilled and our needed contributions to God's Kingdom and the Good News of the Gospel of Jesus Christ has completed its course.

As the **Apostle Paul said**,

If we live, we live to the Lord; and if we die, we die to the Lord. So, whether we live or die, we belong to the Lord.

For those who die without the assurance of God's saving love in their lives a Christian can only say, "We commit their soul to the care and mercy of Almighty God."

We can be confident that a perfectly loving and merciful and just God will always, in the end, bring about that which is loving, merciful and just. "In God we Trust" is not only a generic motto printed on a nation's currency, it is, for a Christian, the central confession of our faith.

With **John Donne** I must declare that, "every man's death diminishes me" and "do not ask for whom the bell tolls, it tolls for thee." The deaths of Don Maurice Airline and Leavander Johnson, men of whom I know nothing except that they have died, are no exception to this rule. Along with their families and friends I must grieve their loss.

As I share these thoughts I can hear **God whispering** in my ear:

"I take no pleasure in the death of anyone," declares the Sovereign LORD. "Repent and live!"

Consider these words the next time you hear someone say, "It was God's will."

BBC: All the News That's Fit to Bend

A BBC headline today reads, "Israel launches Gaza air strike."

"What?" you say. "Why would Israel violate its agreement with the Palestinian Authority? Why is Israel so eager to break the peace?"

Well, I suppose the answer to these questions ought to be found in the small print, underneath the headline where we read:

> *Israel launches its first air strike on Gaza since its withdrawal...*

Well, there you have it. It would appear that this unprovoked attack may well be the first of many, after all, this is only the "first" since the withdrawal. But what was the point of the attack? What was Israel's motivation for this violent incursion into Gaza?

Oh......even further down in the small print....what do we find?
...after Palestinian militants hit an Israeli town.

Huh? What? You mean to say that Palestinian militants attacked Israel first? They attacked a town inside of Israel? Israel was responding to being attacked first?

Then why in the world didn't the headline read:

Palestinian Militants Attack Israeli Town

> *Palestinian militants flagrantly violated the cease-fire agreement today as rockets were sent flying from Gaza into a civilian residential area inside of Israel. As is usual in such circumstances, Israel responded with and air strike in Gaza, targeting known centers of militant activity.*

That is really what happened. That is the real story. But the BBC apparently wanted everyone who glanced or skimmed the headlines to believe that Israel had acted badly today. Why?

The grotesque irony of this misleading headline (which seemingly blames Israel for the day's violence) is that the photograph displayed directly below it shows the smoke rising from an explosion in Gaza during a celebration parade marking the israeli pullout last week. Apparently a truck in the parade, loaded with militants and at least two large rockets on display, blew up while surrounded by large crowds of parade watchers.

The death toll from the explosion is presently 15, including numerous children. Many other people were injured, some seriously.

I searched in vain for any headline that read:

Weapons Explosion Kills 15 During Palestinian Parade--Children Are Among the Dead

So, in summary, let's see.....the two biggest stories of the day are:

1. Palestinian militants attack Israel in violation of the mutually agreed cease-fire; and,

2. At least 15 Palestinians are killed by a weapons explosion during a parade in Gaza.

Yet the headline reads:

Israel Launches Gaza Air Strike

Oh, those Brits....always pulling onc's lcg!

Rita Sings a Familiar Song

Poor Louisiana. Two massive hurricanes in less than a month.

Rita, like her older sister, Katrina, is, like most kid sisters, just sorta tagging along, wandering just a bit but keeping close enough behind so as to be in the same general area.

Unfortunately tonight, that "same general area"

happens to be Louisiana.

Tonight, through the wind, I could faintly hear these words:

.....I'm goin' to Louisiana, my true love for to see....
.....it rained so hard the day I left.....
.....Oh, Susanna, oh don't you cry for me....

Rita, I doubt very much that we will cry "for" you. I am much more confident that we will be crying "because" of you for a very long time.

For once in my life I am tempted to say, "Why don't you just go somewhere and dry up!"

SATURDAY, SEPTEMBER 24, 2005

12-Year Old's Suicide Over Two-Cents In India

A twelve-year girl committed suicide after her impoverished mother refused to give her 1 rupee (worth 2 cents) to buy lunch at school.

India's Telegraph newspaper said Sania was tempted by the sight of classmates eating puffed rice and oil cakes.

Ms Bewar told the newspaper: "I did not give her the money as I did not have it. I snapped at her when she insisted on it."

Today's Anti-War Protest In Washington D.C.: How Many? & Does That Really Matter?

Calculating how many protesters marched in the Washington D.C. anti-war demonstratiion today does not appear to be a simple matter.

Associated Press, whose article appears on the FoxNews, and CNN web pages state that,

"Police Chief Charles H. Ramsey, noting that organizers had hoped to draw 100,000 people, said, 'I think they probably hit that.'"

The Washington Post, on the other hand, estimated even more:

Police (estimated) *the count to about 150,000.*

The organizers themselves are quoted in the Washington Post:

Protest organizers estimated a crowd of about 200,000 rallied at the Ellipse, then marched around the White House and along Pennsylvania Avenue

Al Jazeera, on the other hand had this to say:

Bill Hackwell, a spokesman for Act Now to Stop War and End Racism (ANSWER) the coalition that organised the march along with another advocacy group, United for Peace and Justice....estimated that 100,000 people attended the demonstration, though that number could not be independently verified.

Reuters stated that:

More than 100,000 protesters flooded Washington on Saturday.

This, in spite of the fact that Al Jazeera (see above) had previously quoted Reuters as follows:

Reuters reported that police on the scene put the figure at roughly 30,000.

USA Today simply said "thousands" but did add:

Organizers estimated that 100,000 people turned out for the demonstration, but police at the scene put the number much lower, from 10,000 to 20,000.

From bloggers who attended we have

-Kris, of Reflections of a Libertarian Republican, who seems to agree with the 100,000 figure and does not hesitate to describe

....the massive scale of the rally....

-Glenn Reynolds at Instapundit quotes emailer Brandon Marx as saying:

100,000? On C-Span I'm seeing a couple thousand tops.

-Michelle Malkin, who has posted many photos she took at the rally, does not even attempt to give an estimate (this might indicate that there were more people there than she would like to admit).

My, oh My! What are we to make of this? I guess that we can safely say that somewhere between 10,000-200,000 anti-war, anti-lotsofotherstuff demonstrators demonstrated in Washington D.C. today.

My take on it is this: Forget the numbers. Liberals tried to mock and deride the so-called "Million Man March" by claiming that fewer than 1 million people actually showed up. This is another example of being "on stupid."

Conservatives should not waste everyone's time on the number's debate but focus on the obvious facts:

1. Lots and lots and lots of people showed up in D.C. today to publically express their opposition to our nation's involvement in Iraq and to roundlyt criticize President Bush for his policy decisions. The anti-thisandthat may not have been as focussed on these matters as the organizers might have hoped, but those two criticisms were the clear intent of the rally.

2. Not too many people came out for the "counter-demonstration." This in and of itself does not

mean much. After all, USA Today reports that people were standing 12-deep during today's parade in Oceanside, California, to welcome back 11,000 Marines in the 1st Marine Expeditionary Force based at nearby Camp Pendleton.

3. While the protests today (not surprisingly) offered more heat than light on the subjects of the demonstration, they did indicate a genuine movement afoot. Whether this movement is derided as simply being nothing more of the "usual suspects" or not will not really matter either. As long as there is a national *perception* of a gathering groundswell of American opposition to the Iraqi War, it will not really matter what was said, who said it or even how many people actually were there.

4. Today's demonstration in Washington D.C. did, in fact, project an image that will most certainly be *perceived* as a gathering groundswell of American opposition to the Iraqi War.

5. Today's demonstration will most certainly signal the green light for further national and international demonstrations of this kind.

6. This will have the effect of strengthening the resolve of those following the (sometimes symbolic) leadership of Al Qaeda internationally and with Zarqawi in Iraq more particularly.

7. It will also weaken the national and international perception of the Republican Party's political strength in both the White House and in Congress.

I believe that the political strength of the Republican Party is not, in reality, seriously threatened by the anti-war movers and shakers. The Republican Base in the United States is not based on emotion (as is the Democratic Base) but on principles, and not simply on one policy matter (such as the Iraqi War) alone.

It is ironic that this demonstration comes at the very moment that the people of Afghanistan and Iraq are poised to take some of the most significant steps towards self-government, independence and genuine freedom in their respective histories.

One can only wonder what effect today's demonstration might have on those who will be voting in those two places.

I can only wonder whether those protesting today are actually hoping that the American & Coalition efforts in Iraq and Afghanistan will fall apart and descend into chaos?

I fear that the answer to this must unfortunately be "Yes." At least among those who have planned and organized the event.

Unlike a similar time in our nation's history, when the anti-war movement helped to destroy two presidents (LBJ & Nixon) and undercut whatever success had been achieved in the war against communist agression in Vietnam, we have a President who will not be swayed by the chantings and slogans of a crowd, no matter how large it may appear to be.

We shall soon see whether Republican politicians in Washington will stand by President Bush or start to waffle and hedge their bets.

I can almost guarantee that those who stand their ground will be reelected and those who waffle will be swept aside in the coming bi-elections next year.

Just as they did in the last election cycle I believe that the American people, while not enthusiastic about the American sacrifices in Iraq & Afganistan, will continue to see these, and other policies and far better than any alternatives that the Democrats are likely to offer.

Americans know that we have come a very long way and have accomplished a great deal in a very short time in the Middle East. They will not want to abandon such an important venture when the third lap of the mile race is almost completed.

It is, of course, in my political opinion, a race worth finishing.

....No matter how many people showed up in Washington D.C. today.

Update: BBC demonstrates the difficulty in estimating crowd size with this little gem concerning the parallel anti-war demonstration in London today:
British police said around 10,000 people took to the streets in London, although organisers put the figure at nearer 100,000.

MONDAY, SEPTEMBER 26, 2005

Orchids In Bloom

Well, it's happened again. More orchids in our garden. Here's the latest. Enjoy. We are!

Spain Convicts Al-Qaeda Suspects for Doing What the US 9/11 Commission Said They Didn't Do!

It's hard to figure this out. When the US 9/11 Commission turned in their final report they concluded that Mohammed Atta, the ringleader for the terrorist attacks on New York City and Washington D.C. had only made certain visits to Europe under certain circumstances (ie. only using his own name rather than an alias) and that he did not meet with an Iraqi agent in Prague, despite of the Czech government's insistance that he did.

Well, today Spain convicted several people of supporting Atta in helping to make the attacks both fully funded, supported and coordinated. Included in the charges is the assertion that Atta was provided with false ID (something which the 9/11 Commission discounted. One of the co-conspiritors convicted was Ramzi Binsalshibh who is important insofar as it was his testimony that convinced the 9/11 Commission that Atta had not, in fact, gone to Prague.

It seems that the Commission might want to rethink some of its conclusions in light of Spain's successful prosecution of these unreconcilable charges. Someone has got to be wrong here and it looks like the 9/11 Commission still has some explaining to do.

If Atta did, in fact, meet with an Iraqi agent in Prague as he was making final preparations for the attacks, then it raises the question....Could it be that Iraq had something to do with the 9/11 attacks after all? And why was the 9/11 Commission so eager to dismiss and discount this meeting?

OTHER NEWS: It is reported that the #2 al Qaeda operative in Iraq was killed today in a gunfight in Baghdad today. Eventually getting Zarqawi himself will not end the "insurgency," of course, but it would break the aura of invincibility that gives the lie to the radical Islamic jihadis that Allah is supporting and protecting them in this reign of terror.

As these top operators are picked off one by one they will be quickly replaced by others, equally commited and passionate but....and this is important.....not as competent. The declining quality of the communications, command, coordination, funding, linking new recruits with existing cells and the like is quickly bringing the Iraqi terrorist networking to a state of collapse.

As long as there are cars, explosives and people willing to blow themselves up there will be acts of terrorism directed against US troops and Iraqis. But the acts will become increasingly random and desparate as the experienced, trained and respected leadership continues to fall by the wayside.

I am hopeful that slowly but surely we are still making progress in creating a safe and sane Iraq. In any case, we should be glad that there is one less person willing and able and eager to blow up worshiping Muslims, bomb women and children and behead infidels.

TUESDAY, SEPTEMBER 27, 2005

China Recycles Executed Prisoners Into Collagen For Facial Cosmetics

You know, when you have a great big country and lots and lots of people it's easy to run out of stuff that you really need.

Take China for instance. It happens all the time. Some poor bureaucrat's wife is having a bad lip day and needs some collagen-based cosmetic to boost up her lip-appeal.

Collagen, at least in China, is not a major natural resource. A quick look through any reference book will show that China has zip....zero....nada collagen mines....even in Tibet and Mongolia which ought to have at least something of value somewhere.

Collagen, unfortunately, does not reproduce. It cannot be grown in a field or even easily manufactured from industrial chemicals in a collagen factory.

Nope. The stuff comes from animals....including people. It's found in the skin, the joints, cartilage and bones.

But the Chinese are no fools. They know the score and they are environmentally sensitive, too. The most prolific animal in China is the human being. They've got a billion of 'em. Many, if not most of them are not really useful or necessary and the folks who really do matter figured out that there was an awful lot of collagen running around and going to waste.

The down side of this was when one of those unnecessary souls was shot by a firing squad and then buried. What a waste! Recycling is a big deal in China. Everything gets used and reused. So, a cosmetics outfit got the idea that it would be patriotic, profitable and ecologically beneficial to make the best of a bad situation and recycle those poor executed folks into something useful for the wives of bureaucrats.

The skin is the best source of PRCDA Grade A collagen and whatever skin is not riddled with bullet holes can be carefully harvested and reprocessed into beautiful and glamorous facial restorative cosmetic products.

The popularity of these "dead man's skin" creams and lotions proved to be so huge that word got out and people outside of China began to beg for a piece of what was making the wives of Chinese bureaucrats look so radiantly stunning, especially in the soft glow of a paper lantern.

Yahoo News reports that Chinese cosmetic products containing collagen extracted from the skin of executed prisoners have already been exported for sale to the notoriously skin-challenged people of the United Kingdom.

It is not yet clear whether those who have purchased these cosmetics are actually aware that they are smearing processed human body parts onto their lips. Could kissing really become an act of unintended cannibalism?

I will not be surprised if similar products begin showing up on the shelves of American stores in the near future. The potential market for such renewable human material is endless. I can see the TV commercials now.......

"Hey, guys, do you....you know....suffer from sexual disfunction....not all the time, of course, but every once in a while and it's really frustrating and embarrassing? Well we have a crushed, dried and reconstituted product that will raise you from the dead quicker than a Rocky Mountain oyster......"

On second thought, maybe we all need to have second thoughts about this before we find ourselves being genetically selected and recycled to provide a healthy-looking shine to the hair of some bureaucrat's wife......

THURSDAY, SEPTEMBER 29, 2005

Hugh Hewitt Goes *Mano a Mano* With Brian Montopoli

On September 28th, CBS's Brian Montopoli ran a post on a subject that he termed, "Journo-Bloggers."

National Master-Blogger extraordinaire, Hugh Hewitt, was not amused by Montopoli's effort (although he said "this is really funny"), especially when it came to this line:
If someone is known primarily as a blogger, even if they've published in traditional media outlets, they won't be on the list – which means people like Josh Marshall, Andrew Sullivan, and Hugh Hewitt are out. (Though Hewitt, who has a radio show, is right on the line.)
The usually effusive Hugh could only manage an almost inaudible "Egad" in response.

Not one to leave any turn unstoned, Hugh brought Montopoli onto his radio show later that afternoon for a friendly grilling.

Hugh attempted to score a quick point by challenging Brian's definition of "Journo-Blogging." The argument fell flat, however, since Brian had coined the term himself and was certainly free to define it in any way he wanted to, Hugh's protestations not withstanding.

Hugh then appeared to hit home with body shot aimed at the "clear liberal bias" represented by Brian's disproportionately liberal-leaning list of bloggers. This was followed by several jabs at Brian's omission of several well-known conservative bloggers from his "Journo" list.

Unfortunately, this seemingly effective assault was quickly disqualified as a "low blow" when Brian explained that he had emailed Hugh asking for his input and that Hugh had failed to respond.

Hugh, stunned by the call, argued that he had not replied to the request because he did not wish to be seen as aiding and abetting anyone at CBS with anything!

At this point the referee should have simply "called the fight" on the basis of "flagrant duplicity" on the part of Hugh.

It was suddenly apparent that Hugh had given Brian the "cold shoulder" and that Brian had "counter-punched" by leaving Hugh "right on the line," and deservedly so.

Had Hugh responded to Brian's email I have no doubt that the article would have included Hugh (and others that Hugh might have suggested) on his "Journo-Blogging" list.

Alas, the "Public Eye" of CBS came out looking more open-minded and noble than the California State Sommelier himself.

One is reduced to uttering the only epithet worthy of this misadventure: "Egad!"

"I Looked Over Jordan, and What Did I See....?

Well, I'm signing off on blogging for the next two weeks. I'll be leaving tomorrow for a two week "study leave" that will take me half-way around the world. I'll be spending well over a week going to, visiting and then returning from the Hashimite Kingdom of Jordan. I'll be joining over 40 other Presbyterian pastors and other assorted Reformed Calvinists on a tour of what the Jordanian Tourist Board has begun touting as, "The Other Holy Land."

Petra, Jerash, Karnak, Amman, John the Baptist's baptizing spot on the Jordan River, the Dead Sea, Mt. Nebo, Medaba, Wadi Rum and more will be my daily fare for the tour.

On my way back I will spend three full days in Manhattan, hanging loose and visiting places I haven't had the time to visit before....Ground Zero (the towers were still there the last time I visited NY), Harlem, Guggenheim Museum and maybe the United Nations Building (last visited there in 1966). I might even purchase a "day of performance" discount ticket to a Broadway show (obviously, one that is not "sold out" like "Spamalot".....still, one can hope!).

When I return and catch my breath I will post some stuff about the trip including some photos.

Until then, Aloha In Jesus. I'll be back soon, I*nsha allah*!

MONDAY, OCTOBER 03, 2005

Trip to Jordan Post #1

Well, here I am in Jordan. I won't take time to say much except that I'm having a great time. I had my hair cut this evening down the street from my hotel in Amman. The hotel wanted 10 JD (Jordan Dinars) but the local barber charge only 3 JD. One of the barber's friends, named Hassan, walked back towards the hotel with me...carrying my shopping bags as a gesture of friendship. Hassan is a Palestinian born in Saudi Arabia but now living in Jordan and attending University studying computer graphics in Jerash. I think he had fun trying out his English on me. His family is originally from Nablus.

Anyway...after one full day here in Amman and northern Jordan here are a few photos of things so far.

This is Wesel. He is a Yemani working hard in the United States to support his wife and extended family who remained back in Yeman. This photo is at JFK just before we flew to Amman. He has not seen his wife in 1 1/2 years.

This is Rory Carroll. He is from Ireland but is a staff writer for the Guardian (UK) newspaper. He is returning to Baghdad where he has been covering the unfolding story in Iraq for the past year. He will return home to England in January. We had much to talk about as we sat together from NYC to Amman.

This is a Jordanian dagger I purchased last evening. I will exchange it for one slightly larger tonight.

This is the Sea of Galilee from the Jordanian overlook at Um Qais. This is the site of the ancient Greek/Roman city of Gadara, the location where Jesus cast out demons from a man and put them into a herd of swine. This is a favorite spot for Palestinians to come and look across at their old homeland, yearning to return. (Click on this one to see the Sea of Galilee more clearly).

Bouganvlilea at the Um Qais cafe/coffehouse where we ate lunch.

At the Roman city of Jerash (like Gadara, one of the Decapolis) we came across Jordanian army musicians playing bagpipes and drums in the Western Roman Ampetheater. Jordan had once been a British protectorate and the late King Hussein had been educated in England, hence the odd juxtaposition of traditional Jordanian/bedouin garb and Scottish bagpipes.

Also in Jerash this evening. Sunset at the Temple of Aphrodite.

This, I think, is a good place to end the post. Aloha and Salaam.

WEDNESDAY, OCTOBER 12, 2005

I'm Baaaaaack!

Yep. I'm back in Hawaii after a 12-day trip that took me over half-way around the world to the Hashimite Kingdom of Jordan. In the days ahead I will be posting some of my thoughts and experiences from this trip. Yes, there will be pictures, too!

Murder Confession Produces Clean Laundry

According to today's New York Daily News, a Brooklyn man confessed to a friend that he had murdered two women and didn't want to go back to jail.

The two women had been found in the man's apartment on Saturday, the day he had moved in with his friend.

So, after hearing that his new room mate had just murdered two women (and had put one of them in his refrigerator for safe keeping) and was considering suicide, what does the friend do? According to the Daily News,

...the friend left to do laundry.

Yeah, that's the first thing that I would do, too....right?

In any case, when the friend returned to his apartment the man had shot and killed himself with a bullet in his head.

I've heard of airing out your dirty laundry, but this is ridiculous!

Bonus Info: In addition to the two dead women, the police, while searching the man's apartment, also found a chain saw and several hockey masks. They believe that the man, "a paroled robber, may have simply stolen the tool to sell."

Sure.

Iraqi Bomb Victim Tells It Like It Is

The New York Daily News (which I read while eating my breakfast in Manhattan this morning) quotes a surviving victim of the suicide bomb blast that killed over 30 Iraqi's in Tall Afar yesterday,

We didn't notice him. He drove so fast in his car. He picked the most crowded area, where people were gathered near the food ration store. I don't thiink those terrorists know the meaning of God, and they don't have the least right to claim that they're religious.

Point One: The injured Iraqi should be told immediately that the bomber was not a "terrorist" but an "insurgent." You would think that those Iraqi folks would have conformed into using the proper "politically correct" euphemisms by now.

Point Two: Al-Qaeda's number two man Zawahiri's worst fears (as expressed in his recently released private letter to Zarqawi) have been realized. Ordinary Iraqis no longer consider that these insane terrorists have anything to do with Islam at all.

Point Three: If this Iraqi man's opinion is widespread among the Iraqi people then it should be obvious that the "insurgent/terrorist" battle for the hearts and minds of the people of Iraq has been lost.

Point Four: If Point Three is correct, then Al Qaeda's dream of setting up a populist Islamist government in Iraq has already been transformed from a dream into a nightmare.

It would seem that the more Iraqis that Zarqawi kills, the sooner the radical, international Islamist movement will fade into historical impotence and oblivion.

These spiritually and morally bankrupt fiends have already lost the war in Iraq. They can continue to kill people (any idiot can do that.....and these people are little more than creative, sophisiticated idiots) but they will never lay claim to any pro-active power in that country.

There are still those, especially among the al Sadr Shi'ites, who pose a potentially divisive threat to the unity and peace of the new, emerging nation of Iraq. But killing people is not necessarily the same thing as fighting a war with the possibility of winning it.

Hopefully, the world media will understand this someday soon.

THURSDAY, OCTOBER 13, 2005

Harriet Miers OK By Me

Do I care who President Bush nominates to the Supreme Court? Yes, of course.

What do I look for in a nominee? They should be demonstrably capable and smart as regards the

law. They should be articulate in their opinions and ideas. They should begin and end their legal opinions firmly grounded in the U.S. Constitution (in between the beginning and the end they can explore any and all the U.S. legal precedent they can find but their conclusion should be tied to the actual wording of the Constitution). They should be respected by their peers....even those who may not agree with them.

Does Harriet Miers meet these criteria? Yes, I think she does...with the possible exception of how she might draw her judicial opinions from the Constitution. This is a big uncertainty but not a worry-some one. Few practitioners of the the U.S. legal profession make use of the U.S. Constitution very often anyway. Even appeals court judges are more concerned with precedents than with a direct examination or interpretation of the Constitution. In most cases, at least, the interpretation of the Constitution itself is deferred to the U.S. Supreme Court.

Miers will have the opportunity to explain what her judicial philosophy will be when she goes before the Senate Judiciary Committee. No doubt she has considered this matter often during her long and distinguished legal career.

I believe that she is qualified. I believe that President Bush is convinced that she will be faithful to his pledge to appoint judges that will tend to read their opinions from the words of the Constitution rather than read their opinions into that document of documents.

Are there other judges or potential candidates for SCOTUS who are demonstrably more convincingly conservative? Sure. But Bush, for one reason or the other, did not choose to nominate them. Why? I don't know. But it is folly to assert that Bush blundered in this nomination as though he simply rubber-stamped the recommendation of others. I am convinced that this appointment represents a more far-seeking vision than those who seem only interested in asserting their personal preferences in the here and now.

I cannot agree with Laura Ingrahm who, on her radio show today, predicted that Bush will soon "do the right thing" and withdraw her nomination in order to satisfy the far-right Republican base.

Half of that base has already expressed their support for Miers. The rest will follow once they have had their say and realize that Bush means what he says and will not change his mind on this matter.

Several leading Democrats (including Harry Reid) have already expressed their support of Miers. It will not do the Republican Party any good for anti-Mier partisans to continue their whining and crying into next week.

Mier's nomination will not be revoked. She will express her judicial philosophy clearly and well to the Senate Judiciary Committee and, in the end, she will be approved by at least the same number of votes that Judge Roberts received at his confirmation.

The nation reelected George W. Bush as President of the United States in part because it trusted him to make good court appointments. It is his job to do so. He has now done so and his candidate does not appear to have any warts or blemishes except those projected onto her by her critics.

Do I wish I knew more about her than I do? Yes, of course. By the time the Senate votes for or against her confirmation I will know a lot more. But I doubt that any of it will change my mind. Or the President's.

FRIDAY, OCTOBER 14, 2005

No More "Insurgents"-- Now, Even the Sunni Call Them "Terrorists"

I have long wondered when the tide would turn. This week, apparently, it has.

What am I talking about? It is this:

The Iraqis are at last referring to those who are bombing and shooting them as "***terrorists***."

They are not calling them "insurgents." They are not calling them "freedom fighters." Whatever it is that the Western news media are calling them, the Iraqis are no longer calling them.

To the Iraqis they are now *bona fide* ***terrorists***. Period.

Two days ago I quoted a man injured in a suicide bombing in Tall Afar as saying:

I don't think those ***terrorists*** *know the meaning of God, and they don't have the least right to claim that they're religious.*

Yesterday, after a bomb had gone off in front of their headquarters, **Alaa Makki**, a senior party official with the largest ***Sunni(!)*** political party in Iraq (the Iraqi Islamic Party) condemned the Baghdad attack, saying the party would "use the political process to fight ***terrorism*** and promote stability in Iraq"

When the Sunni leaders in Iraq start referring to the "insurgents" as ***terrorists*** it should be time for the US news media to wake up and take notice.

Unless we know something that the average, ordinary, man-in-the-street Iraqi doesn't know, we should respect their judgement and join them in calling these terrorists ***terrorists***!

But don't bet on it.

SATURDAY, OCTOBER 15, 2005

"Iraq the Model" Posts a Pre-Election Celebration of Freedom

The Iraqi blogger who posts at "Iraq the Model" wrote these words yesterday in anticipation of today's voting. They moved me so deeply I am posting them here in their entirety. (Note: Be sure to visit the site for today's postings as well).

Iraqi's preparing to decide...

Only hours separate us from a major historic day for our nation (too many historic days for Iraq in these two years!).

Tomorrow will draw a line that would mark the beginning of a new era in Iraq; a constitutional Iraq will become reality. It's only a beginning since there will be more steps to go but it's the right beginning because it's a transition from temporary laws to a permanent-though amendable-constitution on which the people will assume control through their elected representatives and through their own direct votes.

It is really amazing how things have changed in Iraq; three years ago Saddam "won" 100% of the votes in a pathetic referendum that he designed in order to give legitimacy to his reign while yesterday even security detainees were allowed to express their opinion on the constitution through voting and the government and parliament are almost begging the 15 million plus voters to say 'yes'! And although many signs indicate that the document is on its way to be ratified, no one can say it is until the people decide which checkbox to tic tomorrow.

Some people would say "Is that all you won, after more than two years of war and violence? That's only one basic right" well, that is the point; we've secured one key right that can help us secure the rest.

Approving this draft is not the end goal, it's a step among others in this process of evolution in Iraq and it's going to be the gate to more steps until we reach the day when we have a constitution that satisfies and serves the greatest majority of the people.

Now let me take you in a short journey in Baghdad; I woke up this morning and decided to take a tour to see Baghdad preparing for the referendum, first thing I saw and surprised me was a leaflet thrown in front of our door.

It was calling for a 'NO' stating 10 reasons for doing that. I read the leaflet that had the Ba'athist tone with five out of 10 of the points said that approving this draft constitution is a Zionist goal. I tried hard to find a connection and of course there wasn't any and it looked like a desperate attempt to use conspiracy theories.
To give you an example of the points in that paper I'll tell you what one point was "what if an Iraqi woman married an Israeli man? Should we grant their children the Iraqi nationality!!!???" and yes, they used way too many exclamation points and question marks.

I walked away feeling more willing to vote with 'yes'. Baghdad's streets weren't crowded as they usually are and checkpoints were everywhere and roads leading to the voting stations were mostly blocked. Most of these stations are located inside the buildings of schools and these in turn are inside residential blocks which makes them easier to protect.

People on the street, TV and radio are all talking about the coming historic event while papers went on hiatus since yesterday but many of them published the document on Wednesday to ensure that more people get to read it.

Although the distribution didn't go perfectly, I doubt there are many who didn't get the chance to take a look as the document was published many times on different outlets including websites and there were many discussions on TV where articles were discusses thoroughly. Add to this the thousands of workshops and lectures organized by NGOs. So I think it's fair to say that only those who weren't interested in the subject would say that they didn't have the chance to read the document.Of course SMSs on cell phones were also utilized for advertising this or that point of view. Yesterday I received an SMS from a Turkmen friend of mine asking me to vote 'no' and to forward the message to 10 other contacts!Actually the Turkmen front decided to reject the draft some time ago and some Assyrian powers in Kirkuk joined them too so it is expected that we're going to see many 'no' ballots in Kirkuk.In Baghdad, some districts witnessed rallies celebrating the agreement between the Sunni and the Kurdish and Sheat leaders on the constitution and people were flying Iraqi flags and firing fireworks.

The walls are covered by many of thousands of posters and banners; most of which encourage a 'yes' while some call for a 'no'. The association of Muslim scholars accused the security forces of tearing their posters but in fact I saw many torn posters from both sides.

On the other hand, the Islamic Party is winning the respect of Iraqis for its courage and role in pushing the process forward; actually it's a rare occasion where secular people thank and support a religious party for doing something. This can be understood when remembering that secular parties will be the ones to benefit more from the aftermath of this after the new parliament is elected.

In my opinion, this morning's attacks on the offices of this party prove our idea when we said that no reconciliation is needed in Iraq and when we said that civil war in Iraq is not a strong possibility. It has shown that the conflict is not between the average citizens themselves but it's rather a conflict between the average Iraqis and the terrorists and it has shown clear that this terrorism is not sectarian in nature but it's in fact one of politics and interests.

I am so excited but a flashback from Saddam's referendum three years ago still hurts; he wanted a 100% as the 99.96% of the previous one shocked the dictator. I was depressed that way and I decided not to go to the voting office and so did the rest of the family but my father was afraid that not going could be dangerous.He said that maybe one member of the family could go alone and cast votes for the rest of us. We looked at each other thinking who's going to volunteer to do this ugly job to protect the family. At that moment my father said "it was my generation that caused the misery we're living in so I'm the one who should do this".

*I couldn't stop him and I couldn't utter a word but I felt sad for him; his sacrifice was big and I had teary eyes when I watched him taking our papers and heading out.
It is different this time father, no more 100% and a 'no' would make me happy just like a 'yes' would do and no one ever will force us to do something against our will anymore.Tomorrow will be another day for Iraqi bravery. May God protect you my people...you have suffered so much and you will still be suffering for some time but I am sure the future will be bright.*

God bless you my people and all the freedom lovers who keep sacrificing to make this world a better place.

It Was a Dark and Stormy Night--#1

Ferd Lewis, sports writer for the Honolulu Advertiser, is normally a very good, insightful and sometimes witty writer. In today's column, however, had he been writing fiction he would have made himself eligible for first prize in the annual Bulwer-Lytton Fiction Contest.* I quote:

> *For in the day and a half preceding the 6:05 p.m. kickoff, time planned to see old friends and dust off memories, the 58-year-old has had ample opportunity to ponder the turn of events that dislodged him from his native Canada and brought him to Hawai'i, which would become an important crossroads in his life just over 40 years ago.*

*This award is named after the writer of the novel that began with this famous opening sentence:

> *It was a dark and stormy night; the rain fell in torrents--except at occasional intervals, when it was checked by a violent gust of wind which swept up the streets (for it is in London that our scene lies), rattling along the housetops, and fiercely agitating the scanty flame of the lamps that struggled against the darkness.*
>
> --Edward George Bulwer-Lytton, Paul Clifford (1830)

Iraqi's Choose Peace In Today's Vote

No matter what the outcome of today's vote on the proposed Iraqi Constitution, the Iraqi people's demonstration of sheer determination to walk long distances and stand in long lines in order to mark their ballot the way *they* want to mark it is a victory worthy of celebration and thanksgiving.

If anything is at all clear today it is that the Iraqi people have emphatically rejected terrorism and have boldly embraced the democratic process for a free and unified Iraq.

Reuters has published many beautiful photographs of the voting from which I have chosen the following as my favorites. As far as I can see these faces do not represent a nation fractured by sectarian fear on the verge of descending into chaos and civil war. Don't believe everything that you read in the generally morbid media. Instead, believe what you see in these photographs...and acknowledge that what took place today was a very good thing for us all!

SUNDAY, OCTOBER 16, 2005

Howard Kurtz Misrepresents Judith Miller's Plame Testimony

In a widely syndicated article for the Washington Post, Howard Kurtz has once again written on the Valerie Plame “outing” investigation. Today’s article (the one I read in the Honolulu Advertiser, which is not available on-line, is similar but not identical to that published by the Post) purports to be a summary review of New York Times writer Judith Miller’s story, published yesterday, concerning her recent grand jury testimony. Miller’s testimony was limited to matters concerning information she received from Vice-President Dick Cheney’s Chief of Staff, I. Lewis Libby.

Kurtz, unfortunately, appears to have misrepresented Miller’s story on at least two important points and implied potential administration misbehavior where none was really possible.

Error #1: Kurtz states, “During two of the 2003 conversations with I. Lewis “Scoote” Libby, Miller said, she wrote versions of Plame’s name in her notebook, although she believes the name came from another confidential source she said she cannot recall.”

The error here is that Miller did not say that she wrote versions of Plame’s name in her notebook during conversations with Libby. She did write them in her notebook, but did not specify that she wrote them during her conversations with Libby. A moot point? Perhaps. But Kurtz' version gives Miller's conversations with Libby a potentially sinister spin that they do not, in fact, deserve.

Error #2: Kurtz states, "Miller said she initially refused to testify about her discussions with Libby because she believed he was signaling her that she should not cooperate in the CIA leak investigation unless her account would clear him."

The error here is, first of all, what Miller "believed" Libby was "signaling" her is of no import whatsoever. She could "believe" that Libby was a werewolf, but, without tangible evidence, her believing something does not make it so. Secondly, the only possible evidence that might be interpreted as a "signal" from Libby was a letter that Miller received from him while already in jail for having refused to testify.

False Implication #1: Kurtz writes that special prosecutor Patrick Fitzgerald "is investigating other crimes, such as whether there was a conspiracy in the administration to discredit Plame's husband, former Ambassador Joseph Wilson IV."

The problem here is that the Senate's Investigative Committee on this matter already has discredited Wilson; a conclusion that was unanimously affirmed by both Democrats and Republicans on the Committee. How, then, can it be a crime for the administration to strategize how to "discredit" someone who had already discredited himself by telling lies and half-truths?

Kurtz is a good writer and it could be argued that his "facts" are fairly correct. But sometimes the way the facts are packaged and selectively chosen can lead a reader to a conclusion that is as every bit wrong as if the story itself had been a lie.

As with any media summary, it is always good to have read thc original source of the story yourself.

Michelle Wie Disqualified In First Tournament As a Pro

Move over TomÃis de Torquemada, the Inquisition has a new leader in the person of Michael Bamberger, a reporter for Sports Illustrated.

Bamberger, following the completion of the LPGA Samsung World Classic Gold Tournament, told LPGA officials that he believed that Michelle Wie, playing in her first tournament as a professional, may have, after declaring an unplayable lie, taken a unfair drop that was closer to the hole than her original lie.

Required to investigate the accusation, officials first reviewed television video records of the incident. They determined that the video was "inconclusive."

Accordingly, they proceeded out to the course with Wie and her caddy and had them show exactly where the ball had been dropped. They then paced off the distance to the hole from the original lie and the drop. This too, apparently, was inconclusive.

Finally, they took string and laid it to the hole from both ball positions. by this means they were able to determine that the ball had been dropped 12-15 inches closer to the hole. (Wie later stated that she believed the distance had been 3 inches). This, according to the "rules of golf," meant that Wie should have added a 2-stroke penalty to her score. Since she signed that round's scorecard without that penalty included she was automatically disqualified.

Now, the 7th hole on the Palm Desert Bighorn Valley Course is a par 4, 400-yard hole. Assuming that Wie hit a 250 yard 3-wood shot into the bush, she would still have at least a 150 yard approach shot to the hole. This means that Wie dropped her ball leaving approximately 149.66 yards to the hole. This is an advantage worth disqualifying someone for?

So, the LPGA now has an Inquisition and a Grand Inquisitor. It has instant replay review and even taped review of actions taken over 24 hours earlier. It can disqualify a player based on possible mis-remembered ball placements nearly two competitive golf rounds earlier.

Can you imagine this being done in a professional baseball game (Sorry, tape review of last week's game shows that Bonds was out of the 1st base running path on his bunt single. His hit must now be recorded as an out, the runner at third did not score. The inning is declared to have been over and it is ruled that the Giants did not fairly win the game. The Dodgers are therefore declared to have won the game. Boxscores and league standings shall be changed to reflect this ruling")?

Professional football ("Sorry, it appears that the coach's left toe was over the sideline on the third play of the second quarter. This should have led to a five yard penalty and loss of down. The game must be forfeited")?

Professional tennis ("Sorry, it appears that the line judge and referee were wrong after all. The point should have gone to Lindsay Davenport. Serena Williams is therefore declared disqualified")?

Professional golf ("Sorry, although video tape review of yesterday's round was inconclusive, we went out with pieces of string, measured out the distance to the hole and determined that Michelle Wie was somewhere between 5/10,000 and 1.9/1,000's closer to the hole than she ought to have been. Wie is herebye disqualified")?

Oops. Sorry about that. They actually do this in professional golf!

You've got to be kidding me!

Can any professional golfer ever be sure they are actually going to be declared ineligible or not, even days after they have completed their round or even the tournament?

The LPGA should investigate and revoke this ridiculous, trivial, vindictive and outrageous ruling. It demeans the sport. It demeans the players. It demeans the spectators and the television viewers. It is a crock and a sham.

In addition, Michael Bamburger should be banned from all professional golf tournaments for years to come. He is a disgrace, a boor and an embarrassment to Sports Illustrated.

The only bright note in this debacle is Michelle Wie who, with grace beyond her just-turned 17 years of age (*note: oops, I meant 16 years of age*), responded to this injustice with humility and restraint. Her public comment after all of this?

"I learned a great lesson," Wie said, her voice choking with emotion. "From now on, I'll call a rules official no matter where it is, whether its 3 inches or 100 yards. I respect that."

The lesson I learned, unfortunately, is this: *The spirit of golf is dead. Michael Bamberger and the LPGA killed it this afternoon.*

Letter to the Editor: Honolulu Advertiser

> *Note: The following letter was sent to the Honolulu Advertiser today in response to this article on the front page of their Sunday paper this morning:*

I am dismayed and disgusted by the sub-headline on today's (Sunday, October 16) front-page story , "Sunnis, millions of others cast vote." The sub-headline reads, "New constitution could face defeat as some provinces back insurgency." This statement is patently false and is neither referenced nor substantiated by the article it purports to summarize.

The largest Sunni political group in Iraq, the Iraqi Islamic Party, urged Sunnis to vote "Yes" on the proposed constitution. The only province that could remotely be considered to be "supportive" of the "insurgency" would be Anbar Province. It is here that the "insurgents" terrorize, threaten and kill those who oppose their barbaric policy of murdering Muslim men, women and children as part of a futile and twisted attempt to assert radical religious and political control over Iraq. The vast majority of Sunnis, as well as Kurds and Shi'ites, publically refer to these thugs as "terrorists" (not "insurgents" or "freedom fighters") and want them to be killed or thrown out of their country.

To imply, as your sub-headline, that "some provinces back (the) insurgency" is a blatant, calculated and easily-refuted lie. Whatever editor wrote or approved this should be reprimanded and, in addition, a public retraction and apology should be printed as soon as possible.

MONDAY, OCTOBER 17, 2005

Ballot Stuffing In Iraq? I Am So Surprised...And So What?

> *Iraq's electoral commission said Monday it intended to audit "unusually high" numbers in results coming from most provinces in Saturday's landmark referendum on the draft constitution.*

It appears that American-style democracy has finally come to Iraq...complete with the "mom and apple pie" tradition of slipping a few extra ballots into the box when nobody's looking.

Does this invalidate the election? Most certainly it will not. But an honest investigation might shed some light on the nascent growth of real, honest(sic)-to-goodness "plumbers" and "dirty tricks" units within the major political parties in the country.

Take Anbar province, for example, the most predominant Sunni population in the country. Thus far, Anbar has reported voter turnout at 77-90% with 97% voting "No" on the new Iraqi constitution.

Former Baathist Party members are most certainly groaning today, dreaming of the "old days" just three years ago when Saddam Hussein managed to get a 100% voter turnout and a 100% voter approval rating, not only in Anbar province but in every other province in the country as well.

Other provinces with smaller Sunni majorities or near-majorities such as Diyala (Baqouba), Ninevah (Mosul) and Tamim (Kirkuk) appear to have approved the constitution by votes of 70% to 20%, 78% to 21% and 63% to 36% respectively.

If these totals are to be believed then it would indicate that half or more of the Sunnis in those provinces voted to endorse the constitution. This would make it all the more difficult to believe that 97% of Sunnis voting in Anbar province would have actually rejected it.

A quick tally of the preliminary, incomplete and unofficial voting reports (with most of the Kurdish, pro-constitution north and four southern pro-constitution Shi'ite provinces in the south not yet included) shows 2,917,000 (84%) of Iraqis voting "Yes" versus 570,000 (16%) voting "No."

I do not think that any amount of ballot box stuffing could change those figures enough to change the outcome. And remember, many of the most pro-constitution provinces have not even reported their vote results yet!

If this does not constitute an overwhelming endorsement of a freely-elected, democratic, representative and constitutional government by the people of Iraq then I don't know what else would.

If the Iraqi people, including Sunni, Shi'ite and Kurd, wanted to stick a finger in the eye of the terrorist thugs they could not have done so more clearly and decisively than they did this past Saturday.

In every election there is a winner and there is a loser.

Today, at least in Iraq, the al-Qaeda, fundamentalist, radical Islamicist, terrorist thugs are losers.

TUESDAY, OCTOBER 18, 2005

Dreams & Visions & God

Yesterday, while leading a funeral service for a dear old friend and charter member of my congregation, one of her sons shared an interesting testimony.

It seems that just last week he was working on a house he owns in Texas. While in the back yard he inadvertantly laid down on top of a nest of fire ants. He was bitten over 100 times, had a severe allergic reaction and, while trying to return to the house to get in some cold water, he collapsed and, as he recalls it, stopped breathing.

He immediately heard voices and saw a brightly lit hallway. He cried out, "I don't want to die. I have my wife and my parents to take care of!"

He then found himself breathing again and, although in great pain, made a full recovery without even seeing a doctor.

He said that this experience brought him great comfort when his mother died two days later because now, without a doubt, he knew that there was, indeed, life after death....and in that life there was a God who knew him and heard him when he cried out to live.

While not an active Christian, he was raised in the faith (in our congregation!) and knew the doctrine and stories of the Bible. But it was this experience that confirmed for him the reality of heaven, of God and of life beyond this life.

He also shared that, still in Texas after he had learned his mother had died here in Hawaii, he offered up a prayer, saying, "Mom, please let me know somehow that you are all right."

Immediately a butterfly appeared nearby, fluttered around for a bit and then landed just in front of him on the lawn. After a few moments the butterfly took off and fluttered away.

This too, brought him great comfort. He saw it as a clear sign from his mother that she was in a "good place."

For a moment or two I pondered whether this man was really on to something or was simply, out of emotional need, mistaking ordinary things for being somehow supernaturally significant.

I have concluded that this man was really on to something.

God has repeatedly spoken to us and revealed his glory to us through ordinary things.

For example: To most everyone in the ancient world the star was just a star. But, to the "wise men from the East," the star was an omen, a clear and straightforward indication that a new King had been born....in Bethlehem!

Jesus had his disciples throw their nets over the other side of the boat when they had not been able to catch a single fish. When the followed Jesus' instructions, the nets became completely full of fish, literally to the breaking point. The disciples immediately understood this as a "message" from God.

In the Old Testament, Gideon wanted God to let him know whether what he had been told was true. So, he put a lambskin outside his tent one night and in the morning it was dewy wet (when he asked for that) and on the next night it was completely dry (which had also asked for). This, he *knew* was a "vision" from God.

Whether it is a star, a fish or a piece of lambskin, God can take ordinary things and use them to speak to us in extraordinary ways.

This is what signs and dreams and visions are all about: Seeing or hearing or experiencing the real presence of God (and, often, his revealed will) in an otherwise ordinary setting or circumstance.

It does no one any good to try and tell someone who has had such an encounter that it was all a figment of their imagination. The experience somehow becomes self-validating. An experience of God of this kind is by no means experienced as an illusion or unreality. If anything, the extraordinary experience is even more real than the ordinary setting or object that served as the vehicle for the vision in the first place!

I myself have experienced several very powerful (and very subjective) experiences of what I immediately understood to be a direct communication from God. On one ocassion I was miraculously delivered from a completely unavoidable traffic accident. At that moment there was so little hope that I actually closed my eyes in resignation. When nothing happened, I opened my eyes and found that the impossibly tangled convergence of cars had completed disappeared. The nearest car was more than 100 feet away. I *knew right away* and without going through any real thought process that my life had been spared for some great purpose.

This incident was a significant step toward viewing my life as being valuable for God and being useful for others.

On another ocassion I had a dream/vision that both chilled and thrilled me. The vision was a overwhelming re-experience of the day of Pentecost when the Holy Spirit entered the room filled with Jesus' disciples like a rushing wind and with tongues of fire.

I woke up *knowing without a doubt* that God had used that vision to assure me that he was empowering me to serve him in some way. At the time I had no idea what that might mean, but I was completely convinced that, whatever God called me to do, I would be given the means to accomplish it.

It is easy, of course, to mistake indigestion for being a message from God. A psychiatrist I once knew was convinced that he had experienced an alien landing and had actually boarded at UFO, travelled with them and then returned to earth.

I cannot prove or disprove that what this man experienced was real or illusory. All I can do is to evaluate his experience from the standpoint of the Bible.

A true vision from God always....and I do mean *always*....communicates a sense of God's glory, power and holiness. Such a vision is always an overwhelming experience that confirms some great truth about God or imparts some sense of calling or purpose leading to a deeper faith and a closer relationship with God....and often with others as well. Such a Biblically authentic experience may or may not include the person of Jesus Christ. But, even if it does not, the vision will in no way lead a person *away* from Jesus Christ as the Son of God and Lord and Savior of the world. In no way will the experience affirm anything that diverges from the Bible as being the only infallible guide to what we are to believe about God and humanity or how we have been called to live in relationship with God and with others.

If a "vision" does not accomplish these things (and my friend's "encounter" with a UFO produced a clear movement *away* from God) then it must be assumed that the experience was a spiritual deception and one that will ultimately produce bitter fruit in the life of the person it has led astray (unless, of course, they repudiate and reject it as being spiritually counterfeit).

I believe that God still "speaks" to people in this way today.

Along with Native American Christian activist Vine Deloria, Jr., I can assert that "a person cannot have a 'mis-experience.' But they *can* have a mis-interpretation of that experience."

In this way many non-Christians, have had a "visionary" encounter with the living God yet do not have the knowledge to clearly understand what they have experienced. Part of Christian evangelism is to reach out to these people and take their spiritual experiences seriously, even as we help them look at and understand those experiences in the light of the one true God who has revealed himself most perfectly to the world through Jesus Christ.

Perhaps you, or someone you know has had a "spiritual" or "visionary" experience. It is important always to, 1. Determine whether it was from God or not (does it lead you *to* God or *away* from God) and then, if it appears to be an authentic God-experience, to, 2. Interpret it in light of Jesus Christ and the written word of God, the Bible.

I do not present myself as an expert in these matters although I strongly believe that many people who *do* present themselves as "experts" in these matters tend to make the whole subject far too complicated and the their interpretation far too legalistic than is actually necessary.

Such experiences should not be a surprise....especially for a Christian. After all, it was Jesus who said that, ".....the Kingdom of God is at hand." This means of course that the real presence of God and the way of life God commends is close enough to touch....or to be touched by!

My life and faith were confirmed by what, to anyone else, were extremely subjective and suspicious experiences. To me, however, and to the man at the funeral who was encouraged and comforted by similar spiritual "encounters," God made his meaning just as clear as he did long ago to those wise men, who looked at a star and saw something that no one else had seen.

WEDNESDAY, OCTOBER 19, 2005

Elizabethtown

In perhaps his most famous parable, Jesus tells the story of a son who leaves his home and father behind to find success in the world on his own terms. When the "prodigal son's" career proves to be a complete failure he decides to return home on his knees, hoping to be given a second chance by a father he has never really taken the time to know.

In *Elizabethtown*, Cameron Crowe has resurrected this time-worn but deeply profound theme and given it a twist: The father dies before the son can return home.

While the son, Drew (played by Orlando Bloom), never really shows guilt or contrition he does radiate an odd combination of depressed fatalism and whimsy (the latter of which serves as the emotional metaphor for the film).

A over-cheerful and bouncy stewardess, Claire (played by Kirsten Dunst), gushes and manipulates her way (whimsically, of course) into his heart; redeeming him from his self-centered "it's all about me" attitude in the process.

A wonderful ensemble of earthy-quirky characters at first mystify and finally endear themselves to Drew as he discovers honest love and affection among his father's family and friends in their hometown: Elizabethtown, Kentucky.

Unlike Jesus' parable, there is no way for Drew to discover his father's love and acceptance face to face. All of that must come second hand from those who knew his father better than he ever had himself. As the unhurried (but never slow) movement of the story unfolds Drew begins to see a depth of character, humor and steadfastness in his mother and others that he has never noticed before....and has most certainly never seen in himself.

The romance between Drew and Claire spirals, joins, leaps and separates much like a man and a woman in a pairs skating performance. In the end, there is a dramatic "lift" which leads to a closing pirhouette. It is, of course, Claire who both "lifts" Drew out of his depression and sweeps him off his feet in the end.

My 16-year old Daughter #3 (who attended the movie with me this evening) rated it an "8" (out of ten). As for myself, even though the whimsy centered on a character who seemed far more saddened by his career failure than by his father's death, the screenplay, dialogue, direction, camera work, editing and soundtrack kept the story moving seamlessly and gracefully along in a tasteful and captivating way.

I did not cry or even feel the desire to cry even though there was a thin layer of emotional sentiment and grief laying close to the surface. I did, however, laugh often and far more loudly than I had expected.

I would rate this movie a 10 for the simple reason that I was entertained without any insult to my intelligence; nor did I feel any inclination to fall asleep even though I had only gotten 5 hours of sleep the night before!

In the end, the movie seems to say that keeping a sense of humor (and whimsy, too, of course) will help anyone overcome saddness and disappointment in life. Especially if that whimsy is accompanied by a caring family and one-special-person who loves you even though you *aren't* a member of their family! This must be the philosphy of Cameron Crowe who is quite open about admitting that the movie grew out of his experience with the sudden death of his own father several years ago.

The title of this new movie will not bring the casual movie-goer into the theater but I suspect that word of mouth will keep this sweet and weepless serious-romantic-comedy around for more than the usual three weeks.

THURSDAY, OCTOBER 20, 2005

Able Danger Strikes Again--Is Anybody Listening?

Last August I posted here on U.S. Congregssman Curt Weldon and his attempts to get some political and news media traction on what appeared to be a Front Page "no-brainer."

Weldon presented compelling evidence that a government intelligence group code named "Able Danger" identified an al-Qaeda terrorist cell along with serveral of the 9-11 terrorist/hijackers (including Mohammed Atta) by name over a year before the actual attacks.

Weldon wanted to know why the information was squelched and by whom and why the Congressional 9-11 Commission did not report on this matter even though the material had been presented to it during its investigation.

Well, after more than two more months of effort, all Weldon has now gathered a total of 7 former Able Danger associates who are willing to swear that this story is true. CIA and DOD Intelligence people are claiming that all Able Danger documents have been destroyed and are forbidding all former Able Danger members who are still under their employment to say anything more about this matter.

One of his witnesses, a Colonel who received a Bronze Star for his intelligence work, has even had threats that his medical coverage, which includes his children, might be revoked.

What is going on here. What is being covered up....by whom.....and why? Certainly there can be little danger to national security since, according to the Intelligence community itself, Able Danger has been defunct for over two years.

Today, (see here (Michelle Malkin), here (Captain's Quarters) and especially here (Sean Hannity interview with Weldon) Weldon added to his accusations, revealing that former ***Able Danger members are also willing to testify that they notified the US Navy over two weeks before the attack on the US Cole in Yemen that there was a plot to attack US military interests there. They told the Navy NOT to allow the Cole to enter the harbor or dock there***.

Two days before the attack they repeated their request and the evidence for it.

The Navy ignored both requests. The Cole entered Yemen. Terrorists attacked just as the Able Danger team had said they would. Seventeen sailors were killed and 39 others were injured in the blast.

IS ANYBODY LISTENING?

Where is the media? Where is the pursuit of truth? Does no one care that the World Trade Center and the passengers and crew of four commercial airline flights might still be alive if anyone had listened to any of these reports?

Not to mention the loss of lives and material in the bombing of the USS Cole?

This story is not going to go away.

People in high places are trying very hard to hide something.

I suspect it must be something very, very important.

But instead, we are "captivated" by the side-show of "who outed CIA 'pseudo-sleuth' Plame."

On a scale of importance from 1 to 10 it seems to me that one of these is a 1 and the other is a 10.

I'll leave it to you to decide which is which.

Apparently the US news media has already cast their vote.

FRIDAY, OCTOBER 21, 2005

Rory Carroll, Kidnapped British Reporter Freed In Baghdad

Rory Carroll, Baghdad-based journalist for the English newspaper The Guardian was released today after being kidnapped on Wednesday.

This might not normally be something I would blog about except for the fact that Rory was my seat-mate on my recent 11-hour flight from New York City to Amman, Jordan, on Royal Jordanian Airlines. (I took the above photo of Rory as we disembarked at Queen Alia International Airport in Amman).

Rory was returning from a 2-week vacation spent with his sister in New York.

I mentioned my encounter with Rory in a previous post here.

Rory has been in my thoughts and prayers often since I met him. It was not until today, when I heard on the radio of his release, that I even knew he had been kidnapped.

In any case, I join with his family, friends, the Guardian and his fellow journalists stationed in Iraq in giving thanks to God for his safe release.

Rory told me he was scheduled to complete his assignment this coming January. He was, he said, looking forward to leaving Iraq and starting a new assignment somewhere else.....presumably somewhere where you don't have to worry about being kidnapped every time you interview someone for a story.

I wonder whether Rory will now get an early ticket home. If offered I would be surprised if he didn't take it.

MONDAY, OCTOBER 24, 2005

Weird News #1 Archimedes' "Death Ray" a Failure

In a sort of "friendly fire" competition, researchers from MIT and the University of Arizona attempted to recreate one of the ancient world's most compelling legends.

The story has it that Archimedes saved Syracuse from a sea invasion by a Roman fleet by creating a series of polished surfaces that reflected and concentrated the light from the sun into a sort of "death ray" that set one Roman ship on fire after another.

According to the AP report, the competition took place in San Francisco this past Saturday, October 22. An old, wooden fishing boat was the target.

The Arizona team failed to do anything more than raise the temperature slightly.

From 150 feet away MIT managed some smoldering but no flame.

When the boat was moved to within 75 feet the MIT team actually managed to start a small fire that, unfortunately for history, quickly went out.

One observer summed it up this way, "We're not saying it can't be done. We're just saying it's extremely impractical as a weapon of war."

Before the U.S. war on Iraq I suppose that most folks figured that "IED's" were also "extremely impractical as a weapon of war." I just hope that the "terrorist/insurgents" don't pick up on this "death ray" idea and figure out some way to made something out of it. There is, after all, an ample supply of sunlight at their disposal.

Wierd News #2 "Syria Says, 'Blame Israel'"

After getting caught in the cross-hairs of a United Nations investigative report on the assassination of former Lebanon Prime Minister Rafik Hariri, Syrian Foreign Ministry advisor Riyad Dawoodi replied, "There's no proof."

In the legendary tradition of the OJ Simpson defense team, Dawoodi then attempted to create a "reasonable doubt" by shifting the blame to......who do you think?

AP writer Donna Abu-Nasir writes,

Seeking to put another spin on Hariri's assassination, Dawoodi implied that the Arabs' longtime foe, Israel, could have been behind the killing.

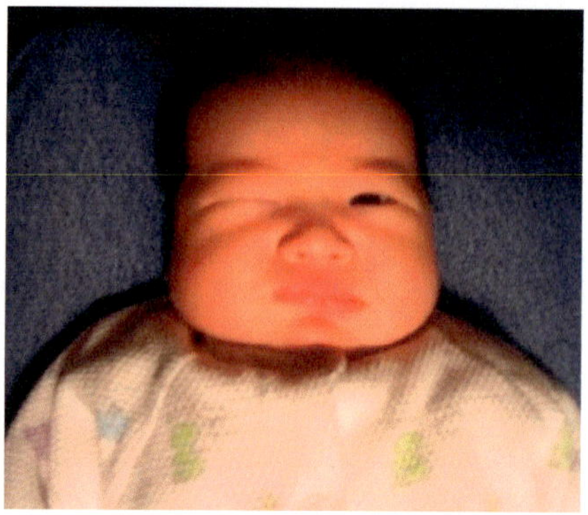

Wink. Wink.

He said (the UN's) report concluded the assassination "could not have happend without a very sophisticated means which belongs to a highly equipped security organ."

"And you just look around you--who is very well-equipped?" he asked, alluding to Israel.

I can just hear Monty Python adding a sly, "Wink. Wink." to this otherwise pathetic moment.

Still, it is refreshing to see Syria publically admitting that its car-bombing capabilities are not "very sophisticated" and that its security organ is not "highly equipped."

Wierd News #3 "Science Almost Loses 'Rat Race'"

In an attempt to discern how introduced species move and spread in a new environment, New Zealand researchers released a Norwegian Rat named "Razza" onto an otherwise "ratless" island.

Although electronically monitored so that the scientists could track the rat wherever it went Razza managed to elude recapture for 18 weeks. At one point the rat disappeared from their monitor completely only to be rediscovered on another island after apparently swimming over 400 yards across open water.

Numerous traps and baits and even sniffer dogs failed to reel in the renegade rat until a suspected area was totally "saturated" with traps. Razza finally met his fate when lured into a fatal liason with fresh penguin meat.

The results of the experiment were so unexpected that the researchers are trying it again to "make sure Razza's race wasn't a fluke."

"We want to check whether this was normal behavior," one scientist said.

Wierd News #4 Honolulu Airport's "Drive Through" Baggage Claim

A man, who police suspect may have been on drugs, drove his car through a glass door and into the baggage claim area of the Honolulu Airport's Inter-Island Terminal on Sunday afternoon.

No one was injured even though the man continued to drive the car for nearly 100 yards before being arrested.

As someone who had frequently driven to and from the Honolulu Airport my theory is this: The man was probably just frustrated after driving around and around the always full parking garag attached to the Inter-Island terminal and, in desparation, was merely looking for a place to park.

Historical Footnote: Some years ago students at MIT found a novel way to solve their parking problems. As a "hack" (practical joke) they managed to put a fully equipped and operational police car on top of the school's signature dome.

Update On South-East Asian Tsunami Recovery

Last night, following a Hawaii Multi-Faith Leadership Forum program that updated us on the disaster recovery process in Indonesia and Thailand (following the earthquake and tsunami that killed over 200,000 people last December), I was privileged to take our two special guests out to dinner.

South-West Coast of Thailand

From **Dr. Bunchar Pangpanich I learned that, in Thailand, at least, the recovery from the tsunami (that killed 5,000 people there, half of them European tourists.....mostly Scandinavian) is going well. Housing has been largely rebuilt and schools are once again up and running. The focus of his agency, the Free Andaman Network, is** on economic and social recovery for the coastal peoples.

Those who live off of the sea in that part of Thailand are largely Muslim. There is also a gypsy-type ocean culture called the Moken who were also dramatically impacted by the devastation.

The first part of Free Andaman plan has been to build and rebuild fishing boats/canoes to replace those that were destroyed. Many boat-building "shipyards" have been financed for this purpose. Some have been so productive that, after replacing local area boats have been contracted by the Thai government to build boats for other areas, too.

Prior to the tsunami, the homes of most villagers stood on land that had never been processed into actual legal title for those who lived there for generations (the title process is too expensive for these poor people). Following the tsunami it has not only been difficult to determine where individual homes had once stood, but business interests, hoping to capitalize on the disaster, have shown up holding legal "documentation" that purports to show that they are the land owners. These folks would like to develop the beachfront land for resorts and other economic purposes. The government smiles on this and, unfortunately, looks the other way, leaving the poor fisher-folks to fight it out on their own.

Fortunately, according to Dr. Pongpanich, the courts are independent enough to sort out the competing claims with some fairness....but only when groups like his intercede and organize the local people to stand up and defend their rights.

As villages become reorganized around these common needs and concerns local, democratic methods of self-government are beginning to emerge, empowering the villagers even more. These people do not want or need a handout any more, according to Pongpanich. Local relief and reconstruction agencies already have more than enough money to finish up the work and the real need is in community organization and development, something his agency is busy doing. ("Perhaps you might consider sending your money to Indonesia where it is more desperately needed," he said.)

Dr. Pongpanich indicated that he did not ever anticipate that his organization would become a permanent "NGO" (non-governmental organization) but was willing to allow it to complete its work over the next 12-16 months and then dissolve.

His personal plan, at that point, is to become a Buddhist monk and develop his spiritual life and disciplines in a deeper way.

As a fully-trained and licensed medical doctor (trained at the Presbyterian Medical School in Changmai) he has already given up that practice in order to serve the larger social and economic needs of the tsunami-impacted coastal communities. It is not surprising to me that he would be willing to give up and let go of this as well for a time of personal and spiritual introspection, refreshment and renewal.

One interesting side note is that his family household includes four Muslims, three Christians (Presbyterians) and three Buddhists, including himself. It is his impression that the recent highly publicized murders by Muslim radicals of local Thai's have been carried out by a very small and marginalized number of people. Local Muslim leaders have publicly condemned such actions. He also shared his belief that at least ½ of these killings have been of a personal nature rather than from religious zealotry.

Aceh Province, Northern Sumatra, Indonesia

The Rev. Dr. Edison Munthe, an Indonesian Lutheran pastor, had a somewhat different story to tell of the situation in Aceh Province in northern Sumatra. Although houses are being rebuilt with both government and non-government assistance, vast numbers of displaced people, (almost all of them Muslim) are still living in tents set up at refugee camps.

The earthquake that followed the tsunami by several months damaged and destroyed many buildings, schools, mosques, businesses and other infrastructure far inland, making the job of rebuilding communities and lives all the more difficult.

As in Thailand, business ventures, with the tacit support of governmental agents and members of the Indonesian military, have seized land that had previously been covered with individual homes and entire villages. This has left thousands of tsunami victims with no place to go home to and no place to rebuild their lives.

Apparently there is a national history of the people of Aceh being treated less fairly than those in other regions of Indonesia. This precedent, enhanced by the presence of drug running and corrupted government officials, has prevented any genuine return to normalcy in the area.

Basic humanitarian needs are still unmet for many thousands of people. Local Christian pastors, while representing a small minority of the population, have been major conduits of money and provisions. They are, in turn, highly respected and accepted by the Muslim majority.

Common Themes

Both men commented on the obvious: Providing support through private agencies (NGOs) is far more efficient than going through government channels. Not all NGOs have local leadership, however, and either are unable to carry through on their plans or are unable to transport needed materials from Jakarta, for example, to Aceh.

For the most part, now that the initial crisis has passed, cash donations are preferred over material ones. Shipping and transporting these materials is costly and difficult. Cash, however, is easily traded for the things that are actually needed in a specific situation. It is not that there is no food or clothing, only that the (ample) food and clothing available cost money that the poor coastal peoples do not have.

It is vital, say Dr. Munthe, that these Indonesian people be allowed to return to their land and reestablish their communities. In the long run both men also agreed that giving too much help and assistance will hurt more lives than it will benefit. “People need to be empowered to rebuild their own lives.....to work together as neighbors and friends and families in the traditional cultural patterns of sharing." People will work and will work hard if given even a small bit of hope for a better future. As long as they remain displaced in refugee camps, sitting idle with nothing to do and little to hope for, a sense of hopelessness and despair will make any future recovery of Aceh all that much more difficult.

Overarching Theme of Our Common Humanity

Both men experienced a similar response to their respective tragedies. In each case, cultural, religious and historic differences that had once separated people became secondary and almost marginal matters as the common needs of a common humanity became paramount.

In Thailand, Buddhists worked with Muslims to establish boadyards (the most successful of which is operated by a Muslim Imam).

In Indonesia, Christians worked and gave freely and generously to support and aid the vast numbers of displaced Muslims.

The spirit of cooperation has been experienced as such a good thing that leaders in the various faith communities are working out ways to continue and sustain their relationships as the crisis begins to lessen and the temptation comes to fall back into old patterns of behavior.

Conclusion

It was good to hear of the successful rebuilding of lives and culture in Thailand.

It was sad and disheartening to hear of the continued suffering of tens of thousands of people still displaced from their homes and communities in Indonesia.

Yet it was inspiring to hear of the spirit of our common humanity transcending those things that would ordinarily be powerful enough to divide people one from another.

Matters of faith and culture are vital and must never be diluted. But when at issue is the survival of our neighbors in need each faith and culture must rise above itself and help usher a mutually-shared vision of peace and prosperity into a tangible reality.

I am so grateful for men and women like Edison Munthe and Bunchar Pongpanich. There are good people in every corner of the world who are willing to sacrifice themselves for the common good of all, even those they do not always see eye-to-eye with. It was a double privilege to not only hear their public presentation but to share a private meal and private conversation with them afterwards.

TUESDAY, OCTOBER 25, 2005

Study Leave Trip To Jordan

I don't want to take up too much space on this page so, if you want to see my pictures and read about my recent one-week visit to Jordan just click here or on the photograph of the Royal Jordanian Airlines plane on which I flew to Amman from New York. At the end of the post are a few miscellaneous photos and a few reflective poems, too.

WEDNESDAY, OCTOBER 26, 2005

Rosa Parks Dies at 92

Rosa parks died on Monday night. She carried to her grave a name that was synonymous with the Civil Rights movement; a name perhaps eclipsed only by the name of the Rev. Dr. Martin Luther King, Jr. himself.

When Rosa Parks refused to give up her seat to a white man on a Birmingham, Alabama, bus on December 1, 1955, she was not simply resting her feet. While her feet may, indeed, have been tired that day, it was her heart that was truly heavy and weary.

"Our mistreatment was just not right, and I was tired of it," she wrote years later.

On December 5 she was fined $14 and put on trial. Black Montgomery, including a young pastor, Martin Luther King Jr., organized a boycott of the city bus system, a boycott that would not end until late December the following year.

That year, 1956, would first find the Montgomery City Council voting to reaffirm their commitment to segregated seating on city buses. Soon after, a Federal Court, and then the U.S. Supreme Court, ruled that the segregation policy was in violation of the Constitution. On December 20, 1956, Federal injunctions were served on the city, enforcing the judicial rulings. The boycott ended the following day. A small, but historically significant, victory had been won.

In 1957 Parks and her husband moved to Detroit, Michigan. In 1963 she participated in the

March on Washington where Dr. King delivered his "I have a dream..." speech.

In 1965 she began working as an administrative assistant to U.S. Representative John Conyers, D-Mich, a position she would hold for over 20 years.

In 1994 Parks published her memoirs, "Quiet Strength." Two years later she is attacked and beaten in her home by a black man looking for money. He did not know at the time who it was he had assaulted.

Afterwards, Park wrote, "I pray for this young man and the conditions in our country that have made him this way."

In 1996 she received the highest U.S. civilian honor, the Presidential Medal of Freedom.

Not to be outdone, in 1999, the U. S. Congress voted to present her with the Congressional Gold Medal of Honor as well.

Rosa Parks was quiet and gentle by nature. But she was stubborn, too. Once she had made up her mind that she was no longer going to accept being a second-class citizen of a country that guaranteed her equality under the law, she sat down on that seat on that Montgomery, Alabama, bus and never left it again.

The forces of bigotry and segregation tried their hardest to get her to stand up and go away but, in the end, it was not the world that caused Rosa Parks to move.....it was Rosa Parks who moved the world.

President of Iran Says, "Israel Should Be Wiped Off the Map"

Every once in awhile a leader stands up and speaks the truth boldly and unequivicably. Two people did that today. But there was a significant difference.

First, Governor Jeb Bush of Florida, in the wake of Hurricane Wilma, publicly declared, *"People had ample time to prepare, and it isn't that hard to get 72 hours worth of food and water, to do the simple things we ask people to do," Gov. Jeb Bush said. The governor bristled in response to criticism of FEMA.*

"If anyone wants to blame anybody, blame me," he said. "I'm not going to criticize anybody and I'm not going to let anybody criticize FEMA for something we accept responsibility for." (as quoted in the South Florida Sun-Sentinel)

How refreshing to seeing a politician accept responsibility instead of trying to blame someone else. How refreshing to see a leader face a problem and promise to find a constructive way to solve it and to do even better next time.

On the other hand, we have Iran's President Mahmoud Ahmadi-Nejad declaring that,

"There is no doubt that the new wave (of attacks) in Palestine will wipe off this stigma (Israel) from the face of the Islamic world," Ahmadinejad told students Wednesday during a Tehran conference called "The World without Zionism."

"Anybody who recognizes Israel will burn in the fire of the Islamic nation's fury, (while) any (Islamic leader) who recognizes the Zionist regime means he is acknowledging the surrender and defeat of the Islamic world," Ahmadinejad said.

Ahmadinejad also repeated the words of the founder of Iran's Islamic revolution, Ayatollah Ruhollah Khomeini, who called for the destruction of Israel.

"As the imam said, Israel must be wiped off the map." (from AP)

For those of you who have never heard this sort of rhetoric before, "A World Without Zionism" means exactly the same thing as, "A World Without Israel."

It is significant that Iran aligns itself with Palestinian terrorism against Israel. Known as a long-time supporter of terrorist organizations such as Islamic Jihad, Iran here publically declares common cause with any group that, in the name of Islam, seeks the physical destruction of the nation of Israel.

Does this qualify as a declaration of war? Would this sort of declaration, taken in the context of Iran's nuclear reactor program, justify a "preemptive strike" by Israel?

I, for one, believe that it is more than likely that Israel will not sit and wait until Western Europe gets around to condemning Iran for either its nuclear ambitions, its incitement to terrorism or its public vow to see Israel destroyed.

When the time is right, Israel will "go it alone" and attack Iran in "self-defense."

Israel will be universally condemned....at least publicly.

The United States, Jordan and Iraq will be excoriated for having allowed Israeli warplanes to pass through their air space.

Iran, in turn, will turn loose at least 10,000 trained jihadi who will be more than willing to martyr themselves in attacks against the US/Iraq, the nation of Israel and any Muslim nation that has or may be considering establishing diplomatic relations with Israel.

Egypt and Jordan will be fair game, of course, but other nations will suffer under the Iranian-style fatwas as well.

Arab governments may well topple under such an assault and the United States, in defense of Israel and other Middle East "allies," may be forced to quarantine and blockade Iran from all trade as part of a world-wide boycott of an entire nation.

In a worse-case scenario, the United States could be forced to actually attack Iran from the air and possibly even send ground troops across her borders.

The religious and governmental leaders in Iran are, of course, counting on their proxies in Palestine to do their dirty work for them. As long as they can pretend that their hands are "clean" they know that they can sucker Western Europe, Russia and China into giving them a "pass."

What is truly frightening this time around is that the President of Iran is talking so boldly that it almost appears as if there is a plan in place....and that Iran actually believes that the destruction of Israel is "doable."

Personally, between the two I would choose Jeb Bush every time.

THURSDAY, OCTOBER 27, 2005

Miers Withdraws As Supreme Court Nominee

Harriet Miers threw in the towel today, requesting the President that her name be withdrawn from nomination to the U.S. Supreme Court. Bush, with regret, accepted her request

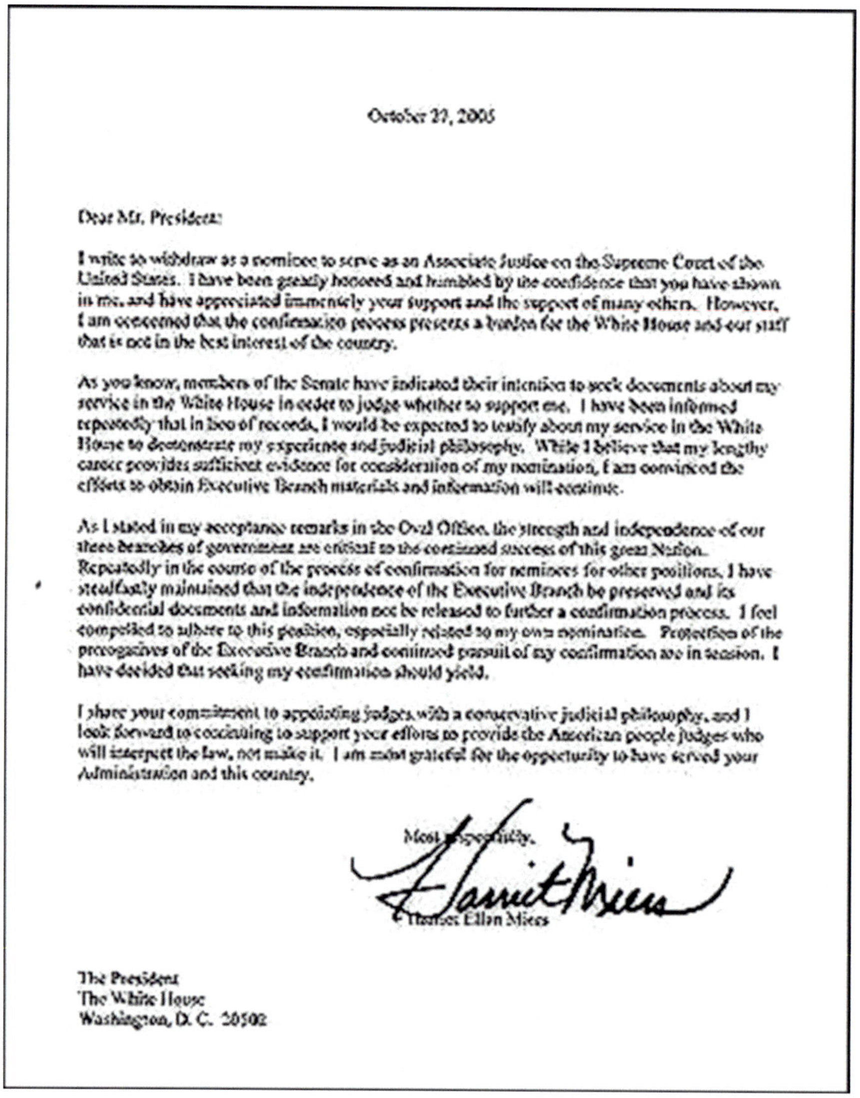

October 27, 2005

Dear Mr. President:

I write to withdraw as a nominee to serve as an Associate Justice on the Supreme Court of the United States. I have been greatly honored and humbled by the confidence that you have shown in me, and have appreciated immensely your support and the support of many others. However, I am concerned that the confirmation process presents a burden for the White House and our staff that is not in the best interest of the country.

As you know, members of the Senate have indicated their intention to seek documents about my service in the White House in order to judge whether to support me. I have been informed repeatedly that in lieu of records, I would be expected to testify about my service in the White House to demonstrate my experience and judicial philosophy. While I believe that my lengthy career provides sufficient evidence for consideration of my nomination, I am convinced the efforts to obtain Executive Branch materials and information will continue.

As I stated in my acceptance remarks in the Oval Office, the strength and independence of our three branches of government are critical to the continued success of this great Nation. Repeatedly in the course of the process of confirmation for nominees for other positions, I have steadfastly maintained that the independence of the Executive Branch be preserved and its confidential documents and information not be released to further a confirmation process. I feel compelled to adhere to this position, especially related to my own nomination. Protection of the prerogatives of the Executive Branch and continued pursuit of my confirmation are in tension. I have decided that seeking my confirmation should yield.

I share your commitment to appointing judges with a conservative judicial philosophy, and I look forward to continuing to support your efforts to provide the American people judges who will interpret the law, not make it. I am most grateful for the opportunity to have served your Administration and this country.

Most respectfully,

Harriet Ellan Miers

The President
The White House
Washington, D.C. 20502

In her resignation letter, Miers offered the reason for her decision as revolving around the issue of "separation of powers." As a White House Legal Council for the past five years she has amassed a wealth of documents that, if released, could provide evidence to her opinions on legal matters and the methodology and legal philosophy by which she forms her opinions.

While the Senate Judiciary Committee is demanding that those documents be released, Miers indicated that she would rather step down than be the cause of a legal headache for the White House that could lead to an unprecedented release of confidential Executive Branch files to the Legislative Branch.

Three thoughts:

1. Bush, with his advisors (including Miers), must have anticipated this particular issue when Miers was nominated. A plan must have been in place to deal with it. Why then, when the issue came up, did it become a reason for her withdrawal? That does not make any sense at all. If, on the other hand, the White House either did not anticipate this matter or, having anticipated it, did not have a rational and reasonable plan to countermand it, then the President and his staff are incompetent buffoons.

I am willing to give them the benefit of the doubt but am still mystified by the lack of a systematic or coherent defense of her nomination. Either something went terribly wrong that has not yet been revealed or else the failure of her nomination was not only anticipated but planned from the beginning.

2. It would appear that Mier's reasoning in her resignation letter would preclude any future Federal Court nominee from having ever served in a White House position OR (using the same logic) in any capacity on the U.S. Supreme Court. If documents related to a nominee's service as White House Counsel can be subpoenaed then so could documents related to a nominee's service as a U.S. Supreme Court intern or aide.

The idea that such confidential memos, correspondence and legal advice could be subpoenaed for something other than a criminal investigation is, to my knowledge, without precedent. Once again I am mystified that the White House would "blink" over a matter that has the full weight of history and legal precedent on their side.

3. I am baffled that the White House went so long and so far with this nomination knowing and observing the political capital they were losing with their conservative base. The immediate negative reaction to Mier's nomination (which I initially supported **here**) should have been anticipated. Even if the reaction caught the White House by surprise, the President should have immediately had second thoughts about the cost of driving a wedge through the Republican Party over one particular nominee when there were many others, equally or more qualified, who would have drawn wide-spread party support.

Unless President Bush can turn dross into gold, even a solid and well-supported nomination will not quickly repair the political damage created by the Mier's debacle.

FRIDAY, OCTOBER 28, 2005

Libby Vindicated & Cleared of Outing Valerie Plame

I just had to write that headline bcause you will not see it anywhere else.

For months a special prosecutor has been persuing the charge that members of the Bush administration leaked information to the press that exposed Valerie Plame as a CIA agent.

After two years, the special prosecuter apparently had not found enough evidence to indict anyone on this charge. (*The indictment for Scooter Libby that* was *released today can be found* ***here***).

During two years involving hundreds of hours of testimony covering hundreds of people trying to recall hundreds of conversations that took place over two years ago with hundreds of different people and with most of these conversations either "off the record" or from an "anonymous source" and being recalled without the benefits of having taken notes on those conversations to assist with recalling exactly what was said when and to whom...... After all of this, the Special Prosecutor was only able to come up with one statement, repeated several times by Scooter Libby concerning conversations with three/four journalists, that appears to be untrue.

In each of these conversations, Libby told the special prosecuter that he was asked a question (which the reporters apparently deny they asked) and that, in his reply, he told them that he did not confirm to them that Valerie Plame was Joe Wilson's wife (which the reporters apparently claim otherwise) but that he had heard suggestions to that effect from other reporters (which the reporters apparently claim he did not say to them.)

The prosecutor presents this evidence against Libby, clearly taking the side of the reporters testimony as being true while believing that Libby intentionally lied, obstructed, falsified and perjured himself with this one statement out of thousands of statements on every other point.

Maybe. Maybe not.

Clearly Libby will have some explaining or clarifying to do when he is given the opportunity to defend himself during his now-pending trial.

If, in fact, Libby made these statements knowing full well that they were not true then he should suffer the consequences of the charges that he now faces.

But, whether guilty of these charges or not, there is no evidence presented that in any way paints the Bush administration as having conspired to do anything unethical or illegal concerning the pathetic case of Joe Wilson and his wife, Valerie Plame.

Curiously, although Barbara Miller of the New York Times is mentioned as one of the reporters who interviewed Libby, her published recollections of her testimony interviews are so vague and and her own integrity and honesty so shaky that her testimony, cited as evidence in the idictments, would appear to be less than authoritative.

This leaves the recollections of NBC's Tim Russert and Time reporter Matthew Cooper as the basis for the indictments against Libby. As I read Libby's testimony in the indictment I am not always certain that he is testifying as to what he *told them and wanted them to believe* (which was clearly obfuscated and untrue but not in any way criminal) **or** to what he actually *knew and believed at the time* (and either lied about it intentionally--which is criminal--or simply mis-remembered--which is not).

At the worst, Scooter Libby was caught in telling a lie to the Grand Jury that has little to do with the charges that initiated the investigation in the first place.

As a reflection of the Bush administration, Captain Ed puts it in persperspective:

If the Times has its sources correct, they can celebrate the second indictment of a Bush administration official.

That only puts the Bush administration 59 behind the Clinton administration, by the way. And that was while he was still in office -- that apparently does not count Sandy Berger's stealing of code-word classified documents from the National Archive and destroying them during the 9/11 investigation.

Right now it appears to be a he/said she/said sort of indictment. A classic case of "left-wing media" vs "conservative republican administration advisor."

With a foundational plot line like that the trial will make a compelling story.

As a matter of national politics it will, however, be "full of sound and fury" but "signifying nothing."

UPDATE: I appears that my thoughts are closely reflected in a **statement** released by Libby's lawyer today.

SATURDAY, OCTOBER 29, 2005

What's Wrong With This Story?

Have you heard about the rioting outside Paris the past three days? Of course not. No one in the American media has printed or said anything about it. Two people are dead, 29 police vehicles destroyed, vandalized buildings and rioters tried to burn down a police station. The situation was so bad that *this was the* good *news in the article:*
There were no clashes with police (last night), unlike previous nights, although 13 people were arrested, mostly while carrying hammers or petrol cans.
Even if you had read the articles written about it in France you might not have understood who was rioting. Read the article here and then ask yourself *what's missing in the article*? (Hint: The only reference to Muslims is complimentary)

UPDATE: The BBC seems to have omitted who was rioting as well. I guess that the identity of rioters is no longer of any interest to readers or, one assumed, the police. It is curious that the word "immigrant" is used. I suppose that could mean that the rioters were expatriate Canadians? Why is the news media so reluctant to give us the news?

Three Girls Beheaded in Indonesia--Inspector Clouseau Is On the Case

A **BBC article** relates the following:

> *Three girls have been beheaded and another badly injured as they walked to a Christian school in Indonesia. They were walking through a cocoa plantation near the city of Poso in central Sulawesi province when they were attacked.*
>
> *This is an area that has a long history of religious violence between Muslims and Christians.*

> *A government-brokered truce has only partially succeeded in reducing the number of incidents in recent years.*
>
> *Police say the heads were found some distance from the bodies.*
>
> ***It is unclear what was behind the attack**, but the girls attended a private Christian school and one of the heads was left outside a church leading to speculation that it **might** have had a religious motive.* (empahasis mine)

Uh....let's see. Christian girls walking to a Christian school in a region beset with conflict between Muslims and Christians. One of the girl's head's is left outside a Christian church....

So, although he is "unclear what was behind the attack," Inspector Clouseau "speculates" that it "might" have had a religious motive.

Whoever wrote this article obviously did not want to cast an negative aspersion against Muslims.....although, way down in the second half of the article (if you take the time to read that far) we learn that the area where the girls were killed

> *was the scene of bitter fighting between Muslims and Christians in 2001 and 2002. More than 1,000 people were killed before a government-brokered truce.*
>
> *Although the violence has been subdued, it has never gone away completely.*
>
> *A bomb in May in the nearby town of Tentena, which is predominantly Christian, killed 22 people and injured over 30.*
>
> *The fighting four years ago drew Islamic militants from all over Indonesia and many have never gone home.*
>
> *Analysts say the militants have targeted central Sulawesi and believe that it could be turned into the foundation stone of an Islamic state.*
>
> *The analysts have warned that the violence could resurface at any time.*

Wow! I am so impressed with these "analysts." Muslims blow up 22 Christians and they actually predict the possibility that "the violence could resurface at any time."

That should give those 22 dead Christians and the three beheaded Christian girls something to worry about...to know that violence "might" be coming along any minute now....

The facts of the matter are clear: Back in 2000-2001 radical Muslims from outside the community stirred up conflict between local Muslims and Christians by attacking Christians and forcing them to defend themselves (against a large Muslim majority population and a government and police force that generally chooses to look the other way).

Christians are then attacked and murdered in "reprisals" for having defended themselves. Just to keep things on edge, every so often a bomb goes off in a Christian area or Christian children are found beheaded.

The message is clear: Christians, get out! Leave your homes and your community where you have lived for over 100 years. Turn your businesses over to your Muslim neighbors. Or you will die.

Until these outside Islamic agitators showed up Muslims and Christians had lived and worked side by side without any hostilities for over a century. The "conflict" is not the will of the local Muslim population but, caught in the middle, they are terrified of what might happen to them if they were to speak out against it.

And the news media, as this article so nicely illustrates, tries to present it as a "conflict between Muslims and Christians" as though some nice mediator could step in and get them to "kiss and make up."

Until we learn how to stand up to these radical Muslim thugs they will continue to terrorize Christians and fellow Muslims, continue to bomb and kill and behead innocent Christians and Muslims, until they get what they want: A world ruled by people like themselves.

We cannot let this happen. Christians and Muslims (and Hindus and Buddhists) around the world must unite to defend against this "theocracy of death" and those who support it.

And the media must begin telling the story straight out, plain and simple, and bury their misguided political correctness in a grave alongside the graves of those three beheaded Christian girls in Indonesia.

SUNDAY, OCTOBER 30, 2005

Saddam Was Willing To Leave Pre-Invasion Iraq

The Australian and Al-Arabiya printed a report yesterday that claims that the United States had negotiated an international agreement with Saddam Hussein for him to leave Iraq and go into exile just prior to the 1993. But Arab nations refused to cooperate:

Deposed Iraqi leader Saddam Hussein had secretly accepted a last minute plan to go into exile to avert the 2003 Iraq war, but Arab leaders shot the proposal down, Al Arabiya television reported today. UAE President Sheikh Zayed bin Sultan al-Nahayan made the proposal for Saddam to go into exile at an emergency Arab summit just weeks before the US-led war began in March 2003. But the 22-member Arab League, led by Secretary-General Amr Moussa, refused to consider the initiative.

"We had got the final agreement from the different parties, the main players in the world and the person concerned – Saddam Hussein – within 24 hours," Mohammed bin Zayed, deputy head of the UAE armed forces and crown prince of Abu Dhabi, told the UAE-based channel in a documentary
A quote from Egyptian President Hosni Mubarak indicates that the United States had agreed to the terms under the conditions that there be a peaceful transition of power in Iraq.

Butwhy would the Arab League refuse to support such a deal? Why did they risk so much suffering for the people of Iraq to preserve a despot who was willing to leave quietly? Could it be that they believed their purposes would be best served by the instability that an Iraqi war would bring? Did they believe that the response of millitant Islam to the invasion would draw attention away from their own national corruption and weakness?

As Captain Ed puts it (and this entire post is a hat tip to him),
Does the Arab League bear ultimate responsibility for the war, and did the US almost finesse Saddam out of Baghdad? We may never know for sure, but if this report is accurate, it would show that the Bush administration was willing to accept a solution short of war that removed Saddam and his sons from Iraq.

Supreme Court Nominee Prediction

I have no idea who the next US Supreme Court nominee will be. The latest news indicates that it is a dead heat between Federal Judges J. Michael Luttig and Alito.

Both men have long track records of judical experience and are both considered to be firmly in the tradition and philosophy of Supreme Court Justice Anthony Scalia.

Both were overwhelmingly approved for their Federal Court positions by the Senate and it would be a real stretch for the Democrats to claim extraordinary circumstances to justify a filibuster on either.

My prediction, if I must make one (and I don't but I will, anyway), is that Alito will be nominated. At 55 he is four years older than Luttig and, based on my reading, be slightly less distressing to the Democrats. His 15 years on the Federal Appeals Court in Philadelphia (in contrast to Luttig's 4 years in Richmond, Virginia) gives plenty of paper trails to follow and, therefore, fewer opportunities for demands from memos or records from the Executive Branch (a situation that Harriet Miers cited for her withdrawal from nomination).

I feel that Bush believes that he will get at least one more chance to nominate to the Court and will be keeping Luttig in his "back pocket." If he gets more than one opportunity look for Janice Brown to get called up. She has only recently been appointed to a Federal Appeals Court position so another year or two on the bench will only serve to ripen her appeal.

I'll probably be wrong on this but no one can say I didn't stick my neck out!

Pope John Paul II's 1975 Ford Escort Sells for $690,000

After the near fatal assassination attempt on Pope John Paul II in 1981 he gave up riding in an open car for sitting in a glass-enclosed Pope-mobile instead. But this had not always been the Pope's favorite means of transportation.

Back in 1975, when he was still the Polish Cardinal Wyzynski he purchased a blue Ford Escort as his personal car. Yesterday, at a Las Vegas auction, the car sold for $690,000. The seller had been hoping the car would sell for as much as $1-5 million.

You could pick up an identical model down at your local used car lot for $1,200.

I'm sure that is what Cardinal Wyzynski would have wanted you to do.

Hugo Chavez Tells Venezuelans--Halloween Is Contrary To Our Way"

Hugo Chavez, Venezuelan President, friend of Fidel Castro and George W. Bush-hater took time on his weekly national radio address to warn his people of a great and looming threat: Halloween. Yes, the American celebration of Halloween is, according to Chavez, a "game of terror" where, "families go and begin to disguise their children as witches."

All of this reflects the American culture of "putting fear into other nations, putting fear into their own people."

The BBC article reporting Chavez' comments adds a side note:
(Chavez) did not refer to incidents earlier this month when lanterns made from hollowed pumpkins carrying anti-government messages appeared in several places in the capital, Caracas.
Are there any skeletons in your closets Mr. Chavez?

NOTE: Chavez is always a good source for a good quote. See here for something he said in September.

MONDAY, OCTOBER 31, 2005

Prince Charles and Looking Good

Well, Prince Charles and Camilla are visiting the United States this week. Charles is expected to tell President Bush all about how he needs to get cracking on the Kyoto Treaty and how people should be terrified about global warming and, oh yes, how the United States should start showing more respect to Muslim countries and how racist, unsophisticated and provincial we are here in the United States.

As a tribute to Prince Charles and in honor of his visit I offer this small portfolio of what Charles would no doubt refer to as his Halloween Costume "haberdashery."

Prince Charles dressed as Count Dracula

Prince Charles dressed as a leprechaun
(probably for St. Patrick's Day) in the hopes of making friends with the Irish

Prince Charles dressed as a Native American to remind everyone that the British once joined with the American Indians to fight off the French in the "colonies" way back when the sun never set on the British Empire and all that.

Prince Charles dressed to kill in his Muammar Ghadaffi costume

And last, but not least, here is Prince Charles in today's Halloween costume looking very convincingly like a Hotel doorman (I am not making this up. This is what he actually wore today, October 31, 2005).

Like St. Paul, Prince Charles clearly believes that he "can be all things to all people." Except, in Charles' case, the people are snickering.

Note to Prince Charles: Please set your own house in order before telling us what to do. You know what I mean....you are aware, of course, that Muslims and Blacks have been rioting against each other in Birmingham, England this past week (Note how the British news calls the rioters "asians" so as to avoid calling them Muslims/Pakistani immigrants). I haven't seen much of that in the U.S. lately. Perhaps we should treat Muslims just like the English do, what?

SATURDAY, NOVEMBER 05, 2005

"T.O."="Tossed Out"--Terrell Owens Suspended by Eagles

No more Sharpies in the endzone. No more dancing in the center of the field, stomping on the opposing team's logo on their home turf. No more cell phone calls while on the field during a game. No more Terrell Owens. At least in a Philadelphia Eagles uniform. At least for the next couple of weeks. Probably forever.

"T.O." is now free to play sandlot flag football with

Brett Favre on Monday mornings.

As for Eagle's quarterback Donovan McNabb, he will be wearing his usual #5 uniform in Sunday night's game against the Washington Redskins. He will not be missing his top receiver. And Terrell Owens will once again learn the hard way that, 1. He is not indispensible; and, 2. Football is a team sport.

Who wants Terrell now? Even Houston and Green Bay have managed at least one win without Terrell Owens. Even if "T.O." would be able to bring them a second win I doubt that any of the players on those two teams would be willing to sell their souls for such a mess of pottage.

As Jesus sort-of said, "What does it profit a team to gain Terrell Owens but lose its good name in the process?"

Oh, Terrell.......have you ever heard of the CFL? Why don't you pull that cell phone out of your sock and give them a call?

TUESDAY, NOVEMBER 01, 2005

Senator Harry Reid Leads Democrats Over the Cliff

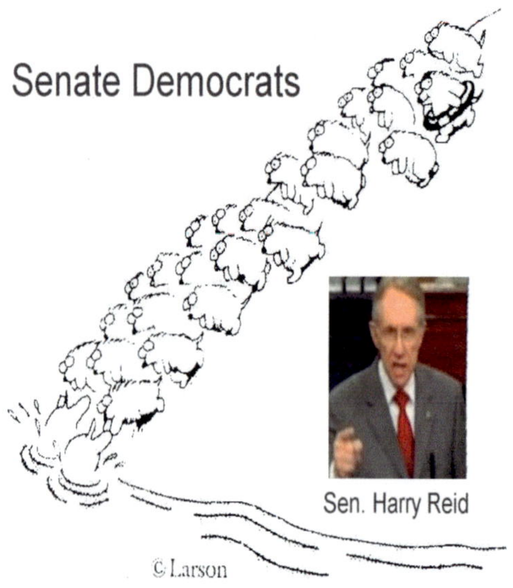

Today the Senate Democrats did what people do who have no power, no influence and nothing to say: They acted outrageously in order to get into the news and they yelled loudly and made noise to create the illusion that they were accomplishing something.

By invoking Senate Rule 21 this morning and calling the entire U.S. Senate into "secret session" for the first time in 25 years (and for the first time ever without a pre-arranged agreement by the leaders of both political parties) Senate Minority Leader Harry Reid led the members of his party "over the cliff" like a bunch of self-destructive lemmings.

To see the Democrats in action today click here and watch the animation carefully. The lemmings clearly represent the Senate Democrats and the judges most likely represent the media they are playing to. Oh...and please...don't forget to laugh. They are very funny. The animation clip, on the other hand, probably isn't!

WEDNESDAY, NOVEMBER 02, 2005

Terror Warnings In Australia and United Kingdom While

Grim announcements in both Australia and the United Kingdomthat reliable information regarding specific and soon-to-be executed terrorist attacks have been received by each government.

In Australia the threat was so specific and so immediate that Parliament convened in emergency session to amend their anti-terrorism laws to allow an immediate response to this particular threat. Even the outspoken opposition party members, after hearing the intelligence reports, voted unanimously in support of the amendment.

Meanwhile, the United States opposition party (aka "Democrats") called an emergency "secret session" of the Senate to discuss.....uh....*Impending terrorist threats?*.......No......Guess again.......*Toughening American terrorism laws?*......Nope........Try again........*The accuracy of US intelligence on Iraqi weapons of mass destruction over four years ago?*......Yep! Gotta hand it to those Democrats.......They sure have their priorities straight, don't they!

THURSDAY, NOVEMBER 03, 2005

Maryland Democrats Say Racism In OK If They Do It

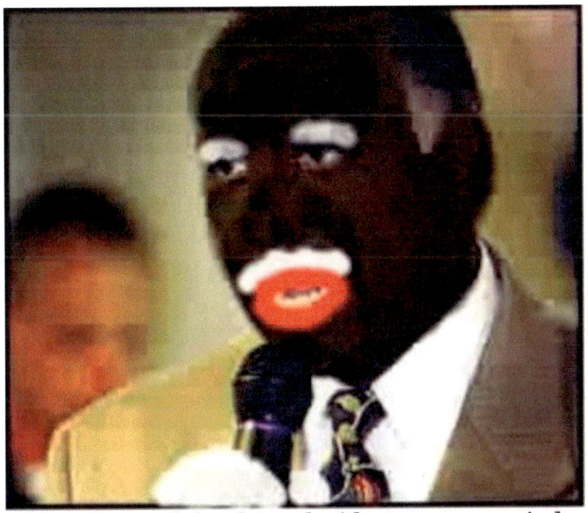

This characature of Maryland Lt. Gov. Michael Steele (that accompanied a blog post entitled, "Simple Sambo Wants Into the Big House") has been declared "acceptable" by Maryland Democrats

John Kennedy, Lyndon Johnson & Hubert Humphrey are no doubt rolling over in their graves today as Maryland Democrats defend their outrageous racist attacks against the first African-American Lt. Governor in their state's history. What's the problem? Michael Steele is a Republican, and he's running for the U.S. Senate.

According to the Washington Times:

> *Black Democratic leaders in Maryland say that racially tinged attacks against Lt. Gov. Michael S. Steele in his bid for the U.S. Senate are fair because he is a conservative Republican.*
>
> *Such attacks against the first black man to win a statewide election in Maryland include pelting him with Oreo cookies during a campaign appearance, calling him an "Uncle Tom" and depicting him as a black-faced minstrel on a liberal Web log. ... "There is a difference between pointing out the obvious and calling someone names," said a campaign spokesman for Kweisi Mfume, a Democratic candidate*

for U.S. Senate and former president of the National Association for the Advancement of Colored People.

State Sen. Lisa A. Gladden, a black Baltimore Democrat, said she does not expect her party to pull any punches, including racial jabs at Mr. Steele, in the race to replace retiring Democratic U.S. Sen. Paul S. Sarbanes.

"Party trumps race, especially on the national level," she said. "If you are bold enough to run, you have to take whatever the voters are going to give you. It's democracy, perhaps at its worse, but it is democracy."

Delegate Salima Siler Marriott, a black Baltimore Democrat, said Mr. Steele invites comparisons to a slave who loves his cruel master or a cookie that is black on the outside and white inside because his conservative political philosophy is, in her view, anti-black.

Speaking of former Democratic Presidents and Presidential candidates, I wonder why we have heard not a single word of outrage from Jimmy Carter or Bill Clinton? Could it be that they actually *condone* this type of behavior within their party? For Shame!

SATURDAY, NOVEMBER 05, 2005

Israeli Archaeologists Hype Discovery of Early Christian Church

Mosaic from newly excavated Byzantine Church in Megiddo (click on picture to enlarge)

One thing that Israel and Jordan do not suffer from are too few Byzantine Christian churches.

When still another one was discovered recently (on the grounds of a major Palestinian terrorist prison near Megiddo) the resulting news release reads as if it could have been formatted from just about any other article ever written about a archaeological discovery in Israel/Palestine:

1. **The writer of the article shows his/her complete ignorance of the subject and gets something wrong in the opening sentence.** (In this case, the AP writer claims that those who discovered the church are saying that "it may be the oldest Christian church in the Holy Land." They said no such thing, of course, although one archaeologist did say it "may be the oldest (Christian church) in our area." (Meaning, no doubt, northern Israel/Galilee and not the entire "Holy Land.")

2. **The one who discovers the site will play it up for all it is worth** (this is because a good dig will generate grant money....lots of grant money). "There is no structure you can compare it to. It is a very unique find," says Yotam Tepper, the dig leader. Others join in, saying the church could be as old as third century.

3. **The writer will try to find a biblical twist that will connect to his/her readers....and they will get this wrong, too**. ("Scholars believe Megiddo to be the New Testament's Armageddon, the site of a final war between good and evil." The link between Megiddo and Armageddon is true, of course, but a "final war between good and evil?" Hardly. Satan and the Anti-Christ gather all their forces in rebellion against God but there is no war. There is no battle. Just take a look at how Revelation 20:7-9 puts it:
7When the thousand years are over, Satan will be released from his prison 8and will go out to deceive the nations in the four corners of the earth—Gog and Magog—to gather them for battle. In number they are like the sand on the seashore. 9They marched across the breadth of the earth and surrounded the camp of God's people, the city he loves. But fire came down from heaven and devoured them.
Yep. That's the great battle of Armageddon! God says, "You're done" and it's over. That's the whole point of Revelation. No one, not even Satan, has any power except for that which God permits them to have...not for *their* purposes but for God's! When God's purpose is complete, the true powerlessness of Satan, evil and death will be exposed and their impotence revealed in a twinkling of an eye. "War between good and evil".....not!

4. **Some real, tangeable value *may* be actually present in the excavation** (This is optional, of course, but in this case, a fine, large mosaic that includes the name "Jesus Christ" makes this church more interesting than most.)

5. **Some archaeologist will challenge the claims of others**, creating at least the appearance of a scientific conflict in the making. (In this case, anthropologist Joe Zias spoils the party by pointing out that Christianity was illegal in the Roman Empire until Constantine granted it full legal status in the fourth century. For this reason there were no Christian churches earlier than the fourth century. "The earliest it could be is fourth century and we have other fourth-century churches," says Zia. Yes indeedy.....he's right!

6. **Someone will find a way to make money off of it**. In this case the Israeli Tourism Board is already drooling. (Israeli Tourism Minister Avraham Hirshzon said the discovery could greatly increase tourism to Israel.
"If we nurture this properly, then certainly there will be a large stream of tourists who could come to Israel," he said.)

So, there you have it. Another reason to visit the Holy Land for the first time or, just like the Disneyland you have been to for a hundred times already, even if you've been there before, you won't want to miss their new, outrageously spectacular "Loopy Daffy's Cartoon Coaster Ride!"--oops--I meant to say, their new, outrageously spectacular archaeological site: "The Basilica of Megiddo!"

(Note: If entrance fee is not included in your tour costs, please pay your 5,000 Shekels at the front gate. Your support of the Israeli economy is greatly appreciated).

TUESDAY, NOVEMBER 08, 2005

Second Thoughts On the Early Christian Church Discovered at Megiddo

My **first post** on the discovery of an early Christian church in Megiddo contained a distinct whiff of sarcasm as I reflected on all they hype that usually accompanies the report of a new archaeological discovery in the Holy Land.

After thinking this over, however, and after reading what little more I could find about this particular site I have found myself becoming more excited about what may have been found.

It does appear that this "church" does not fit the model of any other known fourth century church previously found in the region. Constantinian-era church were almost always built on a site with distinct and specific historical or traditional ties with either Old or New Testament events. Such churches were always built in some variation of a basilica, a Roman architectural layout with an east-west axis and an apse in the front of the worship space (facing east).

In some cases, churches of this period and later were also built on top of the ruins of older Roman or Greek temples, often in ruins from earthquakes and subsequent abandonment.

The Megiddo "church" does not fit any of these expected criteria. It stands in the middle of what must have been part of the Megiddo sprawl, on an otherwise un-noteworthy plot of land and being essentially a simple square in design.

So far as I have heard, it does not appear to "match up" with any Byzantine chronicles or journals kept by Holy Land pilgrims nor did the preliminary reports indicate the usual sort of accompanying artifacts that would indicate that the "church" had at any time been a pilgrimage site or shrine.

Indeed, the only evidence that it might have been a Christian church at all is the large mosaic (covering 576 square feet or 24'x24') that covered an interior floor (or possibly a courtyard). This remarkable mosaic was without any doubt whatsoever created by a Christian community and intended to establish a uniquely Christian environment for those who, for whatever reason, made use of that area.

This evidence is tantalizing in its uniqueness and in the way it can fit reasonably into a time of history when Christianity was officially "illegal" but frequently tolerated during the 2nd and 3rd centuries AD of the Roman Empire.

From the New Testament we know that, while "church" buildings were built for that specific purpose, local Christian communities did meet together in designated places. Most often these meetings would take place in private homes large enough to accommodate the gathering.

Is it possible that what has been discovered at Megiddo is a 2nd or 3rd century "house church?" Could the local Christian community, along with the owners of the "house" have provided culturally appropriate decoration for the place where they gathered for worship and fellowship each week? Could various members donated the cost of the mosaic and other furnishings and their names have been incorporated into the mosaic inscriptions as a means of honoring their gifts?

One inscription declares,

"The God-loving Aketous has offered this table to the God Jesus Christ, as a memorial."

It is already being speculated that this may refer to what is now called (in Protestant churches) the "Lord's Table" or "Communion Table" where the Sacrament is celebrated as either a "remembrance" or as the "real spiritual presence" of the Lord. This would be in contrast to the Roman Catholic use of an "altar," which denotes a place of sacrifice, where Jesus Christ is actually sacrificed again and again as the "real presence" of his body is broken and the real presence of his blood is poured out during the celebration of the Mass.

(Note: This last sentence was honestly challenged in the comments section as misrepresenting the Roman Catholic theology of the Eucharist. I encourage you, the reader, to read both that comment and my reply in the "comments" for this post.)

Is it possible that the early Christians celebrated the Sacrament of the Lord's Supper (as commanded by Jesus when he said, "Do this...") on a table instead of an altar? If so, this would have important and far ranging implications theologically and provide new and exiting insight into the beliefs and practices of the early Christians.

Also curious in this discovery, is that the vast majority of the names recorded in the mosaic are those of women.

It is a fact that, before the universal acceptance and accreditation of Christianity by Emperor Constantine in 386 AD, those most attracted to the Christian faith were the poor (especially widows), slaves and women. This is not surprising since the Good News of the Gospel raised all of these people to the level of equals with everyone else ("For all who have been baptized in Christ have put on Christ. There is neither Jew nor Greek or male or female. For we are all one in Christ Jesus.") . Men, on the other hand, had to take a step down in status when they became a Christian. Within the Christian community they were now equal to women, slaves and the poor. The world changing teachings of this gospel was accepted, of course, by many men who sensed the truth in what it contained. According to the culture of the times, it was these men who took the leadership and teaching roles in the faith communities.

Even so, just as it was Jesus' women disciples who provided much of the support and (possibly) much of the funding for his ministry, it appears that it was the women who provided the support and funding for the decoration for whatever it is that has been unearthed in Megiddo.

According to a "Dr. Beeri," who submitted a comment to an article on this subject in Haaretz.com,

> *the... article states the women's names (listed in one inscription) were Primilia, Kirikea, Dorothea and Kresta...*

Of interest to me is the fact that all the names of Greek (or Latin) names. None has even a remote resemblance to a Hebrew or Jewish name (as was the case with all of Jesus' disciples and apostles).

The Washington Post

This might indicate that, even in these earliest centuries following the fall of Jerusalem by Trajan in 70 AD, the Jewish-based identity of the first Christians in what we now call the "Holy Land" had already been "taken over" by Gentile (or at least Greek-speaking) believers.

Dr. Yotan Tepper, who is heading up the excavations, pointed out another of the inscriptions (from the Washington Post**)**,

"Gaianos, also called Porphyrio, centurion, our brother, having sought honor with his own money, has made this mosaic. Brouti has carried out the work." Tepper said the inscription refers to a Roman officer -- many officers were early converts to Christianity -- who financed the structure's (or at least the mosaic's) *construction.*

Also of interest is the fact that a Byzantine era church was sitting on top of the structure with the mosaic. Dr. Tepper indicated that, although one artifact found contiguous with the mosaic could be dated to late 3rd century AD the actual date for the mosaic would not be determined until datable artifacts could be excavated from beneath the mosaic.

As a Christian pastor with an interest in biblical archaeology and early church history, I am almost overwhelmed by the potential implications of this discover. It could, of course, turn out to have been worthy of my earlier sarcasm. On the other hand it could wind up reshaping everything we know about the Christian churches of the 3rd century AD.....at least in Megiddo!

Other substantive articles on this subject can be found **here** and **here**.

A HUGE hat tip to Archeoblog

WEDNESDAY, NOVEMBER 09, 2005

Israelis Evacuated From Radisson Hotel In Amman BEFORE Blast

Update 11/10: ***Haaretz now says that the report noted below was not true. But their new story muddies the water even more. See here for the story.***

The Israeli news service Haaretz is reporting that Jordanian security forces evacuated Israeli citizens from the Radisson Hotel in Amman hours before the terrorist attack, "apparently due to a specific security alert."

The story continues to add that, "They were escorted back to Israel by security personnel."

If this is true it raises a whole lot of questions. Including:

-What did Jordan know and when did they know it?
-Were some hotel guests warned and evacuated while others were not?
-Why were Israelis singled out for evacuation?
-Was Mossad involved in tipping off the Jordanian security forces along with a demand to evacuate all Israelis?

The story reports good news for Israelis:

The Foreign Ministry stated Wednesday that no Israeli tourists are known to have been injured in the blasts. Representatives of Israel's embassy in Amman were in contact with local authorities to examine any report of injured Israelis, but none were received. There are often a number of Israeli businessman and tourists in Amman, including in the hotels hit Wednesday.

Meanwhile, the questions remain unanswered.

THURSDAY, NOVEMBER 10, 2005

Haaretz Changes Its Story Re Israeli Radisson Evacuation

Haaretz now declares that there is no truth to the story that Jordanian security evacuated Israelis from the Radisson before the attacks (see yesterday's post on this report here).

Curiously, the new article has the same by-line as the original writer, is given the same web address as the original article (meaning when you click on the link you now bring up the new article) and there is no mention that this is a "correction" of a previous report or even a mention that there WAS a previous report in Haaretz that said something different.

Is this a simple case of getting the story wrong and trying to make it right? Or is there a cover-up here. It smells bad to me simply because Haaretz is being neither honest or transparent about the matter. What do you think?

"We report. You decide!"

FRIDAY, NOVEMBER 11, 2005

Pat Robertson's Ridiculous Religious Rhetoric Returns

On May 5, 2005 I posted a story entitled, "Pat Robertson Speaks for Himself, Unfortunately."

On August 22, 2005 I added a second post, "Pat Robertson Shames the Body of Christ."

Today I am forced to proclaim that Pat Robertson has done it again.

It seems that Dover, Pennsylvania, recently voted out eight school board members who had voted to allow the theory of evolution to be questioned in their schools and to suggest that students might want to read a book on the "theory" of "Intelligent Design." Roberts, apparently, felt that this was something worthy of the "wrath of God."

According to Reuters,

I'd like to say to the good citizens of Dover: if there is a disaster in your area, don't turn to God, you just rejected Him from your city," Robertson said on his daily television show broadcast from Virginia, "The 700 Club."

"And don't wonder why He hasn't helped you when problems begin, if they begin. I'm not saying they will, but if they do, just remember, you just voted God out of your city. And if that's the case, don't ask for His help because he might not be there," he said.

So much for the Bible, which declares God to be "an ever-present help in time of trouble."

Note: Even though I am not certain that God has yet stated his position on either evolution or Intelligent Design I might speculate that God would likely take at least some small offense to a theory of *Un*intelligent Design!

Golden Gate Bridge Photo Brings Back Memories

I grew up in Daly City, adjacent to San Francisco. While browsing through BBC News online today I came across this photograph. What a great picture! I can feel the chill just by looking at it! Beautiful!

Deborah Monks: "Golden Gate Bridge, San Francisco, in early morning mist."

SATURDAY, NOVEMBER 12, 2005

Suicide Bombers Are People, Too

Khaled & Said dream of blowing themselves up

"Suicide Bombers Are People, Too." **That's the headline to a story coming out of** MSNBC/Newsweek. Yep. It's true. I didn't make it up.

The story promotes a recent film by Palestinian director Hany Abu-Assad entitled, "Paradise Now." In the film two otherwise ordinary young Palestinian men growing up in a Nablus refugee camp are selected to take their turn in a suicide bombing mission in Tel Aviv. They encounter a young Palestinian woman who decries that sort of violence and seeks peace in other ways.

According to the article,

"Paradise Now".... is one of the first feature films that tries to show the potential killers/martyrs as people.

People? Sure.

Normal people? Uh.......no.

Is it normal human behavior to want to blow oneself up?

Is it normal human behavior to want to kill innocent men, women and children?

I can imagine the movie dialogue.......

Said: How's things?

Khaled: Not too bad. Mom had me go down to the corner store to pick up some cigarettes for Dad. The toilet's broken again and my baby sister seems to spend every day either crying or messing her diaper.

Said: I know what you mean. My Mom and I spent most of this morning trying to decide what sort of water filter to install in our house. Here, have another puff on the hookah. It's your turn.

Khaled: Thanks. (He takes a puff) You know....growing up as a displaced Palestinian refugee isn't all it's made out to be. What sort of future is there for us anyway?

Said: Yeah. I guess we could both finish school (unless the Israelis close it or bomb it again). But then what? There's no work around here? Israel isn't hiring any West Bank Palestinians any more. It's hopeless.

Khaled: If only......... (he sighs).

Said: "If only" what?

Khaled: I was just thinking that if we could be free and independent in a country of our own without Israel pushing us around and destroying everything that we try to build up around here.......I was just thinking that things would be a lot better.

Said: How? What do you mean? That there would be no more poverty? There would be plenty of jobs? There would be........would there be more girls?

Khaled: Stop it. Knock it off. That isn't what I was talking about. I was talking about, well, you know........about our signing up for being suicide bombers. How that will supposedly make everything better for everybody.

Said: Except for the Jews of course!

Khaled: Yes. Sure. But.......uh......I was thinking that how can blowing myself up and killing a restaurant full of Israelis make anything better for us back here? The more I've been thinking about it the less sense it makes.

Said: Hey, stop thinking that way. You know how we both hate this place and how we want something better. You and I know that its never going to get better. We're doomed to live our lives in existential angst. Frankly, I'm filled with angst up to here! (He gestures to his forehead) The only way out of this is to go out in a blaze of glory! Freedom at last! A paradise awaits us, Khaled.

Khaled: Maybe. Maybe not. I'm not as sure as I used to be about all that. Maybe there really is some purpose and meaning to our lives besides killing, dying and hating the Jews. Maybe, just maybe the Prophet (blessed be his name) not only believed that "struggle" is good but that there are more ways to struggle for salvation and peace than just violence and killing infidels and Jews. Maybe the suicide bombing thing isn't really what is going to get us to the freedom and peace we are really looking for.

Said: Huh?

Khaled: I mean, maybe it's better to live and hope and........

Said: (Interrupting) Oh! Now I get it! It's a joke! You're joking! Good one, Khaled. You really had me going there for a minute!

Khaled: No. No. I'm not joking. I'm having second thoughts. I'm so confused. Why don't the people sending us out with suicide bombs ever send themselves out? Or their own children? Why is it always someone else's children? Like you and me? Why do the people on the other side of the wall always seem so happy, prosperous and....so.....so free?

Said: Because they are living off of our suffering. They steal everything we have ever had and destroy what they can't take with them.

Khaled: And that is what makes them happy? I don't think that's it. We have been killing and trying to destroy Israel for a long time. It doesn't seem to have made anyone around here very happy. What do they have that we don't have?

Said: Freedom.

Khaled: So it comes back to that again. Freedom. You know, I have never known freedom. Ever since I was born...and you, too...Israel has been here. (He spits) Maybe we could move to Jordan or some other place where there is freedom already. Maybe.....
Ali: (A man wearing a traditional Palestinian head scarf walks up and says): Hey....I have some good news for you. You have both been chosen to be sent into Israel tomorrow. Be at my house in 60 minutes and I'll fill you in on your mission. This willl be a glorious day for our people when the blood of Jews flows freely in the streets of Tel Aviv! Go home, get your business in order and say your "goodbyes" the way I taught you. You know, so they know what you are going to do but without you really telling them anything specific. Oh, by the way.....if you've written out your farewell speech you might want to bring that, too. We'll be videotaping it later this evening. (He leaves)

Said: God is Great, Khaled. What an honor to have been chosen. And so soon, too! Think of it! The freedom! Paradise at last! No more Nablus. No more squallor. No more oppression. No more......

Khaled: (Interrupting with a small smile) ....I know....no more angst! Said....I want freedom, too. You know that. But there has got to be another way. There has to be......

Said: Dreams and wishful thinking are not realities, Khaled. The only true reality is death; that and the paradise that awaits those who die in a martyr's glory! Well, what about it? Khaled? What about it? Are you coming?

I guarantee that the movie will have a lot of that kind of dialogue in it.

But does that make these folks human? Are they just people like you and me?

To imply that they are does a great disservice to the reputation of humanity. Such casual conversation about killing one's self and innocent others is not normal.....it is pathological. By pathological I mean that normal, healthy human thought has been twisted and warped by indoctrination and/or circumstance to the point where something close to a psychosis has taken effect.

Interestingly, the MSNBC article on "Paradise Now" is linked to a "Related Story" identified as "Dickey: The Pathology of Suicide Bombers."

Young men sitting around and talking in any way resembling what I have "made up" are of the same ilk as those who kill and eat their victims (like Jeffery Dahmer) or those who, although serial killers, manage to live otherwise normal lives...including being married and raising their own children (like the BTK Killer, Dennis Rader).

For a movie to become celebrated for showing us the "human side" of such monsters is disgusting.

For such a movie to make tons of money and be submitted for consideration as a nominee for an Academy Award is, or should be, criminal.

Note #1: I have not (yet) seen this film but am basing my comments on what others have said, including what appeared in the (mostly favorable) MSNBC/Newsweek article cited above.

Note #2: If you think that my fabricated dialogue must be way off base, consider this: The MSNBC article actually says that, in the movie, the young men

"...discuss such mundane things as water filters with their mothers just hours before they're chosen by a militant group to carry out a suicide bombing in Tel Aviv."

The article concludes with a snippet of dialogue from the movie itself. Compare it with what I have written and then reread this post in light of what you find:

Khaled: *"If we can't live as equals, than at least we can die as equals. As long as there is injustice, someone must make a sacrifice."*

Suha: *"There's no sacrifice in revenge. If you kill, than there's no difference between victim and occupier."*

Khaled: *"At least in death, we have paradise."*

Suha: *[she slaps the back of his head] "There is no paradise! That only exists in your head."*

Khaled: *"I'd rather have paradise in my head than live in this hell."*

Normal? Sure.....

Note #3: (Update) BBC has posted a **photo essay** on the making of this film. Several of the captions seem to have been lifted straight out of my "fabricated" film diaglogue. It's almost uncanny.

SUNDAY, NOVEMBER 13, 2005

Drunk Mother Smothers Infant While Breast-Feeding

A 27-year old woman, on probation for child neglects, had six double-shot alcoholic beverages before attempting to breast feed her 4-month old daughter. She says she must have fallen asleep and, when she woke up an hour later, the child was unresponsive, apparently suffocated from having a face-full of her mother's love.

The woman's husband, apparently sober when he drove her home from the bowling alley where she had consumed the alcohol, went out and got drunk himself afterwards, finding the child dead when he returned.

According to the **AP story**, the mother "was on probation for neglect of the same child, and was prohibited from drinking alcohol."

The police said that the mother's blood alcohol level was between .15 & .27 at the time the death took place. I can only guess what the alcohol content of the breast milk must have been!

All children deserve better. Foster parents are needed everywhere to help protect and save children like this from their parents. But what to do with a neglectful, irresponsible mother who is still breast-feeding her child?

Next time I suspect and hope that the judge in this case will err on the side of caution instead of once again making a decision that would allow such a child to be retained by such a mother.

SUNDAY, NOVEMBER 13, 2005

Cross-Dressing Michael Jackson Spooks Woman in Dubai Ladies' Restroom

According to the Khaleej Times (Dubai), Michael Jackon was discovered working on his makeup in the Ladies' Room in a Dubai Mall last night. A woman, who had entered the restroom for the usual reasons was surprised to find that the person wearing the traditional Dubai woman's head scarf was a man.

The rest of the story can be found **here** but the best part is that it seems that the woman and her response was considered to have been a problem while Jackson, in the ladies' room wearing women's clothing, was not.

ht:lgf

WEDNESDAY, NOVEMBER 16, 2005

Avian Flu Virus Reaches Anaheim (Not)

Once in a great while a joke forwarded by someone by email brings a smile. This one from my father-in-law did just that. I smiled so much that I decided to post it for your pleasure.

The photo caption is, of course, "Avian Flu Reaches Anaheim."

PS: I don't want some nit-picker commenting that the picture is not Disneyland in Anaheim. I know that. It's obviously a Cinderella Castle from a different Disneyworld somewhere. But that's not the point. It's a joke! It's a joke! Go ahead......smile! You are even permitted to laugh!

Aussies Blind-Sided by Glow-In-The-Dark Pork Chops

Leave it our friends from Oz to find a scandal where no one else in the world would ever think to look for one.

Most refrigerators have a little light in them. Apparently this is not the case with some folks Down Under.

It seems that reports have come in from people who opened their refrigerator only to find their pork chops glowing in the dark.

Concerns were raised amidst fears of radiation poisoning of irradiated meat.

"No worries," says the food experts. The glow is caused by "the harmless pseudomonas fluorescens bacteria."

It was explained that thebacteria were safe and were "not known to cause food poisoning."

Nonetheless, Aussies were told to "Remember this simple advice - if it glows, throw it."

(unless, of course, his name is Rudolf....)

Italians Celebrate Dead European Constitution With Commemorative Coin Anyway!

No matter that the proposed European Constitution is dead in the water and sinking fast after being voted down by the Belgians and the French.

That didn't stop the Italians from issuing a Two-Euro coin commemorating the 1st anniversary of the completion and endorsement of the Constitution by the leaders of the European Union.

BBC quotes Marco Niadi, London correspondent of the Italian financial newspaper Il Sole 24 Ore, as saying,

"We all know the constitution is not going anywhere at this moment, so to make a commemorative coin is a bit odd,.

However, he said Italians would accept the new coin without fuss, as they would a rainstorm.

"In the UK, people would ask about the cost to the tax payer and question whether it was a sensible thing to do. ***In Italy we are used to the many ways of wasting public money,****" he said.*

THURSDAY, NOVEMBER 17, 2005

Mother Goose & Grimm Go Blogging

Here is today's comic strip from Mother Goose & Grimm

You can click on the picture to enlarge it if you'd like. You can also smile!

US Congressman John P. Murtha Says, "Bring Them Home!"

U.S Representative John P. Murtha (D/PA) made several debatable assertions in a speech today, calling for the immediate "redeployment" of American troops in Iraq (the speech in its entirety can be found here).

The gist of his speech can be found in his opening and closing paragraphs:

The war in Iraq is not going as advertised. It is a flawed policy wrapped in illusion. The American public is way ahead of us. The United States and coalition troops have done all they can in Iraq, but it is time for a change in direction. Our military is suffering. The future of our country is at risk. We can not continue on the present course. It is evident that continued military action in Iraq is not in the best interest of the United States of America, the Iraqi people or the Persian Gulf Region.

....Our military has done everything that has been asked of them, the U.S. can not accomplish anything further in Iraq militarily. IT IS TIME TO BRING THEM HOME. (emphasis his)

He gives many reasons for his conclusions and I encourage you to read them. Unfortunately, his reasons are based far more on public emotion and partisan political aspirations than on any objective reality...especially in Iraq or among our US military.

Rep. Murtha is a veteran with 37 years service in the US Marine Corps. He is to be commended and respected for his service.

His military service does not, however, categorically give his opinions on US military involvement in Iraq any more weight those of anyone else who is in elected or appointed office with authority over US foreign policy and defense.

The point he makes may be worthy of debate but the evidence he musters in support of that point is shaky at it best and dead wrong at its worst.

For example, he states,

....the intelligence concerning Iraq was wrong. It is not a world intelligence failure. It is a U.S. intelligence failure and the way that intelligence was misused.

Now no one is going to argue that the US intelligence on pre-war Iraq was anything but a total failure. It is wrong, however, to say that, "It (was) not a world intelligence failure." US intelligence was gathered from many allied sources including Italy, United Kingdom, Germany and many other intelligence agencies. All came to similar conclusions. Even the United Nations was convinced that the intelligence was accurate and did not dispute it.

Murtha is also incorrect in his charge that the intelligence was "misused." The Senate Intelligence Committee saw the same intelligence that the White House saw and came to the same conclusions about its significance. This has been affirmed in several reports, including a bi-partisan investigation by the US Senate. There has been no evidence of any kind that the Bush Administration either pressured the intelligence communities to skew their data or that they White House in any way twisted or excluded intelligence that did not support some "predetermined" conclusion.

Murtha continues to comment on the morale of US troops, especially those he has personally spoken with at Bethesda and Walter Reed Hospitals in the Washington DC area:

...what demoralizes them is going to war with not enough troops and equipment to make the transition to peace; the devastation caused by IEDs; being deployed to Iraq when their homes have been ravaged by hurricanes; being on their second or third deployment and leaving their families behind without a network of support.
I have no doubt, and no sane person would deny, that these are all concerns that eat away at the morale of our troops.

What Murtha conveniently leaves out, however, is the one thing that overwhelmingly frustrates, outrages and demoralizes our troops in Iraq and Afghanistan. And what is that? The anti-war bias of the mainstream media and the non-stop criticism of the President, the conduct of the war and of the soldiers who are serving their country with such honor and distinction by both the anti-war fringe and by the leadership of the Democratic Party....including Senators Ted Kennedy, Harry Reid, Dennis Kucinich, John Kerry and.....John Murtha.

If our troops are demoralized, it is because of the sort of speech that John Murtha gave yesterday...and the news coverage that it generated. Murtha might have served honorably in the Marines but I doubt that he could be elected "Dog Catcher" by any active Marine unit in Iraq, Afghanistan or on American soil.

In Vietnam, where Murtha served, the soldiers were the disillusioned ones who saw no point to what they were being asked to do. In Iraq and Afghanistan, ironically, it is the troops on the ground (volunteers soldiers to boot) that see the point about what they are doing, support what they are being asked to do and have frequently re-upped their service with the full knowledge that they will be required to return to Iraq or Afghanistan for second and third tours of duty.

No soldier wants war. No soldier likes war. No soldier will freely choose to fight a war that they believe to be "a flawed policy wrapped in illusion." But that is exactly what members of the US armed forces are doing. Murtha's point is refuted by the actions of the very soldiers he claims to represent.

Murtha continues,

Our military has been fighting a war in Iraq for over two and a half years. Our military has accomplished its mission and done its duty. Our military captured Saddam Hussein, and captured or killed his closest associates. But the war continues to intensify. Deaths and injuries are growing, with over 2,079 confirmed American deaths. Over 15,500 have been seriously injured and it is estimated that over 50,000 will suffer from battle fatigue. There have been reports of at least 30,000 Iraqi civilian deaths.

First of all, what does he mean by, "Our military has accomplished its mission?" The Democrats have been ranting over and over again saying either that there was not legitimate mission in Iraq to begin with ("Bush lied. People died.") or that the President has never given a clear explaination of how we would know the mission was completed even if we had completed it!

Amazingly, Murtha seems to know what no other Democrat has dared even say exists: An actual goal for our invasion of Iraq.

Murtha, of course, doesn't believe there is one, either. But he does show his creativity in making one up out of thin air.....a purpose and goal that just happens, by coincidence, to support his preconceived notion that we need to get our troops out of Iraq now.

He reminds me of those good-old-days of Vietnam when critics of the war said, "Why don't we just declare "victory" and bring everybody home?" In essence, this is what Murtha is proposing. It was a lie then and it is still a lie today.

To his credit, he does not embrace the infernal urban legend that over 100,000 Iraqi civilians have died in the past 1-1/2 years. His estimate of 30,000 has widespread support.

His statement that, "Over 15,500 (US troops) have been seriously injured" is, however, a complete misrepresentation of the facts as Greyhawk at Mudville Gazette so exquisitely demonstrates. It seems that there *have* been 15,000 troops wounded but...... 8375 returned to duty within 72 hours.....7347 troops were wounded severely enough to require over 72 hours recuperation..... 2,791 Soldiers were wounded seriously enough to require evacuation to Stateside Army Medical facilities..... and 280 amputees have been treated in Army facilities as a result of the war.

As Greyhawk puts it,

A lot of unscrupulous types who just want to pretend to "support the troops" ignore these facts in favor of the less correct (and more impressive) claim that 15,500 troops have been seriously wounded, or maimed, or mutilated. The real numbers are big enough - I just can't understand why some feel the need to pad them.
I'd also like to comment on Murtha's assertion that

> *A poll recently conducted shows that over 80% of Iraqis are strongly opposed to the presence of coalition troops...*

This may be true but Murtha conveniently overlooks the fact that another recent poll showed that only 12.56% of residents of Baghdad "support the pull-out of foreign troops 'at once'." In spite of this, claiming to speak on behalf of the Iraqi people, that is exactly what Murtha proposes to do! I suppose he should be encouraged that as many 12.56% of Iraqis agree with him!

This post is already longer than I had planned and there is more in Murtha's speech that is worth debating and/or criticizing. But I shall close out this post with reference to a comment that Murtha made in response to a question at a press conference today as noted in the New York Times:

When asked about Mr. Cheney's remarks on Wednesday, Mr. Murtha replied sarcastically: "I like guys who've never been there that criticize us who've been there. I like that. I like guys who got five deferments and never been there and send people to war and then don't like to hear suggestions about what needs to be done."

In the Vietnam era, Mr. Cheney had five deferments and did not serve in the military.
Hugh Hewitt responds to this by saying,

That's fever swamp stuff, the old "chickenhawk" charge that would be equally applicable to hundreds of Democrats in Congress as well as great war time leaders like FDR. It discredits the Congressman, not his targets.

In that same post, Hugh quotes an email he received from from someone who described himself as an "active duty officer with significant combat experience":

As to the Congressman's remarks regarding our Vice President, that is a direct assault on the Constitution of the US which clearly gives the civilians control over the military. You will not meet ONE officer in our Armed Forces who does not believe in this as an article of faith. We have sworn our very lives to its protection. I find it interesting that Cong. Murtha would attack that precept of our governing document. One caller mentioned FDR. What about President Clinton? Was he unqualified to conduct the war in Bosnia due to his contempt for our Armed Forces? NO. He was the president and that makes him the commander in chief, PERIOD. Murtha should be pilloried relentlessly for his seditious remarks and he should never be taken seriously again.

Captain Ed adds his own comment to Murtha on this point,

When will Democrats get through their head that our military comes under civilian control? This isn't Starship Troopers, where only veterans make decisions on war and peace, and most Americans wouldn't want to live in that kind of society. All due respect to Murtha's Viet Nam service, but being an enlisted man in Viet Nam doesn't make him the reincarnation of von Clausewitz, either. Dick Cheney has served as a Secretary of Defense and has his own expertise on military matters, even if Murtha doesn't want to admit it.

Considering that Rep. Murtha was posing as one soldier speaking on behalf of the other soldiers in the US Armed Forces, he sure seemed to tick off most of them.

Ironic?

No.....Just pathetic. Especially when a soldier cannot even tell when his side is winning.

FRIDAY, NOVEMBER 18, 2005

U.S. Congress Says, "Leave Them There!"

What a difference a day makes!

Yesterday's poster child for the Democratic Party as the voice of both the people and the military was Representative John P. Murtha (D/PA). At a well-attended and well-covered press conference Murtha demanded the "immediate redeployment" of U.S. troops in Iraq, claiming that their mission had been completed.

Today the House Republicans took Murtha up on his demands and submitted a bill that would demand the President to begin immediate withdrawal of troops beginning as soon as possible.

So, the bluff was called. The bill submitted for a vote. And those squawking Democrats, including Kucinich, Pelosi and, yes, even Murtha, all voted unanimously to prevent any vote on the measure at all.

Unfortunately for the Democrats, enough Republicans voted to ensure that the House would immediately proceed to an actual vote.

At the end of the day, only three Democrats voted for the immediate withdrawal of American troops from Iraq(McKinney (GA) Serrano (NY) & Wexler (FL)). And SIX (Capuano,Clay, Hinchey, McDermott, Nadler & Owens) refused to enter a vote at all--simply listing themselves as being "Present." The final vote? 3 against the immediate withdrawal of US troops from Iraq.

This is the party that wants to be in control of United States foreign policy? A party that says one thing for political effect but, when it comes down to a vote, backs away from just about the only policy suggestion they have made during the past two years.

Watching this play out today I was reminded of the wonderful scene in Monty Python and the Holy Grail where, under heavy resistance during a seige on a castle, the good knights retreat to the rear, crying out, "Run away! Run Away!"

If nothing else, Rep. Murtha (who voted twice against what more or less amounted to his own suggestion) has been effectively discredited as a US military policy wonk. Today's defeat was so complete and the beating, humiliation and embarrassment of the Democrats in general and Murtha in particular was so severe that it may well qualify Murtha for his third Purple Heart for injuries sustained in combat.

When the water starts to boil over on my stove I pour some oil on it to help "simmer it down."

Today the Republican Congress not only poured a little oil on the Democrat's head of steam but probably threw a bucket or two of cold water on the fire under their kettle as well.

Note: Yes, I know that the Republican resolution did not match Murtha's proposal in any but a general sense....and, yes, I know that one Republican Representative quoted a Marine in a way that insinuated that Murtha is a "coward." And, yes, these two things dampen any Republican claim to have taken the "high road" today. Nonetheless, the matter of "immediate withdrawal" demanded by so many on the far left wing of the Democratic Party actually got a hearing and an opportunity for some comments directly related to this matter to be permanently recorded in the Congressional Record. In the end, while the Republicans did not come out looking very good, the Democrats came out looking pretty bad.

Iraq Ranks #4 in Middle East Freedom Index

Each year the British-based Economist Intelligence Unit (EIU) ranks countries according to an Index of Political Freedom.

When applied to 20 Middle Eastern countries the EIU ranked them as follows (with the most free getting the highest score):

INDEX OF POLITICAL FREEDOM
Israel: 8.20
Lebanon: 6.55
Morocco: 5.20
Iraq: 5.05
Palestine: 5.05
Kuwait: 4.90
Tunisia: 4.60
Jordan: 4.45
Qatar: 4.45
Egypt: 4.30
Sudan: 4.30
Yemen: 4.30
Algeria: 4.15
Oman: 4.00
Bahrain: 3.85
Iran: 3.85
UAE: 3.70
Saudi Arabia: 2.80
Syria: 2.80
Libya: 2.05

First of all, note that the nation most criticized and excoriated and censured by the United Nations and by all other Middle Eastern countries is also, by far, the home of the freest people in the region--Israel.

Also not the irony of having Lebanon ranked second from the top...having just recently been liberated from the oppressive occupation of Syria...which is ranked second from the bottom!

Iraq, which only a few years ago would have ranked at or near the bottom has, like an unbeaten/untied college football team, moved up in the regional rankings with amazing speed! Could it be that the United States military intervention in that country has had anything to do with this?

I find it remarkable that "Palestine" receives the same score as "Iraq." Yes, Iraq is not yet either stable or secure....but neither is Palestine. Everyone who claims that Iraq is in the process of becoming a representative democracy would be given some measure of credibility by most people...even those who may disagree with that assessment.

But what about Palestine? Does anybody really believe that people are being governed by the people they have freely chosen? Does anyone truly believe that the Palestinian government is anything but corrupt, inept and powerless to even police its own streets? Does anyone truly believe that there is any semblance of multi-party participation in the government?

In Palestine the voters are threatened and cowed by local terrorists.

In Iraq, however, the voters have *defied* the threats and attempts at coercion by local terrorists.

I suspect that next year's list will bring about a well-deserved and growing gap between Iraq and Palestine. The one going up....the other....well...you know.

By the way, here is the criteria used for making the list:

FREEDOM INDICATORS
Election of head of government
Election of parliament
Fairness of electoral laws
Right to organise political parties
Power of elected representatives
Presence of an opposition
Transparency
Minority participation
Level of corruption
Freedom of assembly
Independence of the judiciary
Press freedom
Religious freedom
Rule of law
Property rights

SATURDAY, NOVEMBER 19, 2005

200,000 Jordanians Publically Condemn Zarqawi

Al-Husseini Mosque, Amman

Between 200,000-250,000 Jordanians gathered in Jordan today to protest the terrorism of the Jordanian-born Palestinian known as Zarqawi. According to reports, the protest began at the al-Husseini Mosque and grew ever larger as it moved 1-1/2 miles from the downtown Suq (shopping area), ending at a large rally at the Amman City Hall.

The people held signs and chanted slogans such as, "Zarqawi, from Amman, we say to you: 'You are a coward.'"

Many other signs identified people as representing the many different tribal groups in Jordan...both Bedouin and Palestinian.

The media reports that, "An anti-terrorist demonstration of such size is unprecedented in the Arab world."

It appears that Arabs themselves are beginning to draw their own "lines in the sand' and declare, "This shall not stand!"

As I have said repeatedly over the past year, there will be no resolution of Islamist terrorism until the Muslim world itself rises up and takes a stand against it.

Certainly, there was no Muslim vs. Muslim sentiment expressed today in Amman (although the act of one Muslim murdering other innocent Muslims is unjustifiable to many Muslims....especially when it happens in YOUR neighborhood!). The issue was more political and nationalistic in nature....a declaration of Jordanian solidarity against an enemy who, by attacking Jordanians and Palestinians in Amman, had attacked them all, personally.

In this sense, the anger directed against Zarqawi today was intensly personal in nature. Each Jordanian there was letting Zarqawi know that he was hated by each of them, personally. A strong message that this al-Qaeda affiated terrorist will most certainly have to take to heart.

In another blunder, this time two-fold, Zarqawi released a statement intended to explain himself but will most certainly only make the Jordanian people even more outraged.

According to CNN, Zarqawi (referring to the Radisson Hotel were over 30 people attending a Jordanian/Palestinian wedding receiption were killed) denied that the wedding party was a target.

Instead, he praised who he called the "three lions (who) left their dens in Iraq and headed to the heart of Amman to carry out the blessed attacks against three targets known to be headquarters of Jews, Crusaders and other enemies of God." (He did not make reference to the would-be suicide wife who was arrested after her failed attempt to blow herself up along with her husband at the Radisson wedding reception).

Zarqawi declared that the evidence that one of the bombers purposely blew himself up amid the crowded wedding party as "baseless lies fabricated by the evil Jordanian intelligence services." Instead, he suggested that the bomb may have exploded on the floor above the reception, causing the ceiling to collapse; then adding,

Oh, our people in Jordan, what do we have to do with explosions amidst wedding celebrations? If we wanted to blow up our bombs in such places, be mindful that wedding halls are all over the country, open to everyone with no guards or security risk.

No doubt these words will fall on deaf ears of a Jordanian population that, following the November 9th bombings, gathered in the streets of Amman chanting, "Burn in hell, Abu Musab al-Zarqawi!"

The evidence is clear and undeniable....and backed up by the full confessions of one of the attackers on the Radisson Hotel....that the suicide bombers freely chose to place themselves in that wedding reception in order to kill and injure as many of those people as possible. Unless they were blind they could have easly seen that there were few, if any, Israelis or Americans in that room that night.

Zarqawi can blame the Jordanian Security folks for lying all he wants. The Jordanian people know better. He has proven himself to be a liar and a traitor to not just the ordinary Jordanian and Palestinian individual, but to the religion of Islam, as well.

The second blunder in Zarqawi's alleged tape message today is to declare King Abdullah of Jordan "an infidel and a traitor." The Jordanian people may well wonder, "A traitor to what? A traitor to who? Zarqawi? Islam?"

The motto for the country of Jordan is, "Allah (God), Homeland, The King: Jordan First."

King Hussein (l.) & King Abdullah II (r.)

By attacking King Abdullah as well as bombing hotels in Amman Zarqawi has hit the people of Jordan where they are the most passionate. Most Jordanians love Abdullah almost as much as they loved his father, the late King Hussein. Abdullah earned his own way through the Jordanian version of Special Forces and, although his power is almost absolute (he can be over-ruled by a 2/3 vote of both houses of the freely-elected National Assembly), he is trusted as one who sincerely puts the interests of the people of Jordan first in all things.

Zarqawi can never hope to attain the level of support in Jordan enjoyed by Abdullah. Given a choice, all but the most marginalized and radical Palestinians living in Jordan would choose Abdullah in a second.

King Abdullah II & Family

This second blunder is compounded by attacking the King personally with this threat,

(King Abdullah) "Your star is fading. You will not escape your fate, you descendant of traitors. We will be able to reach your head and chop it off."

This final charge will be particulary galling to Muslims since Abdullah is the Great Great Grandson of the Sharif (religious leader) of Mecca and a member of the Hashimite tribe which traces its roots back to the Great Grandfather of the Prophet Muhammad himself. (...a "descendent of traitors" ....hmmmm.)

If you listen very carefully you can hear the sound of millions of Jordanians scratching Zarqawi's name off of their 2005 Christmas lists.

Catholic Catechism For Laughs

Is it possible that the Roman Catholic Church has finally found a way to lighten up just a little bit? Has the Vatican given its imprimatur to this idea? Will Catechists have to stifle their giggles during class?

Check it out. Go to Amazon.com and type in "Church Humor" and then look at what pops up at number 18! (Yes, it's a copy of the Roman Catholic Catechism).

Coming soon: "St. Chuckles of Chalcedon Cracks the Comic Code of Aquinus!"

By the way, have you heard the one about the priest the rabbi and the Presbyterian minister . . .?

SUNDAY, NOVEMBER 20, 2005

Time Magazine Skewers Islam With Cartoon of the Week

LFG mentioned this in a post today. I checked it out and can not believe the political cartoon I found at the Time Magazine site. If this cartoon had appeared on Little Green Footballs Charles Johnson would have been immediately condemned as a bigot or worse.

It will be interesting to hear how Muslims and the "lovers-of-tolerence" folks will react to a political cartoon like this....one that I, personally, consider to have fallen over the edge of propriety.

Writer/Blogger Michelle Malkin Has Had It Up To HERE!

Conservative blogger *extraordinaire* Michelle Malkin has finally called out the racist hate-filled supposedly liberal bottom-feeders who have repeatedly called her a "whore" and made derogatory attacks on her race (Asian), her husband (a Jewish professional who, since his wife's career took off, now stays at home and helps with their two children) and have called her conservative views a pathetic attempt to mimic her "white masters."

You can read her stirring and empassioned response here.

As for me, perhaps I have lived in Hawaii for too long (13 years). Even though she has her photograph posted at the top of her blog-site (which I visit often) I had never realized until today that she WAS Asian!

Ah, me. Perhaps if I was a true liberal such things would matter to me. Sigh.....

New Evidence: Man Executed 12 Years Ago Was Innocent

An apparently innocent 17-year old Cantu in 1984

Ruben Cantu was only 17 in 1984 when he was accused of murdering one man and nearly killing a second man in Texas. During the trial his fate was sealed when the only eyewitness (the man who survived) identified him as the killer and his co-defendent chose not to tell prosecutors that Cantu had not been with him the night of the killing.

In 1993, at the age of 26, Cantu, who always had claimed he was innocent, was executed.

Recently both the eyewitness and the co-defendent signed affidavits swearing that Cantu had been wrongly charged, convicted and executed.

The eyewitness (who was an illegal immigrant) said he had been pressured by police to identify Cantu and the shooter.

The co-defendent did not say why he failed to waive prosecutors away from Cantu. Perhaps it was because he might then have been charged with the murder? Or that he had been threatened by the real killer not to reveal anything to the police?

In any case, I was struck by the story for this reason: If either of these two men had done the right thing during the trial, Cantu would be alive today. Whether pressured by police or not....whether threatened by the real murderer or not....they were the ones who held Cantu's life in their hands.

So, what does the eyewitness to the shooting, who knowingly falsely identified Cantu as the killer, say?
You've got a 17-year-old who went to his grave for something he did not do. Texas murdered an innocent person.
Yes, my friend, but you led him to the slaughter. You kissed him on the cheek. You and the co-defendent collected the 30 pieces of silver and it has taken you 21 years to come to the same conclusion that took Judas Iscariot only hours.

The news report did not make any reference to a Potter's Field.

Note: Although I do not consider the "death penalty" to be inherently immoral, this story illustrates one of the reasons I oppose its use in our legal system. I believe it should be abolished because it is frequently applied unjustly.

Locked Door Hinders Bush's Escape In China

In Beijing, China, and wanting to conclude a press conference today, Bush said, "Thank you," and walked stage right to a large set of double doors. He grabbed the handle to open the door and abruptly laughed. The door was locked.

With a slow Jack Benny deadpan and then a shy grin, Bush faced the reporters and said, "I tried to escape....but it didn't work!"

As the reporters laughed, Bush exited behind the stage backdrop.

The incident was very human and even amusing. You can read about it and even watch the video. But first you have to go to the BBC.

MONDAY, NOVEMBER 21, 2005

CNN Slaps "X-Rating"On Cheney During Speech Today

According to Drudge Report, when CNN did a live telecast of Vice-President Dick Cheney delivering a speech at the American Enterprise Institute this morning, a mysterious, large, black "X" appeared superimposed over his face at regular intervals, each time for less than a second.

The photo at the top of the post was taken from a "freeze frame" on a video of the broadcast.

CNN has not yet responsed to enquiries nor yet offered any explaination.

I suppose that someone at CNN will lose their job over this.....unless they are given a promotion, instead!

UPDATE: After a good airing out on the internet (bless their pajama-bottomed souls) the concensus is that the "X" appeared as part of a video/electronic glitch. You can just hear the sound of air being sucked out of everyone who thought they had discovered another MSM conspiracy! Michelle Malkin has the final update and Hugh Hewitt has some good links to wrap this story up good and tight.

Teen Killer of Girlfriend's Parents, "I Intended to Kill Them. And I Did."

18-year old David Ludwig has confessed to having killed the father and mother of his 14-year old girlfriend after her father refused to allow him to see her anymore.

Kara Borden also confessed that she saw Ludwig shoot her father. As she ran away she saw him point the pistol at her mother. Soon after, she says, she ran to Ludwig's car and voluntarily drove away with him. According to her statement, Kara said that she wanted to get "as far away as possible, get married and start a new life."

I can't wait to stay home and miss the movie.

Poor Embattled France Now Hit By Rail Strike

French rail workers went on strike today, shutting down nearly 60% of the country's rail service. The workers want reassurances that the government is not planning to privatize any of the national railroad system. The assurances were, of course, immediately given....no doubt with a defiant apology for the misunderstanding and a brave and courageous pledge to increase the worker's pay by whatever they suggest.

The timing of the strike is believed to have been triggered by the realization that, in the wake of the recent national riots, there were only 39 unburned (although slightly singed) cars left in the entire country, leaving commuters held hostage to the rail system.

A spokesman for the nation's disenfranchised, unemployed immigrant youths, begged to differ, saying that his sources had reported that there were at least 48 cars still operable in France and that, working in solidarity with the rail workers, his group would try and finish off the remaining cars within the next two or three days.

Meanwhile, a spokesman for Renault vehemently denied rumors that company executives had been seeing torching Renault dealerships in the hopes of increasing their declining production levels.

A British (Tongue-In-Cheek) Take on the Panther's Cheerleader Escapade

Golly gee, I just love British humor. Even British journalism is so grounded in satire that sometimes you can't tell whether you're hearing the truth or a little fib, slipped into the narrative just for fun.

This article on the two Carolina Panther's Cheerleaders (who were allegedly "holding hands" with each other in a toilet stall in a night club's women's room) is a perfect example.

Fact and fiction and glittering pom-poms give the article the sort of "savoir faire" and "joie de vivre" that invariably eludes American writers.

Click on the link and give it a read. You'll be laughing with a stiff upper lip in no time.

Note: Sorry, no pictures. At least no real good pictures. Sorry.

Gaza Palestinians Launch Fake Kosher Products Into Israel

A "Krembo" is a round biscuit topped with foamy cream and chocolate. It is a seasonal kosher treat popular with Jews all over the world.

No one at the border crossing between Gaza and Israel had ever heard of "Sambo's Krembos" before (I'm serious....I am not making this up!). After some investigation the Krembos were found to have been made in Gaza and packaged with forged kosher lables and certificates.

When the question arose as to whether the "Sambo Krembos" might possibly have been successfully exported overseas, one man claimed that he had seen them in a kosher store in Cooper City, Florida.

It is not true that Israeli border guards spent several hours checking out each fraudulent Krembo to see if plastic explosives, ammunition or suicide bombers had been hidden inside.

When questioned concerning this rumor the guards were unable to answer. It seems that they were still too busy licking their fingers.

(*Sambo's?* Krembos? You've got to be kidding...Right?.....)

WEDNESDAY, NOVEMBER 23, 2005

Hugh Hewitt's Pol Poll Poses Problematic Positions

I love taking on-line polls. I think this is because I scored well on standardized tests when I was younger. In some subliminal way, taking a poll sort of makes me feel like I might win something. But, of course, I never do.

Hugh Hewitt, the "Hockey Commissioner of Minnesota," has posted a poll at his blog today. I have no issue with the lists of "usual suspects" who may or may not be contending in the 2008 Presidential campaign.

I do, however, wonder at the choices we are given in the two multiple-choice responses at the end of the poll.

The first question gives three ways to finish this sentence:" The Republican majority in the United States Senate is: "Too Confrontational," "Just Right" or "Too Collaborative with Democrats."

Surely none of these choices comes close to representing the clear consensus of Conservatives, which is to say: "A bunch of wimps."

Regarding ANWR, we are told that one can either believe it to be "A national security issue of supreme importance," "A useful bit of exploration that will bring oil prices down in a few years" or "A disastrous despoiling of the wilderness that should left as it is for future generations."

I cannot agree with either the second of the third choices but why does the only choice left seem to be so extreme?

Most conservative folks would agree with Hugh that ANWR is a security issue. But of "supreme importance?" Probably not. Supreme means, the "highest," as in, "there is no other security issue that ranks higher than this.

Hyperbole may score points in a debate but, in a poll, it puts words into people's mouths that make the answer taste as though there was too much chili or thyme in the entree than the recipe called for.

Japanese Spacecraft DID Land on Asteroid

Last Sunday, Japanese space officials lost track of their Hyabusa Space Probe for three hours during what they later said was a failed attempt to land the probe on an asteroid. Today, however, they have determined that the craft DID, in fact, land on the asteroid and remained on the surface for at least a half-hour before taking off again.....but without any rock or soil samples.

The probe's shadow is clearly seen on the asteroid last Sunday

The fact that the landing was a success is a great acheivement, technologically. Scientifically, however, it was a great disappointment.

As a result, the craft is being maneuvered back to the asteroid for an attempt at a second landing.......this time with the hope that it will pick up some rocks or gravel or *something* for scientists to analyze when, and if, it safely returns to earth.

Christian Top 1000

Christian Top 1000 is a blog aggregator that bills itself as "The Ultimate Christian Directory." I discovered it while reading another blog recently and decided to sign up. Blogs are listed in order of visits per day. I landed at #251 out of 2300 blogs listed.

I am seven spots above "Teen Girl Hangout" and five spots behind "Jesus--About My Return." Personally, I would think that Jesus' blogsite would have been ranked higher than that. But, then again, I am only ranked 10 places below "The Word of God" which, I should think, places me in some good company.

Dying for a Drink--England Volunteers To Help

Two news stories today struck me as somehow related.

The first, from BBC, tells of new regulations in England and Wales that will permit 1000 pubs, clubs and supermarkets to sell liquor 24-hours a day. In these establishments there will never again be anyone to say, "Sorry, mate. We're closing up. Time to go home."

In the second story, we read of a 34 year-old man in Norway who downed 19 shots of tequilla in 90 minutes. He then fell into a coma and died. The bartender who served him the drinks was sentenced to 6-months in jail.....not for causing his death, but for serving drinks to an intoxicated man.

The story also noted that the bartender apparently tricked the man into thinking he was engaged in a drinking contest by downing shots of water to encourage the other man to keep drinking!

I suppose that popping into the pub for a "quick one" at 3 am might seem better than draining a bottle of vodka in your apartment by yourself. On the other hand, if you were already home, you wouldn't have to drive anywhere afterwards.

Note: As some sort of a public service the BBC attached a link to an article entitled "How Much Is Too Much?" Apparently the man in Norway hadn't read it. Too late now......

Brazil's Police 'Execute Thousands'

A BBC investigation has determined that "hundreds, if not thousands," of Brazilians are executed" by Brazilian police each year.

"Around 60% of the bodies of people that were killed by the police had more than six shots," explains (Former police ombudsman Professor Julita) Lemgruber.

"Most of them [were shot] in the head and in the back - mostly executions."

It was reported that "in the state of Rio alone, the police killed 983 people last year. The figure is similar for Sao Paulo."

A former military policeman, Gordinho (not his real name), says executions by police death squads are common.

"Everyone knows the police here in Rio de Janeiro... nearly all of them abuse their authority," he says.

Most people killed by police are criminals caught up in raids, officials say "When you get excited you feel you are the law... The shooting cases you hear about, most of them are executions.

"It's all premeditated--very cold-blooded and calculated."

The story is quite chilling. It makes Iraq seem like a safe place in comparison!

THURSDAY, NOVEMBER 24, 2005

Being Thankful In Hawaii

Today is Thanksgiving and the Honolulu Advertiser published two pages of letters to the editor from local people telling what they are thankful for. The names of the letter-writers have their own stories to tell. Their names represent the story of Hawaii. Indeed, they *are* Hawaii. For the privilege of living among them....for this I am Thankful!
Hale, Buss, Medeiros, Yang, Spadavecchia, White, Mori, Rieben, Perry, Gibbons, Lui-Kwan, Choy, Lihilihi, Eng, Powell, Sussman, Ruidas, Sawyer, Koki, Tenn, Villalino, Sandry, Cassen, Levey, Ballucanag, Grotstein, Aldenderfer, Aki, Abraham, Cazinha, Guerrero, Rarangol, & Fujiyoshi.

HAPPY THANKSGIVING!

Jordan Becomes the First Arab State To Declare War On Terror

(Note: This may be the most important article I have ever posted. It has been written with fear and trembling).

AP has released remarkable story today. It is so full of hope and is such a wonderful Thanksgiving Day present that I'm about to bust....and I haven't even eaten dinner yet!

On the other hand the implications of this story may be almost apocalyptic.

I have always known that, at some point, an Arab nation would be pushed to the point of saying, "Enough!" to the likes of bin Laden, Zarqawi and the so-called theological school of thought that justifies their use of lethal force against anyone that may be considered to be an infidel....even other Muslims.

Well, today the time has come. King Abdullah II of Jordan has said, "Enough!"

Here are some excerpts from the story:

AMMAN, Jordan (AP) -- Jordan's King Abdullah II appointed a new prime minister Thursday and urged him to launch an all-out war against Islamic militancy in the wake of the deadly triple hotel bombings earlier this month....

(We reaffirm) our need to adopt a comprehensive strategy to confront the Takfiri culture," Abdullah said, referring to the ideology adopted by al-Qaida and other Islamic militants who condone the killing of those they consider infidels.

Abdullah said the strategy should "not only deal with the security dimension, but also the ideological, cultural and political spheres to confront those who choose the path of destruction and sabotage to reach their goals."

The king called for a "relentless war on all the Takfiri schools, which embrace extremism, backwardness, isolation and darkness and are fed on the ignorance and naivete of simple people."

I have no doubt that Abdullah's father, the late King Hussein, would be proud of his son today. I am, too.

By God's grace, other Arab nations will follow suit.

War has been declared. As a direct result there will be much violence in the Arab Middle East.

Egypt, Jordan and Saudi Arabia will be hit hardest at first. It is uncertain whether the government in Egypt, in particular, will be able to stand.

The goal of the Bin Laden's, the Zawahiri's and the Wahabbi, Takfiri, Muslim Brotherhood and Taliban ideologies is to remove the governments of every Muslim nation, replace those governments with a unified rule under Sharia law, and, ultimately, to remove national boundaries entirely, thereby creating a vast, pan-Muslim "empire" that will sweep across the world for Islam.

To use a word that is anathema to them, these folks are "crusaders" in the worst sense of the word.

Western nations will be hard-pressed to step in and assist these soon-to-be embattled nations, yet great restraint must be shown lest the Muslim populations be swayed on impulse to join the Islamists simply to resist the "non-Muslim infidels."

This new "war" must be fought between Muslim and Muslim; Imam and Imam.

The violence, however, will likely spread across Europe and Asia (including the southern republics of the former Soviet Union) all the way to the Philippines.

It is also likely that the intentional and strategic freeze on direct attacks on the United States (a strategy designed to prevent any rise in support for the war in Iraq) will also be swept away.

In the end, only God and Muslims will be able to resolve this matter.

Until now, however, it has all been pre-game warm-up.

What King Abdullah has done today may, in retrospect, be seen as the game's opening kick-off.

Pew Poll Results Predetermined by Who They Chose To Ask

Powerline's John Hinderacker has a wonderful post today in which he dissects what, on the surface, are polling results that appear to show overwhelming lack of support for the war in Iraq.

Based on what is revealed about the demographic status of the pre-selected subject samples it becomes clear that the results of ths Pew Poll were pre-determined from the start.

Read the poll. Read the post. We report....You decide.

Court Rules Girl Will Not Be Returned To Her Parents...Huh?

When Anna Mae He was born in Tennesee back in 1999, her parents, immigrants from China, were facing financial and legal problems.

Shaoquiang "Jack" He and Qin Luo "Casey" He did not feel that they could provide stable care for their first-born child until these matters had been resolved. Accordingly, they arranged for Jerry & Louise Baker to have what they believed was temporary custody of her.

When, some months later, the Hes returned to get their daughter, the Bakers said, "No."

At issue was the fact that the girl's parents had not visited her in over four months. The Bakers declared something to the effect that this constituted legal abandonment.

When the courts became involved, they ruled on behalf of the Bakers.

Yesterday, a state appeals court upheld that ruling.

Shaoqiang He, who now works as manager of a Chinese restaurant in Memphis, responded by saying, "We don't understand why it is so difficult for our family to be reunitied."

The Hes, who still hold Chinese citizenship, are still wondering, after five years of legal battles, what they did wrong?

I also wonder about this.

Anyone who has ever worked with the child welfare system, the child protective services or the foster care programs know how hard it is to permanently take a child away from their natural parent or parents.

Parents must be proven to be unfit in a court of law.

Before the legal ties that naturally bind child to parents can be broken, the parent/s are given repeated opportunities to "get their act together." They may go through drug rehabilitation programs...even serve out a jail term. The child, in the meantime, is placed in foster care only if there are no other family members or close friends willing and able to care for them.

Even when the decision has been made, a process that often take years, the parents are given numerous rights to appeal that decision.

In every case the legal responsibility rests with the county or state to prove that the parents are unfit.

When there is any uncertainty at all, courts will almost always err on the side of the child's parents.

Even when a newborn child has been legally released for adoption, the birth-parent has a relatively long period of time to reconsider their decision and to revoke the legal declaration that they had signed earlier.

What is it about this case in Tennessee that makes it so different?

The He family is now stable. They have regular income. They have two other children that they are providing for. There is no record that they have ever abused any of their children and there is no evidence that they have ever acted out of anything short of having their children's best interests in mind.

Why, I wonder, are the Bakers so defiant? Why do they demand to keep someone else's child as their own? Is "possession" 9/10 of the law in Tennessee?

The Chinese Embassy has publicly supported the He's attempts to regain custody of their daughter and has led Chinese community groups to complain of cultural bias in Tennessee courts.

The He's are already planning their next appeal which will be to the State Supreme Court. It is unlikely, I think, that it will go beyond there as I cannot see any Constitutional matter at issue. I'm sure that route will be pursued, however, if the He's should lose again at the state level.

Pray for Anna May. Pray for her parents. Pray for the Bakers. Pray for the Tennessee Supreme Court justices who will hear this case. Pray that God will "works for the good" in this sad, sad and seemingly unnecessary impasse.

Thanksgiving In Hawaii

Thanksgiving dinner in Hawaii brought together an interesting group of people this year.

JJ was born in Korea, was a prima ballerina and speaks four languages. She has also recovered from a heart attack that left her without a heart-beat in the emergency room.

Dorothy was born in mainland China, has nearly recovered from a stroke and just returned from a trip to China where she keeps in touch with members of her family. As always, she took plenty of Christian Chinese literature to give away to Christians there....(she knows people in both the state-endorsed and the unapproved and often persecuted house churches).

Sean was, a few years ago, a member of the Hawaii State Champion High School Football Team at St. Louis High School in Honolulu.

Quinton and Kalen are brothers who are swim champions and Eagle Scouts. Kalen is also a triathlon and cross-country champion in his age group.

Barry is an expert on submarines

Judy leads and teaches the Hawaii Bible Study Fellowship (BSF) in Honolulu.

Not to mention a U.S. Navy officer, a tile and ceramic wholesaler, four nurses, a university faculty member, a retired military meteorologist, a church organist, an administrative assistant (for a US Congressional-sponsored international relations project that brings future political, diplomatic and military leaders together for seminar training from the Pacific Basin, South and South-East Asia and the Middle East), a U.S. Postal Service employee (aka "mailman" or "letter carrier"), and an assortment of children and young people.

And me, Bird of Paradise (aka "Pastor").

What a great group of people to share Thanksgiving Dinner with this year.

As you can imagine, there were plenty of interesting conversations taking place around the various tables.

Everyone filled out a card and listed something they were thankful for:

The most frequent reason for being thankful was family, followed by knowing God's saving love in Jesus Christ, being a part of a loving church family and then a mix of health and other assorted blessings.

What are your reasons for being thankful this year?

Ordinarily my Wonderful Wife and I host the "open-invitation" dinner at our home each year. With my wife still recovering from a hospital stay less than two weeks ago, the Submarine guy and his BSF/nurse wife were kind enough to offer their home instead.

So....the bad news is that we didn't get to keep all the left-overs when everyone left....but...the good news is we didn't have to set up the house and clean it up afterwards!

Usually I have a snack in the evening before going to bed. Tonight I am too filled with turkey and the blessings of friends and family to even think of adding anything more.

Jihad Comes To Oakland Like "A Clockwork Orange"

The security videos capture the African-American men, all dressed in suits and bow-ties, as they enter the grocery stores in Oakland. They also capture them smashing the stores to pieces (with special attention to the liquor and beer displays) with their hands and with metal batons.

The arrogant coolness of these "men with a mission" is chillingly reminiscent of the gang of thugs in Stanley Kubric's "A Clockwork Orange."

No one was badly beaten or raped, however, but Charles Johnson at LGF notes that the men's sartorial splendor looks suspiciously similar to that worn as the unofficial "uniform" of members of the Nation of Islam.

Store owners were accused of "poisoning our neighborhoods;" a clear reference to the selling of alcohol, a beverage forbidden in Islam.

Has sharia law come to Oakland?

My guess is, "Yes."

FRIDAY, NOVEMBER 25, 2005

Michael Jackson: "Jews Are Leeches" and I'm Converting To Islam

Well, the King of Pop is soon to be a Muslim living in Bahrain. At least that's the story coming out of that small kingdom today.

American pop star Michael Jackson has officially announced that he has been following the five tenets of Islam and intends to convert to Islam, according to a report on the website of Arab-Israeli newspaper Panorama.

The report is based on information elicited from sources in Bahrain.

According to the report, Jackson's announcement noted he is moving to Bahrain and has purchased some real-estate on an artificial island there. The singer said he decided to convert to Islam because he is convinced it is the closest religion to his personal beliefs.

According to a phone recording released last week, among Jackson's "personal beliefs" is one that considers Jews to be "leeches."

According to that story,

Jackson is heard saying that "they're like leeches...I'm so tired of it. They start out the most popular person in the world, make a lot of money, big house, cars and everything. End up penniless. It is a conspiracy. The Jews do it on purpose."

I suppose that fits in with most Muslim attitudes these days, at least in the Middle East.

The story of Jackson's conversion to Islam continues,

Jackson also noted he intends to soon move all his assets and his studio from the U.S. to Bahrain, and expressed his hope to be rid of various legal troubles and enjoy the kind of freedom he says he does not have in America.

Considering that Jackson is supposed to be flat broke, how does he come up with enough money to buy and artificial island and house in Bahrain? And what assets does he have that are not already claimed by creditors?

In any case, it looks as though Neverland will be left behind for good.

I wonder if we have an extradition treaty with Bahrain?

I also wonder if child molestation is considered to be a crime there? Maybe Jackson will name his new home, "Pleasure Island."

Jackson has been a creative and talented entertainer. He is also, as I have stated before, a very troubled man. I cannot, in good faith, wish him well in the new path he appears to be taking. I would prefer to see him submit to the judgement of God, repent and be "born again" into a new and improved Jackson rather than to see him pick a religion because it "comes close" to agreeing with his own beliefs.

What about his hope that he will "enjoy the kind of freedom he says he does not have in America"? Well, when you have enough money, you can enjoy freedom without accountability in just about any corrupt, despotic country you care to choose.

It is only in nations that believe all individuals are to be held equally accountable under the law that a rich man or woman loses the freedom to do whatever they want.

If this is freedom for Michael Jackson, then perhaps it is better for all of us for him to live in Bahrain.

Japanese Spacecraft Lands On Asteroid....Again!

According to BBC News,
Japan's space agency says it believes its Hayabusa probe has become the first to collect samples from the surface of an asteroid.

The craft made a successful landing on the asteroid Itokawa and fired a small metal ball to loosen surface material for collection, the agency says.

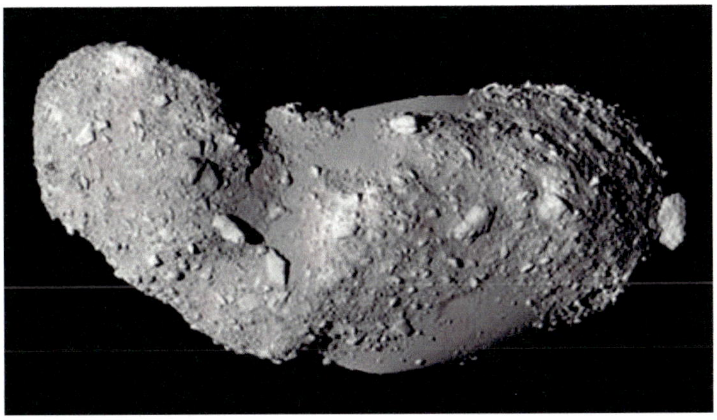

But scientists will only be sure the probe picked up the loose matter in 2007, when Hayabusa return to Earth.

I don't know about you but this story convinces me of two things:

1. Modern technology is amazing and not limited to the United States, and

2. There is no need to send men and women to Mars when research and exploration can be done nearly as effectively, far more safely and much more inexpensively by unmanned space probes.

It is my opinion that the Japanese engineers that designed and built this asteroid mission have the "right stuff!"

I congratulate them and join them in hoping for a successful conclusion to the mission in 2007.

SATURDAY, NOVEMBER 26, 2005

Help! We're Running Out of Sea Water!

In today's Honolulu Advertiser there is a letter to the editor that is worth posting simply because of its unassailable logic.

It seems that bottled, purified, desalinated deep-sea water is a big thing in Japan these days. It's a fad thing, like the Pet Rocks of legend.

On the Big Island of Hawaii at least two commercial outfits have plugged into this gold mine and are pumping deep-sea water to the surface where they (surprise!)desalinate, purify and bottle it.

This is, most certainly, the inspiration for this letter. I honestly cannot decide if it is a sincere, but naive, effort from a child or sarcasm written by an adult. Read it and decide for yourself!
Selling Hawai'i's sea water is a no-no. To read that our precious sea water is being sold for commercial profit is very disheartening and needs some soul-searching.

Taking Hawai'i's sea water could eventually cause environmental danger to shorelines and also to seaweed, fish, crab and so on.

Sea water is in this world for many special reasons; selling it is not one of them.

Hmmm....

Boston's 'Holiday Tree' Captures the True Spirit of Secularism

Boston Mayor Thomas Menino has declared that he will keep calling the city's 48' Nova Scotia spruce a "Christmas tree" regardless of the fact that the city is officially calling it a "Holiday Tree" this year.

"I grew up with a Christmas tree, I'm going to stay with a Christmas tree."

Many conservative Christians are not happy with the removal of "Christmas" from the seasonal symbol.

Neither is the Nova Scotia man who cut the tree down for donation to Boston, a tradition of "thanks" since 1917 for Boston's help in the aftermath of an explosion in Halifax that killed 1,900 people.

Donnie Hatt was indignant and said he would not have donated the tree if he had known of the name change.
"I'd have cut it down and put it through the chipper," he told a Canadian newspaper. "If they decide it should be a holiday tree, I'll tell them to send it back. If it was a holiday tree, you might as well put it up at Easter."

Sorry, Donnie, but you can't celebrate Easter anymore, either. You might call it a "Spring Holiday Tree" but that's about as far as you can go these days, at least in the law-suit-fearing, politically correct, secularist cities on the outer fringes of the United States.

Just wondering..... what other holiday tradition besides Christianity puts up a hewn evergree tree and decorates it with lights, ornaments and tinsel every year in December? Kwazaa? Hannukah? (my Jewish friends had "bushes")

Oh, I see. We just take the symbol and remove what it symbolizes! As a Christian I consider that to be a rape of my faith. The tree is a symbol for the everlasting life that is ours in Jesus Christ whose birthday we celebrate on December 25 each year.

How dare a city take my religious symbol and strip it of its significance. What right does government have to step into my religious tradition and manipulate it for its own commercial purposes.

Whatever happens to the so-called "separation of church and state" when the state can mess with my religion but will not permit me to express my faith in a public place?

If the city of Boston does not want to have a "Christmas Tree" this year then they should not have a tree at all! Period!

Let them put up a totem poll and offend other people for a change.

"Merry Holiday?" Bah.....Humbug!

SUNDAY, NOVEMBER 27, 2005

Personal Correspondance from al-Anbar Province, Iraq

A friend and former member of my congregation is a Marine officer currently deployed in al-Anbar Province in Iraq.

In reply to a recent email, he writes:

I enjoyed getting your letter and I, and all the Marines, soldiers, sailors and airmen, are very appreciative of all the prayers and good wishes that are sent our way. I think you might like the article below – I was directly involved with this Operation and can attest the validity of the reporting . . .

This is a very good article that needs to be highlighted. For those of you that have spent time over here, you know what I mean. For those that have not, this article speaks to what is really going on that, of course, is not reported in the mainstream media. Americans need to hear the truth, the whole truth, not just what CNN / Headline News want them to hear.

Semper Fi, (name withheld)

The Badlands of Al Anbar

Cutting the ratlines and quashing the insurgency in Western Iraq
By W. Thomas Smith Jr.

Insurgencies are not put down in a fortnight. But considering the successes in the recent counter-insurgency sweep in Iraq's Al Anbar Province, one fact becomes obvious to anyone with so much as a sliver of an understanding of ground combat operations: Eliminating the insurgency in Iraq is best left to those who best know how to do it.

Not the White House: Americans learned the hard way in both Vietnam and the Iranian desert that the Oval Office should never call the tactical shots once forces are committed to action. President Bush understands this, and thus — to all of our benefit — does not micromanage his commanders in the field.

Certainly not the House and Senate: Many on Capitol Hill seem more concerned about scoring points with their stateside constituencies than they are the Marines and soldiers who must battle the enemy on the ground. And make no mistake, the ground along the Euphrates River valley and up along the Syrian border has been the stage of an ongoing series of running gun-battles between insurgents and coalition troops for months.

Therein lies the obvious: The troops on the ground, taking the fight to the enemy, are the ones who best know how to quash the insurgency. They are doing so systematically. The proof is in the results of their work (whether opponents of the war want to believe it or not), and the vast majority of those troops express no intention of abandoning that country with work to be done.

(Don't miss the rest of the article. Click here to read it all!)

Hanging of the Greens

Tonight our church held its annual "Hanging of the Greens" service. In 30 minutes we sing carols and decorate the Worship Center. When it is beautiful for the Advent Season we head off to the lanai for our first taste of Christmas cookies since last year. Our Preschool children and Adult Choirs also sang. But the evening is especially wonderful for the children.

Here are some photos I took this evening. Click on them to make them bigger! Enjoy....

...

.......................Before.............. ....After..........

...

....Preschool Children Sing

...

.............Decorating the Tree

...

...

...

...

Creche.................

....Worship Elders

ANNIVERSARY

Panama Canal Miraflores Locks Video Cures Bordom

Bored? Never fear....hope is on the way!

Just click here and watch one week of shipping traffic at the Miraflores Locks on the Panama Canal condensed down to just over 11 minutes.

BoingBoing describes it as hypnotic...
Watching the stately dance of the giant ships, day and night, passing through the locks, is like watching ogres waltz -- their grace is perfectly offset by their hulking, container-stacked brutal unloveliness.
As a bonus, watching this video is guaranteed to cure insomnia.

FOX News Analyst Gets Un-Fair & Un-Balanced Treatment vs Cindy Sheehan

The Daily Star reports that anti-war zealot Cindy Sheehan will receive $11,000 in student fees to speak at the State University College at Oneonta.

FOX News military analyst and Iraq war veteran Lt. Col. Scott Rutter, who will counter Sheehan in a separate presentation, will receive $600.

Now that's what the far-out left would call, "Fair and Balanced...You Decide."

ht:Michelle Malkin

News Flash: George Bush & Tony Blair Forced Clinton to Bomb Serbia!

The Opinion Journal caught this mind-bender this past weekend:

Simon Jenkins, a columnist for London's Sunday Times, comments on reports that President Bush and Prime Minister Tony Blair toyed with the idea of bombing al-Jazeera, the Qatar-based TV network:

> *That Blair and Bush should have discussed bombing the Al-Jazeera building in Qatar is hardly surprising. They agreed to bomb the headquarters of Serbian television during the Kosovo war.*

Well, color us impressed. Who knew President Bush was already conducting foreign policy back in 1999, when he was still governor of Texas?

ht:Instapundit

Move-On.Org Screws-Up On Anti-War Ad

So many soldiers who have served in Iraq or Afghanistan have told me how much they resent the biased and skewed reporting by the American media in their coverage of the conflict.

Opinion Journal has a report from a returned soldier who saw something that left him wondering whether he should laugh or cry:

Yesterday we got an e-mail from an old friend who is a captain in the U.S. Army. He writes:

"I just got back from my third deployment from Iraq on Friday, and I happened to be at the dentist and saw a completely offensive ad from the idiots at MoveOn.org this morning. Anyway, it is a Bush-bashing ad that pretends to be arguing for American soldiers families as they will miss the holidays and it shows turkey and crying wives and blames Bush for it all. Here is the crucial part of the ad that I would like to bring to your attention. As they pretend to argue on my behalf, they show a group of soldiers standing around a table in the Middle East."

Here's the scene to which our friend refers:

"A hundred and fifty thousand American men and women are stuck in Iraq," according to the narration that accompanies this scene.

Our friend (we've cleaned up a bit of his language for civilian consumption) continues:

"These are not your normal everyday U.S. soldiers though. If you look at the frame they are actually British soldiers. One is in shorts (we don't have shorts as a normal combat uniform) and the others are all clearly wearing British pattern fatigues. So, my point is that these [turkeys] pretend to argue on my behalf and bash the president in the name of my crying wife, and they don't even know what an American soldier looks like! Anyway, it really [ticked] me off.

"The only thing that would have made this more galling is if the ad had mentioned that the liberation of Iraq was "unilateral."

ht:Instapundit

Update: Not only did MoveOn get the wrong soldiers in their ad but, when they realized their mistake, their first response was to literally "cover it up!" That tell-tale Brit wearing the shorts just had to go, so the MoveOn folks PhotoShopped some camoflage fatigues onto his bare legs and posted the altered photo on their web page......at least until the news media, being tipped off by dozens of bloggers, started calling them for interveiws on the debacle. With (one would hope) red faces, they have removed both the video ad and the photo from their web site. Score one more for the blogosphere! You can see the altered photo at **Michelle Malkin** and many other sites as well.

Suicide Bomber in Iraq Was Belgian Woman

The Jawa Report records this sad story....one that I expect we will hear more of in the future: A convert to the ROP (ie. "Religion of Peace" aka "Islam") left FranceJunior (Belgium) to become a suicide bomber in Iraq. Here's the saddest part: her Muslim husband is said to have talked her into it.

According to UPI:

> *A woman who carried out a suicide attack in Iraq two weeks ago was identified Tuesday as the first European female suicide bomber.*
>
> *The Belgian anti-terrorism unit has confirmed that the woman was a Belgian citizen who converted to Islam after her marriage to a Muslim fundamentalist, news service RTL reported Tuesday.*
>
> *American military forces identified the woman at a combat scene in Baghdad. She was carrying recently issued Belgian identity papers which revealed she had traveled via Turkey. There are no traces of her radical husband who is believed to have organized her trip.*

One Jawa reader left this pithy comment: "Divorce. Sharia-style."

Sad. Sad. Sad.

Osama bin-Laden Dead? Did Senator Harry Reid Blab Top Secret Report?

Update: It appears that the actual \audio of the Reid interview shows that he did not imply that he had been "informed" of the "bin-Laden is dead" idea; simply that he had "heard" it. Where? Through the grapevine?On the web? At the Senate barbershop? This seems to diminish the charge (written below) that Reid had somehow improperly revealed classified information gotten in some sort of "briefing."

I have frequently criticized bloggers who either just "go" with whatever the daily story is or those who simply ape the bigger bloggers who they look up to and follow like "groupies." It seems that I did the same thing with this story. I should have spent a little time confirming its accuracy. For this I apologize.

"Loose lips sink ships," they say. If that's true then some ship somewhere is filling up with water at this very moment!

The source of this leakage is none other than Senate Minority Leader Harry Reid, who appears to have suffered a relapse of his seemingly chronic "Loose Lips Syndrome."

Last May he publically made use of an unverifiable reference to a confidential FBI file to damage the reputation of a Bush judicial nominee to the 6th Circuit Court of Appeals.

Now, as reported by John Fund,

Is Senator Harry Reid all that swift when it comes to U.S. Intelligence matters? Last Wednesday, the Minority Leader appeared on KRNV-TV's "Nevada Newsmakers" program and dropped a stunning revelation. He had been informed just that day that Osama bin Laden was killed in the giant Pakistan earthquake last month.

"I heard that Osama bin Laden died in the earthquake, and if that's the case, I certainly wouldn't wish anyone harm, but if that's the case, that's good for the world."

Intelligence analysts tell me that the only proper action by a top U.S. Senate leader who has been given such information is radio silence. If the report is true, such information is best released at a moment of the U.S. government's choosing. For one thing, as long as the information is tightly held, it can be used to sift out electronic intercepts that might lead to other Al Qaeda leaders. On the other hand, if Mr. Reid's public speculation proves groundless, it only embarrasses the U.S. and contributes to enemy morale....

If the Navy ever launches a USS Harry Reid I can guarantee that it will sink straight to the bottom. Glub.

ht: Michelle Malkin

WEDNESDAY, NOVEMBER 30, 2005

Hawaii Supreme Court Ruling Has Important Abortion Implications

From today's Honolulu Advertiser:

The Hawaii State Supreme Court unanimously (5-0) overturned the conviction of a . . . *woman whose newborn infant died because she smoked crystal methamphetamine during her pregnancy.*

The high court ruled that the homocide prosecution of Tayshea Aiwohi did not fall under state law because her unborn child was not a "person" when she smoked the drug.

This will no doubt come as a surprise to Scott Peterson who, just one year ago, was conviced of 2nd Degree Murder in the death of his unborn son, Conner.

In the Hawaii case, the mother. . .*said she used ice the three days fefore the birth and took a "hit" on the morning of (her son's) birth.*

The baby died two days later of what the city medical examiner's office found was high levels of methamphetamine and amphetamine in his system.

The implications of this ruling are far-reaching.

As one Justice stated in an opinion signed by four of the five Judges (the fifth wrote a separate opinion), the "logical implication" is that a person cannot be prosecuted for causing the death of a child by injuring the pregnant mother.

The reason for this is clear: An unborn child cannot be a "person" when someone other than the mother causes his/her death at the same time that the same child is NOT a "person" if the mother causes his/her death.

I should think that in Hawaii, at least, this would mean that a Doctor who does something prior to a baby's birth that either kills, permanently maims or otherwise injures the child cannot be prosecuted because, at the time of the incident, the unborn child was not yet a "person" under the law.

This would mean that a drunk driver who slams into the car of a pregnant woman and causes either the death of her unborn baby or a miscarriage cannot be prosecuted for the same reasons.

There can be no doubt that this ruling will create years of litigation chaos in Hawaii.

If an unborn child is not yet a "person," what is it? The property of the pregnant woman? (Note: She can't be called the "mother" because there is no "person" to be a mother of!) Does a father have any claim on "ownership" of his unborn child? Or is the unborn child simply an extension of the womans body, like her are or her legs?

Could the person causing harm to the unborn child be charged with personal injury against the pregnant woman? Or with destruction of property?

It is all absurd, of course. And the reason for this absurdity is this:

The Hawaii Supreme Court knows (and almost every other US Appeals Court knows) that to rule that the unborn child is a "person" would have a profound impact on the legality of abortion. Because the law permits a woman to voluntarily dispose of her unborn child at virtually any time during her pregnancy, it MUST follow that the unborn child is not a "person" and is, therefor, not in possession of any personal legal rights, including the rights of "life, liberty and the pursuit of happiness."

Because of the illogic of the decision of the U.S. Supreme Court in Roe v. Wade, the courts must twist and bend and contort common sense in order to protect this so-called phantom "Constitutional Right" for a woman to have an abortion without legal penalty.

The solution to this is clear.

The U.S. Supreme Court must revisit Roe v. Wade and revoke the Constitutional interpretation on which that ruling was based.

This does not mean that abortion need be declared unconstitutional, of course. The most simple respose is to erase the ruling from Federal jurisdiction completely. All existing state laws (all of which permit abortion in varying degrees) would be untouched. This would return the abortion debate to state legislatures and, if necessary, to the U.S. Congress to determine whatever limits or boundaries should be set both nationally and regionally.

It would appear to me that the definition of what constitutes a "person" under the law should be a Federal matter rather than a state decision. This has precedence in the Federal abolition of slavery, a decision that effectively removed the right of the states to make arbitrary distinctions between what constitutes a "person," half of a person or when a non-person can be deemed to be property (slavery).

The logical solution to this mess is to rule that an unborn child is indeed a "person" but without the full constitutional rights of a full-born person. Perhaps the age of viablility could be considered a legal turning point.

If the law allowed, a woman could be given the legal option of terminating her pregnancy at certain times under certain circumstances. This could even be voted into state constitutions as a "right" if the legislatures and the voters agreed.

In this scenario state law could clearly state that the "right" of the woman to terminate her pregnancy trumps the "right" of the unborn child to be carried to full term and birth.

Such a law would preserve some status of "personhood" for the unborn; allowing for the prosecution of those, other than the prospective mother, who might injure or cause the death or miscarriage of the unborn child.

Until people realize that the Gordian Knot and the legal mess that is Roe v. Wade cannot be unraveled but must be cut to pieces and disposed of entirely at the Federal level, we will continue to have confusion and chaos in every legal matter that pertains to an unborn child.

Personal Note: As a Christian I believe abortion to be a grave moral sin; not an unforgivible sin, certainly, but a sin nontheless. Within the pluralistic context of American society I will do all I can, within the law, to affirm the personhood and protect the human rights of the unborn.

Even so, it is not the Christian Church's role to impose its moral standards on those who have not accepted the Christian faith. It is, however, our Christian moral duty to attempt to pursuade and to influence public opinion on this and many other important matters.

With abortion and other difficult issues, Christians should be very careful to remove the beams from their own eyes before even thinking about pointing out the specks in everyone elses.

Roman Catholics No Longer In "Limbo?"

Captain Ed Morrisey gives all of us Christian folks a "heads up" with a post that offers an inside look into some important stirrings in the Vatican

Specifically, rumor has it that a special theological advisory group will soon be suggesting to

Pope Benedict that he declare an end to the teaching of the existance of "Limbo" in the Roman Catholic Church.

Limbo is a non-biblical, theological construct from the Middle Ages, created, in part, to explain the destiny of dead, unbaptized babies.

Captain Ed suggests that, if Limbo goes into limbo, the doctrine of Purgatory may step up to fill in the gap.

Update On White, Middle-Class, Belgian Suicide Bomber

Here is an update on the Belgian woman suicide bomber I wrote about yesterday:

MIREILLE, who was born in Belgium to a white, middle-class Christian family, blew herself to pieces last month in a suicide attack against American troops near Baghdad. In one of the most extraordinary tales of Islamic radicalisation, she is thought to be the first white Western woman to carry out a suicide bombing.

Belgian investigators, who arrested 14 people associated with her, are keeping the 38-year-old woman's true identity secret, but details have started to emerge. She was from the southern Belgian town of Charleroi, married to a Moroccan and converted to an extreme form of Islam.

"This is how she came into contact with the organisation which allowed her to become a fighter for jihad," said Glenn Audenaert, the federal police director. Her Belgian documents show that she travelled with her husband to Iraq. On November 9 she blew herself up in a car bomb attack on a US military convoy, killing — according to conflicting reports — either only herself, or six people. Her Belgian passport was near by. Her husband was killed by American troops in a separate incident.

As I said yesterday...Sad. Sad. Sad.

HT:lgf

TUESDAY, DECEMBER 06, 2005

Do Muslim Extremists Control 80% of American Mosques?

Personally, I think this figure is way too large. I'd guess more like 40%. But Yehudit Barsky, an expert on terrorism at the American Jewish Committee, seems to believe that the 80% figure is (unfortunately) very accurate.

You can read about why he feels this way and also learn why he feels this way by checking out this summary story at Little Green Footballs.

P.S. I hope he's wrong. But I don't think I'll lay down any bets on it.

John Dean Says Iraq War Cannot Be Won

In an interview yesterday on **WOAI San Antonio**, John Dean, the Chairman of the Democratic Party, said that,

(the) idea that we're going to win the war in Iraq is an idea which is just plain wrong.

Dean went even further, comparing Iraq with Vietnam:
I've seen this before in my life. This is the same situation we had in Vietnam. Everybody then kept saying, 'just another year, just stay the course, we'll have a victory.' Well, we didn't have a victory, and this policy cost the lives of an additional 25,000 troops because we were too stubborn to recognize what was happening.
He then added,

President Bush got rid of Saddam Hussein and that was a great thing, but that could have been done in a very different way. But now that we're there we need to figure out how to leave. 80% of Iraqis want us to leave, and it's their country.

My summary:

1. We are not winning in Iraq and will never win;
2. Therefore, the sooner we cut our losses and leave the better;
3. It was good to get rid of Saddam, but a military invasion was not necessary;
4. The sooner we leave the happier the Iraqi people will be.

My response:

1. What does "winning in Iraq" look like? Does Dean have a definition of this? If not, how can we know if winning is possible or not? Does he offer a definition? No. Has the Bush administration offered a definition of "winning in Iraq?" Yes. Is it acheivable? The administration says, "Yes." Does Dean disagree or disagree with the Bush administration's definition and prediction? We don't know. He won't comment on it. Does Dean offer any context to indicate what in the world he is talking about? No.

2. Let's see....Korea was an "unwinnable war." Actually, no one won and no one lost. It sort of was put on hold as a tie. If the United States had "redeployed" our troops two years earlier we could have saved many American and Korean lives. As a bonus, we would have had a unified Korea, too! Just like Iraq was unified before we invaded it! Think how many American lives could have been saved if we had not invaded Okinawa during WW II. We had pushed Japan back on every front....back beyond where they had been before WW II even started. We could have just called it quits right then, called it a victory (which it was) and just gone home. By doing this we could have avoided that atomic bomb mess, too. Dean's logic is unassailable!

3. Yep! Sanctions and inspections were working. Surely Saddam would have grown weary of them eventually and quit or retired or surrendered sooner or later, right? Or, perhaps Dean envisions a well-aimed missile from an unmanned Predator drone.....That would have shaken things up in Iraq! Maybe Uday and Qusay would have stepped up to take their Dad's place and chosen the United States and the rest of the free world as their ally! Hey, anything's possible! And the sad thing is we'll never know because we never tried.

4. Oops. One small detail overlooked here. The Iraqi government, made up of elected leaders

from every race, sect and district in the country.....the only folks with any legitimacy to speak on behalf of the country.....want us to stay a while longer. When I was in the hospital years ago I desparately wanted to be somewhere else and wished that the nursing staff would leave me alone! If I had been asked some polling questions on the subject I would have said so. But, on the other hand, I probably would have died. What we want and what we need are not necessarily the same thing. A national leader who does not know the difference between wanting and needing something should not be a national leader.

My Conclusion:

1. As Party Chairman, John Dean represents and speaks on behalf of all Democrats.
2. John Dean is nuts and so is everything he says.
3. Therefore: ______________________ (you get to fill in the blank)

THURSDAY, DECEMBER 01, 2005

Too Much Narnia?

I have read through the Chronicles of Narnia three times and the well-worn first volume more often than that! Every time I have been enchanted and charmed by the vivid themes and imagery or this C.S. Lewis classic.

As a Christian I have also enjoyed the many Christian themes of sin, evil, goodness, beauty, courage, sacrifice, atonement, resurrection, redemption, salvation, pilgrimage, and even the creation of a new heaven and a new earth that Lewis has so deftly and creatively woven into the stories of Narnia.

With my now-grown children my wife and I watched and were wondrously impressed with the imaginative and faithful translation of these books into visual reality by means of the creative genius of WonderWorks, which produced the first three books as a BBC mini-series back in the late 1980s.

On December 9 the new movie, "The Lion, the Witch and the Wardrobe," will be released by Disney. I trust that this version will also be true to the original. If it is it will be a wonderful addition to the legacy of C.S. Lewis and Narnia.

Unfortunately, along with a major movie release comes all the commercial tie-ins that will make a lot of money but will, ultimately, also have the potential to cheapen the substance and compromise the character of the movie and the book that inspired it.

Consider this list of Narnia-related products being sold at Christian Book Distributors:

*-**The WonderWorks Chronicles of Narnia** DVD Set;*

*-**The World of Narnia Collection** (children's illustratedabridgmentt);*

*-**The Chronicles of Narnia** CDs (a British-made audio set complete with Sir Anthony Quail, Claire Bloom, Michael York and Ian Richardson);*

*-**The Narnian: The Life and Imagination of C.S. Lewis**, by Alan Jacobs;*

-The Chronicles of Narnia*, 7 volume set (both a movie tie-in set with photos from the new movie and a set without the tie-in);*

-a ***One-Volume edition of the entire Chronicles of Narnia****;*

-The Official Illustrated Movie Companion *(for The Lion, the Witch & the Wardrobe);*

-Inside Narnia: A Guide to Exploring The Lion, the Witch, and the Wardrobe*;*

-Knowing Aslan *(an evangelism booklet to help interpret the movie to non-Christians);*

-The Lion, the Witch, and the Wardrobe--2006 Wall Calendar*;*

-The Chronicles of Narnia, Limited Edition: Focus on the Family Radio Theatre-- *CDs;*

-The Lion, the Witch & the Wardrobe Board Game*;*

-Stratego, Chronicles of Narnia Edition*;*

-The Chronicles of Narnia Activity Books *(for children ages 4-8);*

-Music Inspired by The Chronicles of Narnia: The Lion, the Witch, and the Wardrobe--*CD;*

-The Chronicles of Narnia soundtrack*;*

-Narnia Book Covers*, including: "Long Live the True King," "Aslan Duotone Bible Cover," "Narnia Map Bible Cover," and the "Narnia Bible Cover."*

I can't wait to see the Chronicles of Narnia action figures in stores just in time for Christmas (Am I joking? Nope! Check out the photo at the top of this post. It is linked to Amazon.com)

I do know that the heirs and Estate of C.S. Lewis put many restrictions on the marketing of the movie and related capitalist product spin-offs. But from what I am seeing in catalogues it appears that there are plenty of Narnia products for consumers to choose from.

My prayer is that the movie will lead even more people to read these wonderful books than have done so previously. No matter how good the movie is, it will never replace the books.
In the recent Lord of the Rings Trilogy, the movie was remarkably faithful but still had to omit many of the most lyric, mythological and transcendent passages for the sake of keeping the action moving. While these movies were an excellent production worthy of the praise they received, they in no way can ever replace the written words of J.R.R. Tolkien as they appear in the books themselves.

My nightmare is that the commercialization of Narnia will relegate it to the status of Winnie the Pooh, which, in the hands of Disney, has become almost a parody of itself and the Milne books that originally brought him to life.

Narnia deserves better. By God's grace we will never see a Saturday morning "Narnia" cartoon program on TV.

I'll see you at the movie.

WEDNESDAY, DECEMBER 07, 2005

Pearl Harbor Day In Hawaii--64-Years Later

Today is December 7th. At 7:55 am my house was rocked with the roar of low-flying military jets. A tight formation of F-16s curled over Mililani on their way to a fly-over of Pearl Harbor and the USS Arizona Memorial.

It was at 7:55 am on this date in 1941 that the Japanese surprise attack on Pearl Harbor began.

Each year Hawaii remembers with a ceremony traditionally attended by representatives of the nation of Japan. Wreaths are laid and flower leis tossed into the water from the Arizona Memorial, that stands astride the remains of the battleship that carried 1,177 sailors to their watery grave on that "infamous" Sunday morning.

Living survivors of that day still gather to remember. Their numbers growing smaller each year. Those who live in Hawaii volunteer at the Memorial every day, greeting visitors and telling the stories of the death and heroism of their friends and comrades. Soon, they will be gone and only their stories will remain.

This year, special honor was given to the USS Ward, a that happened to be on patrol off the entrance to Pearl Harbor that morning. At around 5:45 am someone on the ship spotted what appeared to be the superstructure of a miniature submarine, heading in the direction of the harbor entrance.

Ironically, the USS Ward was hit by a Japanese kamakazie plane on December 7, 1943, exactly three years after the attack on Pearl Harbor

The command was given to fire. The ship fired twice. Because of good aim or good luck, the sub was hit and sank to the bottom, taking its two Japanese crew members with it.

Historically, this is considered to be the first formal engagement between the United States and Japan in WW II....one hour before the attack on Pearl Harbor began.

The remains of the miniature submarine were discovered not too long ago, in 1200 feet of water not too far from where the USS Ward's log said it would be. Its exact location has not been revealed to protect it from scavengers. It is now protected by law.

Those who have visited the USS Arizona Memorial over the years know how emotional that

experience can be. I, personally, have visited it five or six times, once for an evening retirement ceremony for a naval officer who is a member of my congregation.

The ship, although under water for these past 64 years, has never been de-commissioned. As such, the USS Arizona is treated as any other active-duty ship in the American naval fleet. Visitors must receive "permission" before being piped "on board" the Memorial.....which is considered to be a part of the ship. Naval personnel offer the appropriate salutes to the ship and to her crew.

If you know where to look a visitor can find bullet holes and shrapnel damage on numerous structures standing at Hickam Air Force Base, Pearl Harbor, Wheeler Army Airfield and Schofield Barracks. It is a sobering thing to walk up a flight of steel stairs in what was once a Hickam barracks and literally step on a hole punched through the 1/4-inch steel by a 20-mm shell on that long-ago day when the United States was attacked by Japan.

There are many beautiful and wonderful natural and historic sites in Hawaii. But for me, and for many others, there are none that impress more than the National Cemetary of the Pacific (Punchbowl) and the USS Arizona Memorial.

Back in 1942 a song called, "Remember Pearl Harbor," became a national hit. I am glad that we still remember. On the one hand, it was a day of defeat and humiliation. On the other hand, it was the day a nation that would soon become the most powerful country in the history of the world "woke up" and roared.

Willow Creek Church Will Close Doors On Christmas Sunday

At Willow Creek Community Church outside Chicago, Sunday morning generally features eight worship services at four locations with 15,000 people attending.

On Christmas Sunday this year, their doors will be closed.

As quoted in USA Today:
Cally Parkinson, a spokeswoman for Willow Creek Community Church in South Barrington, Ill., said church leaders decided that organizing services on a Christmas Sunday would not be the most effective use of staff and volunteer resources. The last time Christmas fell on a Sunday was 1994, and only a small number of people showed up to pray, she said.

"If our target and our mission is to reach the unchurched, basically the people who don't go to church, how likely is it that they'll be going to church on Christmas morning?" she said.

According to Willow Creek the only reason to worship God on Sunday is to reach the unchurched? I thought that Christians worshipped God on Sunday in order to......uh.....worship God!?

Sure Christmas is a busy day....for families in particular. There are stockings to poke through. Bicycles to assemble. Presents to unwrap. Food to cook. Guests to accommodate. Trips to make. When Christmas falls on a Sunday, like it does this year, how can people be expected to squeeze in a morning worship service in the middle of all that?

Christmas, after all, is about families, isn't it? Or is it about God....and Jesus....the Incarnation...the Word become flesh....the advent of the Son of God....Immanuel....the Prince of Peace.

On that first Christmas,

-Angels took the time to form a choir, and;

-Shepherds took time off in order to find the baby Jesus and worship him.

It seems to me that the Christmas story provides a clear guide to what should be a Christian's priority on a Christmas Sunday morning.

After all, the only present really worth celebrating on Christmas Day is the gift of Jesus himself.

Come to think of it, Easter morning is a busy time for families, too. All those egg hunts and Easter baskets and family gatherings and travel plans and cooking big Easter meals.

Perhaps Willow Creek should close down on Easter, too. It's a real bother that Easter has to land on a Sunday every year.

Note: It's almost enough to make **this parody** seem like the real thing!

ht:Captain's Quarters

FRIDAY, DECEMBER 09, 2005

Sentenced To Death for Self-Defense

Everyone's talking about Stanley "Tookie" Williams these days.

Will California Governor Arnold Schwartzeneger commute his death sentence for having murdered four people in cold blood during his gang days (which was pretty much all that he did before being convicted and sent to prison)?

The news media and Hollywood stars are having a field day with this story.

Meanwhile, down in Mississippi, a man sits on Death Row, convicted of a crime he almost certainly did not commit.

Cory Maye was asleep in the middle of the night in his duplex apartment, alone with his young daughter, when his front door was suddenly kicked in by men wearing black. Fearing for his life, and the life of his daughter, he grabbed a gun he kept near his bed (the house was not in a genteel neighborhood) and shot the first man in the door as he approached.

Unfortunately for Cory, the men were police officers participating in a drug raid on the other apartment in the duplex. It is not clear whether the police identified themselves or not as they entered. Most likely they did not since they had already identified themselves as they had entered the neighbor's apartment moments earlier. The men entering Cory's apartment had thought they were entering the same first apartment through a side door.

But they were wrong; and the officer shot by Cory died as the bullet entered his lower abdomen just beneath his bullet-proof vest.

Even more unfortunate for Cory, the slain officer was the son of the Police Chief. Both were white. Cory was black.

Cory was eventually charged and found guilty of the willful murder of a police officer and sentenced to death. Previous to the night his home was unlawfully invaded Cory had never in his entire life been arrested or charged with a crime.

Evidence points to a incompetent and biased jury, an inept public defender and a charlatan hired by the family to file appeals briefs (which were not filed in a timely fashion). And, of course, a charge of murder that should never have been brought in the first place.

You can read more detalils about Cory Maye's tragedy here and here and here and here. (Note the last two links are news articles that do not even mention that Maye's apartment was not the one identified in the search warrent. In fact they infer that Maye was the prime suspect in the drug raid.)

You can also feel free to contact Haley Barbour, the Governor of Mississippi, and politely request that he consider doing the right thing and pardon Cory.....before he gets a lethal injection for the crime of defending himself and his family.

Governor Barbour's address and phone # are:
P.O. Box 139 Jackson, MS 39205
Phone: 601.359.3150 or 1-877-405-0733

PS: Silent Runnings has posted an "open letter" to Governor Barbour. I'm sure you will be permitted to copy it and send it as your own if you are either not creative enough or have enough time to write your own.

Was Missile Fired at AA Flight 612 Over LA Last Month?

Check out this story now making the internet rounds.

A missile or rocket may have been fired at American Airlines Flight 612 as it gained altitude after take off from Los Angeles International Airport late last month.

ABC Radio twice aired a news story on the subject. After that the story disappeared.

Is their a government cover-up? Are American passenger jets in danger from shoulder-fired surface-to-air missiles?

This story is scary.

Whether it is scary like a Stephen King novel or scary because it is true we do not, as of today, know for sure. Follow the link and decide for yourself.

Be sure to check out the internal link to the LAX airport monitor. Really creepy.
As for the internal link to the air traffic controller recording with AA 612, the relevent bit is literally the last thing on the recording.

Mainland China Troops Shoot Down 20 Unarmed Demonstrators

Here is an excellent NY Times article (plus an update AP release taken from CNN)describing a horrible slaughter of poor Chinese fishermen farmers in a village in Southern China.

Is this simply an unfortunate error in judgment or a strategic display of authority to curb future demonstrations?

Is the demonstration itself a rarity or something becoming more and more common in recent months? Does it represent a growing dissatisfaction in China with the current government regime? Does it constitute a legitimate threat to the stability of the country?

SATURDAY, DECEMBER 10, 2005

A Christian Dialogue With Muslims:The Trinity, Forgiveness & Jesus Christ

An article on Michael Jackson I posted two weeks ago at blogcritics continues to generate dialogue (it is still on the "Hot Topics" list). The comments have, over time, morphed into a dialogue between an Orthodox American Jew living in Israel, several very "evangelical" Muslims (who are determined to convert me to Islam), and myself.

Recent conversations have spurred me to post several responses that I thought I'd share with my readers. What follows are the opening sentences of six postings. If you want to read all of a post, just click on the link and you will arrive at the rest of it. (Note: For tes print edition I have included the entire texts).

Thoughts On God's Forgiveness #1

I wrote the article that started this thread. I am a Christian Pastor in Hawaii. I have Muslim friends. I am part of the Hawaii Multi-Faith Leadership Forum that includes the President of the Hawaii Muslim Association/Mosque President and am friends with the Muslim School Headmaster who I have twice invited to share what Musllims believe with my adult Sunday School class (he as also proofed the Islam portion of my World Religions material and affirmed it as accurate). I correspond on matters related to Islam with a Muslim Professor at a Major American University. I have read the Qur'an twice(yes, I spell it Qur'an...sorry Noanchor...just like I spell Aqaba and Qatar properly) in two English translations and refer to it in study often. I do not believe that I have the integrity to speak about another person's faith unless I personally know it as well or better than most believers.

Having said that, I must express my personal belief that the God of Islam is distant, impersonal and unreachable. The God revealed to us in the Old Testament and more clearly in the Injil is near to us by his Holy Spirit, personal in his desire to love and be loved and reachable through the incarnation, death, resurrection and ascention of his eternal Son, Jesus Christ.

From this I conclude that either the Muslim concept of God is a regressive one (such as is found in American Unitarianism) or is simply a different God altogether from the God of Abraham, David and Jesus.

The Christian God is both perfectly merciful (in forgiving our sins) and perfectly holy and just (in requiring penalty for our sin).

The Muslim God can neither be perfectly merciful mor perfectly holy or just. For at judgment, Allah only forgives the sins of those whose righteousness exceeds their sin (refusing to extend mercy to those whose sins exceed their righteousness) and also fails to impose any penalty for the sins committed by those whose righteousness exceeds their sin.

This is as though a Judge in a court of law told a convicted child molester, "Well, you have done more good things than bad things in your life so I'm going to let you go free. Your sin? Forgetaboutit. No Penalty. Next case."Such a God may be merciful to some but, in so doing, makes a mockery of justice and permits the unchanged sinner into Paradise along with their sin.

For the sake of brevity, one final thought. If Islam is so willing, open and confident in its intellectual, historical and spiritual superiority, why are other faiths banned, restricted or persecuted in Muslim countries? What are they afraid of? If Islam is so "open" and "civilized" why does it impose the death penalty (shirk) on those who, of their own free will, desire to convert to another faith?

I find it ironic that this dialogue on the relative merits of Islam and Christianity are taking place in a forum and a country where the freedom to do so is grounded in the Christian principals of individual live, freedom and the pursuit of happiness and truth.

This dialogue could not even take place in a Muslim nation, especially one governed by Sharia.In this manner the superiority of Islam is demonstrated by its denial of the very rights that we are here enjoying.Jesus said, I am the Way, the Truth and the Life, no one comes to the Father except by me.

He also said, You shall know the truth and the truth shall set you free.

May it be so. Insha Allah. Salaam.

Salvation Is a Gift from God Received Through Faith In Jesus

Kashan, In my Christian faith my eternal salvation has been "purchased" for me by Jesus Christ. I receive this "gift" by faith and repentence of my sin. This salvation is assured as a "covenant promise" from God.

In Islam, I must earn that salvation through my own righteousness. That is impossible since God requires that we "be holy" as God is holy. Jesus himself states that we must "be perfect as our Father in heaven is perfect."

Jesus once asked his disciples why they did not leave him. They replied, "You have the words of eternal life."

This is why I follow Jesus as Lord and Savior. This is why Islam, with all its requirments and uncertain hope, will never lure me away.

Shalom. Salaam. Aloha. Peace.

Thoughts On God's Forgiveness #2

Kashan says "it is not true" that Jesus took our sins because we must bear our own burdens.

In the Christian faith this is not true. And it is not because of Paul. Jesus himself says, "Come to me all you who are weary and heavy-laden, for my yoke is easy and my burden is light." Here Jesus clearly tells us that when we are yoked with him he will bear the burden that we are not able to carry ourselves. This burden is, of course, sin.

The prophet Isaiah prophesied that a day would come when there would be one of whom it would be said,
"Surely he took up our infirmities and carried our sorrows, yet we considered him stricken by God, smitten by him, and afflicted.

But he was pierced for our transgressions, he was crushed for our iniquities; the punishment that brought us peace was upon him, and by his wounds we are healed.
We all, like sheep, have gone astray, each of us has turned to his own way; and the LORD has laid on him the iniquity of us all." Isaiah 53
The holiest day in Judaism is Yom Kippur, the Day of Atonement. On this day, God commanded that the blood of a sacrificed goat be sprinkled on the people as a sign of the forgiveness of their sin (the goat symbolicaly suffered on the people's behalf for their sins.) On a second goat, by the laying on of hands, the sins of the people were symbolically laid upon the animal, which was then set loose to carry the sins away into the wilderness.

God teaches us clearly that we are not able to carry the burden of sins by ourselves. For our sins to be forgiven God requires "atonement" or the payment of a price by means of suffering or sacrifice. No mere animal is sufficient for this, of course, and no mere human can endure the suffering or, in righteousness, pay the price for the atonement of the sins of the world. God alone, who is Life and Light is able to bear that suffering and provide the righteousness needed to satisfy the forgiveness of sin.

Christians believe that Jesus Christ was without sin (something that God and his prophets have taught us is not possible for any mere human to accomplish) and took our sins upon himself on the cross so that we might be relieved of the unbearable burden of them.

Jesus himself "forgave sin" during his ministry....something that no "prophet" has ever done before or since. Only God can forgive sins that offend God.

Christians believe that in Jesus Christ, God revealed his very self to us. Jesus was, as the Injil itself tells us (again quoting from Isaiah), that Jesus was Immanuel...a title that means, "God with us."

When asked if he was the "Christ (Messiah), the Son of the Most High God," Jesus replied, "I AM." A response that not only affirms the answer to the question but also claims for himself the Divine name of God revealed to Moses.

I suppose the the prophets, the Injil and Jesus, himself, were completely wrong on this point...which would mean that they were not prophets at all. The alternative is that Jesus was who he was prophesied to be and that he was who he claimed to be.

If Jesus does not fulfill God's requirement for the atonement of our sins by a sinless "other" then who does? If there is no one to fulfill this requirement then we are still in our sins and as righteous as a bunch of "filthy rags" (Isaiah again).

That does not bode well for a final judgement.

This post is too long already. I'll add something on the Trinity shortly and separately.

Aloha

Thoughts On the Doctrine of the Trinity

(On a more serious note, it seems that the concept of the Trinity is the major stumbling block between Christians, Jews and Muslims.)

Here is a thought about the concept of the Trinity. First of all we must dismiss the argument that the idea of the Trinity is absurd or illogical.

Pretend I am holding a dime in my hand. There is just one dime. Yet it also has a "heads" and a "tails" as well. One dime yet two surfaces. How can one dime be two different things? This would easily fit in with the Torah and Prophets who teach that God is present with us by the Holy Spirit. Clearly God cannot be present with us in his fullness lest be be destroyed, yet, by his Spirit, that which is truly God can indeed be "with us."

The coin is both heads and tails. But the coin has one more surface as well: its edge. How can one coin have three parts? Well, it is obvious that it does. If you remove any one of the parts you are left without a coin. The three parts are inseparable from the coin. As long as the coin has existed there have been these three parts. The "heads" is just as much the "coin" as is the "tails" and the "edge." Each part is fully and only composed of the unique essence of the coin.

Yet each of the three parts is unique and distinct from the other two parts.

This is what Christians mean when we say that we believe in One God in Three "Persons," Father, Son & Holy Spirit. The Father is God; the Son is God and the Holy Spirit is God. Yet each is distinct in their own right.

The prophets teach us that "God is not a man." This means that God is not to be thought of as we would think of a person. God is somehow more than singleness. Genesis tells us that God created Man in the image of God...not "Man" in the sense of one person, but in the combined sense of "Male and Female God created them."

The word often used for God in Hebrew is "el" which is singular. "One God." But the word is also used in its plural form, "elohim," to describe God. Not that there are more than one God but that the very nature and substance of God is somehow plural.

Islam denies this. Christianity affirms it. We also affirm that the eternal person of God that we call "the Son" entered this world in human flesh ("incarnate") and, in his human form, suffered and died for our sins and rose again to life to demonstrate God's power over sin and death, assuring us those who believe that we, too, shall experience resurrection and the gift (not earned, but given) of eternal life.

Folks are free to reject the idea that God is a Trinity of Persons but it would be a clear mistake to insist that the concept is illogical or absurd. It is, in fact, more illogical and absurd to require that God's nature be, of necessity, a singularity in some anthropomorphic sense. The very nature of God is shrouded in mystery. We can only glimpse God as God chooses to reveal himself to us. Everything else is guessing.

Aloha

PS I am not debating or trying to prove anything here...just explaining.

Thoughts On God's Forgiveness #3

Ghazan,

The Muslim and Christian view of God/Allah is, in fact, very similar. The names of God as recited in your faith (a traditional list with commentary can be found **here**) are all acceptable to Jews and Christians as descriptive of God's nature.

Yes, of course God is a merciful and a forgiving God. But God is also a holy God; pure and spotless and perfect in righteousness. None of us come close to this. We all fall short of the glory of God. This is what Christians call sin...falling short of the holiness that we were created to enjoy.

Besides the nature and person of Jesus Christ, one of the biggest differences between Muslims and Christians is how we believe God deals with our sin.

You, Ghazan, and Kashan before you, have described the relationship between our sin and the attitude of our heart towards God. Christians agree with this, too. When we turn away from our sinful nature and set our eyes on loving, serving and pleasing God, this is what we call "repentence." For Christians, this is the first step a person takes in faith....it is a step that is necessary for a person to receive the assurance of God's forgiveness and salvation.

The difference between us is that you state that God can forgive who he pleases.... God declares that he will forgive the sins of a man or woman whose heart is inclined towards him......whose goodness and righteousness exceeds their sin.

Chrisitians also believe this. But we also recognize something more. Our sin may have been forgiven but we are still sinners. No matter how good and righteous we may be, we will still carry that sinful part of us into Paradise where we will, like Adam and Eve in the Garden of Eden, begin the fall of humanity all over again by sinning again.

This raises an interesting question: If Adam and Eve were righteous prophets and yet sinned against God, why did God expel them from his presence. Why did God not simply forgive them in the same way that you believe God will forgive you and let them back into the garden?

The reason is that, once back in the garden, they would have sinned again.....and again....and again....

Sin was imbedded in Adam and Eve in the same way it is embedded in us today....like a malignant tumor that eats at us and eventually brings death to us....even if 80-90% of the rest of our body is healthy and fit.....Yet because of the tumor, we will still die, just as a mostly righteous man will also die because of the sin that is in him. No matter how small the sin, it will still be enough to kill him.

Forgiveness was not enough. God's holiness and perfect righteousness requires that we also be holy and righteousness if we are to ever stand in his presence in Paradise. Holy and unholy, righteous and unrighteous cannot stand side by side.

This is why Christians believe that Jesus is the Savior of the World. At the time of his baptism, John the Baptist prophesied of Jesus, "Behold the Lamb of God, who takes away the sin of the world." Note that Jesus does not just take away the sins of the world, the bad things that we do....John declares that Jesus takes away the SIN of the world....Sin itself is taken away.

Forgiving a sin is like treating a symptom of a disease. What Jesus did was to remove the disease itself. Jesus cured us of sin. He removed it from us. Where did the sin go? The Injil tells us that Jesus took our sin upon himself and died with it.

When, in resurrection, we stand before God in judgement, the risen Jesus will stand alongside us and declare us to be not only forgiven but cleansed and purified totally and completely so that in holiness and righteousness we can live with God forever.

You ask, If Jesus took our sin, then he died a sinner and therefore he was neither a prophet nor was he sinless. How can this be?

My answer: Being righteous and holy, Jesus was immune to sin. He could embrace it and take to himself but it could not infect him. When he died on the cross, the sin, along with his body, died and was buried with him in the tomb. When he arose from the dead, the sin remained in the tomb (so to speak) dead and buried forever.

How can Jesus be righteous and holy? No human being can be righteous, holy and good. Jesus himself said so. When someone once called him, "Good teacher," Jesus replied by saying, "Why do you call me 'good?' There is only One who is "good." (meaning God). It is important to note that nowhere in this teaching does Jesus tell the man that he was wrong to call Jesus "good." He just wanted the man to know what he had unwittingly done, he had declared Jesus to be holy, righteous and good as only God can be holy, righteous and good.

Either Jesus was a sinner like you and me, and therefore could not bear our sin on the cross (in which case we are not saved) or else he was holy, righteous and good as only God can be holy, righteous and good....in which case he is not only our Savior but is also our Lord. This is exactly what Jesus taught his followers when he said, "I and the Father are One." And again, "He who has seen me has seen the Father."

This is what every Christian confesses to believe when they claim Jesus to be their Lord and Savior.

Islam, however, does not offer a Savior.

God may indeed forgive your sins in the final judgement, Ghazan, but that forgiveness will not make you holy, righteous or spiritually clean. How do you think you can enter Paradise in the presence of God and take sin along with you? Is Paradise populated by millions of people who are "mostly good" but still doing "just a few" evil things against God and one another from time to time? How can a holy and righteous God tolerate such rebellion within his people. Surely they all will be cast out just like Adam and Eve were in the beginning.

Thoughts On God's Forgiveness #4

Kasham asks, So, if I am forgiven by Jesus of all my sin then I can do anything I want and it won't matter, I'll still enter Paradise.

Some of the first Christians also were confused on this very matter and actually claimed what you say to be true. They were severely chastised and rebuked for this. In Romans 6:1-6 we read, *1What shall we say, then? Shall we go on sinning so that grace may increase? 2By no means! We died to sin; how can we live in it any longer? 3Or don't you know that all of us who were baptized into Christ Jesus were baptized into his death? 4We were therefore buried with him through baptism into death in order that, just as Christ was raised from the dead through the glory of the Father, we too may live a new life.*

"5If we have been united with him like this in his death, we will certainly also be united with him in his resurrection. 6For we know that our old self was crucified with him so that the body of sin might be done away with, that we should no longer be slaves to sin—

This is very simple for a Christian to understand. It is what our faith is built on. This why the New Testament declares of Jesus, "that there is no other name in heaven and on earth by which we must be saved."

A good, sincere and faithful Christian will, by their free choice, try to please God in all things....to be obedient to his commandments (especially the command to Love God and Love Neighbor)...and to avoid the things that might tempt them to turn astray.

Christians need not do this in order to enter Paradise....but because they have already received the promise of God that Jesus Christ has saved them from their sin. Christians live good lives out of gratitude for what God has *already* done for them.

This is why Christians are not "fatalists" (at least not as regards salvation). Christians are, or ought to be, optimists as regards to their eternal destination because, as the Bible tells us, our hope is "certain." Why? Because,

"God is not a man, that he should lie, nor a son of man, that he should change his mind. Does he speak and then not act? Does he promise and not fulfill?" (Numbers 23:19)

Through faith in Jesus Christ as Lord and Savior, God has promised me eternal life. (John 3:16) I, for one, am happy to hold God to his Word!

SUNDAY, DECEMBER 11, 2005

Enormous Oil Refinery Explosion & Fire In England

England's "Sky News," under the headline, "Massive Explosions At Fuel Depot," states the following:
A huge fire continues to burn at the country's fifth largest oil storage depot near Hemel Hempstead where a series of explosions injured 43 people early this morning. A fire chief has described it as the largest peacetime incident of its type in Europe(emphasis mine).
Police authorities almost immediately assured the public that the explosion was not caused by terrorists or an airplane. One can only wonder how they have ruled out terrorism when they also admit that they do not yet know the actual cause of the expolsion and subsequent blaze.

Apparently, just a week ago, some Islamist terrorist group urged British Muslims to strike against the country. Among the targets singled out for special attention were.....yep, you guessed it....oil refineries.

If you are looking for video, click on the link at the top of this post and you will find plenty of it there.

MONDAY, DECEMBER 12, 2005

English Oil Depot Fire Almost Extinguished

The fires resulting from yesterday's massive explosion at an English Oil Depot are almost out. At least this is what the fire department spokesman is saying. Next will come a careful examination of the ruins to see if the cause can be determined. A anti-terrorist team is in place just in case the original and emphatic denial that terrorism was involved proves to have been wrong.

In any case, the explosion and fire created many memorable photographs. Here is one of my favorites:

TUESDAY, DECEMBER 13, 2005

Pro-American Iraqi Voter In Detroit Says "Go To Hell"

The Mainstream Media and Democratic Congressmen keep telling us how the Iraqi people want Americans out of their country and the sooner the better.

Well, one Iraqi voter in Detroit doesn't seem to fit the media's stereotype of your average Iraqi.

While being interviewed by a Detroit TV News station, Betty Dawisha, an Iraqi citizen who had just finished voting, had this to say:

Anybody who doesn't appreciate what America has done and President Bush, let them go to hell.

If Betty gets her way there are sure going to be a lot of Democrats and Al Qaeda supporters crammed together in a very hot place someday soon.

You can watch the interview on video by visiting The Political Teen.

TUESDAY, DECEMBER 13, 2005

President of Iran Says Holocaust Is a "Myth"

Iranian President Mahmoud Ahmadinejad said today that the murder of millions of Jews under Nazi Germany during the Second World War is a "myth."

In a live television broadcast he stated, "They have invented a myth that Jews were massacred and place this above God, religions and the prophets."

According to BBC,
Mr Ahmadinejad also called for Europe, the US or Canada to create a Jewish state there, instead of the Middle East.

Mr Ahmadinejad's latest declaration reiterates comments he made last week in which he said he did not accept six million Jews were killed by the Nazis, remarks which were widely condemned.

The president also sparked international outrage in October when he said Israel should be "wiped off the map".
This is the same man who boasts about Iran's nuclear "power" program and threatens the United Nations if it decides to enact sanctions against his country.

Israel, of course, has once again condemned Ahmadinejad's remarks as being totally unacceptable and inexcusable.

Why is the rest of the world silent? Must Israel stand alone? Like Pontius Pilate are the Western powers "washing their hands" of the matter and leaving the President of Iran free to incite mob violence and mass hysteria without so much as a "Drop dead" response?

I fear that Israel will be used by the Western Nations as a scape goat, being forced to attack Iran on its own in order to ensure its own self-preservation.

Iran and North Korea continue to be the world's deepest wells for the propogation of world terror.

Sooner or later something will have to be done about Iran's nuclear ambitions.

If this creepy ideologue cannot unify the nations of the world in their attempts to curtail Iran's nuclear enrichment program, nobody and nothing can.

Historically, nation's exhibiting an evil intent against their neighbors invariably discover their leadership descending into irrational madness.

Iran does not appear to be an exception.

WEDNESDAY, DECEMBER 14, 2005

Rock, Paper, Saddam

The language is crude but the actual courtroom photos of Saddam's trial give this short, fictional demonstration of arrogance an aura of creepy reality! It may also give you a good laugh. You'll find it all here.

ht:HH

Updated & Corrected Info On Death Row Prisoner Cory Maye

Five days ago I posted on Cory Maye and his unbelievable conviction and death sentence for shooting a policeman who crashed in his door at 11 pm at night while he was sleeping in his room with his 18-month old daughter.

Today, The Agitator has put up a corrected summary of the facts in Maye's case.

A key point that was earlier misrepresented is that the police *did* have a warrant for Maye's apartment....but without his name on it.

The facts still speak for themselves and they speak quite loudly in Maye's favor (at least they do to me!). Click the link and decide for yourself. If you decide that an injustice was done, you can contact Mississippi Governor Haley Barbour to demand a rehearing of the case or the extension of a full pardon.

Governor Barbour's address is:

P.O. Box 139 Jackson, MS 39205
Phone: 601.359.3150 or 1-877-405-0733

THURSDAY, DECEMBER 15, 2005

CNN Loses Interest In Historic Vote In Iraq (Yawn)

Today the Iraqis gave birth to a new government and a new future. It will take a few days or a week before the details of the new "baby" are known.

In many ways it could be said that over 2,000 American soldiers died so that this day could come. It is a day made holy, if not to God then at least to democracy, in their blood.

Many billions of American taxpayer dollars have been spent to rebuild the country and make it safe and hopeful for this election. The controversy of America's leadership in the invasion and occupation of Iraq has stirred the headlines day after day for three years. No one can utter even one criticism of the Bush administration's policy in Iraq without it becoming the top news story of the day.

So, what are the headlines on CNN online today? "Iraq Vote a Success?" Nope.

The headline story is, "Freezing Rain Blasts Across Southeast."

How about the list of "More News" in the upper-right corner? There are 10 supposedly important stories there (including, "Sex con dupes Amish senior, police say") but not one of them refers to Iraq.

There is a two-minute video news clip about the election that you can watch...but the only news story is buried at the bottom of the page under the heading, "World."

There is an old saying that, "Victory has a hundred fathers but defeat is an orphan." The new Iraq has many brave and worthy parents. CNN is not one of them.

Juan Cole's Anti-War View Gives Two Thumbs Down On Iraq Vote

As a representative of the left-wing, anti-war branch of the Democratic Party, University of Michigan professor Juan Cole is always good for a quote.

His posting on today's historic Iraqi elections has, as usual, hit gold.

The LA Times probably reflects the thinking of a lot of Americans in hoping that these elections are a milestone on the way to withdrawing US troops from Iraq. I cannot imagine why anyone thinks that. The Iraqi "government" is a failed state. Virtually no order it gives has any likelihood of being implemented. It has no army to speak of and cannot control the country. Its parliamentarians are attacked and sometimes killed with impunity. Its oil pipelines are routinely bombed, depriving it of desperately needed income. It faces a powerful guerrilla movement that is wholly uninterested in the results of elections and just wants to overthrow the new order. Elections are unlikely to change any of this.

Hey, it's possible he'll turn out to be right. In fact, I'm sure he was right about something once...a long time ago...but I can't remember what it was....

In any case, Protein Wisdom has a rundown on what the anti-war blogs are saying about the Iraq elections today....the answer? Not much. Surprise.

French Are Surprised To Find Islamic Terrorist Arms Cache Just Outside Paris

Oh, those French. They "Oolala" their Muslim friends and cozy up to Saddam Hussein and take his oil for food money and courageously stand up against American aggression towards the Iraqi people and, with their heads in the sand, say, "Ah...If only America was as wise and noble and principled as we French there would be no problem with Islamic terrorism. After all, we even side with the Palestinians agains Israel! We even let Arafat come here so we could try and save his life!

So, when Muslim youth riot for more than two weeks and burn buildings and destroy nearly 10,000 cars it cannot possibly have anything to do with Islam. Non, non, non! It is socio-economic issues, mon amis. Certainment!

Today, however, French police announced that they have uncovered a large cache of millitary assault rifles, dynamite and TNT hidden in a storage room attached to an apartment building in a Paris suburb.

According to Reuters, the discovery was "part of a probe into an Islamic militant group said to have indirect links to al Qaeda's leader in Iraq (Zarqawi)."

"Thanks to (several) arrests, an arms cache has just been discovered which reveals the seriousness of this matter. They are very determined people, with links between terrorist extremism and major crime," (French Interior Minister) Sarkozy told BFM TV.

"We think they have indirect links, at a fairly high level, with al Qaeda," he said.

But, mon dieu! What are they doing in France? We are their friends! We are on their side...uh...non...n'exactment pas...I mean, we like all Muslims, no matter who they are...and, uh...these folks have really...I mean really embarrassed us by taking advantage of our hospitatlity like this. Most certainly they were planning to use these weapons somewhere...against somebody...perhaps the English...Oui, les Anglais...or the Americans...after what they have done they deserve it (d--m I miss all those oil options)...After all, why would they want to attack moi? I mean, France? C'est pas possible!

We the French have a word for this, of course, because our language c'est tres superior, n'est pas? Oui...and the word is...NUTS!

Muslim Brotherhood's Gains In Egypt's Parliament Viewed As "Move to the Center?"

Mehdi Akef...a Centrist?

An AP report tells us the following,

Minimizing election gains by the Muslim Brotherhood, Egyptian Ambassador Nabil Fahmy said Thursday his country was moving toward a centrist and not an Islamist political position. Mohammed Mehdi Akef, the actual leader of Egypt's Muslim Brothers, seemed to have a different perspective, however. **In an interview** with the state-owned English language Ahram Weekly, he said,
"I declared that we will not recognize Israel which is an alien entity in the region. And we expect the demise of this cancer soon."

Yep. That sounds centrist to me!

Note: The banned but tolerated Brotherhood won 20 percent of the seats in the 454-strong (Egyptian) parliament, making it the largest opposition bloc in the house.

ht:**lgf**

FRIDAY, DECEMBER 16, 2005

Church Preschool Christmas Program

Christmas and children go together like bagels and cream cheese only better! At our church preschool Christmas Program the children stole the show as usual. But I took a special interest in the parents this year and captured some of their enthusiasm for posterity. I guess every child is worthy of a paparazzi or two...especially when its their Mom & Dad! I hope you enjoy these photos.

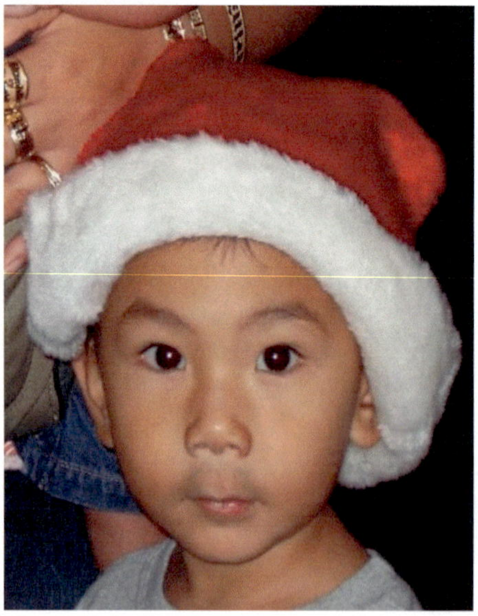

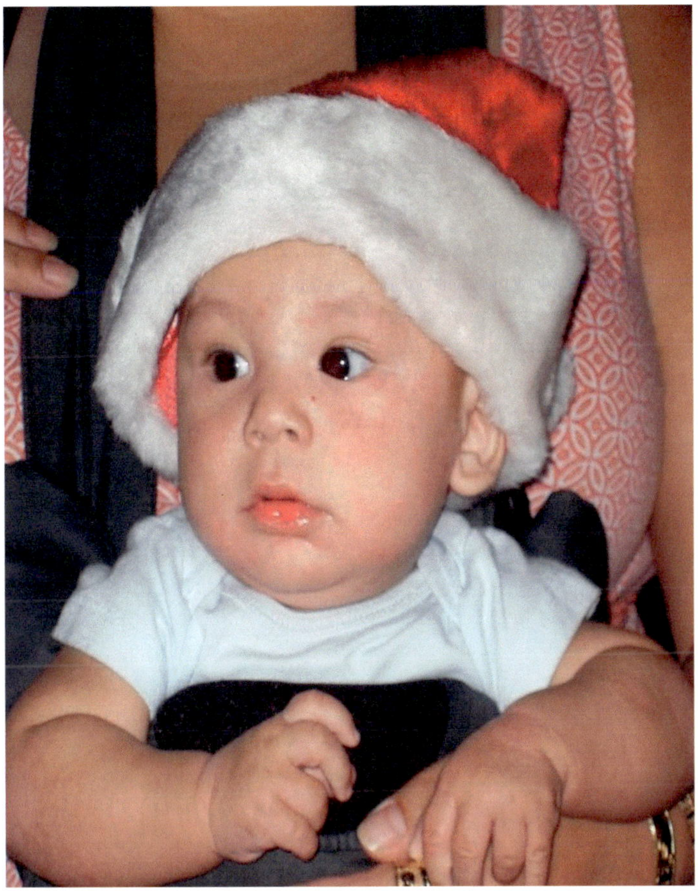

Merry Christmas

NY Times Dramatically Reveals That President Bush IS DOING HIS JOB!

The NY Times thinks it has come up with another hit piece on President George W. Bush. Spilling the classified, top-secret beans concerning a Presidential order permitting the NSA to eavesdrop on certain, approved international contacts from or to the United States without a court order was intended to show how much our personal rights have eroded under Bush's watch.

The news has sent the anti-Bush crowd scurrying around like choreographed bit players in a Broadway musical, spouting predictable lines such as Democratic Senator Chuck Schumer who declared that,
Today's revelation that the government listened in on thousands of phone conversations without getting a warrant is shocking . . .

Also "shocked" was Sen. Russell Feingold, D-Wisconsin, who said,
I can't imagine a more shocking example of an abuse of power.

Personally I am "shocked" that Senator Feingold is not capable of imagining anything more shocking than this.

But this was not the end of Feingold's thoughts because there was so, so much to be shocked about. Here he goes again,
This shocking revelation ought to send a chill down the spine of every American.

Somewhere there just has to be a Democratic Party memo with the phrase, "act as though you are 'shocked' by this revelation by the NY Times."

The memo would be important. Otherwise the Democratic leadership might just slip up and remember that the President long ago informed the appropriate Senators of both parties regarding this matter and received their consent.

Personally, I think that this particular leak of classified information to the NY Times ought to be investigated and the leaker(s) charged with whatever crime is involved with the unauthorized release of such information.

On the other hand, this revelation can only benefit Bush in the long term. No matter what spin the Democrats and the media will try to put on this I believe that most Americans will get the clear message that our President is just doing his job protecting us all from intentional acts of terrorism.

A President who would not seek a way to react swiftly and thoroughly in probing individuals identified from seized terrorist documents has no business being President.

I wish to be the first in the blogosphere to thank the NY Times for making Bush look very competent, decisive, resourceful and.....well....Presidential!

I suspect that, like so many things the liberal wing has tried to use in their attacks on the Bush Administration, this one will create a short-term negative effect that will quickly rebound into even higher satisfaction ratings for Bush.

After all, he promised us that he was going to "hunt them down." Now we know that he has kept his promise. Good on you, President Bush.

SATURDAY, DECEMBER 17, 2005

Spy Scandal? Bush Speech Clears the Air and Crushes Critics

President Bush told it like it is this morning. It was a speech that harshly criticized Democrat opposition to the renewal of the Patriot Act and, with brutal honesty, defended the NSA eavesdropping policy revealed by the NY Times and excoriated those who leaked this information to the media.

I'll let his own words (with my highlights) speak for themselves:

In the weeks following the terrorist attacks on our nation, I authorized the National Security Agency, consistent with U.S. law and the Constitution, to intercept the international communications of people with known links to al Qaeda and related terrorist organizations. Before we intercept these communications, the government must have information that establishes a clear link to these terrorist networks.

This is a highly classified program that is crucial to our national security. Its purpose is to detect and prevent terrorist attacks against the United States, our friends and allies. Yesterday the existence of this secret program was revealed in media reports, after being improperly provided to news organizations. As a result, our enemies have learned information they should not have, and the unauthorized disclosure of this effort damages our national security and puts our citizens at risk. Revealing classified information is illegal, alerts our enemies, and endangers our country.

As the 9/11 Commission pointed out, it was clear that terrorists inside the United States were communicating with terrorists abroad before the September the 11th attacks, and the commission criticized our nation's inability to uncover links between terrorists here at home and terrorists abroad. Two of the terrorist hijackers who flew a jet into the Pentagon, Nawaf al Hamzi and Khalid al Mihdhar, communicated while they were in the United States to other members of al Qaeda who were overseas. But we didn't know they were here, until it was too late.

The authorization I gave the National Security Agency after September the 11th helped address that problem in a way that is fully consistent with my constitutional responsibilities and authorities. The activities I have authorized make it more likely that killers like these 9/11 hijackers will be identified and located in time. And the activities conducted under this authorization have helped detect and prevent possible terrorist attacks in the United States and abroad.

The activities I authorized are reviewed approximately every 45 days. Each review is based on a fresh intelligence assessment of terrorist threats to the continuity of our government and the threat of catastrophic damage to our homeland. During each assessment, previous activities under the authorization are reviewed. The review includes approval by our nation's top legal officials, including the Attorney General and the Counsel to the President. I have reauthorized this program more than 30 times since the September the 11th attacks, and I intend to do so for as long as our nation faces a continuing threat from al Qaeda and related groups.

The NSA's activities under this authorization are thoroughly reviewed by the Justice Department and NSA's top legal officials, including NSA's general counsel and inspector general. Leaders in Congress have been briefed more than a dozen times on this authorization and the activities conducted under it. Intelligence officials involved in this activity also receive extensive training to ensure they perform their duties consistent with the letter and intent of the authorization.

This authorization is a vital tool in our war against the terrorists. It is critical to saving American lives. The American people expect me to do everything in my power under our laws and Constitution to protect them and their civil liberties. And that is exactly what I will continue to do, so long as I'm the President of the United States.

This speech supports what I wrote about this "scandal" yesterday.

You can watch Bush's speech here.

ht: Powerline & HH

Honolulu Advertiser Editorial On Bush Is the "Most Ridiculous Item of the Day"

The Editorial in today's Honolulu Advertiser (Saturday, December 17) scores a 10 on the "Ridicul-O-Meter." After putting it into the context of President Bush's speech this morning it could even go off the chart and ring the bell ("give the editor a cigar!")! Here are some highlights:

President Bush hid behind the free elections in Iraq this week when a news report revealed that in 2002, he authorized a "Big Brother"-type spy operation that infringed on the freedoms of hundreds, if not thousands, of Americans here in the United States.

How diabolical of Bush to anticipate yesterday's story in the NY Times and arrange a national election in Iraq to distract us!

As great as the Iraq elections were, it (sic) didn't leave Bush much of a fig leaf. Signing a secret order to allow the government to spy on Americans doesn't cut it in the land of the free.

I can only wonder if the editorial was written by Hans Christian Anderson (ie. fantasy instead of facts.) Not to mention the unmitigated gall in using the Iraqi elections as a metaphor for the covering of someone's genitals. I'm sure the Iraqi people and the US soldiers in the field will appreciate this attempt at journalistic sophistication.
But it was a shortcut that short-circuited (sic) the Constitution.

As in "electrical short-circuit?" or as in a "short-cut" across the center of a race track? I'm sure this means something but I'm not sure what... In any case the sparks are flying at the Honolulu Advertiser Editor's office. It would be helpful if the Editor had cited what part of the US Constitution has been short-circuited and how. But that would mean actually doing some research into facts...and facts only get in the way of opinion, I suppose.

But Sen. Ted Kennedy, D-Mass., called the program "Big Brother run amok."

It's always good to quote from an unbiased, authoritative and respected analyst to prove your point. Too bad the Editor couldn't find one.

Now the president must come forward. Misdirecting attention to the free elections in Iraq isn't good enough, nor is hiding behind some vague sense of national security.
That about sums up the Democratic, anti-Bush, anti-war position on national security, doesn't it. "Vague." The rest of America has a clear sense of what "national security" means. It means exactly what President Bush is trying to do... protect us from terrorist attacks by Islamist groups like Al Qaeda.

Bush needs to come clean.

Dear Editor: The President "came clean" this morning (see here).

Now it is the Honolulu Advertiser's turn to wash their hands of the mud they've been throwing and, while they are at it, take the beam out of their eye.

Iran weekly advertises “application form” for suicide operations

From IranFocus:

Tehran, Iran, Jul. 23 – The following is the translation of the text of an advertisement that appears regularly in the hard-line weekly Parto Sokhan as part of a recruitment drive for suicide operation volunteers.

English translation below:

In the Name of God, the Most High

“Martyrdom-seeking operations embody the pinnacle of a nation’s greatness and the apex of its epics”

His Eminence the Supreme Leader Ayatollah Ali Khamenei

Statement for Recruitment of Martyrdom-seeking Forces

In order to achieve all-round readiness against the enemies of Islam and the sacred Islamic Republic and to protect the foundations of Islam, the Lovers of Martyrdom Garrison plans to organise “a martyrdom-seeking division” for each province in the country from the martyrdom-seeking and brave popular forces of that province and give them specific and specialised training. We therefore request all our pious brothers and sisters, who are committed and determined to defend Islam, if willing, to submit two photographs of themselves, a copy of their identity cards, and the filled-in application form below to the following address, so that preparations for their organisation and training could begin:

P.O. BOX 16535-664, Tehran

It should be noted that for the forces of the martyrdom-seeking division from each province, the training and preparations for martyrdom-seeking operations will be implemented in that province.

Membership request application

I, ____________, son/daughter of___________ ID number ________ Date of Birth _______

Address: ___________________________Telephone: _____________________

Request membership in the Martyrdom-seeking Division in the province of ....

Signature: _________________________________

And these folks want to "wipe (Israel) off the face of the earth," are developing ballistic missiles and are close to acquiring nuclear weapons. Not cool.

Assassination Attempt on Iranian President Mahmoud Ahmadinejad?

No doubt there are many folks in the world who would like to see the crazy President of Iran breathing something besides oxygen.

During a well-publicized visit to a region of Iran with many persecuted Sunni Muslims today, an attack by "bandits" caused the death of President Mahmoud Ahmadinejad's driver and one of his body guards.

The story does not say whether Ahmadinejad was in his car at the time of the attack.

SUNDAY, DECEMBER 18, 2005

New Orleans Asks France To Come Back, Please!

I just came across a very amusing "letter" to France from a homeowner in New Orleans. I found it at Jeliel3 who hat tips other sources going back to nola.com. I agree with Jeliel on this one, it's funny!

Joan Fox of New Orleans writes:

Dear France,

Greetings from Louisiana! We are shopping for new owners, and we immediately thought of you! Our present rulers haven't been taking very good care of us and we are looking for a better deal. They are spending all our money in a place called Iraq (somewhere in the Middle East). We thought that perhaps you might want to revisit an old land deal you made long ago.

If you've been reading the papers lately, you may have noticed that we have had a few problems with "water". No, we're not offering you a deal on a damaged water park. (Althouugh that's what it looks like from the air) Seriously, we need help, and fast.

Some things you might like here:

1. We named the state after your King Louis
2. We named the city after your city, Orleans
3. We have lots of French names on the streets
4. We still have Napoleonic law (maybe you can explain it to us!)
5. A lot of our citizens speak French (the accent will grow on you)
6. We like French food and wine

What we can offer you:

1. a toehold (rather wet!) on the continent
2. an incredible port
3. Lots of oil and gas
4. Lots of restaurants
5. Jazz
6. Mardi Gras (you won't believe what we do with this!)
7. Some of the most beautifu houses in the world (very, very wet)

What we need from you is simple:

1. Wetland redevelopment
2. New levees
3. Lots of new houses (but we want them to look old like the ones we lost)
4. We need schools and hospitals rebuilt
5. If you insist, we wouldn't mind some more outdoor cafes like you folks are famous for.

Please think this over carefully. Our current owners are so busy in other countries, they might not even notice if you come down here and take a look around. We'll put you up in grand style in a place we call "The French Quarter" (yeah, really!) and you can have lunch at a place we built for your very own Napoleon, which we call (you guessed it!)Napoleons". You'll be right at home.

Oh, just remember, we would like the levees and the wetlands taken care of ASAP, sometime just after lunch if not sooner.

Yours sincerely,
A homeowner in New Olreans
Joan Fox

Christmas Caroling In Hawaii

There isn't any snow and we wore shorts but around 25 or our church youth and adults went Christmas Caroling this evening. Each year we do this at an apartment complex down the street from our church. The people there actually look forward to our visit and this year presented us with two boxes of chocolates and three batches of cookies as a reward for our singing.

A good time was had by all. As we sang our last carol the rain came down in buckets. We shouted, "every man (and woman) for themselves, " and ran back to the church soaking wet. The youth then had their own party while the adults went to a home for theirs.

After caroling we have a tradition to phone former church members on the mainland (it is 2 am on the East Coast), wake them up and sing *Mele Kalikimaka* to them over the phone. That's what friends are for, isn't it?

In any case, here are some photos of what it looks like to go Christmas caroling

...

Bali Bomber Says Mohammed Killed Infidels

According to The Australian, "BALI bombings commander Mukhlas has written a fanatical call-to-arms from his death-row prison cell, exhorting Muslims to kill Westerners."

Some of his comments are revealing as to how some if not many Muslims view their faith and the founder of their faith. Here are two excerpts from the 60-page document:

You who still have a shred of faith in your hearts, have you forgotten that to kill infidels and the enemies of Islam is a deed that has a reward above no other . . .

Aren't you aware that the model for us all, the Prophet Mohammed and the four rightful caliphs, undertook to murder infidels as one of their primary activities, and that the Prophet waged jihad operations 77 times in the first 10 years as head of the Muslim community in Medina?

Uh...if Mukhlas is correct it would appear that Islam, by imitation of Mohammed and the first Caliphs who followed him, is a faith that demands and rewards violence towards infidels and unbelievers.

Other Muslims insist that they are a religion of peace, tolerance and...well...all those other nice things.

Who is right? This is the question whose answer tauntingly eludes us.

I wonder how many Muslim hymns begin with, "I've got peace like a river in my soul!"

ht:lgf

MONDAY, DECEMBER 19, 2005

Rethinking the Border Wall With Mexico, Call It a "Welcome Wall"

Mexico's President, Vicente Fox, has called American plans to extend the security fence along the Mexican border, "Shameful."

According to BBC, Fox condemned the proposal saying it is too focused on securing the border and does not acknowledge the "enormous contribution" that Mexican workers make to the US economy.

Perhaps Presidente Fox has a point. Maybe the new fence could be reconfigured and redesigned with a more welcoming ambiance.

Perhaps if the United States could celebrate the regular arrival of Mexican immigrants in a more affirming manner. After all, in the past, servants, slaves and hobos were always required to enter a home by way of the back door. By forcing so many Mexicans to enter the United States by way of the "back door" we have been treating them as somehow inferior to the rest of us.

By all means, Mr. Fox, let us recognize the "enormous contribution" that Mexican workers make to the US economy by treating them as equals. Let us, with this new fence, and perhaps even more of it, close off the back door completely! Let us vow to never again degrade, demean and insult our neighbors to the south by forcing them to shuffle, bow and scrape their way into our national house.

I suggest that the new wall be designated the "American/Mexican Welcome Wall." Large signs should be erected facing Mexico at regular intervals along the wall stating (in both English and Spanish),

We are grateful for your contributions to the economy of the United States.

We want to make you feel welcome and appreciated. Accordingly, we invite and ecourage you to enter our house through the front door so that we may receive you with honor.

Please follow the arrows to the nearest open door where we will just run a few checks to affirm that you are, in fact, willing and able to make a positive contribution to our economy.

We will also, of course, check your criminal record and make sure that you are not carrying any illegal drugs, weapons, explosives or nuclear devices.

America is and always has been the 'Land of the free and the home of the brave.' If you are brave enough to enter through the front door we will welcome you, honor you and grant you the freedom of our home.

Viva Mexico! Viva Estados Unidos!

If that won't satisfy Presidente Fox, I have no idea what will!

TUESDAY, DECEMBER 20, 2005

Nancy Pelosi Invokes Religious Litmus Test In House Vote

Unbelievable!

Last night, House Democrat Leader Nancy Pelosi spoke in opposition to a bill that would trim $40 billion out of the Federal budget over the next five years. According to news reports Pelosi decared that those who voted for the bill would, in essence, be voting against what the Bible teaches and would be slapping God himself in the face. She then explicitly urged the U.S. House of Representatives to join her in worshipping God on the House floor.

Her actual words are as follows,

As the Bible teaches us, to minister to the needs of God's creation is an act of worship, to ignore those needs is to dishonor the God who made us . . . Let us vote no on this budget as an act of worship and for America's children.

I doubt that such incendiary words of a partisan religious nature have been uttered on the floor of the U.S. Congress for over 100 years. In passing judgment on the religious integrity of those voting differently than herself, Pelosi has, without any doubt, uttered the single most arrogant, blasphemous, outrageous, impolitic, rude, insulting, inappropriate, insensitive, divisive, offensive and intolerant statement I have ever heard spoken by an elected representative holding such a high political leadership position.

The Democratic Party should demand that she issue an apology and/or resign as the House Minority Leader immeditely.

I shiver to imagine what would become of the U.S. Congress should everyone begin talking like this. The floor of the House of Representatives would begin to sound like a bitterly divided religious convention instead of a body politic.

Is Pelosi now a self-appointed arbiter of whether a fellow Representative's positions are religiously acceptable? If Pat Robertson or James Dobson had uttered these words they would have been excoriated by people like Pelosi even if they had uttered them from inside a church. What hypocracy!

I am so appalled that I honestly do not know how to express my feelings. I do not know whether to rant or rage or weep or simply sit quietly in stunned numbness.

If a Republican Representative had spoken these same words I would feel the same as I do towards Pelosi. There is no excuse, no justification for such a thing.

If you think Pelosi simply spoke off-the-cuff without thinking the matter through and should be excused for a slip of the tongue, consider that she has said much of this before...word for word.

Shame! Shame! Shame! Shame! Shame!

WEDNESDAY, DECEMBER 21, 2005

Pope Benedict Dons Medieval "Santa" Hat for Advent

Pope Benedict looked like he was pretending to be Santa Clause sans beard today as he rode his popemobile through St. Peter's Square. The red velvet hat trimmed in white fur (called a "camauro") is a traditional 12th century piece of Papal wardrobe not seen in public since the days of Pope John XXIII in 1963. By the time Benedict stepped out of the vehicle the hat was gone, replaced by the familiar white skullcap.

The current Pope is known for a dry sense of humor and it is not likely coincidental that he chose to wear this satoral throwback just five days before Christmas.

Someday soon we may well see the Pope reciting the Sanctus as, "Ho- Ho- Ho-ly, Lord God of Hosts....."

Newsweek Compares Bush With Botha and Apartheid Oppression

A Newsweek commentary by Arlene Getz today parallels and compares President Bush's "warrantless wiretapping" with the civil rights and human rights violations of South Africa's President Botha in the final years of apartheid.

"Why," she asks, "have (Americans) reacted so insipidly to yet another post-9/11 erosion of U.S. civil liberties? . . .the nasty echoes of apartheid South Africa should at least give them pause. While Bush uses the rhetoric of 'evildoers' and the 'global war on terror,' Pretoria talked of "total onslaught."

She also parallels South Africa's systematic torturing and murdering of detainees with Bush's emergency eavesdropping policies:

"Botha liked to tell South Africans that the country was under 'total onslaught' from forces both within and without, and that this global assault was his rationale for allowing opponents to be jailed, beaten or killed. Likewise, the Bush administration has adopted the argument that anything is justified in the name of national security."

What a nice word, "likewise." Such an easy way to create moral equivilency between the policies of George W. Bush and the morally bankrupt human rights abuses of one of the most repressive and constitutionally racist nations of 20th century Western Civilization.

What Arlene Getz is talking about bears little or no resemblance to either the legal or actual issues and reality of the President's NSA survellience policies. It is as though she completely omitted the facts of the case in order to create an illusion of something she has conjured up out of her own imagination.

The Getz article is entitled, "Where's the Outrage?" and carries a subheading that reads, "Bush's defense of his phone-spying program has disturbing echoes of arguments once used by South

Africa's apartheid regime. Why Americans should examine the parallels."

Ms. Getz has, of course found the same "parallels" that any half-wit could see: Both South Africa and the United States are governed by governments with presidents and, as a matter of national security, operate survellience and intelligence gathering operations both within and outside their national borders.

That's it. That's the parallel we are asked to examine.

Memo to Ms. Getz: There is not a single nation or government in the entire world that does not do this. Just because South Africa abused their security operations does not mean that every other nation is guilty of doing the same nor does it follow that what President Bush is doing is the moral equivilent of "jailing, beating and killing" his political opponants.

Ms. Getz asks, "Where's the outrage?"

The outrage, Ms. Getz, is that you have dared to present your twisted, biased and hateful blather as informed commentary and that the editors of a leading national "news" publication have seen fit to publish it.

That, my dear Ms. Getz, is outrageous.

New Rembrandt Has Legs

A new painting by Rembrandt has been discovered and is expected to sell for up to $4 million at an upcoming auction. This photo by AP photographer Kirten Wigglesworth shows off the work of a Master with a twist of whimsy.

FRIDAY, DECEMBER 23, 2005

Who's Leaking All the National Security Programs?

Is it just me or is anybody else wondering who leaked the radiation testing project being conducted by the FBI? US News and World Report carried the story so somebody had to let them in on it.

So far we've had CIA airplane transportation systems outed, secret terrorist holding facilities in Eastern Europe revealed, warrant-less international communication monitoring of US residents/citizens by the NSA uncovered on the front page of the NY Times and now the FBI radiation testing program.

This is more than just a leaky ship...this is a conspiracy to destroy the Bush Administration at the cost of American security.

Is it treason?

If this sort of information was given or sold to a foreign country it would be considered to be an act of espionage...but it would still be "secret," at least from other nations and from the public. To publicly release this information for the sole purpose of undermining the effectiveness of our nation's War on Terror is unconscionable.

This is something that an enemy of the United States would do. It is not something that a patriot or loyal American citizen would do.

A lifetime in Leavenworth might be too easy a sentence for these traitors.

Where is the investigation? Who will conduct it? It must stop. It is nothing short of terrorism in our midst.

SATURDAY, DECEMBER 24, 2005

Advent Calendar from the Twilight Zone

Every year our church hands out small Advent Calendars to the children and their families. The calendars are inexpensive and now I know why. Last night my daughter #1, home for Christmas from graduate school in Los Angeles, pointed out a few unusual scripture verses slipped into this year's Christmas story .

*December 7--"**Lord, teach us to count our days**." (Psalm 90:12) I suppose that this could be a "Pearl Harbor Day" reminder that our lives can change and even come to an end in an instant. But what does this have to do with Christmas?*

*December 11--"**John wore clothing of camel's hair with a leather belt around his waist**." (Matthew 3:4) Note: John was born only a few months before Jesus. Is this description of what he wore 30 years later supposed to remind us that he was "Elijah" who had come to prepare the way for the Messiah? If so, what a strange and cryptic way to say it...especially on a child's Advent Calendar!*

*December 17--My favorite: "**A multitude of camels shall cover you**." (Isaiah 60:6) Note: Having seen camels and ridden on camels the last thing in the world I would want to ever happen would be to have a "multitude" of them "covering" me! I suppose that this could be another cryptic reference, perhaps to the Messiah being surrounded by animals as a result of being born in a stable...but, come on...give me a break here!*

*December 18--"**Simeon took him in his arms and praised God**." (Luke 2:28) Note: This ocurred after Jesus was born...hardly an Advent verse!*

The back of the calendar says that the scripture verses were "compiled by Peter Mead." All I can say is, "Peter...you are one wild and crazy guy!"

Judge Alito Memo Not Related to NSA Surveillence Controversy

The old memo written by Judge Alito over 20 years ago and making headlines everywhere has little or nothing to do with the present issue of the Presidents ordering warrantless surveillence of international communications to and from the United States by the NSA. The memo was addressed to a specific issue.

The issue and the memo's irrelevence is clearly laid out by John Hinderocker at Powerline.

Apparently journalists are so intent on uncovering an expose that they do not even take the time to research their story before going to press. What a sham.

Accusations of Fraud and Reported Disqualification of Sunni Candidates Creates Election Confusion in Iraq

Many Sunni leaders have been joined by secular Shi'ites and the party of present Prime Minister Allawi in making charges of massive fraud in the recent Iraqi elections.

A coalition group, calling itself Maram, has gathered at least 20,000 demonstrators in Baghdad to express their reservations on the votes legitimacy.

Publius feels these charges have great merit, at Iraqi Bloggers Central Jeffrey believes that the vote looks fairly accurate but Mr. Ghost believes that an intransigent Islamist government is being created. On the other hand, Iraq the Model is encouraged by Shi'ite willingness to discuss an inclusive coalition government to soothe the Sunnis and secularists.

So far, conversations between the various factions have been fairly civil (although the leader of the religious Shi'ite coalition that appears to have won a huge victory says that the "sore losers" may be guilty of "terrorism" if they threaten to disrupt the elected government or demand a new election).

More ominous is a report today saying that the "Anti-Baathist Commission" has declared that as many as 90 Sunni candidates have been disqualified because of previous association with Saddam Hussein's ruling party. One of those reportedly disqualified was the Vice-Chair of the committee that drafted the new Iraqi constitution. If true, this would only serve to further disestablish Sunni voters who may come to the conclusion that they will have nothing to do with the new government.

This, of course, would be a disaster of the highest magnitude.

Somehow, some way, this must all be sorted out peacefully and in a manner satisfactory to all the parties involved. I'm not sure I can see how this will all turn out to be a good thing. Time will tell. In the meantime I am praying for the Iraqi people (including Sunni, Shi'ite, secularists, Christian and Kurd) who deserve good, stable, just and honest leadership in their new government...whoever they may turn out to be.

Christmas Eve In Hawaii

This evening we will celebrate the birth of Jesus Christ with a candlelight worship service. There will be special music, traditional carols and the Christmas story will be read from Scripture. The Welcome, Prayers (including the Lord's Prayer), the lighting of the Christ Candle and the Benediction will all be done in both English and Korean as we share worship together with the Korean congregation that nests in our facilities.

One of the things I do each year is to write a poem and set it to music. This is then included as part of my short sermon message. This year's Christmas music is a quartet that includes one verse sung as a round. I can't share the music but I can share the words.

Since tomorrow is Christmas Day I will not be blogging unless something extraordinary comes along! So, I leave you with a "Merry Christmas, Christ Is Born!" and the following words:

Bethlehem Was Still That Night

Bethlehem was still that night;
Darkness pierced by one bright light.
Mary, birthed a son.
Our salvation had begun.
.....Our salvation had begun.

Jesus in a manger lay
In a stable filled with hay.
Mary, Joseph, too,
Know that Christ was born for you.
.....Know that Christ was born for you.

See him sleeping, hear him cry.
Know that one day he will die.
Buried in a tomb and then
He will rise to life again.
.....He will rise to life again.

He will wash our sins away;
He will turn the night to day.
Jesus, Savior mine.
Child of Mary; Child Divine.
.....Child of Mary; Child Divine.

Words & Music by Jim Tweedie
December, 2005

MONDAY, DECEMBER 26, 2005

Gerrymandering for Dummies

What is "gerrymandering?" It is the drawing the boundaries of state electoral districts (for U.S. Congress) in an unnatural and artificial way so as to gather together as many residents of a common socio-economic and political bloc as possible (to ensure the election of either a Republican or Democrat as their Representative).

A perfect example is the 12th District in North Carolina (ht: Mary Katherine Ham at Hugh Hewitt).

Iraq Election Update

You won't read it in the American press because it takes more than a sound-bite and a 3rd-grade education to follow the story line....but the dramatic aftermath of the Iraqi National Election earlier this month continues to unfold.

The best summary to be found anywhere can be found at Iraq the Model. His report is encouraging in the sense that both the winners and losers are working hard to keep the peace as they haggle over the future government like they would over the purchase of a carpet. The Middle East clearly has a cultural dynamic with its own unique style and flair.

Those of us who are not part of that culture should be patient as this seeming brinkmanship moves slowly along to what we all hope will be a peaceful conclusion, satisfactory to all...except, of course, the insurgents.

You can find my previous post on this subject here.

WEDNESDAY, DECEMBER 28, 2005

Dumbest Vacation Ever--Part 2

Last September I posted on what I considered to have been the dumbest vacation ever. Today comes news of one even dumber.

It seems that Juergen Chrobog, a former German Ambassador to the the United States has been kidnapped, along with his wife and three adult sons, while touring in a remote area of Yemen.

Chrobog and his family were visiting Yemen at the invitation of the former Yemeni Ambassador to Germany.

Chrobog took the trip in spite of the fact that (as reported by the Washington Post),
Two Austrians and two Swiss were abducted in Yemen in the past two months. All were released unharmed a few days later.

The German Foreign Ministry had posted a travel advisory for Yemen, warning visitors that they could be abducted by ransom-seeking tribesmen and noting a general risk of terrorist attacks against Western interests in the country.

Because Chrobog was vain enough to thumb his nose at the warning from his own Foreign Ministry he has now created an international headache for his own country.

This is doubly ironic since Chrobog once negotiated the release of 14 European hostages (9 of whom were German citizens) held y "Islamic radicals" in North Africa just two years ago. It is reported that Chrobog personally carried several $ million in cash to intermediaries as part of the settlement that led to the hostages release.

This generous response to hostage taking has, apparently, given both Germany as a nation and Chrobog as an individual, the reputation of providing a quick way to make an easy million bucks or two.

Recently, German archaeologist Susanne Osthoff, was kidnapped and held hostage by insurgent/terrorists in Iraq. Germany managed to negotiate her release but refused to state what sort of settlement was offered in return.

Curiously, Germany released Mohammad Ali Hammadi, convicted of killing Navy diver Robert Dean Stethem during the 1985 hijacking of a TWA flight to Beirut and sentenced to life without parole, just a few days before Osthoff was also released.

Captain Ed at Captain's Quarters asks,

Coincidence? Not likely....

I am inclined to agree.

I must also agree with the Captain today when he more or less says that Germany has now hoisted itself by its own petard. Having negotiated with terrorists for the release of hostages and having caved in to demands for ransom and for the release of prisoners, should anyone be surprised that German citizens are now prime targets for international kidnapping?

No doubt Chrobog is hoping that someone back home will come up with a few $ million to help bail himself and the rest of his family out of their unfortunate predicament.

In contrast, it is my hope that, when all have been safely released, Chrobog will, out his own pocket, repay the money that was paid to his captors.

I also hope that he will also issue two apologies. One, to the German government for being so stupid as to get himself into this mess in the first place, and, Two, to those German citizens who have now been placed at even higher risk of kidnapping because of his own personal irresponsibility.

Chicago Tribune Concludes: "Bush Didn't Lie About Iraq"

An interesting article in the Chicago Tribune re-examines the nine claims for attacking Iraq that were raised by President Bush and the White House. Their analysis and conclusions will most certainly be welcomed by Republican pundits as well as by the White House itself.

I suppose, however, that we will soon hear charges that the Tribune writers were paid by the RNC.

THURSDAY, DECEMBER 29, 2005

Kathleen Parker and "Lord of the Blogs"

Syndicated columnist Kathleen Parker posted an article today entitled, "Lord of the Blogs." She has some critical things to say about blogging in general but some polite recognition for the skills and accuracy of others.

Her general thesis is nothing new: Blogging gives uninformed, unskilled and unaccountable journalist-wanna-bes the freedom to write all sorts of useless junk, most of which is stuff criticizing others for their mistakes. She compares this corner of the blogosphere with the anti-nomian descent into barbarism that William Golding so graphically depicted in his book, "Lord of the Flies."

I must confess that there is some truth to this thesis. Many blogs are tediously imitative of the big blogs, mindlessly aping their proclamations, endorsing their opinions and joining in their battles with little concern for accuracy or self-control.

Bloggers persist no matter their contributions or quality, though most would have little to occupy their time were the mainstream media to disappear tomorrow. Some bloggers do their own reporting, but most rely on mainstream reporters to do the heavy lifting. Some bloggers also offer superb commentary, but most babble, buzz and blurt like caffeinated adolescents competing for the Ritalin generation's inevitable senior superlative: Most Obsessive-Compulsive.

I would say that this is a fairly accurate description of far too many blogs floating around in cyber-space these days. But, when Parker gets specific she reveals that her main concern is to protect the professional hard work and unbiased of those who labor in the mainstream media.

...Many bloggers seek the destruction of others for their own self-aggrandizement. When a mainstream journalist stumbles, they pile on like so many savages, hoisting his or her head on a bloody stick as Golding's children did the fly-covered head of a butchered sow.

...When someone trips, whether Dan Rather or Eason Jordan or Judith Miller, bloggers are the bloodthirsty masses slavering for a public flogging. Incivility is their weapon and humanity their victim.

What Parker fails to note, however, is that, if the mainstream media types would print accurate, unbiased news for the American public to read, digest and debate, there would be no need for the "public flogging" of folks like Rather, Jordan or Miller.

The biased, arrogant abuse of power that each of these has shown was neither corrected nor denounced by the media for whom they worked. It was right and good that their errors and outright lies were caught, exposed and debated in the blogosphere.

Parker also fails to note that those she criticizes, especially on the conservitive right, are largely fighting what is essentially a defensive struggle against the very media that Parker glorifies.

Conservative bloggers attack the media because it is the members of the MSM who, all too often, are the ones who "seek the destruction of others for their own self-aggrandizement."

The head of President George W. Bush and the heads of members of his Administration and

Party are daily hoisted aloft like trophy's by the New York Times, Washington Post and the Los Angeles Times. Bloggers fight back because there is no one else to do so.

Still another point that Parker fails to note is that the blogosphere is the epitome of a free-market economy. Good stuff sells. Bad products do not. Inaccurate and bloviating blogs quickly become marginalized by any serious reader. The "Adults," as Parker calls them, are like the cream in the milk bottle: They have risen above the rest by virtue of their quality and taste.

She asks her readers to "ignore" the "ego-gratifying rabble who contribute only snark, sass and destruction." . There is no need for her to say this since bad blogs, whether expressing opinions on the political right or on the political left will be ignored by just about everyone looking for honest and accurate news, information and commentary.

To her credit, Parker does express her respect for the "Adults" who write and post on the internet:

> *. . . I've been a blog fan since the beginning, and have written favorably about the value added to journalism and public knowledge thanks to the new "citizen journalist" . . .*
>
> *I mean no disrespect to the many brilliant people out there - professors, lawyers, doctors, philosophers, scientists and other journalists who also happen to blog . . .they know who they are.*

Once again, however Parker misses the point as she fails to note that the blogosphere never was, is not and never will be a replacement for the MSM. The business of blogging is something entirely different. For her to criticize bloggers for not following the same journalistic methodology of newspapers, magazines and television is to miss the point of the blogosphere entirely. It is something different. She could just as easily slam the hardback book industry for failing to be as "current" as the morning edition of the Wall Street Journal. Anyone with any knowledge of the book publishing industry would know that such a comparison is silly. Those who blog will no doubt come to the same conclusion after reading Kathleen Parker's article.

In the end, it is ironic that the media Parker defends is fast-sinking into a black hole full of cancelled subscriptions while the leading blogs are not only holding their own in "readership" but are even drawing advertising revenue away from the MSM.

Financial capital always follows where the people are putting their money. Lately, that place is the blogosphere.
Whether Kathleen Parker likes it or not.

NSA "Cookie" Caper

So, the NSA has been downloading persistant cookies into the computers of folks who have dropped by the NSA web-site for a visit. Yawn.....

Privacy advocates think its a big deal but come on, almost every retail company on the internet downloads persistant cookies onto user's computers (Note: Persistant cookies are those designed to remain imbeded even after shutting down and re-booting). Ad-ware and Spy-ware are downloaded so often that software companies make a fortune off of selling programs that can find them and delete them.

Strange to say, but virtually every computer OS has a "remove cookies" program built into it. Personally, I delete all cookies on my computer every evening before I turn it off. NSA cookies disappear with all the rest.

Even so, today's "cookie" story declared that the practice of downloading persistant cookies by the NSA was "illegal."

According to today's AP story,

In a 2003 memo, the White House's Office of Management and Budget prohibits federal agencies from using persistent cookies — those that aren't automatically deleted right away — unless there is a "compelling need."A senior official must sign off on any such use, and an agency that uses them must disclose and detail their use in its privacy policy.

Peter Swire, a Clinton administration official who had drafted an earlier version of the cookie guidelines, said clear notice is a must, and "vague assertions of national security, such as exist in the NSA policy, are not sufficient."

Daniel Brandt, a privacy activist who discovered the NSA cookies, said mistakes happen, "but in any case, it's illegal. The [guideline] doesn't say anything about doing it accidentally."
Now I am not a privacy expert like Daniel Brandt, but for something to be illegal there has to have been a law enacted that makes it so.

A government policy enacted by an Executive Branch agency simply does not have the force of federal law behind it unless the Legislative Branch (Congress) enacts legislation that backs it up.

The "cookie" story does not indicate that any actual laws have been broken. It may be that a policy was violated, however. This could, of course, result in an investigation, a reprimand or termination of employment but not a charge of violating criminal law.

I certainly hope that "mistakes" like this NSA "cookie" caper are the exception rather than the rule. Even so, I am glad that there are policy guidelines that have been established to keep a short leash on what these governmental agencies are doing with what is, perhaps, too much spare time on their hands.

Which Chronicles of Narnia character are you most like?

Here's a web site. A fun spot to see if you like to "roar" or shoot arrows. It's the "Which Chronicles of Narnia character are you most like?"

For some reason I thought that I would score high as "Mr Beaver" but, as you can see, the child in me won the day! Lucy! I can live with that!

You scored as **Lucy Pevensie**.

Which Chronicles of Narnia character are you most like?
created with QuizFarm.com

A Follow-up to "canceling Worship On Christmas Sunday"

Some weeks ago I posted on the news that several mega-churches were canceling worship services on Sunday morning because it landed on Christmas! Most of these churches had planned extensive pre-Christmas and Christmas Eve programs and worship services as simply wanted to given their staffs a rest day with their families.

Jolly Blogger covered this story, too, and has now posted two very different responses from Pastors of two churches that received a great deal of criticism for canceling Christmas Sunday worship this year. (One of said that folks like me were being "stirred up" by the "devil.")

WEDNESDAY, JANUARY 04, 2006

Mark Steyn Predicts the Collapse of "The West"--Sadly, I Agree

Last April, in a post entitled, "Is Europe As We Have Known It Beginning To Disintegrate?" I predicted the collapse of Europe as a distinctly Western culture within the next 25-30 years. Today, in a long, rambling article entitled, "It's the Demography, Stupid--The Real Reason the West Is In Danger of Extinction," Mark Steyn predicts the same thing and for the same reasons.

In April I wrote,

National (European) identities seem to be hanging by a mere thread in countries such as France, Germany and the Netherlands. As immigrant "minority" groups grow in strength (particularly Black & Arab Muslim) they have begun flexing their muscle and letting the rest of their "countrymen" know how much they dislike those who have treated them so condescendingly for so long . . .

Clearly the Arab Muslim communities pose the greatest threat to the political, economic and social stability of Western Europe. Many local Imams regularly preach that Europe must and will become a Muslim continent. Given the continuing influx of Muslims into Europe and their high birthrate compared to the negative birthrate of the historically European peoples, something is going to have to give sooner or later. It looks like it is starting to happen sooner!

In today's article, Steyn begins by bluntly stating what, for many of us, has already become obvious,

Most people reading this have strong stomachs, so let me lay it out as baldly as I can: Much of what we loosely call the Western world will not survive this century, and much of it will effectively disappear within our lifetimes, including many if not most Western European countries.

For Steyn, the reason is two-fold:

1. The Western liberal embrace of secular multi-culturalism has created a culture of short-sighted "live and let live" mentality coupled with a complete inability to judge one cultural world-view as being "better" or "worse" than another.

This cultural relativism has left the liberal West (including most of Europe and Canada) with a philosophy of existance founded upon the premise of non-judgemental embrace and toleration of virtually every cultural, political or religious view EXCEPT for those that created Western civilization in the first place. To endorse Western civilization would be, of course......well.....it would be bad....very bad!

2. The birthrate in Western nations have fallen either below or very below the rate necessary to sustain an idiginous population. As Steyn puts it,
When it comes to forecasting the future, the birthrate is the nearest thing to hard numbers. If only a million babies are born in 2006, it's hard to have two million adults enter the workforce in 2026 . . .

Steyn tells us that it takes 2.1 children per female to sustain a population. He then gives us some numbers to digest:

Some countries are well above (2.1): the global fertility leader, Somalia, is 6.91, Niger 6.83, Afghanistan 6.78, Yemen 6.75. Notice what those nations have in common?

Scroll way down to the bottom of the Hot One Hundred top breeders and you'll eventually find the United States, hovering just at replacement rate with 2.07 births per woman. Ireland is 1.87, New Zealand 1.79, Australia 1.76. But Canada's fertility rate is down to 1.5, well below replacement rate; Germany and Austria are at 1.3, the brink of the death spiral; Russia and Italy are at 1.2; Spain 1.1, about half replacement rate. That's to say, Spain's population is halving every generation. By 2050, Italy's population will have fallen by 22%, Bulgaria's by 36%, Estonia's by 52%.

The bottom line is this. Europe and the West need sustainable populations to sustain their economies. Immigration will be necessary to provide the labor force. This labor force has and will continue to come from Third World countries, especially (in Europe's case) from the Muslim world.

The Muslim birth rate is extremely high. It is already the driving force for population increase in Europe today.

While Mr. Steyn does not put it this way, it could be said that, what the Arab Muslim world failed to do in its failed attempt to conquer Europe by force in the 9th-15th centuries, it is today on the verge of doing quitely and simply by immigrating and having babies.

If folks believe that one culture is no better or worse than any other then this should not be any cause for concern. If Europe and West becomes dominated by Muslim religious and cultural beliefs, then....maybe that would be a good thing!

If, however, folks (like myself) believe that there is a great deal of difference in values between one culture and another and that some values are worth preserving, then this current state of affairs should be a cause for great concern indeed.

In Pakistan last year (which is, by the way, Muslim but not Arab) there were over 800 cases of physical gang rape against women and girls in order to shame, punish or "send a message" to others concerning behavior not acceptable to the men in the family. Many, if not most of these cases, enjoyed the support of the local Imams.

This version of Sharia (Qur'anic) Law is growing in popularity among Muslim populations not only in the Middle East and South-East Asia, but in Germany, France, Belgium, the Netherlands, Sweden, Britain and Canada.

It will become the law of the land unless enough folks who value Western culture and values (derived from Christianity) stand up and, with determination, devise some strategy of opposing what will otherwise become the inevitable suicide of Western civilization.

As I put it nearly a year ago,

. . . by 2030, Muslims could potentially become the majority population of......Sweden! Yes, I said, "Sweden!" Say good-bye to those thin, trim, long-haired, blonde, tanned, blue-eyed Scandinavian girls. If some of the "new Europeans" have their way they will be wearing burkas in less than 25 years.

While Steyn lays out the problems and, with a certain sense of defeatism, hopes for some plan of response, I would like to offer him some concrete encouragement with the same specific suggestion I made last April.

I am not trying to sound some sort of alarm (for that alarm has already gone off and nations are either trying to deal with it, as in the Netherlands; compromising with it, as in Spain; pretending that "it will never happen to us because we're the French," as in.....well.... France; or simply being too overwhelmed by a dizzying myriad of social fragmentations to know what to do with any of it, as in Germany).

I am also not trying to stir up distrust, hate or bigotry against Arabs or Muslims. I am simply pointing out that it is the (mostly Arab) Muslims who are becoming the primary provocateurs (the French do seem to have the vocabulary for this sort of thing, don't they?) of social unrest and conflict throughout Western Europe.

It is vital that we in the United States should strive mightily to prevent this sort of "Balkanization" of the population to occur here. There must be a concerted emphasis (in education especially) to balance out the current bias towards "diversity" with at least an equal dose of "unity." As Lincoln once famously said (paraphrasing Jesus), "a nation divided within itself cannot stand."

As I have said many times as a church Pastor, what holds us together as a church is our unity of faith. ***It is what we hold in common that unifies us****...whether as Christian believers or as members of a bridge club or as citizens of a nation.* ***"Diversity" always divides and separates people from one another into "us" and "them." Unity turns everyone into a "we."***

*Whatever it is that has inspired us to say, "**We**, the people of the United States of America...." must be distilled and taught and ingrained in every one of us regardless of what our age, race, faith or culture might be....*

That's all I have to say on the matter today . . . except to encourage you to read all of Mark Steyn's article alongside all of mine. Then I would ask you to seriously consider whether there is anything is Western civilization that you believe is worth saving...and, perhaps, even laying down your life for. In the not too distant future it may well come down to that.

Israel's Sharon Fighting for His Life Following Massive Stroke

The details are still rolling in as the Israeli Prime Minister undergoes more surgery following the one lasting six hours. A good summary of the situation and a concise summary of its political implications can be found **here**.

Palestinian Anarchy In Gaza Kills Egyptian Border Guards

If there was ever any doubt about the utter collapse of social order in Gaza today's events have provided enough evidence for even the most fervent supporters of the Palestinian people to break into tears.

There is both tragedy and irony in what has been happening today. **Captain Ed** has an excellent summary and even better commentary.

THURSDAY, JANUARY 05, 2006

Pat Robertson Suggests God Struck Down Sharon for Disobedience

Today, on TV, Pat Robertson suggested that Israel's Prime Minister Ariel Sharon's stroke may have been a sign of God's displeasure, a punishment for the abandonment of Gaza.

In light of other, similar spiritual insights revealed by Robertson in the past (see here, here & here), perhaps he and Iran's President Mahmoud Ahmadinejad should consider getting together and comparing notes. (By the way, was that an aura surrounding Robertson as he spoke? Is it true that no one in the broadcast studio blinked once during the program?)

I previously have said that Pat Robertson "shames the Body of Christ" by what he says. Today I do not believe that the living Body of Christ, the True Church, the Elect of God, even care anymore. Pat Robertson has become to the Church what Pat Buchanan has become to the Republican Party. He is living in his own little spiritual world created out of his own imaginings.

On the other hand, if what Pat Robertson said today is true, then I fear that I will most certainly suffer some terrible calamity tomorrow as punishment for my sin of disbelief.

We shall see.

FRIDAY, JANUARY 06, 2006

Please Help Return Anna Mae He To Her Parents

A little over one month ago I posted about the strange and surreal case of little Anna Mae He who has, for all practical purposes, been "stolen" from her parents through a series of legal maneuvers that, to be honest, seem like something from our of a Franz Kafka novel.

You can read a good summary of the case here.

Even better, you can sign this petition to restore legal custody to her parents.

If you are not convinced that you should support this petition I also encourage you to read the following Christmas greeting that the He's have written to Anna Mae....who the courts are now planning to give up for adoption with all contact with her parents being legally forbidden!

Pray for the He family. And, at the very least, sign the petition.

A greeting letter to our beloved daughter, Anna Mae, during the holiday season.

Dear Anna,

Happy Birthday!

Your mother, father, sister and brother want you to know that we love you and that you are always with us in our hearts, especially during this time of year when we celebrate your birth that is also Chinese New Year.

A Judge that you will probably never meet decided in May 2004 that you would no longer live with us, but live instead with the Bakers. We do not know why the Bakers believed they could love you more than your mother and father. We continue to pray they take good care of you.

Always remember that your mom is Qin Luo, is a good woman who loves all her children. When you get older you will read her name on your birth certificate. She wanted you before you were born and will want and love you every moment for the rest of her life.

Always remember that your dad is Shaoqiang He, a good man who loves all his children. When you get older you will read his name on your birth certificate. He loves you now as he has from the moment he knew you were to arrive in this world.

Your mom and dad always wish you the best in your health, but in the event you need blood transmission or any part of our body for medical reason, we will always be available to you.

Your brother is Andy and your sister is Avita. Just like you, they are lovely and adorable. Your brother and sister have faces that always remind us of you, though it has been a long, long time since we last saw your face.

We wish we could look at the faces of all three of our beloved children. We wish we could watch you all grow and learn together. We wish all three of our children could wake up in the same house, see each other—and smile.

Always remember, too, that you are Chinese. We wish you were with us so you could learn not only about your country, America, but also learn about your Chinese culture. We wish you could, just like your brother and sister, speak both English and Chinese. We wish when you wake up each morning you were surrounded by people look like you—the two people who created you--your mother and father.

If you were with us we would love you everyday of your life. Even in your heart-breaking absence that does not change. We love you and always will. You are not in our home (your home), but you are always in our hearts.

Mom, Dad, Andy and Avita

SATURDAY, JANUARY 07, 2006

Three Things About Islam That Should Concern You and One Thing That Will Encourage You

As I have mentioned on several occasions, Islam is quickly moving towards becoming the dominant faith and political force in Europe. Three things that should give all non-Muslims a reason to worry and then one positive thing to ponder:

1. Father Joseph Fessio, Catholic Priest and founder of Ignatius Press, was interviewed on Hugh Hewitt's radio show yesterday. The interview was important in the insights it gives to Pope Benedict XVI's view of the rise of Islam in the West. One simple point, however, stood out as worthy or repeating here:

" I think there are 98 Islamic countries in the world, and 97 of them do not have religious freedom . . . And that's what's going to happen to Europe. Once there's an Islamic majority, it is . . . going to eliminate religious freedom . . . and therefore, Western civilization as we know it."

(Read the whole interview here and Hugh's excerpts and comments here).

2. Part of that lack of religious freedom includes the fundamental tenet of faith that, once a person has become a Muslim, they are never allowed to renounce it apart from being under a sentence of death. A corollary to this is that the freedom to practice other religious beliefs in Muslim countries is either restricted or forbidden. (Read more about this here)

3. Some radical Muslim gang members in England have apparently carried this concept even further, telling another youth, in June 2004, that if he did not convert to the Muslim faith by the following Wednesday they would kill him. On Wednesday the boy's mother heard gunshots coming from a nearby park and wondered if it might have been her son. It turned out it was. He had been shot to death in the head. This sort of threat has few historical precedents in Islam. But it does show the level of radical insanity that is accompanying this new, intolerant and lethal strain of grassroots Islamisicism around the world.

The bright spot?

Father Fessio passed on to Hugh Hewitt one other, more hopeful, thought:

". . . (I)n the United States, we also are not having children. There's abortion. There's contraception. There's the ideal of a one or two child family. But where is our immigration coming from? From Ecuador, from Mexico, from Cuba, from Guatemala. And these people are Christians. And so, I believe without being...you know, having hubris as an American, I believe that Christians in the United States are the ones who will be able to save not just Christianity, but Western civilization, if we maintain our fidelity to the scriptures, our fidelity to Christ, our fidelity to family life, and our fidelity to fertility and fruitfulness in marriage. So I believe we are in a world historical century, which is going to depend upon the strength of Christianity in these United States."

Is it possible that, within the next two generations or less, it could come to this?

It is possible. It is likely. Yes.

I Am More Optimistic Than the Pope Concerning the Threat of Islam to the West

According to a Hugh Hewitt interview with a priest friend of Pope Benedict XVI, the Pope is not hopeful that Islam can adapt to "modern" ideas as embodied in the fundamental tenets of Western Civilization; especially insofar as they have been derived from Christian faith, thought and tradition. The Pope's premise, that the Koran is, for Muslims, an unalterable expression of the eternal will of Allah, is well articulated and can be found at the end of Hugh's posting on the interview **here**.

The history of Islam, however, presents a more hopeful and less predictable prognosis (and I am, on this subject at least, an avowed pessimist!).

From the time of Mohammed himself, there has been a historical ebb and flow between progressive and regressive Islam. Today, radical regressive Islam seems to be in the ascendancy . . . a movement emerging by means of a well-planned and well-funded program of world-wide terror and havoc spread by means of grassroots education and indoctrination.

Many Muslims see a hope of mystical liberation and a vindication of Islam in this movement. Most do not. As time passes, the inherently self-destructive path of this theocratic malignancy will become more obvious even to many of the conservative and traditional practitioners of Islam.

History shows that repressive regimes of any and all sort sooner or later collapse under their own intellectual, moral and functional bankruptcy. In order to survive, such regimes must, over time, either become more repressive in order to suppress dissent, or else open a few windows to vent the steam of pent up cultural and economic frustration and restlessness. This later tactic is, like the USSR's *glasnost*, no less than an admission of defeat and convincing evidence of impending implosion. Iran is, at the moment, following the first of these options; China has been cautiously experimenting with the latter.

In any case, we can be confident that the ascendancy of radical Islamism, driven by a vision of a world-wide caliphate, will sooner or later come to a dismal end. When the end comes, however, it will come from within Islam itself and not from without.

Until that day arrives, those of us who are not Muslim must do all we can to ensure the survival of Christian faith and values along with all that is good and worth saving in so-called Western Civilization.

We must also recognize and remember that there is much in our Western culture that is worthy of the scorn and repudiation of Islam. There are (it should not be surprising to say) many moral values held in common between Islam, Judaism and Christianity. Our differences primarily lie in how we believe these values should be instilled and enforced in society.

We who are not Muslim must begin the task of reforming our own culture while, at the same time, defending our God-given vision of freedom and liberty against those who would take it from us.

We who are not Muslim must also make a concerted effort to offer friendship and support to those Muslims in our communities (and around the world) who share our fear of the cultural regression and terror of radical Islamist ideology.

We should pray for those more moderate Imams who are caught between a rock and a hard place in their own spiritual communities. There are many who are under threat from radicals and are overwhelmed by the Wahhabist theology propounded and spread by the wealth derived from Saudi oil.

The very soul of Islam is at stake and we would do well to pause for a long moment before we assume that Islam itself is the enemy. It is true that our terrorist enemies are virtually all Muslim. It does not necessarily follow, however, that every Muslim is our enemy.

Alongside most ordinary Muslims there are many powerful and influential Muslims in every corner of the world who are our potential allies in this fight. We must seek them out and encourage them. The threat to them is even greater that it is to us...at least in the immediate future. A minutes thought reveals that it is the moderate Muslims who must be terminated before the rest of the world can be brought under submission to the Islamist caricature of Allah.

So then, be very, very worried. But do not be discouraged. God is the God of history as well as of creation. These times, as with all times, belong to God and are in God's hands. We who stand for God's freedom, peace, mercy, justice and redemption must stand boldly, hand in hand with all who will stand with us . . . even, and perhaps more so, if the hand we hold is the hand of a Muslim.

WEDNESDAY, JANUARY 11, 2006

Alito Jumps Hoops With Ease

When I was younger someone once told me that acheiving your goal required a lot of "jumping through hoops." "Hoops" turned out to be those obstacles that had to be endured or overcome to get where you wanted to go....perhaps a BA degree or a particular job.

Some hoops serve a good purpose but many seem to have been created simply for the sake of jumping or crawling through them. Certain hoops even seem to have been created soley to bring humiliation to the aspirant and some kind or frat-boy initiation-rite joy to those who have already passed that way before.

Back in my Boy Scout days we had a hoop called "snipe hunting" that served this purpose quite well.

This week Judge Alito is jumping through his irrelevent and largely purposeless hoops in the United States Senate. The Democrats have been doing their best to turn it into a frat-boy initiation-ritual and seem to be taking perverse pleasure in trying to make the President's nominee to the Supreme Courts squirm or at least look humiliated.

Unfortunately, what the world is seeing instead is a bunch of campus bullies throwing their (not inconsiderable) weight around in trying to make life miserable for what they view as some young, nervous Freshmen.

Even more unfortunate for the Democrats is that Alito is proving to be a better man than they are (and this includes the women, too!). The contrast is striking. Senators bloviating and posing and ranting and raving over jots and tittles and motes and specks while beams the size of Pacific

Coast Redwood trees can be seen planted firmly in their eyes. Alito, meanwhile, sits and tries his best to be civil and patient, demonstrating why he was nominated as a qualified Supreme Couirt Judge instead of the many wanna-be former lawyers who, facing him, pretend to be his betters.

The world is watching. Americans are watching. They are seeing the quality of leadership representative of the conservative, Republican Party. They are also seeing the quality of leadership representative of the liberal, Democratic Party. It should be clear to all that there is a difference. And the difference is not flattering to the liberals.

I think, when it is all over, the Democrats will look back and realize that, in some ironic twist of fate, they were the ones who were jumping through the hoop...and missed it.

Then again, the naked Emperor continued to insist that he was richly clad in spite of the wind and cold and all the other evidence to the contrary. Sometimes folks have a hard time getting their own jokes...especially when they are unwittingly the butt of them themselves.

American News Media Blacks Out Story of Italian Terror Arrests

Its been several days since this story broke throughout Europe. Headlines in every major paper.

It seems the Italians captures a terrorist cell planning major attacks in the United States.

Why, you may ask, has the American media not covered this story?

Perhaps this phrase in the story has something to do with it:
Italian authorities recently announced that they had used wiretaps to uncover the conspiracy to conduct a series of major attacks inside the U.S.

The story is scary in its implications.

On the other hand, it makes President Bush's defense of his Homeland Security policy look pretty convincing.

It also makes the New York Times and its expose on the President's wiretapping look rather pathetic.

You can read the whole story of what the Italians discovered in many different news sources. I'll follow Powerline's lead and refer you to the Abyssinian International News Agency.

General Hillary Clinton Demands More Body Armor For U.S. Troops

A Pentagon study apparently found that as many as 60%+ of combat-related deaths in Iraq and Afghanistan might have been prevented had a full complement of superior body armor been worn.

Senator Clinton sees this, of course, as a failure on the part of the military and the Bush Administration, saying, "We perhaps could have avoided so many of these fatalities with the right body armor..." adding that she was "just bewildered as to how this president and this vice president continue to isolate themselves from different points of view."

If General Clinton (as Michelle Malkin calls her) had spoken to any of the troops in the field she might have kept her mouth shut. It appears that each soldier is already lugging around over 40 pounds of "stuff" (including armor) and that a balance has to be made between safety and the ability to move. The full armor suggested by Hillary would potentially save lives but would also bring the weight total to nearly 100 pounds, effectively rendering the soldier immovable.

Soldiers' replies to Clinton's huffing and puffing can be found here and many other places on the internet.

This does not mean that more can and ought to be done to protect our troops but, in light of the troop response, it does not appear that the good Senator picked up too many votes from military families on this particular issue.

An anonymous source released this sample illustration of what Hillary believes will provide the protection needed by our troops.

The halberd, apparently, was Colonel Chelsea's idea.

THURSDAY, JANUARY 12, 2006

Six Suspects Arrested In Last October's Mini-Jihad In Oakland

Last November I posted on the attack on stores selling liquor in Oakland. The stores were vandalized by African-American men nattily dressed in suites, white shirts and bow-ties. The incidents were graphically captured on security cameras.

The men's attire led me to conclude that they were members of the Nation of Islam or, at the least, considered themselves to be "Black Muslims" of some flavor or variety.

It turns out that this was the case. Six of the men have now been arrested. A recent news story from Oakland states that at least one of them is a "Black Muslim." No mention is made, however, of the Nation of Islam. Take a guess as to whether the other five men were "Black Muslims." I am still left to wonder whether they are also members of the Nation of Islam and, if so, did they act on their own? (highly unlikely) or ordered to do this by someone "higher up?" (highly likely).

In any case, they were wearing the "uniform" of members of the Nation of Islam. I suspect that the Oakland prosecutor will not want to get entangled in a criminal case that could implicate Nation of Islam leaders. I have little doubt that the case will be based on these men acting on their own as individuals and not as representatives of any group larger than themselves.

The news story linked above turns the issue into one over the issue of the selling of alcohol...how much, if any at all, is enough. There also appears to be conflict between Black Muslims and Middle Eastern Muslims (the latter are the owners of the stores that were attacked).

Ah, me. I do hope that the law, whatever it may be in Oakland, is equally applied and fairly prosecuted against all people whether they are Black, White, Muslim, Christian, big-shot or whatever else one might come up with.

Regardless of whether their motive was "pure" and "well-intentioned" or not, these men broke the law and destroyed property not belonging to them.

I hope they will be prosecuted to the full extent of the law. I hope that, if others are implicated, they will be also.

But I'll believe it when I see it.

In Iran: Rape Victim Sentenced to Death for Killing Attacker

One of two women attacked by three men who attempted to rape them was sentenced to death by hanging by a court in Iran this week.

The girl, 17 years old at the time of the incident in March 2005, said that she first stabbed one of the men in the hand when she was forced to the ground. As they attempted to run away, the men tried to grab them again. It was then that she stabbed one of them in the chest. It was not her intent, she said, to kill anyone.

The girls had been sitting in a park with their boyfriends at the time of the attack. The boyfriends jumped on their motorbikes, drove off and left the girls behind.

The story does not say whether either of the two surviving attackers were charged with any crime.

Choice Quotes From Muslim Radical On Trial In England

According to the London Telegraph, Muslim preacher, 47-year old Abu Hamza, *who was born in Egypt and has lived in Britain for several years as a British citizen, is accused of nine counts of soliciting to murder, four counts of using threatening, abusive or insulting behaviour and two counts of possessing abusive recordings with a view to distribution and possession of a document useful to preparing terrorism.*

According to the story, Hamza's apartment contained plans to blow of Big Ben, skyscrapers, airports and football stadiums.

Most disturbing to me are recordings of Hamza's preaching and teaching. The Telegraph article includes the following citations:

In one speech, delivered to a meeting in Whitechapel, east London, in 1997 or 1998 Hamza said the role of women should be to encourage their husbands to train children as young as 10 so they could become mujahadeen (holy warriors).

In a tape aimed at young people he said: ***"When you meet Allah you will be asked who was killed at your hands?"***

Britain and Western nations were "100 per cent anti-Islam", he said in another tape, calling on his followers to spread Islam "by the sword" and adding: "European leaders only respect those that are strong."

He said: ***"Killing the kafir for any reason is OK, killing the kafir for no reason is OK,"*** *and he specifically singled out those that granted licences for "wine shops".*

Hamza added: ***"We like blood and are addicted to it. When they say they love Allah they must ask themselves how much kafir blood they have spilt for Allah."***

Describing non-believers as "germs and viruses" in another tape he added: ***"There is no drop of liquid loved by Allah more than blood of Serbs, Jews or any other enemy of Allah."***
If you are wondering what a "*kafir*" is, it probably means **you**! Any person who refuses to submit himself to Allah (God), who disbelieves in the message of Mohammed and in Mohammed as the Prophet of God is a "*kafir.*"

Isn't it nice to know that God loves your blood? Especially when it has been happily and blessedly shed by a follower of someone like Hamza?

The saddest part of all this is that, as you can see in the photograph at the top of this post, Hamza seems to have many supporters in front of the courthouse protesting his trial.

Am I Anti-Muslim? Am I Racist?

Am I anti-Muslim or racist? Some folks seem to think so. I have received comments on other sites where I have posted some of my thoughts on radical Islamist terrorism accusing me of this.

Personally, of course, I do not consider myself to be either of these. Just in case you have your doubts I am printing a reply I recently made to several of my accusers over at Blogcritics. They had been responding to my post entitled, "Steyn Predicts the Collapse of 'The West'- Sadly, I Agree." (also posted on this site here).

Greetings. As the author of this post I see that Aaman and Swingpuss have chosen to describe it as "racist." That is all well and good. But labeling the article as racist does not even address the issues being presented. That sort of name calling does not rise to the level of adult dialogue. It more resembles the behavior of otherwise inarticulate children in an elementary school playground. Please, can't we raise the level of conversation a little bit.

Frankly, I am puzzled over the term "racism." I don't seem to find any reference to "race" in my article at all. Islam, whether the more radical kind found in Shi'ite Iran or in the Muslim Brotherhood/Wahhabist/al-Qaeda Sunni varieties, is not a matter of race but of sectarian religious beliefs.

I am merely critiquing a particular version of Islam that seeks to replace "Western Civilization" with a completely different set of values.

As you well know, Muslims come in all shapes and sizes and races and there are many different ways in which different Muslims apply the teachings of the Qur'an to life in the 21st century. To call a critique of a particular viewpoint within the Muslim world "racist" demonstrates that the person bringing that charge has absolutely no idea of the subject at hand...or, more charitably, has misunderstood the subject as presented.

As to xenophobia, this is a word defined as, "Fear or hatred of strangers, people from other countries, or of anything that is strange or foreign." I am not aware of anything in my article that reflects any of this. While it may be xenophobic to have a fear of anything that is strange or foreign it is most certainly not xenophobic to have a critically informed fear of a "strange or foreign" religious sect that would like to see my country and all it represents swept away into oblivion.

This is not xenophobia but common sense...assuming there is a reasonable foundation for the fear...which I believe is easily demonstrable.

Yes, I completely agree that India is a remarkable example of how an experiment in Western-style Democracy is (thus far) successfully evolving and adapting to an Asian multicultural and multi-faith context.

The success of democracy in India actually supports the point of my article. By its constitution, the government in India (as it is in the United States) is required to be secular. Under secular law, Muslims and Hindus and Christians and Buddhists are, at least theoretically, considered as equals.

Under the religious Muslim law of sharia, Muslims are granted one legal status, Jews and Christians another and all the rest still another. The Qur'an does not readily adapt to the concept of secular law and secular government (although that experiment continues in such places as Turkey). What most historic and theological interpretations of the Qur'an envision are variations on the political practice of theocracy, where religious and civil matters are inseparable.

I personally believe that most Muslim versions of a sharia theocracy are not a good thing...at least in light of the freedoms and rights I value as part of Western Civilization and the Judeo/Christian propositions that undergird this world view.

If having a healthy fear of someone's philosophy, political beliefs or religious pracitice is "racist" and "xenophobic" then a critical view of communism, nazi-ism, anarchy or even the Klu Klux Klan must be "racist" as well.

And this, of course, is absurd.

I look forward to continuing with this dialogue. I am also publishing two follow-up articles related to this subject. They will appear whenever the blogcritic editors choose to publish them.

Aloha.

Note: ome six months ago I wrote a post attempting to answer the question, "I Thought This Was a Christian Blog? Why All the Muslim Stuff?" If you are wondering the same thing, follow the link and read my answer.

FRIDAY, JANUARY 13, 2006

Krauthammer's Review On "Munich" Worth a Careful Reading

I have chosen not to pay money to see the movie "Munich." This is not so much because of the controversy over the film but simply because the subject matter does not interest me. Fictionalized history, especially of the still-warm-in-the-morgue variety rarely gets me all excited.

I have, however, read many negative reviews and comments of the film, but none as clear and succinct as in Charles Krauthammer's syndicated column this morning entitled, "'Munich,' the Tragedy."

His most devestating indictment of the movie can be found in these two consecutive paragraphs:
It is an axiom of filmmaking that you can only care about a character you know. In "Munich," the Israeli athletes are not only theatrical but historical extras, stick figures. (Director) Spielberg dutifully gives us their names--Spielberg's List--and nothing more: no history, no context, no relationships, nothing. They are there to die.

The Palestinians who plan the massacre and are hunted down by Israel are given--with the concision of the gifte cinematic craftsman--texture, humanity, depth, history. The first Palestinian we meet is the erudite poet giving a public reading, then acting kindly toward his Italian shopkeeper--before he is brutally shot in cold blood by the Jews...
You get the idea. I got it and I will be content to let others pay good money to watch history and humanity disfigured and bludgeoned to death in the name of "art" or whatever else Mr. Spielberg wishes to call his movie.

The Green Bay Packers' Curious Choice of a New Head Coach

Based on intuition and a quick scan of the statistics of measurable success I do not believe that I would have chosen Mike McCarthy as an NFL head coach as the Green Bay Packers did yesterday.

As a Quarterback Coach for the Packers back in 1999, McCarthy managed to coach the Football Hall of Fame-bound Brett Favre to a stellar 8-8 season.

This past year, as the San Francisco 49ers Offensive Coach, McCarthy managed to give his team a power ranking of 30th out of 32 NFL teams.

His offense managed 17 touchdowns in 16 games averaging 242 yards of total passing & rushing offense per game. His team finished 4-12, dead last in the NFC West, a division which pitted them against such powerhouses as the 6-10 Rams and the 5-11 Cardinals.

According to AP, Packers General Manager Ted Thompson touted McCarthy as someone who could return the franchise to a championship level.

"We feel very good about our future going forward," Thompson said.
Thompson, unfortunately, is not managing a fantasy league team next year.

Three Things I Would Hope To See Happen With Alito On the Supreme Court

With "muddled middle" swing-voter Sandra Day O'Conner soon to be replaced by Sam Alito on the Supreme Court I would hope and expect to see a few changes in the High Court's rulings over the next several years.

1. With new Chief Justice Robertson leading the charge my first hope would be a flat-down overthrow of the insane ruling in last year's ***Kelo v. New London*** concerning the right of **emminent domain**. By a 5-4 margin the Court ruled that municipalities have the right to commandeer private property in order to cater to the needs of private business... all in the name of economic development, of course.

The Bad News is, unfortunately, that all five supporters of this ruling are still sitting on the court. One can only hope that fresh insight from the two SCOTUS newbies will be persuasive enough to lead one of those five to reconsider their previous opinion.

2. One can also hope for a slow reduction of a woman's current "right" to choose to have an abortion in any way and at any time she would like, even if she is a minor with a pregnancy created by abuse or incest.

Eventually, the Constitutional illogic of **Roe v Wade** will crumble into dust. A new ruling would one day, hopefully, identify what legally constitutes human life (this is most certainly a Federal matter) and then leave the debate of the morality/legality of abortion and to what degree it may or may not be available to the States where it belonged in the first place.

3. The issues concerning the separation of **Church and State** have also become unnecessarily muddled over the past 30 years of Supreme Court innovation and wishful thinking. I'm not sure what direction the new Court will take on this and I really do not care, as long as the decisions are rendered intelligibly and in accordance with the plain meaning of the Constitution. Hopefully, the so-called "Lemon Test" will be replaced by something more objective and grounded in legal clarity.

4. The Supreme Court cannot seem to make up its mind concerning the Constitutionality of **Affirmative Action**, either. In a ruling concerning academic Affirmative Action in the admission practices of the University of Michigan, Justice Sandra Day O'Conner, who provided the swing vote endorsing affirmative action, wrote in her decision, "Effective participation by members of all racial and ethnic groups in the civic life of our nation is essential if the dream of one nation, indivisible, is to be realized." She also said that affirmative action is "potentially so dangerous" that it should be eventually phased out.

Such loopy logic must be killed off and buried forever. It is hard to believe that, if the late Chief Justice Reinquist couldn't bring the Court to ground on this matter, Robertson and Alito will be able to do any better.

If nothing else, there will be some snappy, blunt and articulate dissentions should the "flighty five" ever gang up against logic and common sense in the future.

While such potential flights of fancy may not advance the cause of *juris prudence*, the dissents, at least, will most certainly be more entertaining and educational to read than in the past!

MONDAY, JANUARY 16, 2006

Why Can't Hollywood Find Any Native American or Japanese Actresses?

First it was "Memoirs Of a Geisha" where the two lead parts went to Chinese actresses. Where there no Japanese actresses to play the roles? Isn't this an insult to Japan and their culture? How does this validate the films authenticity? Most Asians and many Americans can tell the difference between a Chinese and a Japanese, even with makeup!

Now it is the soon-to-be-released movie, "The New World." Colin Farrell will play Captain John Smith (will he have an English accent?). I can live with this but what about the important role of Pocahontas? The then 15-year old Q'orianka Kilcher was chosen for the part. She is Native American, right? Well....sort of. She is Swiss/Alaskan on her mother's side (I'm not sure what "Alaskan" means) and was born in Germany. On her father's side she is part Quechua/Huachipa, indigenous tribal groups from Peru.

This, I suppose, would suit the role if she was meeting up with Pizarro in the Inca Empire. But, isn't there a single young actress from a North American Native American tribe (especially from the East or North East tribes that could have filled the roll? I'm sure that she does a fine job playing her role. But....

Remember when the blue-eyed Swede, Max von Sydow, played the role of Jesus in "The Greatest Story Ever Told?" Would Hollywood hire a dark-complexioned Italian to play the role of a Scandinavian Viking? I'm afraid the answer is "yes."

I just don't get it. Next will we see an African-American playing the leading role in a movie about George Washington? or a Vietnamese playing the role of Abraham Lincoln?

It makes just about as much sense as just about everything else Hollywood is doing these days. They expect the rest of the American people to be "politically correct." Why can't they try it themselves?

I don't plan on seeing any of these films but....just maybe...I might have if I had thought that they had gotten more appropriate actresses to play these parts.

I'm sure that "Geisha" will be a big hit in Japan, too! Right? Wrong!

MONDAY, JANUARY 23, 2006

Nothing To Say

I've been gone for the past week attending a two-day seminar and church meetings in Los Angeles. I also enjoyed some time with Daughter #1 including a long visit to the Getty Museum.

Now that I am home I have scanned all the past week's newspapers and major blog sites for all the news that I missed while I was gone. There wasn't any.

I suppose that the election results from Iraq (which left the Shi'ite/Kurd coalition short of an outright ruling 2/3 plurality) was worth a positive mention. And there are, of course, the Seahawks and the Steelers heading to the Super Bowl (I had hoped for this!). Mostly, it seems, the blogosphere and newspapers were mostly talking about each other, ignoring each other and spinning whatever little piece of information they could find about....well....just about anything (especially if it had the word "Washington D.C." in it).

Today's news can be best summarized as this: "Way to go, Canada, eh?" Now that the Tories are (more or less) in power we should see some melting of the cold shoulder the Canadian government and press have been giving the United States for the past several years.

Now I will stop. I had nothing to say and have undoubtedly proven it.

TUESDAY, JANUARY 24, 2006

LA Times Column: "I Do Not Support the Troops"

Joel Stein's column in this morning's LA Times has caused a fire-storm of criticism. All I need to do is print a few paragraphs and you will see why:

I DON'T SUPPORT our troops. This is a particularly difficult opinion to have, especially if you are the kind of person who likes to put bumper stickers on his car. Supporting the troops is a position that even Calvin is unwilling to urinate on...

But blaming the president is a little too easy. The truth is that people who pull triggers are ultimately responsible, whether they're following orders or not. An army of people making individual moral choices may be inefficient, but an army of people ignoring their morality is horrifying. An army of people ignoring their morality, by the way, is also Jack Abramoff's pet name for the House of Representatives.

I do sympathize with people who joined up to protect our country, especially after 9/11, and were tricked into fighting in Iraq. I get mad when I'm tricked into clicking on a pop-up ad, so I can only imagine how they feel...

I'm not advocating that we spit on returning veterans like they did after the Vietnam War, but we shouldn't be celebrating people for doing something we don't think was a good idea. All I'm asking is that we give our returning soldiers what they need: hospitals, pensions, mental health and a safe, immediate return. But, please, no parades.

Seriously, the traffic is insufferable.

Personally I have little to say although many are asking folks who take the LA Times to cancel their subscriptions.

The LA Times may or may not endorse what Stein has written but they were under no obligation to print it. That they chose to publish and distribute this column at their expense, however, is perhaps one of the most dishonorable things I have ever seen in a major American newspaper.

Astonishingly, in an interview with Hugh Hewitt today, Stein acknowledged that he did not know anyone in the U.S. Military. As Hugh summarized,

Mr. Stein really doesn't know anyone on active duty, hasn't been to any bases or any of the service academies, hasn't met with wounded or returning troops, and generally admits to being blissfully ignorant of the military. He could not recount a single book he has read about the military, and doesn't even know how big it is. He thinks the soldiers, sailors, airmen and Marines who have died in the GWOT have died in vain. He does not feel grateful for their service.

These are not illegal opinions, of course, but they are deeply repulsive ones.
How sad to think that Stein's opinions may represent those of many in our country. Clearly, the LA Times would do better to publish columns written by those who have some credible idea of what they are talking about. Perhaps a soldier, sailor, airman or Marine?

I won't hold my breath either.

Mexican Government Distributes US Border Survival Maps

The **AP story** begins with this:

A Mexican government commission said Tuesday it will distribute at least 70,000 maps showing highways, rescue beacons and water tanks in the Arizona desert to curb the death toll among illegal border crossers.

A few paragraphs down we read this:

Officials said the maps would help guide those in trouble to rescue beacons and areas with cell phone reception. The maps will also show the distance a person can walk in the desert in a single day.

And then comes the kicker:

"We are not trying in any way to encourage or promote migration," said Mauricio Farah, one of the commission's national inspectors.

I suppose the Mexican government could also print a brochure detailing the easiest ways to rob a bank. No doubt their response would be: "We are not trying in any way to encourage or promote bank robberies. We do know that robbing banks can be very dangerous and we simply want to provide information that, if someone should decide to do such a thing, will help them avoid injury or death."

How kind of them.

Note to readers: *I am not in any way mocking the many tragic deaths and the suffering endured by those attempting to enter the United States illegally from Mexico. Unscrupulous "coyotes" frequently abandon illegals if they sense any danger of being caught. Men, women and children will often find themselves disoriented in the middle of a desert landscape. It is wrong, of course, to not attempt to help such people but there is a fine ethical line between assisting a person in need of food and water and assisting a person in the act of commiting a crime.*

To provide food and services to entering illegal aliens for the express purpose of assisting them in entering the United States successfully is against the law and wrong, no matter what idealistic justifications are offered in its defense.

Google Succumbs To Self-Censorship In China

With the announcement of its new deal with China, Google has become the latest corporation to cave in to the dubious pseudo-ethics of economic globalization. Call it the "New World Order" if you want, but whatever you call it "it" has arrived.

It is virtually impossible for international businesses to adopt a "one size fits all" ethical standard when each national market sets conflicting standards and restrictions.

In the case of China and Google, the mega-search engine giant agreed to China's demands that a long list of subjects (such as "Tianamen Square" and "Taiwan Independence") be blocked.

There is precedent for this, of course. In Germany, for example, Google already blocks Nazi-related items for sale from its search engine in accordance with German law.

In many countries a precondition for doing business has been to offer bribes to certain favored individuals within the government. Most international corporations have entered into such agreements willingly and wholeheartedly in order to gain the advantage over competitors.

Faust learned that there is a way that one can sell his soul. In the area of international business there are innumerable ways.

While such business dealings may increase the corporate "bottom line" it is the average person on the street (who number in the billions) who become the losers. Corrupt and despotic regimes are propped up by such business practices. Personal freedom to acheive success and self-sufficiency are almost always crushed.

In the end, the world, taken as a whole, is the big loser in these international transactions.

It reminds me of the man offered $ 10,000 to kill someone. He took the money with a clear conscience because, as he put it, "The person was going to be killed anyway, by somebody. So I figured that I might as well get the money instead of them."

That, my friends, is as good a summary of the transaction of international business as I have found.

Google is simply the latest example.

Some company was going to get the China contract anyway, so it might as well be . . . well, you get the idea.

Palestinians Are Voting Today

Usually I am an optimist. When it comes to the leadership of the Palestinian people I am, however, a certified pessimist.

Take the elections taking place in Palestine today as they elect representatives to the legislative body of the Palestinian Authority. For most voters, they have the choice of voting for a representative of Fatah (the political arm of Arafat's old PLO) or a representative of Hamas.

Fatah, which supposedly condemns terrorism, recognizes Israel as a nation (sort of), negotiates with Israel and professes to be secular (more or less), has militant affiliates who routinely kill Israeli civilians when it strikes their fancy. Fatah does nothing to disarm them or punish them in any way.

Hamas, on the other hand, does not recognize Israel as a legitimate nation and has, as its only core value, a determination to reclaim Israel for the Palestinian people (at least the Muslim ones who support their "our way or the highway" political philosophy). Hamas leaders have, in recent years, been effectively targeted for assassination by Israel. Even so, from time to time they still seem able to do a fairly good job blowing themselves up along with Israeli civilians as part of their pursuit of an all Muslim united Palestine.

Who is Israel rooting for today? I suspect that, at least privately, they are rooting for Hamas. This would provide Israel with a clear enemy that they can ignore as a political pariah and militarily attack with impunity as an organization that is openly "at war" with Israel.

The current Israeli strategy of unilaterally deciding which settlements to close and which to incorporate into its newly drawn and enlarged national borders is best served by a good showing by Hamas.

Publicly, however, Israeli's will be cheering for Fatah, a corrupt and powerless parody of what it claims to be. With Fatah Israel and the Palestinian Authority would no doubt be condemned to continue the never-ending dance of deception that, for world consumption, they can refer to as "peace talks" and "negotiations."

Pessimist that I am, I see the only hope of any peace settlement predicated on Hamas eventually gaining full control of the Palestinian Authority. If, with such power, Hamas continues its attitude of "war" with its neighbor, then Israel can, with some justification, systematically attack and destroy it. It will only be by being beaten into submission that the suffering Palestinians will ever be forced into conceding the existence of Israel as a legitimate state and be satisfied with creating and accepting a separate state for themselves.

While Israel's 1948 war of independence turned a goodly number of the Palestinian people into refugees, their greatest suffering has been inflicted upon them by those pretending to be their advocates.

What did Arafat ever do to relieve the suffering of "his people?" Nothing.

Neither will Hamas. Their very existence requires that the Palestinian people continue to suffer and to eat and breathe hatred for Israel and the Jews every day of their lives.

My heart aches for these poor, abused people. If Hamas and Fatah and all the other groups motivated more by hate for Israel than by any measure of love for the Palestinians were to disappear then I have no doubt that Israel, the United States and any other nation that really, truly has the best interests of the Palestinian people at heart, would willingly share their own wealth and resources to create a Palestinian State that would provide for the needs of its people and protect them from themselves.

Never, perhaps in the history of the world, has a group of people worked so hard for so long to hurt themselves as the Palestinians.

Perhaps today's elections will begin to turn the tide in a more positive direction.

As a pessimist, however, I say, "fat chance."

THURSDAY, JANUARY 26, 2006

Hamas Wins--Will "Govern" Palestine

It's time for "Good News Bad News." First, the bad news.

Hamas won the Palestinian elections.

And the good news? Uh.....I'm thinking, I'm thinking.......

Hamas has, of course, a public policy calling for the violent destruction of the State of Israel and the establishment of an Islamist Palestinian State (that would include the land presently "occupied" by Israel).

Hamas has backed up this policy by successfully sending at least 60 suicide bombers into Israel during the past few years.

Some Israelis are trying to put a positive twist into the election results by saying things like, "Hamas was not elected to carry out attacks against Israel. It was elected to bring about change."

Others are not so sure, such as the travel guide who said, "It is hard not to be even more pessimistic now about peacemaking prospects here. We could see this whole place engulfed in even further chaos. Israel has to tread very carefully."

With Iran building nuclear weapons while saying that it's official policy is to have Israel "wiped off the map;" with the Iranian-backed Hizbollah continuing to defiantly maintain its well-armed presence and control of southern Lebanon along Israel's northern border, and; with Hamas controling the West Bank and Gaza and all the border check-points between Jordan, Egypt and Israel the threat of a devastating, armed conflict in the region is perhaps greater today than at any time since the 1973 Yom Kippur Arab-Israeli War.

And the good news? One positive note in all of this is that Fatah, with all of its lies, corruption and posturing for "peace," is out of power and, perhaps, gone forever as a credible representative of the Palestinian people.

Hamas, on the other hand, seems to know how to use its power and authority to gain and maintain control over a population. It has taken a preeminent lead in providing health services, support and education (especially of the "get a good Muslim education so you can blow yourselves up so as to take as many Israelis with you as possible" sort of curriculum). Whatever Christian Palestinians remain in Gaza or the West Bank will surely be the biggest losers since Hamas, as an Islamist group with ties to the Muslim Brotherhood, will now count non-Muslim Palestinians as second-rate citizens even though they have lived there for hundreds of years longer than the Muslims themselves.

On Tuesday, I posted on another piece of "good news" of a more macabre kind that could result from a Hamas victory. Israel now has an enemy that it can deal with up front and personal. No more games need to be played. There are clear positions on each side: Israel wishes to continue to exist alongside a peaceful Palestinian State and Hamas wishes to kill every Jew in Israel and end its existance as a nation.

Neither Israel nor Hamas recognize each other and have vowed that they will not speak or negotiate with each other.

Only time will tell. At least it is a place to start from!

My feeling is similar to when a fresh breeze clears the smog only to reveal the true ugliness of the surrounding landscape.

Please join me in praying for peace. Surely, no mere mortal is capable of unravelling this knotted web of anger, bitterness and sin.

As the Psalmist (traditionally identified as David) once wrote, "Some trust in chariots and some in horses, but we trust in the name of the LORD our God."

To that I say, "Amen."

Iran Wants Direct Flights to the U.S.

No, this idea didn't originate at The Onion or in the late-night monologues of Jay Leno or David Letterman. Strange as it sounds, Iran has indeed asked the United States to allow direct flights between the two countries.

Reuters reports that:

Iran has asked the United States to allow direct flights between the two countries after a break of more than two decades, a senior civil aviation official said on Thursday. . .

"We sent a letter to the relevant American officials on Wednesday, announcing Iran's willingness to resume direct flights," Nourollah Rezai-Niaraki, head of Iran's Civil Aviation Organization, told state television.

He said the decision to make the request was taken by hardline Iranian President Mahmoud Ahmadinejad due to demand from the large Iranian community living in the United States.

"They have repeatedly complained about wasting time and losing their baggage on connecting flights," the official said.

Just what we need-- an Iraqi airliner flying direct from Tehran to JFK International loaded with suicide bombers and nuclear or "dirty" bombs.

"I hope American officials do not adopt a political stance in making a decision on this request," said Iranian civil aviation spokesman Reza Jafarzadeh.

A "political stance?" Why in the world would the United States want to adopt a political stance on this matter?

I wonder how you say "Nuts!" in Farsi?

ht:lgf

FRIDAY, JANUARY 27, 2006

White Guy Experiences Preaching at African-American Church

I am, of course, the "white guy" mentioned in the title of this post.

Last Sunday, while in Southern California attending several denominational events, I preached at **Angeles Mesa Presbyterian Church** in Los Angeles.

Pastor Timm Cyrus and I have been friends for nearly 20 years. He preached at my Mililani church when the Presbytery of the Pacific met in Honolulu two years ago so now it was my turn to preach at Angeles Mesa. The church is African-American and thrives on emotion and enthusiasm centered around the saving Lordship of Jesus. I had never preached in such a venue before but had attended and experienced such worship on many occasions.

I took a sermon I had recently preached in Mililani and added an introduction and expanded a section in the middle but left it more or less the same otherwise. I preached for 40 minutes (a luxury and a departure from my usual 20 minute message) but did not expect the response I received.

The vocal support from the congregation was far more than I had anticipated. At one point I had to pause and wait for the enthusiasm to subside before I could continue. By the time I approached the end of the sermon more than a few in the congregations were actually standing on their feet praising God and encouraging me on with my message. (Note: This is *not* a pentecostal church!)

What a wonderful experience to have the power of the Holy Spirit pour out of the pulpit only to have it returned in full by the response of the congregation. That is so different from the usual Sunday morning where the power of the Holy Spirit flows from the pulpit only to seemingly disappear into thin air and silence.

In any case, I found my ministry and preaching to be wonderfully affirmed and I flew home that evening feeling strangely uplifted and encouraged.

I can assure you that there are no "frozen chosen" at Angeles Mesa. But there are plenty of "chosen!" I praise God for Timm's wonderful ministry and for the warm welcome I received from the members of his congregation.

P.S. They have one of the best small gospel choirs in Southern California. Awesome! Worship is at 10:00 am.

SATURDAY, JANUARY 28, 2006

Nicole Kidman Becomes UN Goodwill Ambassador--No Joke!

According to AP:

Nicole Kidman has a new role - working to advance women's rights around the globe as a goodwill ambassador for the U.N. The Oscar-winning actress will work with the United Nations Development Fund for Women, UNIFEM, on critical gender concerns such as ending violence against women.

Some years ago everyone wanted to have a pot bellied pig for a pet. Today, in Hollywood at least, everyone wants to be a United Nation's Goodwill Ambassador.

It appears that one of the qualifications for this position is that you must, 1. Be female; 2. Be a beautiful female; 3. Be a famous and wealthy actress, and; 4. Be willing to take all your clothes off and be seen totally naked by millions of people around the world.

Thus we have had Angelina Jolie and, as of yesterday, Nicole Kidman chosen for the honor.

Kidman, of course, has stripped to full-frontalhood in such films as "Birthday Girl," "Eyes Wide Shut" and, most recently, "Cold Mountain."

This experience, of course, has given her exemplary credibility on "Women's issues" and "gender concerns" around the world, particularly in Muslim countries and in most Third World countries, which are notoriously conservative and purient when it comes to public exhibition of female flesh.

Personally, I do not quite see how running around naked on movie screens around the world and playing a starring role as a tabloid sex symbol helps Nicole in being taken seriously as she presents her concerns over "violence against women."

I'm sure that she is a nice, sincere person who has a certain amount of passion for the needs of women. As a UN Ambassador I also have no doubt that she will be given many free trips to exotic places and be feted and wined and dined at embassies and government offices and noted five-star restaurants around the world.

There will also be, of course, the mandatory photo ops with victimized women in South-East Asia and Africa. How this will help these women is not exactly clear. Perhaps shaking hands or being hugged by Nicole will lift their spirits and inspire them to enter movie careers. Perhaps the blue jeans and pre-washed white shirts covered with a pre-worn light denim jacket will convince those who exploit these women to have a change of heart and become film directors in Hollywood.

Dearest Nicole: If you really want to address the issues of violence against women and honestly desire to raise their status in the eyes of world culture (and of men, in particular), the very best thing you could do would be to begin by addressing the debased, degrading and stereotypical image of women as sex objects in the Hollywood movie industry.

Say what you will....but until you renounce your own career and take on the industry that made you a celebrity, there will not be one man in the entire world who will take you seriously. Indeed, in many places you will need to be protected from men would would otherwise spit on you for your indecency. To much of the world you are a poster girl for the immoral depravity of so-called Western civilization. For you to go anywhere outside of the United States or your home country of Australia and point your finger in accusation of the abuse of women or the suppression of their "human rights" will generate nothing but disdain.

Your selection as a United Nation's Goodwill Ambassador for women's issues mocks the very subject for which you were chosen as a spokesperson.

The fact that the United Nations chose you also mocks what little sincerity, integrity and reputation remains in that thoroughly discredited institution of international corruption and self-service.

Where is Shirley Temple Black when we need her!

Should a Christian Blog Post a Semi-Nude Photo?

My previous post on Nicole Kidman prompted the following comment:

Please take off the semi-nude photo of Nicole. Why promote sin in men to lust? IS this not a "Christian" blog?

I appreciate this comment because I spent a long time debating whether to post that photo or not. There were, of course, many photos available which were far more revealing and these I did reject without question. In the end, however, I chose to post this more modest photo to illustrate and validate the point I was making. It did not occur to me that this particular photo might "promote sin in men to lust." For me it simply served as a ironic representation of both her primary qualification and primary disqualification for being a UN Goodwill Ambassador.

Throughout history Christian painters have used the exposed human body both to represent the natural beauty, goodness and innocence of God's creation and the association of the self-conscious shame of nakedness with the reality of human sin.

The famous painting of "The Creation of Adam" in the Sistine Chapel and the Statue of David, both by Michelangelo, are examples of the former while Massacio's "Expulsion from the Garden" is a good example of the latter (note that the original did not have the "fig leaves" on it...they were added later).

The naked human form has also been used to illustrate the hapless powerlessness of those condemned in the final judgment. The macabre paintings by Hieronymus Bosch, the Last Judgment by Michelangelo (also in the Sistine Chapel) and the medieval figures over the doors of the Cathedrals of Bourges and Autun all use nudity to emphasize the horror of damnation.

The naked images of the infant Jesus and the near-naked exposure of his body on the cross are also examples of the human body being used to communicate other, quite different, feelings and emotions from scripture.

I'll confess that some artists have utilized the biblical iconography of Bathsheba taking a bath as an excuse for painting a sensual image that might well "promote sin in men to lust." Since that was, of course, the entire point of the story of David and Bathsheba it seems that even a painting such as this can serve a useful purpose in reminding male viewers that they are just as vulnerable to sexual sin as King David was.

In the context of the Christian gospel and in the context of my post, the photo of Nicole Kidman serves to "expose" the fallacy and lie of pretending that what Nicole Kidman does in her movies is somehow admirable, sophisticated or liberated.

In context, the photo "exposes" Kidman as a fallen woman, shameless in her sin, in "stark" contrast to Adam and Eve, who (at least) made "aprons" to cover their nakedness.

She, like those expelled from Eden, is in need of repentance, forgiveness and new birth.

It is not just our souls and hearts that are in need of salvation and redemption, however. God created us in his image...male and female he created us. Our bodies of flesh, with all of their sexual distinctiveness, are also in need of transformation.

It is important to remember that Jesus entered the world "in the flesh," suffered and died on the cross "in the flesh," was, by means of the physical transformation of resurrection, raised to life "in the flesh" and, forty days later, ascended into heaven "in the flesh."

It was, in part at least, for our flesh that Christ died.

Nicole, like every one of us, is in need of the Good News of God's saving love in Christ Jesus her Lord.

Because of this, her nakedness should generate feelings of embarrassment and pity in us rather than admiration, envy or respect.

The Bible itself is quite graphic in its description of human sin. While linguists translate the words into other languages, artists translate scripture into painting, sculpture, theater and music. It is sometimes helpful to see sin presented in some way other than words alone.

Like Massacio's painting of Adam and Eve, I intended the photo of Nicole Kidman to serve that purpose being fully aware that, like Massacio's painting, there will always be those who will find the subject matter tintillating instead of edifying.

Paul, in Corinthians, warns us to limit our freedom for the sake of those who are weak in faith lest we cause them to stumble. While I seek to be obedient to this admonition I am also of the opinion that, should we attempt to avoid anything and everything that might cause others to "stumble," our lives, our world and the Gospel itself would become sorely impoverished.

So....I've decided to leave Nicole's photo on my site as a witness to her fallenness and to our own.

And I am glad that the photo offends some people because, after all, that was the very point I was trying to make.

Note: Strange to say, but whatever photo I originally posted showing Kidman partially nude has disappeared from my blog's archives. I have no idea what it was. I suppose I will just have to leave it to the readers' imaginations!

SUNDAY, JANUARY 29, 2006

LA Times Column Blames Israel for Just About Everything--Including the Palestine Election Results

In an LA Times article entitled "Hamas In Charge" Beshara Doumani follows the new left-wing liberal mantra that says that it is all Israel's fault.

Beshara, who is an associate professor of history at UC-Berkeley, manages the twin feat of twisting reality into an indictment of Israel while, at the same time, ignoring and hiding the fact that Hamas' stated policy (and Fatah's official, behind the scenes policy) is the total destruction and annihilation of the nation of Israel.

One of two key paragraphs begins with what might appear to be a reasonable opening:
In terms of the relationship with Israel, nothing fundamental will change, but the mask will be off.
Yes, you will say, while Fatah was duplicitous, corrupt and disingenuous in its policy toward Israel, at least with Hamas the "mask will be off." But you would be wrong.

Beshara's point is that now the world will see Israel for what it really is, a hateful, racist and intransigent block to any and all efforts by the Palestinians to negotiate a peace agreement.

You see, according to Beshara,

It wasn't really Hamas that eviscerated Palestinian Authority President Mahmoud Abbas and Fatah in the elections. It was the Israeli governments that engineered the failure of the "peace preces" to produce fruit, and the the Fatah leadership's gluttony that blinded them to the consequences of their own failures. Still, the Hamas victory will make it much easier for Israel to sell the "no partner for peace" line.

Not once does Beshara even hint at the fact that Fatah (and the PLO it emerged from) and Hamas are still fighting the 1948 war of Israel's independence. They do not want peace with Israel, they want Israel to vanish and disappear forever. Such groups do not exist to be "advocates" or "friends" of the Palestinian people. They exist to destroy Israel. Period.

Fatah proved this by investing billions of dollars in international aid for the Palestinian people in their own Swiss savings accounts and allowing attacks on Israel that destroyed what had previously been a mutually beneficial economic exchange between Israel and the Palestinian people. Fatah has, wherever it has gone (ie. Jordan, Lebanon, West Bank & Gaza) created a legacy of poverty, social ruin, corruption and despair. The economy and standard of living in the West Bank and Gaza was far better off (relative to the times) 40 years ago (pre PLO/Arafat) than it is now.

Can Hamas do any better? Only time will tell whether they will have any interest in improving the living conditions for the Palestinian people now under their watch. Politically, it is to their advantage to follow the reasoning of Professor Beshara and continue to leave their people in squalor while blaming Israel for everything even as they send Kassam rockets and suicide bombers across the borders (which they now control) into Israel.

Even if they develop an inclination to govern and improve living standards and security in their territory they will probably achieve those ends by suppression of freedom and the imposition of social change by threats and by force. Some form of *sharia* is inevitable and the next wave of fighting will not only be between Fatah and Hamas but between the more "extreme" and the more "moderate" leaders within Hamas itself.

Beshara concludes his article with these words,

But there is a larger truth: After Oslo, the daily life of Palestinians in the occupied territories deteriorated to almost subhuman levels, largely because of Israeli policies. The best that people hope for is to keep their heads above water and pray that their society will not suffer a complete collapse. At times like these, people turn to God and to each other. Hamas has helped them to do both , and it has something to show for it.

Here Beshara not only reasserts his claim that Israel is the cause of "subhuman living conditions" in the "occupied territories" but that Hamas has extended the promise of hope by calling people to "turn to God and to each other."

As a Christian, I believe that we "turn to God" with repentance and remorse for our sin. In obedience to Christ we would then "turn to each other" in sacrificial love, putting the needs of our neighbor above those of our own. We would "bear one another's burdens and so fulfill the law of Christ" and we would "exercise forbearance and love towards one another."

When Hamas says it, however, they are speaking of God's command to destroy the infidels and, by force if necessary, restore the land upon which Israel sits to Muslim rule and to then spread that rule to every nation on earth....by force if necessary.

To kill your infidel neighbor and yourself as well on behalf of Jihad is pleasing to God and even encouraged by a blessing of immediate salvation to Paradise.

It appears to me that Beshara eloquently writes and speaks as though he were a spokesman for Hamas. The article is a one-sided, anti-Israel propaganda piece that the LA Times should have been ashamed to have printed in their paper. That is, of course, unless the LA Times agrees with him.

Hamas To Institute Shari'a Law In Palestine

Last Friday I wrote,

Hamas, on the other hand, seems to know how to use its power and authority to gain and maintain control over a population. It has taken a preeminent lead in providing health services, support and education (especially of the "get a good Muslim education so you can blow yourselves up so as to take as many Israelis with you as possible" sort of curriculum). Whatever Christian Palestinians remain in Gaza or the West Bank will surely be the biggest losers since Hamas, as an Islamist group with ties to the Muslim Brotherhood, will now count non-Muslim Palestinians as second-rate citizens even though they have lived there for hundreds of years longer than the Muslims themselves.

Earlier today (Sunday) I wrote,

Even if they develop an inclination to govern and improve living standards and security in their territory they will probably achieve those ends by suppression of freedom and the imposition of social change by threats and by force. Some form of sharia is inevitable and the next wave of fighting will not only be between Fatah and Hamas but between the more "extreme" and the more "moderate" leaders within Hamas itself.

Now I read that Hamas leaders are, indeed, planning to institute shari'a law in Palestine, beginning with the education system.

Mr. Abu Teir, who was No. 2 on the Hamas list of candidates for Wednesday's election, said introducing sharia -- a controversial moral and legal code based on the Koran -- would be the first act of the new Hamas-controlled Palestinian Legislative Council.

"The No. 1 thing we will do is take sharia as a source for legislation. Sharia has a soul in it and is good for all occasions,"

He made it clear that one way Hamas planned to encourage the next generation to follow sharia was to revamp the Palestinian education system, separating girls' and boys' classes and introducing a more Islamic curriculum.

Hamas leaders indicated that they were not planning on imposing full shari'a law in the West Bank and Gaza. Alcohol would still be permitted, they said, and women would not be required to wear the *hijab* (Islamic head covering).

Teir also declared that,

"We are centrists, we are against any kind of extremism. The motto that we operate on is that in religion, you cannot force people."

Palestinian Christians, many of whom have expressed concerns about being ruled by Islamists, have nothing to fear, he added.

Sure.

Smiles In Worship

Well, it happened. The sort of thing you read about in Reader's Digest. The sort of thing that keeps ministers up at night in cold sweats. This morning I happened to me.

During the responsive reading of our Call to Worship (Pslam 150) I was supposed to read the text as follows:
Let everything that has breath praise the LORD.
What I read, however, was something like this:
Let everything that has breast's. . .
At that point, realizing my error, I came to an abrupt halt. But the damage had been done. There was no real "out loud" laughing but there were a few soft giggles and lots of smiles.

Pro that I am, I simply started the line over again and moved on with our worship of God.

Later, after giving the matter some thought, I have decided that "everything that has breasts" *should* "praise the LORD."

Even if the pslamist didn't really put it that way!

Quotes from Screen Actor's Guild Awards

"Oh, my God, y'all. Sometimes, I can't just shake the feeling that I'm just a little girl from Tennessee." Reese Witherspoon, Best Actress, "Walk the Line"

"It's important to say that actors can't act alone, it's impossible. What we have to do is support each other. Actors have to have each others' backs. It's the only way to act well is when you know the other actor has your back, and these actors had my back, and I hope they know I had theirs." Philip Seymour Hoffman, Best Actor, "Capote"

"I can't imagine a greater honor than being acknowledged by my peers. Being an actor is a hell of a thing. It's a hell of a thing. It's up and down. It's great, but I found the best thing about it is hanging around the craft-service table with other actors and crew people, eating doughnuts." Paul Giamatti, Best Supporting Actor, "Cinderella Man"

"I love actors. I married one. OK, I married a fantastic one." (referring to husband William H. Macy) "But even more than acting, I love the community of actors. I love the green room. I love the hair and makeup trailer. ... I'm so happy I can make a living at it, because I was never very good at math." Felicity Huffman, Best Actress Nominee, "Transamerica"

"A friend of mine always says if you don't have something nice to say about someone, say it. This is the saddest collection of climbing, grasping, paranoid, back-stabbing, screen-grabbing schmoozers and losers that you ever saw in your life. But we love each other very much." Terry O'Quinn, co-star, Best TV Dramatic Ensemble, "Lost"

And that, my friends, is why they normally read from scripts.

Quotes courtesy of AP

A Near Mid-Air Collision? You Decide

A photographer captured this dramatic photograph over East London yesterday. He started taking photos of the DHL and Japan Airlines jets, he said, "after seeing the planes apparently coming together 'on a collision course'."

But a spokesman for DHL said photographs could be "incredibly deceptive".

"In the picture, they look like they are close together but it doesn't mean they are. And in fact they were not," he said ..... The spokesman said there was no question that either aircraft had strayed from its proper path, which should mean there was a distance of some two and a half miles between them.

The planes both landed safely at Heathrow Airport with no reports of any safety violations.

Hmmmmm...We report, you decide.

Story and quotes taken from BBC

MONDAY, JANUARY 30, 2006

Bull Jumps Wall At Bullfight--Dramatic Video

A 1,000 pound bull jumped into the stands during a bull fight in Mexico City today. Several spectators were injured. If you watch the dramatic video of the incident here, you will join me in wondering why no one was killed! No doubt there are many very grateful folks thanking God for their lives tonight.

Orchid In Bloom

Well, our orchids have gone and done it again. It seems that here in Hawaii we couldn't stop them from blooming even if we tried! All we do is just leave them alone sitting alongside the house and they have the nerve to do *this* to us! Nice, isn't it!

TUESDAY, JANUARY 31, 2006

State of the Union Is Good

President George W. Bush stood his ground before a brazenly defiant bi-partisan Congress this evening and laid out what has to have been one of the most timid and unambitious speeches of his presidency.

His defense of "freedom is on the march" seemed like it came out of a can and, in light of the Hamas victory in Palestine and the gains of the Muslim Brotherhood in Egypt, its tone of triumphalism rang almost hollow.

His challenge to Iran seemed particularly bland and innocuous. He almost sounded like an echo of John Kerry in linking US policy and a resolution of the Iran nuclear crisis to our European allies.

He spoke nicely to the Iranian people themselves but gave them nothing to hope for in the way of American intervention or even any cause for optimism that the United States would step in and help them should they attempt civil unrest or a counter-revolution against the ayotollahs.

North Korea was mentioned only in passing, alongside Zimbabwe and Burma. On the other hand, Israel was not mentioned at all, an omission that, frankly, concerns me .

The tributes to US military personnel and their families were, perhaps, the most sincere and effective parts of his speech. For the most part, they received bi-partisan support. The father, mother and widow of SSgt Dan Clay, killed in Fallujah last month, while appropriate, also seemed somewhat staged to counter the Cindy Sheehan outraged-mother-as-a-victim media circus. The word "exploited" even flitted (momentarily) through my thoughts.

Cindy herself had received a gallery pass from a Democratic Congresswoman but was, according to news reports, hurried away in handcuffs before the President entered. Why? It's not exactly clear but apparently she had a rolled-up banner of some sort on her lap that she was either actually beginning to unfurl or appeared to be preparing to do so, perhaps later, during the speech.

Bush did lob a few shots over the Democrat's bow but with little effect. He effectively defended his warrantless NSA "terrorist surveillance" policy (providing an opportunity for the cameras to zoom in on an almost bemused Hillary Clinton, who remained seated as the Republican side of the aisle rose in a standing ovation.

The response was similar when Bush called for the full reinstatement of the "Patriot Act." The Democrats took a direct hit to the chin but did not seem overwhelmed by the jab.

On the matter of Social Security reform Bush handed the Democrats a birthday present when he reminded everyone that his reform proposal had been defeated. The entire Democratic side of the aisle rose with applause, cheers and, for the only time during the evening a celebration of triumph.

Perhaps Bush believed that his demand that Congress face up to the issue would provide a counter punch. It didn't seem to have any effect. But it did allow him to call for a bi-partisan committee to seek out a solution to the Social Security fiasco that could actually accomplish something tangible. Both sides rose with applause in response....so maybe it wasn't such a bad gesture after all. As regards Social Security, it shouldn't be politics but public interest that is served. I believe that Bush scored a point here but was, perhaps, unnecessarily subtle about it.

As should be obvious to just about anyone, the single most favorable domestic issue to the Bush administration is the state of the US economy. Surprisingly, unless I fell asleep for a moment, I heard nothing about this, either. A little bragging on this score could have segued into a recognition of outgoing Fed Chairman Alan Greenspan and his replacement, Ben Bernanke, who had been confirmed by the US Senate earlier in the day.

Appropriate acknowledgment was made to Coretta Scott King, widow of Martin Luther King Jr., who passed away at home in her sleep early this morning.

Appropriate also was the effort that went into the hurried swearing in of new Supreme Court Justice Samuel Alito this afternoon, whose nomination had also been confirmed by Senate vote earlier today. His presence, and that of new Chief Justice Roberts (sans "stripes" thank God) among the "nine" was, perhaps, the most visible example of Bush's ascendant political influence during the entire evening.

Alito's admission to the Court also gave Bush the pleasure of announcing the retirement of Sandra Day O'Connor; an announcement that brought polite applause from all sides (although not, perhaps, for the same reasons).

There were, of course, a number of "initiatives" concerning litigation against OBGYN physicians and energy policy. But, while sounding substantive, it is unlikely that either will be prosecuted during an election year.

All in all I was disappointed in tonight's speech. The lack of a bold clarity on Iran and the lack of mention of our nation's firm commitment to the continued existence of Israel seemed to project an air of confusion and uncertainty into our foreign policy.

Even though I would give the speech little more than a C+ or a B- I still enjoyed one statement more than all the others combined. With a firm and steady stare fixed on the Democrats, Bush declared,

"...hindsight is not wisdom and second-guessing is not strategy."

That, at least, was a home run deep into McCovey Cove.

Coretta Scott King 1927-2006

Blogcritics.org

Culture Pick of the Week

Coretta Scott King, who died this morning from the effects of stroke and ovarian cancer, was a woman thrust onto the world stage through no effort of her own.

When she married the Rev. Martin Luther King, Jr. in 1953 she no doubt planned to live a quiet life as the wife of a Baptist pastor. Her husband was clearly cut from special cloth from the start and she knew this and admired him for the clearness of his vision and the eloquence of his voice.

During her husband's rise to international fame and influence Coretta kept a quiet profile, raising their children and trying to make life as "normal" as possible for a family frequently the target of death threats. She knew that each day might well be her husband's last. There were so many who wanted him dead.

By God's grace, Dr. King survived until 1968 when a sniper's bullet killed him in Memphis, Tennessee.

Following a time of mourning, Coretta felt the pressure of the Civil Rights Movement to step up and carry on her husband's legacy. Her leadership, while effective and inspiring, was more than anything symbolic of the still considerable influence of her late husband.

It is doubtful that she ever again had any personal identity separate from that of being the widow of the late "Rev. Dr. Martin Luther King, Jr."

Even so, she carried this heavy burden with grace and dignity. Even though there were many who would have rejoiced if she had fallen in disgrace, she rarely even stumbled and remained standing tall and straight until the end.

She was, for all of America, a role model for being a wife, a mother, a widow and a public figure. She was all this and more; and not just for the African-American community; but for all Americans.

I only heard her speak in person once, back in the early 1980's when she spoke at a Colloquium at Utah State University. I remember her presentation as being sincere and passionate but not particularly uplifting or inspiring. Even then she seemed more like her husband's shadow (as in Peter Pan) than herself.

Coretta Scott King is the perfect example of the "what if" scenario. What if her husband had not moved to Montgomery just 3 months before Rosa Parks got arrested for not moving to the back of the bus? What if her husband had not risen to national prominence? What if her husband had not been assassinated?

I suspect that deep in her heart, gifted though she was, Coretta Scott King's personal dream would have been to simply be a Baptist pastor's wife, mother to her children and, perhaps, one day stepping out into some vocation of her own choosing when the children had grown. Instead of choosing her own destiny, however, destiny chose her.

It is to her credit and worthy of our gratitude that she took the mantle of her fallen husband and served us all so well until the end.

We now trust her spirit to the care and mercy of Almighty God in the sure and certain hope of resurrection to eternal life.

"Free at last! Free at last! Thank God Almighty, we are free at last!"

Amen.

WEDNESDAY, FEBRUARY 01, 2006

A Thought On Gasoline Prices--Rats . . . Maybe They Sorta Make Sense

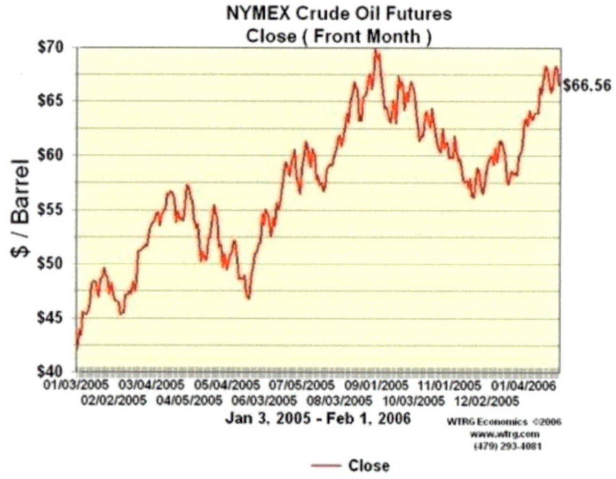

Mexican Crude (click to enlarge)

Instead of listening to talking heads or talk show callers to learn about gasoline prices I decided to just sit down for ten minutes and do a little math. You know...the kind of math we learned in elementary school?

In any case, I first checked out some facts on the internet (all figures are rough estimates rounded off):

2004 average cost of a barrel of crude oil: $37

2004 average cost of a gallon of gasoline at the pump: $1.85

Cost of crude oil as a percentage of the total: 47%

This means that the crude oil cost came to .87 per gallon of gasoline

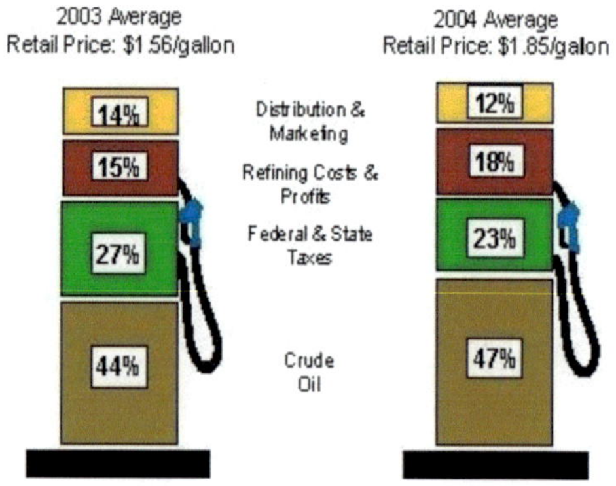

Percentage cost breakdown for gallon of gasoline

I then compared this with this past year:

2005 average cost of a barrel of crude oil (last 6 months): $65

2005 average cost of a gallon gasoline at the pump: $2.50 - $3.00

Cost of crude oil as a percentage of the total: (here is where the math comes in)

The cost of crude increased by $28

$28 is an increase of 76% over 2004

This means that the cost of crude alone added .66 to the cost of a gallon of gasoline. Therefore:

This one factor alone would have raised the cost per gallon of gasoline to $2.55 without factoring in any resulting increase in taxes (which, at an average of 23% of cost per gallon would have risen from .42 to .58, an increase in .16), refining costs (there was a hurricane, remember?) and transportation costs (those delivery trucks had to buy diesel at higher prices, too).

My guess is that with all these factors weighed in that the average price of a gallon of gasoline in 2005 ought to have been somewhere around $2.75 or so.

As it turns out that was just about what it was.

Now the cost of crude oil did fluctuate above and below that $65 per barrel figure even as the selling price of a gallon of gasoline stayed relatively stable.

Over the course of the year, the oil companies probably made an above average profit increase because of those fluctuations. But keep in mind, they had to increase prices ahead of costs because they did not know just how high the cost per barrel could go.

In short, they had to plan on the worst-case scenario or else they could have run out of cash to purchase the oil!

Fortunately for us all (you and me as well as the oil companies) the cost per barrel of oil peaked at $70 in September 2005. The national average for a gallon of gas stands today at $2.37 which sort of reflects the fact that crude dropped to around $55 at the end of last year. This past week it rose up to $66 so we can expect that gallon of gasoline to cost a little more in the weeks ahead.

Personally, I'd rather see the oil companies taking a healthy profit than "running on empty." The success of this "free market" approach to the price of gasoline does have its good side....In Europe, where much of the refinery business is still under government control, the cost of a gallon of gasoline last year went up to the equivalent of $8 US.

So, Exxon had a good year.

As a nation, we did too.

So stop complaining about the cost of gasoline and try focusing all of your energy on rising health and pharmaceutical drug costs. My simple math just doesn't add up when it comes to health care!

Note: Lest you think I've gone nutters, you should know that I live in Hawaii where today's average cost for a gallon of gasoline is $2.87, the highest in the nation. (The national average is $2.37). Ouch!

THURSDAY, FEBRUARY 02, 2006

Winnie-the-Pooh Takes On the Muhammed Cartoon Furor

Unless you have been in hibernation you will have heard of the Muslim uproar over the publication of several **cartoon drawings featuring images of the Prophet Muhammed** in a Danish publication. Muslim tradition does not permit the reproduction of any image of Muhammed or of Allah. The fact that these cartoons mostly featured the Muslim prophet in the context of Islamic terrorism did not particularly ingratiate the Danes with the Muslim world.

The death-threatening and Danish-boycotting has caused a rare liberal backlash in Europe with several **publications in Germany, France, Italy and Spain reprinting the cartoons** in defiance of the attempt to suppress what they view as the freedom of speech.

The editor of the French publication has already been fired and the Danish government is full of apologies. But it seems as if Europe has had enough of mollycoddling (which means bowing and scraping to) the Muslim fundamentalists who believe that any action by an infidel that does not conform to the standards set by their particular brand of *sharia* is worthy of the death penalty.

Today's Day By Day, a popular on-line cartoon drawn by Chris Muir, captured the controversy with an admirable combination of sensitivity, disdain and wit.

Click to enlarge

If you would like to see the offending cartoons for yourself you can see them **here.**

If you would like to see the sort of anti-Semitic cartoons that are printed daily in the Arab-Muslim press you can see them **here**.

If you would like to see a collection of depictions of Muhammed throughout history you can see them **here**.

And, if you want to know my opinion of such matters, I'll tell you:

As a Christian I do not believe that it is helpful or appropriate to publicly insult or ridicule historical figures who are revered by other faith groups.

As an American citizen I support the right of publications and individuals to do so under the protection of the First Amendment.

I can't say that I particularly like to see a crucifix submerged in a bottle of urine or to see Jesus depicted in a movie as engaging in intimate sex with one of his disciples but...I believe that God has given us the freedom to embrace him in faith or to reject him in disbelief. I would be denying the very freedom extended to us all by God should I become intolerant of another's decision to mock Jesus, God, Allah, Muhammed, Moses or Buddha.

Even so, acting out our freedom does have consequences that we must be willing to accept. The publication of these cartoons was bound to stir up anger among many Muslims. The fact that these cartoons were intentionally misrepresented in the Arab world in order to produce the anger that we are now seeing does not negate the publisher's responsibility to "reap what they had sown."

In any case, we in the "sophisticated and cerebral" West are getting a heady education in the emotional displays that are part and parcel of daily life in the Arab world. Anger, friendship, grief and passionate love are not only deeply and profoundly felt in this culture but are publicly expressed in a manner that can only be described as "way over the top" by our more privatized standards of "politically correct" social behavior.

Somehow, with the Arab Muslim population growing in our midst (especially in Europe), it will be useful to separate the need for mutual respect of different cultures and beliefs from the equally important need to totally reject the radical adherents of those beliefs whose goal is to foment terror and fear and to forcibly impose their faith upon the rest of the world.

Multiple hts:lgf

Washington Post Responds to Joint Chiefs' Complaint With disdain

The following is a paraphrase of the Washington Post's responseto a letter of criticism written by the Joint Chiefs of Staff in response to a political cartoon published in that paper earlier this week:

Dear Patriarchal, Jack-booted Joint Chief Generals and Admirals of the So-Called United States Military-Industrial Complex Currently Waging War On Behalf of the Oil Industry and At the Command of That Lying Commander-In-Chief Who Only Got Us Into This Mess To Avenge His Father: Greetings.

What? The Joint Chiefs of Staff criticizing a political cartoon in the Washington Post? Actually sending a letter signed by the five ranking military leaders of the United States during a time of war? Who do you think you are? Really! Of all the nerve. It's not as though this war is popular or anything. Young men and women are being killed and maimed in large numbers day after day after day.

The image of the four-limbed amputee was not intended to imply any disrespect to American troops who have been injured in this unjust and illegal conflict while they have been under orders to torture innocent civilians in Abu Graib, terrorize the Iraqi people in their homes and who were deployed to destroy and mutilate a country that DID NOT HAVE ANY WEAPONS OF MASS DESTRUCTION in the first place.

There is nothing to apologize for. Your complaints and criticisms are completely lacking in merit and totally unfounded. Any intelligent person, such as those on our newspaper editorial staff, could have told you that if you had only given us a phone call and asked for clarification.

What are you, after all? Just military hawks shuffling America's poor, uneducated underclass who, in the face of economic injustice and rampant racial prejudice, had no other choice than to join the military, around like pawns on a chessboard for your own blood-lust pleasure!

How dare you morons criticize US! We are the power of the people! The corporate embodiment of the First Amendment and defender of everything that is good and honest and moral and legal and Democrat in America!

To criticize us is to criticize the very freedoms you are supposed to be fighting for! Such hypocrisy leaves us almost, but not quite, speechless.

We've actually taken an objective poll of all the people who were responsible for publishing that cartoon and you will be surprised to note that not one of them, NOT ONE, saw anything offensive in the cartoon at all.

At the very least you should all schedule a visit to your favorite optometrist as soon as possible because it is obvious that you do not view the world the same way as we do!

Oh, before we sign off with our response to your letter, "Now that (you) have addressed the insidious threat cartoons pose to our troops, perhaps (you) can move on to less pressing issues like getting them their damn body armor."

Sincerely and Respectfully Yours,

The WaPo Editorial Staff

FRIDAY, FEBRUARY 03, 2006

When It Comes to Islamic Radicals Truth & Fiction Sometimes Converge

Consider this photograph of a Muslim protester in London the other day. He clearly takes the matter of defending Muhammed's honor against Danish cartoon caricatures very seriously.

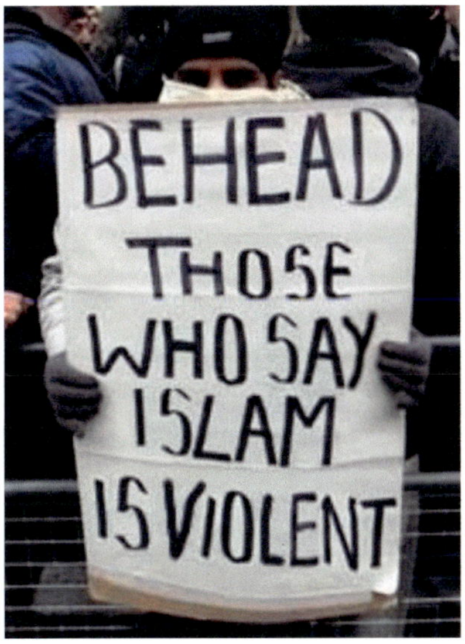

Consider the same photograph photo-shopped by some anonymous blogger.

I think this second "sign" speaks closer to the truth of the protestor's misplaced religious fervor than the one he wrote himself.

The irony, of course, is that most of the controversial cartoons depicted Muhammed (as representative of radical Islamist terrorists) as being inclined to violence.

Is Muhammed's character and reputation so shakey and unstable that the only way to defend him is to murder his detractors?

The intellectual and moral sophistication of this brand of Islam does not yet appear to have risen above the level of "brain stem" intelligence.

As I have said so many times before, the West may be forced to defend herself against this onslaught of moral and spiritual bankruptcy but, in the end, it will be the responsibility of Muslim leaders to moderate and contain this movement by projecting and demanding a higher vision for the Muslim faith.

If Muslim leaders are unable or unwilling to stand against this sub-human response to competing world views then Islam, as a whole, and those who practice it, will, of necessity, be forever branded as barbarian....in the lowest and worst usage of this term.

I pray that those who represent the highest and noblest ideals of the Muslim faith will rise up and convince me that I am in error.

In all honesty, I would be very happy if that should that happen.

SATURDAY, FEBRUARY 04, 2006

Where Did All Those Burning Danish Flags Come From?

Charles Moore raises an interesting point in regards to all the Denmark-bashing going on in front of cameras throughout the Muslim world:

It's some time since I visited Palestine, so I may be out of date, but I don't remember seeing many Danish flags on sale there. Not much demand, I suppose. I raise the question because, as soon as the row about the cartoons of the Prophet Mohammed in Jyllands-Posten broke, angry Muslims popped up in Gaza City, and many other places, well supplied with Danish flags ready to burn. (In doing so, by the way, they offered a mortal insult to the most sacred symbol of my own religion, Christianity, since the Danish flag has a cross on it, but let that pass.)

Why were those Danish flags to hand? Who built up the stockpile so that they could be quickly dragged out right across the Muslim world and burnt where television cameras would come and look? The more you study this story of "spontaneous" Muslim rage, the odder it seems. Moore has plenty more to say that is worth reading and pondering over.

Hmmm...and, by the way, why are there so many Muslim men (usually young men) with nothing to do except be angry and burn things on CNN and Al-Jazeera? What do they do in their spare time? Ah...yes...it comes to me now...they spend their free time working on their international flag collections!

SATURDAY, FEBRUARY 04, 2006

"Preventive Security" In Palestine

According to a BBC report Israel has retaliated for a rocket attack out of Gaza that wounded three Israelis yesterday. An Israeli helicopter hit a Gaza building where they said rockets were prepared for use against Israel. A car fleeing the attack was struck by a rocket killing three men. The building was being used by the al-Aqsa Martyr's Brigade.

Palestinians said the building was an al-Aqsa sports club and sports training camp. (I suppose that constructing, practicing and shooting off rockets into Israel could qualify as a sport in Palestine. Hopefully it will not become an Olympic event anytime soon).

According to hospital officials, four of the five men wounded were security personnel guarding the Palestinians' Preventive Security headquarters near the al-Aqsa facility.

You just have to love that name: "Preventive Security." It just about perfectly sums up the political platforms of both Hamas and Fatah and, to their credit, they have successfully "prevented security" for the Palestinian people for a good many years!

SUNDAY, FEBRUARY 05, 2006

Super Bowl Prediction: Steelers 34 Seahawks 24

Pittsburgh will win 34-24.

Why? Because Seattle has not played on the road for a long time and because Detroit is as good as a home game for Pittsburgh. If they played in Seattle I would pick the Seahawks. It could well be tied at half-time.

It will be a good game...probably better than the commercials this year.

SUNDAY, FEBRUARY 05, 2006

U.S. Media's Double-Standard (Or Should I Say Hypocrisy) Concerning Muhammed Cartoons

This evening I emailed off the following letter to the Honolulu Advertiser:

There was irony in your article, "U.S. Media Debate Cartoon Furor," on Sunday, February 6th. First you quote the Associated Press as saying that they chose not to carry pictures of the Danish cartoon caricatures of Muhammed "because they didn't meet AP standards for acceptable content . . . our practice is to not move material that is known to be offensive" Then, quoting Advertiser Editor Saundra Keyes, you cite your own paper's decision to not print the cartoons: "Taste is an issue we always consider in content decisions, as is respect for the beliefs of diverse faith communities."

You then, on the same page, print a photograph of an extremely anti-Semitic Palestinian poster showing the Danish flag as a hateful face with a snake (a well-known and often-used derogatory symbol of Jewish Zionism) coming out of its mouth. If you are completely naive about such matters then the juxtaposition is ironic. If you are well-informed then perhaps the word "hypocrisy" would be more appropriate.

In either case I suggest that the Advertiser owes an apology to the Jewish community in Hawaii for publishing this offensive and disrespectful photograph.

By the way, the photo was courtesy of . . . you guessed it . . . Associated Press.

Here is the offending photograph (click to enlarge):

A22 | Sunday, February 5, 2006 The Honolulu Advertiser

HATEM MOUSSA | Associated Press

Palestinians in Gaza City yesterday held copies of the Quran next to a poster caricaturing Denmark. The protest was part of what some see as a new culture war pitting the Muslim world against the West.

Just to provide some support for my assertion that the snake is a derogatory symbol of Jewish Zionism I briefly scanned the internet and found the following pictures and quotations:

This photo is of the entryway to the U.S. Holocaust Memeorial Museum. Note the prominant display of a picture of a snake.

The following is taken from an article relating a visit to a Book Fair in Germany:

Last week at the Frankfurt Book Fair, I happened to find myself in the International Publishers section and was simply astonished. At the stand of the Iranian publishers, in plain view, was the text that influenced Hitler's Holocaust fantasies like no other: "The Protocols of the Learned Elders of Zion," published in English by the Islamic Propagation Organization of the Islamic Republic of Iran. The first page of the tract makes clear that Israel is the target of this new edition. It shows a ***snake*** *made of triangles, enclosing an area labeled "Greater Israel" that includes large areas of Egypt, Syria, Lebanon, Jordan, Iraq, parts of Turkey and northern Saudi Arabia. Each triangle, according to the annotation, symbolizes the "Freemason's Eye," supposedly a "symbol of Jewry.*

Mr. Küntzel is a political scientist in Hamburg and author of "Djihad und Judenhass" (Jihad and Jew-hatred), published in 2002 by Ça Ira Publishers. Belinda Cooper translated ***this article*** *from the German.*

The following pictures are taken from an **exhibition of drawings**done by students at the Palestinian-operated Hajah Rushdah girls schools in the Beit Ain Alma refugee camp in Nablus (August 18, 2004).

(Note that the snake has been a classic anti-Semitic symbol since the 19 th century but gained popularity at the beginning of the 20th when "The Protocols of the Elders of Zion" were published.)

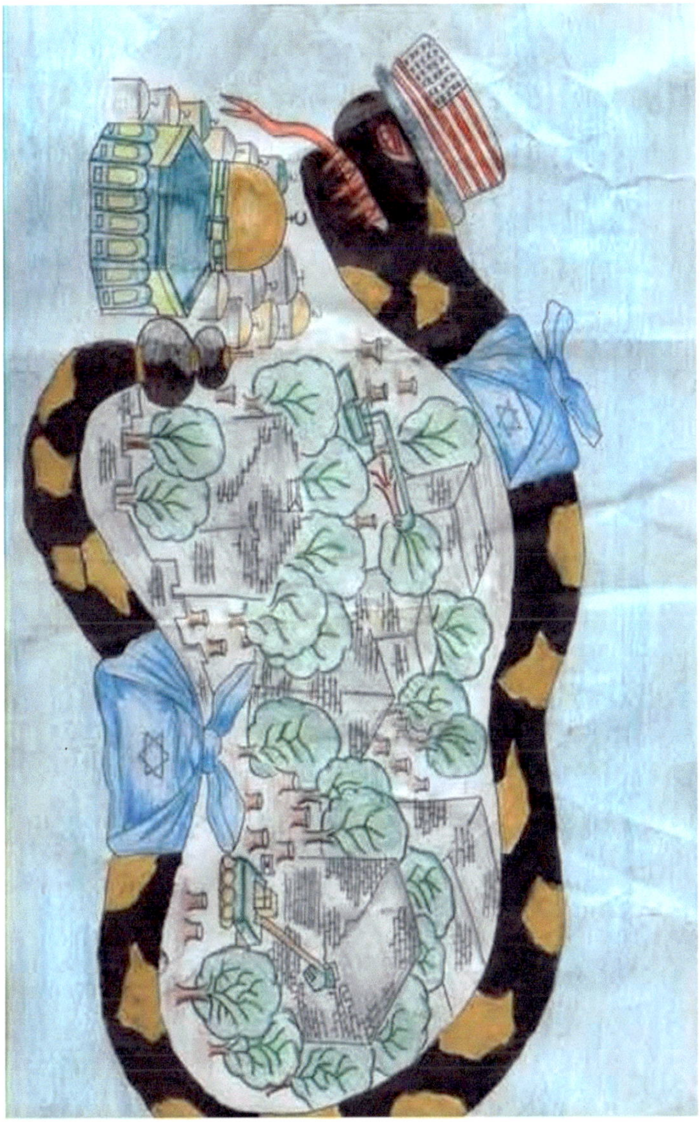

The Jewish snake (wearing a hat made out of the American flag) threatening to swallow the mosques on the Temple Mount and all Palestine. The drawing was done by Ghadam Hijawi, a student in the 9th grade.

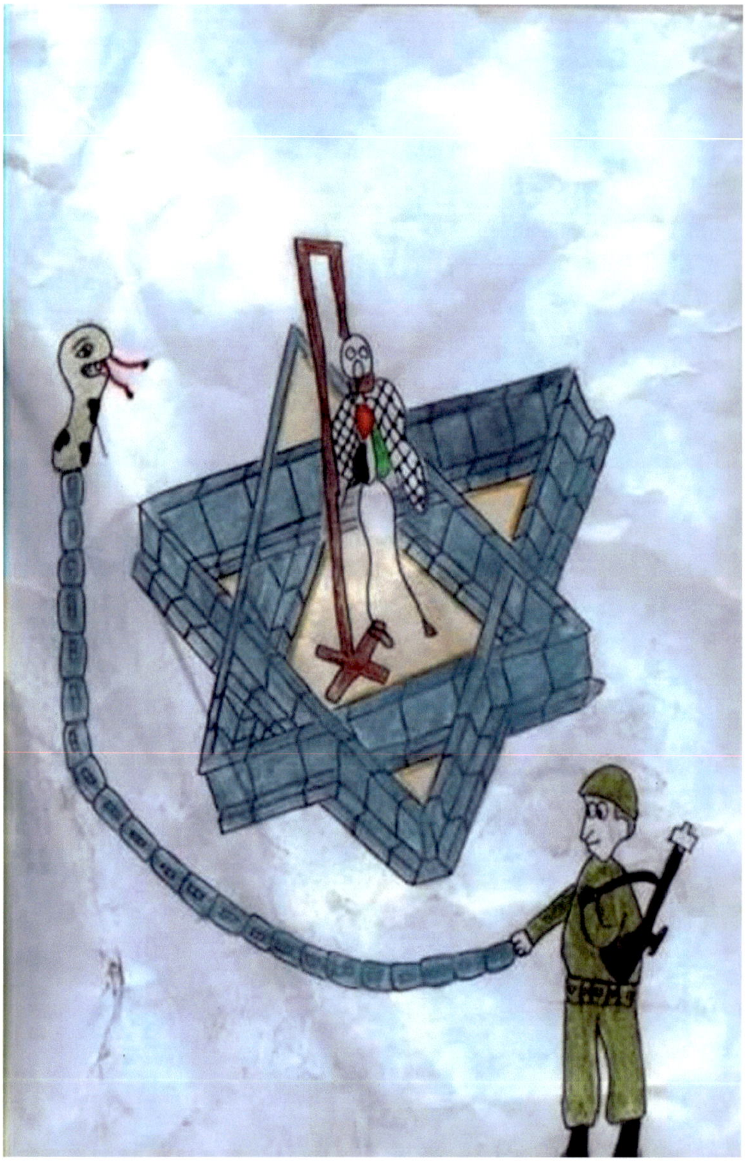

A snake and a Magen David (Star of David) wrapped around a Palestinian hanging on a gallows .

Anti-Israeli and anti-Semitic hate propaganda in cartoons published in the official Palestinian Authority newspaper Al-Hayat Al-Jadeeda:

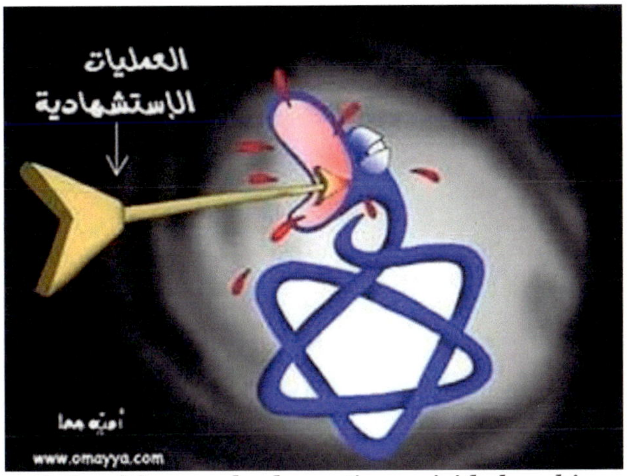

A cartoon combining anti-Semitism and advocating suicide bombing attacks against Israel. The inscription above the arrow reads "suicide bombing attacks" and is stuck deep in the mouth of the Jewish snake to choke and kill it.

A cartoon, this one showing Jewish control (the snakes) of the UnitedStates.

متن پروتکلهای دانشوران صهیون برای
تشکیل حکومت جهانی یهود

Sobh, *a monthly periodical identified with radical Islamic elements, published selected excerpts from the Protocols under the heading "The text of the Protocols of the Elders of Zion for establishing the Jewish global rule" (December 1998 – January 1999 Issue). The publication was illustrated with the notorious symbol of the Jewish snake swallowing the globe (click on picture of the magazine to enlarge it).*

German Nazi propaganda slide entitled "Jewry, Freemasonry and Bolshevism," featuring a poisonous snake with bared fangs, which served as the title slide for an anti-Semitic lecture series. [Photograph #49819]

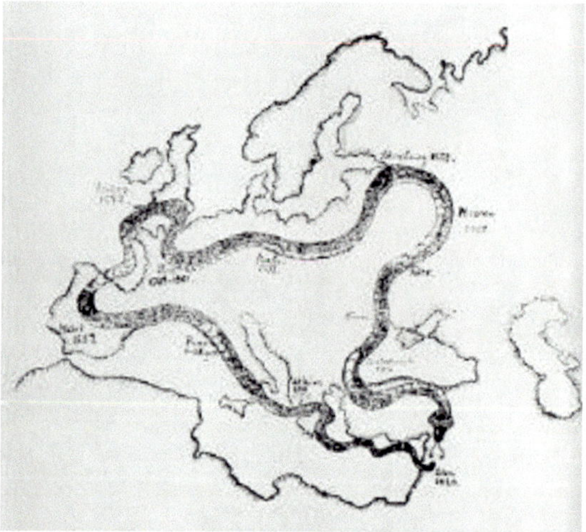

Antisemitic "symbolic snake" imagery, which was supposed to represent the purported "Jewish plot" to take over the world. Pictures and descriptions of the snake have accompanied the "Protocols of the Elders of Zion" throughout its history.

A poster depicting Alfred Dreyfus as a snake. In 1894, Captain Alfred Dreyfus--the only Jewish member of the French general staff--was accused and convicted of spying for Germany. He was exonerated of all charges a decade later, but only after strenuous protests on his behalf. The case was widely followed in the U.S.

The following is taken from an article at The American Thinker(emphasis mine):

Christian Identity groups (a.k.a – white supremacist) and others like them use the Protocols as a commentary to the Bible. In Religion and the Racist Right, Michael Barkun, quotes a Christian Identity Pastor. This Pastor's message of hate comes from Revelation 2:9, and these are his rhetorical questions:

"If Cain were not the offspring of Satan, there is no basis for the age-old conflict between Jews and Christians. Moreover, there are no reasonable grounds for the Jews themselves claiming to be from Cain. Why is the ***snake*** *chosen as the symbol of the serpent's seed in The Protocols of the Learned Elders of Zion?" (191)*

It does not require a scholar to understand this anti-Semitic Pastor has taken the pure word of God and interpreted it, wrongly so, through the racist eyes of the Protocols. This anti-Semitic rhetoric taken from the pen of Nilus, the Russian clergyman who released the Protocols:

The learned men decided by peaceful means to conquer the world for ZION with the slyness of the ***Symbolic Snake****, whose head was to represent those who have been initiated into the plans of the JEWISH PEOPLE – the administration was always kept secret, even from the JEWISH NATION itself. (Protocols, Intro.).*

This idea, the Jewish people are a lineage of the **snake** or better known as the **Seed of the Serpent** is commonplace and dogmatic Theology in the Christian Identity movement. It is upon this Theology that the white supremacist religious groups (a.k.a Christian Identity) find a justification for hatred and violence against Jewish people.

This is the actual citation from "The Protocols of the Learned Elders of Zion" (a 19th century Russian **anti-Semitic hoax** purporting to articulate the ancient plot of the Jewish people to take over the world) that initiated this sybolism in the first place (Note that the "Protocols" are taught and widely read in the Arab & Muslim world as historical fact):

PROTOCOL No. 3.1

1. To-day I may tell you that our goal is now only a few steps off. There remains a small space to cross and the whole long path we have trodden is ready now to close its cycle of the ***Symbolic Snake****, by which we symbolize our people. When this ring closes, all the States of Europe will be locked in its coil as in a powerful vice.*

Lastly, a photo of an Arabic copy of the "Protocols:"

Satis Est.

Note: Links on this post are for source information only and are not intended to be construed as endorsements of the sites that are linked.

MONDAY, FEBRUARY 06, 2006

Super Bowl Prediction Just About Right

Let's see...I predicted that,
It could well be tied at half-time.

The score was 7-3 Pittsburgh.

I predicted that Pittsburgh would win by 10 points (34-24).
They won by 11 points (21-10).

I missed my own spread by 1 point.

Not bad for a rookie.

MONDAY, FEBRUARY 06, 2006

NBC To Ridicule Christ's Crucifixion On Maundy Thursday

UPDATE February 6th at 7 p.m.: Apparently I missed the fact that this last Friday NBC announced that ***"some erroneous information was mistakenly included in a press release describing an upcoming episode of 'Will & Grace,' which in fact has yet to be written. The reference to 'Cruci-fixin's' won't be in the show, and the storyline will not contain a Christian characterization at all. We value our viewers and***

sincerely regret if this information has offended them."

Thank you NBC for clearing this "misunderstanding" up so quickly!

According to Associated Press NBC is "fixin'" to insult, degrade, mock and ridicule the death of Jesus Christ on Maundy Thursday, the evening that Christians around the world celebrate Jesus' Last Supper with his disciples and his subsequent betrayal which led to his crucifixion the following afternoon.

The news story begins as follows:

Britney Spears will guest star on an episode of "Will & Grace," NBC announced Tuesday.

The pop star will appear as a Christian conservative sidekick to Sean Hayes' (honosexual) character, Jack, who hosts his own talk show, on the April 13 episode, the network said.

Jack's fictional network, Out TV, is bought by a Christian TV network, leading to Spears contributing a cooking segment called "Cruci-fixin's."

An email making the rounds asks for Christians or others who may be offended by this story-line to do the following:

1. Call your local NBC affiliate and ask them not to air the April 13 episode of Will and Grace. Ask others to call. Click here to find your local NBC station.

2. Click here to send a letter to NBC Chairman Bob Wright.

But please, PLEASE, do not threaten to kill anyone, do not threaten to boycott everything related to the United States and do not attempt to burn down the NPC offices in New York City. After all, it was on Maundy Thursday that Jesus said, "A new commandment I give to you, that you love one another as I have loved you." John

Interestingly, this is why that day is called "Maundy," from the Latin word *mandanum* which means, "commandment."

If you correspond with NBC (as I have already done) do so in a way that honors Jesus Christ and reflects his love.

TUESDAY, FEBRUARY 07, 2006

Faith & Politics Mix At Coretta Scott King's Funeral

Dr. Martin Luther King Jr. was roundly condemned for mixing politics and faith. "Just stick to preaching the Gospel and leave the politics to the rest of us" seemed to be what his many critics demanded.

But for Dr. King, politics and faith went hand in hand or, even more accurately, politics sat under the judgment of faith and was accountable to the One who declared freedom and liberty to be an "unalienable right" for all people of all colors, rich and poor alike.

Today, at the funeral of his wife and widow, Coretta Scott King, Dr. King and his vision for a world blessed with peace and freedom for all was remembered and celebrated. Coretta was honored and eulogized as the good, Godly and almost iconic figure she became.

For all the faults in the lives of Dr. & Mrs. King, their greatest glory was how, when given a choice, they almost always chose the "high road" in getting their message across.

By this I mean that they proclaimed the vision of the way things ought to be. They lifted up the high ideals of the founding documents of the United States and grounded them on the Biblical foundations of justice, forgiveness, equality, freedom, hope, love and peace. "Look to the good," they seemed to say, "and the good will both judge and condemn the injustice and oppression that dwells among us."

President Bush, in his brief presentation, took that same high road, extolling Coretta for her faithfulness to the vision of her husband that has made our country a far better place than it had been before. He referenced God, Moses, the Old Testament prophets and, without using the name, the guiding hand of the Lord Jesus Christ in world events. Given the church setting his words were uplifting, positive and uniting.

Those who followed, at least for the most part, followed the same high road. But there were noticeable exceptions. Regrettably, one of them was Jimmy Carter, one of three former presidents to be present (the other two being the elder George Bush and Bill Clinton).

Carter, who has apparently adopted the worldview of the international elite and deluded into thinking that he speaks on behalf of the poor, the oppressed and the Arab Muslim "street" injected two sour notes in his presentation.

The first contained a "low road, low blow" at the current Bush administration when he said, "It was difficult for (Dr. & Mrs. King) personally, with the civil liberties of both husband and wife violated as they became the target of secret government wiretapping."

This not-so-subtle reference to the current NSA terrorist communication warrantless intercept program brought thunderous applause from the politically partisan gathering. A "cheap shot" at the man who had come to represent the American people at a national event honoring a national figure. On an occasion such as this, a partisan attack on the President is nothing less than an attack and an insult on the entire nation. For shame!

Later, according to a Fox News/AP story, "(Carter) said that Hurricane Katrina showed all are not yet equal in America, and made a veiled reference to the war in Iraq and the existing government's international strategies."

A second "low road" comment came from Joseph Lowery who, with Dr. King, had founded the

Southern Christian Leadership Conference.

"We know now there were no weapons of mass destruction over there," he said in a boisterous, rhyming oration. "But Coretta knew and we know that there are weapons of misdirection right down here -- millions without health insurance, poverty abounds. For war, billions more, but no more for the poor."

If the "high road" had been taken these anti-Bush slams could have been transformed into remembrances of just how far we have come and into visions of just how far we still need to go.

Even so, a smiling and gracious President Bush reportedly rose and gave Lowery a warm embrace following his eulogy.

The irony is that, at the funeral service for the widow of Dr. Martin Luther King Jr., it was those pretending to represent the legacy of Dr. King's non-violence who struck out with anger at the President of the United States.

But it was President Bush who quietly took the blows and turned the other cheek.

WEDNESDAY, FEBRUARY 08, 2006

Cartoon Contest Fights Against Jihad With Humor

As some of you may already know, in response to the Danish cartoons that caricatured Muhammed as a terrorist a newspaper in Iran has begun a macabre cartoon contest:

Iran's biggest-selling newspaper has chosen to tackle the West's ideals of "freedom of expression" by launching a competition to find the 12 "best" cartoons about the Holocaust, the Associated French Press reported on Monday.

In response, the World Union of Jewish Students has initiated its own contest but the rules are quite different.

We decided on nuclear energy for strictly economic reasons. After all, at $70 per barrel, who can afford oil anymore?

The World Union of Jewish Students in conjunction with editorial cartoonists, Edward Margolis and Noah Crissey, has announced an International Editorial Cartoon Competition for students called "Fight Hate with Humor. . ."

According to cartoonist, Margolis, "the whole thing about the Iranian Contest would be hilarious if it weren't so terrifying."

Their web site has some examples of the sort of cartoons they are hoping to get.

I couldn't help myself so I have submitted one of my own for them to consider. I don't have any chance of winning but, what the heck, a little humor never hurt anybody . . . at least not yet, anyway! (click on cartoon to enlarge)

WEDNESDAY, FEBRUARY 08, 2006

Islam Means "To Submit" . . . So, You Cartoonists . . . SUBMIT . . . NOW!

Several days ago Daniel Pipes published a cogent essay on the subject of the Muhammed Cartoon Controversy. The article, entitled "Cartoons and Islamic Imperialism," provides an insightful context for the current unrest.

With remarkable accuity, Pipes summarizes the situation in this way:

The deeper issue here, however, is not Muslim hypocrisy but Islamic supremacism. The Danish editor who published the cartoons, Flemming Rose, explained that if Muslims insist "that I, as a non-Muslim, should submit to their taboos...they're asking for my submission."

That's it in a nutshell. "Memo to the West: Submit to Muslim law, tradition and culture as we interpret it or we will kill you, boycott your products and burn down your embassies."

For the radical Islamists who are fanning the flames of this non-controversy, the words "Islam" and "submission" mean just one thing for the non-Muslim world: "oppression."

There is only one way to respond to demands such as these: "Just Say No!"

And don't forget to support Denmark by buying anything that has that nation's name on the label.

ht:powerline

FRIDAY, FEBRUARY 10, 2006

Where Are All the Muslim Women In the Middle East?

Where are all the Muslim women in the Middle East? What do they have to say about Intefada, terrorism, jihad and insurgents? How do they feel about their husbands, brothers, fathers and sons who have been dying by the thousands at the hands of American Troops, Muslim terrorists and as volunteer "mujahadeen" and suicide bombers?

Televsion pictures show hundreds and thousands of Muslim men demonstrating every day . . . especially on the holy day of Friday. In Palestine these men wave AK-47s, cover their faces with their head scarves and dip their hands into the blood of their terrorist leaders when they have been blown to pieces by an Israeli missile.

How do the women feel about all of this?

How do they feel about their second-class status? Are they glad that they do not have to run around in a mob, shouting angry and hateful slogans against Jews, Americans and the degenerate West? Do they feel shut out and cut off from wielding influence in the midst of the unrest and death? Are they being abused by the angry men who seem to surround them? Have the ongoing conflicts in Iraq, Afghanistan and Palestine lowered the number of men to the point where there are large numbers of widows and orphans left behind and alone?

Do the women want peace? Or are they as fanatical about Islam as the Islamist radicals seem to be? What are their hopes and dreams for the world? Do they want every other woman in the world to be as they are? What do they think about honor killings of wives and daughters? Is this part of their culture and faith that they accept without complaint?

Recently we have seen how the women in Palestine seem to feel. In a pre-election poll (see 2-18, 19), more than half of the women supported the continuation of suicide bombings against Israel. Indeed, the women were more supportive of this than the men! (Here is a post-election poll with similar results--but not specifically by women--here. A completely opposite poll result can be found here. Which are we to believe?)

Beyond the taking of polls is there no way to discover the thoughts and opinions of Muslim women in the Middle East? Are there any who blog?

If there is a way, why has no one asked them? Is it because no one in the West cares? Are there no women journalists who could investigate and report on what over half the Muslim population feels about faith, conflict, jihad, hopes, dreams, children, husbands, America, freedom and all the rest?

If there is no way to discover the thoughts and opinions of Muslim women in the Middle East then what does that say about the culture and religion that imposes this mass silence, isolation and invisibility upon them?

Personally, I am tired of watching the Muslim men shout and scream and chant bloody murder day after day after day. Just for once, I'd like to hear from the women. I am confident that they have something important to say. After all, in more than a symbolic way, they represent the "home front" for the Islamist war against the world. History has shown that it is often on the home front that wars are won or lost. Why the silence?

Note: An interesting story about a "feminist play" in Gaza provides some insight and can be found here. Note the story appears in an Israeli newspaper!

SATURDAY, FEBRUARY 11, 2006

Microphone Blunder Reveals Bush To Be . . . a Gentleman?

There's an old British saying, "A true gentleman is one who uses his butter knife when he dines alone."

The point is that a person of true character is the same in private as they are in public.

Yesterday, President George Bush proved to be a man of character . . . a true gentleman.

Here's what happened: At a House Republican strategy session in Maryland, President Bush appeared and spoke publicly and on the record to the Representatives and other party leaders. The press and all visitors were then asked to leave while the President addressed the gathering privately.

Oh! What the MSM would pay to hear what Bush was saying. To get that story would be to get a

Pulitzer! The headline would read, "President Caught In the Act . . . His Hypocracy Revealed!"

Well, as it turned out the MSM got to hear what the President said in private without paying a cent. It seems that some audio flunkey forgot to turn off the live microphone feed to the White House Press Room. So, Bush spoke in private and the world listened in. And what did they hear?

Not much and nothing new!

Bush simply repeated to the Republican gathering what he had already said publicly concerning the NSA warrantless surveillance situation. And that was all.

The old song said, "Nobody knows what goes on behind closed doors..." Well, now we know: President Bush uses his butter knife in private.

As Captain Ed puts it, "Bet this doesn't make the front page tomorrow."

Michael Jackson Now Homeless? An Update

According to Fox News,

Today will be the seventh week in a row that employees at Michael Jackson's Neverland Ranch have not received paychecks.

And now I have really bad news for them: Jackson has been cut off and kicked out by Prince Abdullah, son of the King of Bahrain. He is no longer, I repeat, not doing it anymore — not funding Jackson, his kids and nanny in an extended stay in Bahrain.

The first clue that this was the case was Jackson's traveling last week from Bahrain to Germany, and then on to Italy — on commercial flights in business class. There was no more private plane.

Well, I guess that, having seen all the sights in Dubai, Jackson is hoping to spend some time researching Michelangelo before . . . who knows, learning how to dance the Karagouna in Thessaly?

SUNDAY, FEBRUARY 12, 2006

Al Gore Proves That There Is a God

All praise and thanks be to God Almighty, Father, Son and Holy Spirit, world without end. Amen!

Surely the goodness and mercy of the Lord was upon the United States of America when Vice-President Al Gore was denied the Presidency following the 2000 election. God's providence served us with blessing upon blessing in providing for us a President who loves this country and has been faithful in his oath of office to "preserve, protect and defend" the Constitution and this country from all enemies, foreign and domestic.

Can anyone in their right mind imagine what the world and our country would be like today had Al Gore become our President?

Consider the latest chapter in Gore's descent into anti-American perdition.

Earlier today (Sunday) Al Gore appeared at the Jiddah Economic Forum in Saudi Arabia. Just this past week the Saudi government withdrew their invitation to a Danish delegation because of the Muslim uproar over the posting of cartoon caricatures of the Muhammed. This blatant insult to the freedom of speech and the diplomatic irresponsibility in acting punitively against a sovereign nation simply because a private Danish newspaper exercised that freedom should have offered Gore an opportunity to demonstrate his solidarity with one of the central and unimpeachable values of Western Civilization by withdrawing from speaking at the Summit.

Instead, Gore not only spoke but used the opportunity to express his solidarity with the radical Arab Muslim world in their demonization of the United States.

Consider this **news summary** of Gore's speech:
Former Vice President Al Gore told a mainly Saudi audience on Sunday that the U.S. government committed "terrible abuses" against Arabs after the Sept. 11, 2001, attacks, and that most Americans did not support such treatment.

Gore said Arabs had been "indiscriminately rounded up" and held in "unforgivable" conditions. The former vice president said the Bush administration was playing into al-Qaida's hands by routinely blocking Saudi visa applications.

"The thoughtless way in which visas are now handled, that is a mistake," Gore said during the Jiddah Economic Forum. "The worst thing we can possibly do is to cut off the channels of friendship and mutual understanding between Saudi Arabia and the United States."

If the United States was at war with radical Islam, and that radical form of Islam was being funded and encouraged with Saudi money and Saudi Muslim clerics, and if most of the terrorists who attacked the United States on 9/11 had been Saudis then a good case could be made that Al Gore had committed treason today.

Oh . . . my goodness . . . We ***are*** at war with radical Islam . . . it ***is*** being funded and encouraged with Saudi money and Saudi Muslim clerics . . . most of the 9/11 terrorists ***were*** from Saudi Arabia . . .

I don't really know what to say . . . except to thank God that Al Gore did not become the President of the United States.

Note: Captain Ed critiques Gore's claims and concludes that "he sold out the U.S." I agree. The man is worse than an embarrassment. He has sold his American soul in exchange for the warm embrace and accolades from an anti-American Saudi audience. The man has no shame. And tragically, there are tens of millions of Americans who would vote for him again if he ran for President in 2008.

MONDAY, FEBRUARY 13, 2006

How The Iraqis REALLY Feel About American Troops

Greyhawk has posted the following letter from the Iraqi Mayor of Tall-Afar. This man has some remarkable things to say about the members of the 3rd Armored Cavalry Regiment and their families.

In the Name of God the Compassionate and Merciful

To the Courageous Men and Women of the 3d Armored Cavalry Regiment, who have changed the city of Tall' Afar from a ghost town, in which terrorists spread death and destruction, to a secure city flourishing with life.

To the lion-hearts who liberated our city from the grasp of terrorists who were beheading men, women and children in the streets for many months.

To those who spread smiles on the faces of our children, and gave us restored hope, through their personal sacrifice and brave fighting, and gave new life to the city after hopelessness darkened our days, and stole our confidence in our ability to reestablish our city.

Our city was the main base of operations for Abu Mousab Al Zarqawi. The city was completely held hostage in the hands of his henchmen. Our schools, governmental services, businesses and offices were closed. Our streets were silent, and no one dared to walk them. Our people were barricaded in their homes out of fear; death awaited them around every corner. Terrorists occupied and controlled the only hospital in the city. Their savagery reached such a level that they stuffed the corpses of children with explosives and tossed them into the streets in order to kill grieving parents attempting to retrieve the bodies of their young. This was the situation of our city until God prepared and delivered unto them the courageous soldiers of the 3d Armored Cavalry Regiment, who liberated this city, ridding it of Zarqawi's followers after harsh fighting, killing many terrorists, and forcing the remaining butchers to flee the city like rats to the surrounding areas, where the bravery of other 3d ACR soldiers in Sinjar, Rabiah, Zumar and Avgani finally destroyed them.

I have met many soldiers of the 3d Armored Cavalry Regiment; they are not only courageous men and women, but avenging angels sent by The God Himself to fight the evil of terrorism.

The leaders of this Regiment; COL McMaster, COL Armstrong, LTC Hickey, LTC Gibson, and LTC Reilly embody courage, strength, vision and wisdom. Officers and soldiers alike bristle with the confidence and character of knights in a bygone era. The mission they have accomplished, by means of a unique military operation, stands among the finest military feats to date in Operation Iraqi Freedom, and truly deserves to be studied in military science. This military operation was clean, with little collateral damage, despite the ferocity of the enemy. With the skill and precision of surgeons they dealt with the terrorist cancers in the city without causing unnecessary damage.

God bless this brave Regiment; God bless the families who dedicated these brave men and women. From the bottom of our hearts we thank the families. They have given us something we will never forget. To the families of those who have given their holy blood for our land, we all bow to you in reverence and to the souls of your loved ones. Their sacrifice was not in vain. They are not dead, but alive, and their souls hovering around us every second of every minute. They will never be forgotten for giving their precious lives. They have sacrificed that which is most valuable. We see them in the smile of every child, and in every flower growing in this land. Let America, their families, and the world be proud of their sacrifice for humanity and life.

Finally, no matter how much I write or speak about this brave Regiment, I haven't the words to describe the courage of its officers and soldiers. I pray to God to grant happiness and health to these legendary heroes and their brave families.

NAJIM ABDULLAH ABID AL-JIBOURI

Mayor of Tall 'Afar, Ninewa, Iraq

I bet you won't see this letter published your morning newspaper.

ht:Powerline

How the Danish "Cartoon Crisis" Was Born

Captain Ed has posted an investigative report by the Danish newspaper, JYLLANDS-POSTEN Sunday, February 12, 2005. This is, of course, the same paper that published the cartoon caracatures of Muhammed in the first place.

Captain Ed concludes that the article supports the view that Danish Muslims had a bigger agenda than simply protesting the cartoon.

After reading the article for myself I did not come to the same conclusion. To me it appears that the article indicates that Danish Muslims simply wanted their voices to be heard and respected...not necessarily acted upon. After having their efforts rebuffed and ignored (Why? Perhaps they are NOT shown respect in Denmark?) they made a fatal decision to take the issue to those with more clout. At this point they effectively lost control of the situation.

The role of Ambassadors to Denmark from Muslim countries remains unclear and, as the article clearly shows, some of the information and claims are either intentional misrepresentations, mistranslations or simply subjective beliefs grounded in personal feelings and emotions rather than objective "facts."

In any case, I find it encouraging that the Danish Muslims apparently made a sincere effort to work "within the system." Democratic governments are supposed to be responsive to the people. It is quite possible that much of the blame for this fiasco is to be shared by the Danish government for ignoring the concerns of Danish citizens who happened to be Muslim.

Here is the article. Read it and make up your own mind.

THE MUHAMMED CRISIS
By Orla Borg and Lars Nørgaard Pedersen

The evening of Novemer 18, 2005 was when they finally decided. All Danish channels were showing a smiling Anders Fogh Rasmussen opening the doors of Marienborg [ED:Downing Street No 10 in Denmark] to the Dutch parliamentarian Ayaan Hirsi Ali.

To the Imams and other representatives of Moslem organizations, who for several weeks had been protesting the Muhammed cartoons in the Jyllands-Posten, it felt like a kick to the face:

So, the Prime Minister welcomed her - this /woman/ who had written the manuscript for "Submission Part 1", a film highly critical of Islam. But the ambassadors of 11 Moslem countries who had asked so pleadingly to meet him regarding the caricatures of the prophet Muhammed, were not granted an audience.

This was the straw that broke the camel's back.

The inflamed Danish Moslems who had organized in the network "Moslems for the Prophet in the Media" decided to enter phase two: The international phase with travelling delegations to the Middle East, since their first strategy - national actions within the borders of Denmark - had led them nowhere.

Since October 2, 2005 - two days after the publication of the drawings - they had tried to make the Jyllands-Posten and the Danish government apologize for the drawings and ensure that there would be no repetitions. They had collected 17000 signatures. They had organized a demonstration numbering more than 3000 on Rådhuspladsen in Copenhagen. They had written to the Ministry of Culture from which they had not even received an answer. And lastly 11 ambassadors had co-authored a letter asking to meet the Prime Minister to discuss the matter.

All in vain.

DEFENSE TURNED INTO AN ATTACK

The 27 organizations called for an emergency meeting where it was decided to put together delegations who would "visit the Islamic World in order to inform them of the danger inherent in the situation and convince them to join

in the defense and the support of our prophet," as the published mission statement of the delegations had it.

But this defensive action evolved into an attack on Denmark - with the connivance of the diplomats of Moslem countries in Denmark.

In the middle of November representatives of the Moslem organizations first met the Moslem ambassadors in Copenhagen. Mona Omar, the Ambassador of Egypt - who was later elected spokesman of the 11 ambassadors - in November received a handful of representatives of the Moslem organizations. They presented to her the plan of sending delegations to the Middle East. The embassy approved of the idea and arranged for them to meet in Cairo

Muhammed Shaaban, an advisor to the Egyptian Foreign Minister, former Ambassador and a member of the board of the Danish-Egyptian institute for Dialogue in Cairo. The Egyptian embassy also helped with visas and provided contact to the League of Arab States in Cairo.

Two main delegations were sent in the first round. The first delegation of five landed in Egypt on December 3, 2005 and returned December 11, 2005. The second delegation comprising four Danish Moslems travelled to Lebanon December 17, 2005 and returned to Denmark December 31, 2005. During that time, Imam Ahmed Akkari from the Lebanon delegation visited Syria to present their case to Grand Mufti Ahmed Badr-Eddine Hassoun. Furthermore a smaller delegation travelled to Turkey while individuals visited Sudan, Morocco and Algeria.

The fact that the two main delegations were sent to Lebanon and Egypt, Imam Ahmed Akkari ascribes to several factors: The Danish Ministry of Foreign Affairs supports 'The Arab Initiative', designed to improve cooperation in the

Middle East, and specifically on Lebanon. Furthermore they noted that Lebanon, in spite of civil war, had diverse religious communities, which might increase the likeliness of their being understood. And when Nicholas Sarkozy specifically had visited the Grand Mufti Muhammed

Said Tantawi in Cairo during the debate over hijabs - headscarves - in France, it had made a great impression on them. And finally, several of the members of the delegation descend from the two countries: The businessman Ahmed Harby and Nour-Edin Fattah of the first

delegation are of Egyptian descent while Raed Hlayhel and Ahmed Akkari of the second delegation are of Lebanese descent.

43 FULL PAGES

According to Ahmed Akkari, one of the goals of the delegations was to avoid "a new Van Gogh-case" - referring to the Dutch director who was murdered by an Islamist extremist in 2004. "The trip to Egypt was needed to create a response to be used in Denmark," Ahmed Akkari says.

The delegations brought stacks of a document 43 pages long containing pages of text and photos. The document contained the 12 cartoons from the Jyllands-Posten, 10 cartoons from the Weekendavisen and 4 derogatory photos, which according to the Moslems had been sent anonymously to Moslems in Denmark.

The delegation to Egypt achieved a great impact. It was headed by Abu Bashar of The Community of Islam and amongst the leaders were also leaders of Pakistani and Turkish organizations. During the meeting with the League of Arab States, which took place on December 11, 2005, the Danish Imam Abu Bashar showed the photo depicting the prophet as a pig.

Alaa Roushdy, the first secretary of Amr Moussa, participated in the meeting. The two Danish-Moslem representatives described the pig photo. They also talked about an announced movie critical of Islam, to be produced by Denmark, says Alaa Roushdy. The alleged movie was later to be one of many untrue rumours to circulate in the Middle East.

The delegation also met the presidentially appointed Grand Mufti Muhammed Said Tantawy, who is also the leader of Al Azhar University, one of the world most renowned institutes for higher learning in the Sunni Moslem world.

THREAT OF A FATWA

The Grand Mufti released a statement condemning the cartoons. A fatwa to boycot Danish goods was threatened unless the drawing were withdrawn. And more important: The Egyptian Foreign Minister promised to raise the issue during the coming islamic conference when the 57 countries of the OIC (Organization of the Islamic Conference) was to meet at the end of December. Symbolically, it was to be in Mecca - the home of Muhammed - that things took a turn.

The second delegation got the Lebanese Foreign Minister, Fawzi Salloukh, to contact his Egyptian counterpart in view of a common response. The third and lesser delegation travelled to Turkey. Led by Zeki Kocer of DMGT - a union of Turkish immigrant organization - it is unknown with whom they met.

In none of the countries visited by the delegations did demonstrators take to the street. But a meeting in Mekka set wheels in motion.

The 57 Moslem countries of the OIC met in the home city of Muhammed in December. The Egyptian Foreign Minister brought the 43 pages from the Danish Delegation. The cartoons of Muhammed circulated in the corridors and became THE topic of conversation during the conference. In the final communiqué, the OIC noted that the 57 countries were worried about the growing hatred against Islam and condemned "the latest incident where the media of some countries have desecrated the holy prophet Muhammed."

Now the case had gained traction.

The end of January saw protests against Denmark erupting volcanically. First came the boycot of Danish products in Saudi-Arabia and Kuwait beginning January 26, 2006 - a boycot which quickly spread to other Islamic countries. After that, the cartoons became the theme of the Friday Sermon everywhere. The same weekend Moslem protesters burned down down the Danish embassy in Syria, attacked the offices of the Danish deputation in Beirut and since then death threats have been made against Danes in several Moslem countries.

Thursday the ninth, the beginning of the Ashura holidays in the Shiite world, the cry went out "Death to Denmark" in Iran, Pakistan, Iraq and Lebanon.

THE INFIDEL DANES

In Denmark criticism of the delegations has grown. They have been accused of showing false cartoons and spreading disinformation. But the 43 pages the delegations brough with them contained a text that has gone unnoticed so far.

The text labels the Danes as "Infidels"

"Though they are nominally Christian, secularization has submerged them to a degree where to say that they are infidels would not be a lie." Furthermore the text contains to specific disinformations.

** Of the situation of the Moslems in Denmark: "Those of the true faith are opressed in a number of ways, mainly the
Islamic faith is not officially recognized in Denmark."*

** Of mosques in Denmark: "Which brings about a series of problems; most significantly permissions to build mosques are not granted and Moslems thus have to reuse old commercial properties and storage facilities as places of worship."*

This information is wrong:

** The Ministry of Religion recognizes 19 Islamic denominations in Denmark.*

** No Moslems are prevented from building Mosques. That it has not happened is caused by fraternal dissent in the Moslem communities: Agreement can not be reached as to who is to run the Mosque and thus sufficient money has not been raised for the building of a mosque.*

The debate about the delegations runs high. Few defend them. Some do, including one of the 11 ambassadors which thePrime Minister declined to meet. The Ambassador wishes to remain anonymous but says: "We encouraged none of the actions the delegations took, nor did they encourage us. They made their own choices and none of the ambassadors participated in any of their meetings. People are now trying to pin it on the delegations but it was already an issue when they left for Egypt."

Alaa Roushdy, First Secretary of the influential leader of The League of Arab States in Cairo defends the delegations too: "I have been following the discussion as to whether the delegations hold responsibility for what is happening in the Middle East. But the truth is that the real reaction came one and a half month after their visit." Roushdy adds that the issue would have exploded under any circumstances once the League of Arab States and the OIC had been informed.

Many criticised the delegations. One of their sharpest detractors is Ben Haddou of Moroccan ancestry, a former City Councillor in Copenhagen for the Centrist Democrats and later the Conservatives. He calls the delegations "half treason" and thinks that the delegations and protests have been staged to attract money from the rich Arab Gulf States. "They are fighting for their own Kingdom in Denmark and their own Mosques. Why does the Community of Islam call press conferences? Why do they so want to go with Danish Industry [ED: Umbrella Organization for Danish employers in the indutrial sector] to the Middle East? Why do they want public servants on the trip? Because it will give them a rubber stamp of approval. If they go to the Middle East with Officials of the Danish State, it will be seen as an official mark of approval and then the flow of money from the Gulf States will be without end."

NOT OUR FAULT

The members of the delegations reject the claim that they carry the main responsibility for the attacks on Danish interests. Most members refuse to comment and refer to spokesman Ahmed Akkari. He has no regrets. "We never wanted this development or the violent actions which we have distanced ourselves from" (SIC).

On the matter of whether the delegations haven't achieved the exact opposite of what they set out to do, if the goal of the delegations was to strengthen the Islamic position in Denmark, answers Ahmed Akkari: "We will not accept that it was our responsibility. When Bush goes to the Middle East it often causes new riots, but nobody tells him not to go. We feel stigmatized as second- or third-class citizens."

Do you feel as a second- or third-rate citizen? "I feel that the public discourse in Denmark is harsh towards the Muslims and that our voice is not heard. That goes for me personally as well."

But you HAVE been heard the last couple of weeks, haven't you? "When finally we do get our say, we are portrayed as villains. We want to be represented properly," says Ahmed Akkari.

He predicts two endgames for the prophet-case: Either Moslems will be properly and fully recognized in Denmark or else portrayal of them as villains will be intensified. "I believe in the former. I am an optimist."

CNN & FoxNews Face-Off In Cartoon Wars

Here you have it, folks . . . the real difference between CNN and FoxNews.

On the left you have CNN's broadcast of one of the Danish cartoon caracatures of Muhammed.

(The image was blurred out)

On the right you have FoxNews' broadcast of the same cartoon.
(The image was not blurred out)

And that, my friends, is the difference between CNN and FoxNews.

FoxNews Reports. You Decide.

CNN Decides For You.

Note: The two images were apparently later censored by Photobucket

TUESDAY, FEBRUARY 14, 2006

Hamas Does Not Think Highly of Rotary International

. . . or of Freemasonry or Lions International for that matter.

According to a new translation of the Hamas Charter provided by MEMRI, Charter Article 28 contains the following remarkable passage:

The Zionist invasion is a cruel invasion, which has no scruples whatsoever; it uses every vicious and vile method to achieve its goals. In its infiltration and espionage operations, it greatly relies on secret organizations which grew out of it, such as ***the Freemasons, the Rotary Clubs, the Lions and other such espionage groups.*** *All these organizations, covert or overt, work for the interests of Zionism and under its direction, and* ***their aim is to break societies, undermine values, destroy people's honor, create moral degeneration and annihilate Islam.***

I am shocked! SHOCKED! I had no idea that my father, as a Rotarian, was working as a Zionist agent for virtually all of his adult professional life! I feel so naive to have thought that Rotary Clubs were simply groups of community professional men and women who met to encourage friendship, cooperation, community improvement and goodwill between the nations and peoples of the world! What a fool I have been!

I think of all those poor, deceived Muslims who have joined Rotary and Lions Clubs all across the world, completely unaware that they had become part of a secret diabollical conspiracy to "create moral degeneration and annihilate Islam."

Freemasonry is, of course, intentionally secretive about its rites and rituals. As one who is not personally privy to such matters I cannot, therefor say "yea" or "nay" about the motives, beliefs and aims of these otherwise very ordinary folks.

In a free society friends are permitted to hold secrets between themselves so, if you want to find out what the Masons believe, you can find out by telling one that you'd like to join (they won't ask you . . . you must initiate the conversation). After you have passed through the First Degree you can email me and tell me all about it. I'll believe every word that you say, too!

If, on the other hand, you want to know what the Lions and Rotarians believe you can attend their weekly meetings as guest or just read what they have to say about themselves on the internet.

You will be shocked to discover, for example, that instead of the Five Purposes of the Church, the Five Pillars of Islam or the Four Spiritual Laws, Rotary boldly adheres to the ***4-Way Test***. Rotarians are forced to memorize and (in a sort of brain-washed way) actually govern their behavior by answering the following questions in the affirmative: ***Is it the Truth? Is it Fair to All Concerned? Will it Build Good Will and Better Friendships? Will it Be Beneficial to All Concerned?***

Even more sinister, Rotarians are urged to commit themselves to abide by their motto, ***Service Above Self***. They are even cajoled into supporting the movement's international goal of eradicating polio from the face of the earth! Since most polio cases are found in Third World countries populated by non-Caucasian people, it seems suspicious that these people would be supporting the injection of biological agents into the most helpless and oppressed people in the world (many of whom, of course, may well be Muslim!).

Members of Lions Clubs are no less open to suspicion of hidden motives. Under the mystic and cryptic motto, ***We Serve***, Lions International has grown into the world's largest civic organization with nearly 1.4 million members in 197 countries. Even more appalling is the fact that they collect discarded eyeglasses for redistribution to unsuspecting and innocent poor people around the world . . . especially taking advantage of those with poor eyesight! And, to make matters worse, many of these "discarded eyeglasses" have been *suspected of having once belonged to dead people*! Even people suffering from River Blindness are not safe from the agressive ministrations of this organization. Blind people have actually been pressured into undergoing (experimental?) surgical procedures that are dsigned to restore their eyesight! What a degrading policy to believe that blind people are somehow "incomplete" or "unhappy" simply because they are visually challenged!

I could go on but clearly, Hamas is on to something here. If what they say is true then it must follow that, among the most important goals of Zionism, are the giving of sight to the blind and the eradication of polio around the world.

If, from Hamas' point of view, such things are "cruel, vicious, vile, anti-social, decadent, dishonorable and degenerate" then, I think, Hamas has given us a very clear sense that the concepts of "love" and "mercy" have no place in their world-view.

Accordingly, when Hamas declares (as they do in Articles Six & Eight of their Charter) that:

The Islamic Resistance Movement is a distinct Palestinian movement that is loyal to Allah, adopts Islam as a way of life and works to raise the banner of Allah over every inch of Palestine . . .

(which includes Israel, of course), and

Allah is its goal, the Prophet its model to be followed, the Koran its constitution, Jihad its way, and death for the sake of Allah its loftiest desire.

then I, for one, am tempted to pray that they will all soon attain their "loftiest desire."

WEDNESDAY, FEBRUARY 15, 2006

Dick Cheney, CNN & the F-Word Network

On Wolf Blitzer's "Situation Room" today we find the following exchange between Wolf and CNN Correspondant Jack Cafferty:

(BLITZER) Let's go up to New York. Jack Cafferty standing by with "The Cafferty File." First of all, Jack, what did you make of Dick Cheney's interview today?

JACK CAFFERTY, CNN ANCHOR: Well, I obviously didn't see it because it hasn't been released in its entirety yet. But I would guess it didn't exactly represent a Profile in Courage for the vice president to wander over there to the f-word network *for a sit down with Brit Hume. That's a little like Bonnie interviewing Clyde, ain't it? Where was the news conference? Where was the access to all of the members of the media? Whatever.*

BLITZER: You still think he needs to do a full-scale news conference and invite all the cameras, all the reporters and ask whatever they want?

CAFFERTY: That's never going to happen. But running over there to the Fox network. Talk about seeking a safe haven. He's not going to get any high hard ones from anybody at the f- word network.
Is there any doubt why 2 to 4 times as many people are now watching FoxNews rather than CNN?

Cafferty should make a public apology to both the Fox Network and to the CNN viewing audience. Wolf Blitzer should be forced to explain why he allows this type of commentary on his program.

WEDNESDAY, FEBRUARY 15, 2006

A Thought About Iran & Nuclear Power

Iran continues to insist that its nuclear power program is only being created to produce electricity.

Baloney.

You do not need weapon's grade enriched uranium to produce nuclear power, yet Iran insists on having the capacity to manufacture weapon's grade enriched uranium.

Some forms of nuclear power (breeder reactors) are associated with the creation of weapon's grade plutonium but others aren't.

What plutonium and highly enriched uranium IS useful for is, of course, muclear weapons production.

Memo to Iran: Liar, liar, pants on fire!

THURSDAY, FEBRUARY 16, 2006

Iraqi Kurds Show What Freedom Can Do

Kurds have been persecuted in both Turkey and Iraq over the years. Now, for the first time in far more than a century, they actually have semi-autonomy as part of the new and improved Iraq.

Although virtually all Kurds are Sunni Muslims they appear to have avoided the scourge of radical Islam and have allowed their own ethnic identity to forge them into a unified community with a clear vision and desire for progress and prosperity.

After seeing the photographs of the Dream City of the Kurds posted by Michael J. Totten I am beginning to wonder if there is something in the Kurdish "brand" of Islam that could form some sort of a model for other Muslims who want to kick out the "insurgents/terrorists" in their midst and get on with building up their own lives instead of tearing down everyone else's.

Check out the amazing progress being made in Northern Iraq. And remember that the Kurd's freedom has been made possible by the sweat, blood, wealth and foreign policies of the United States. It makes me feel just a little bit proud. Especially when I remember that it was these same Kurds who were murdered by Saddam Hussein with chemical weapons just a little over 15 years ago.

Amazing. It gives me hope.

Newborn Babies Are Living Poetry and Art and Much More Wrapped Up In Human Flesh

As a Pastor I get to visit newborn babies and their happy parents. Often I even get to visit them in the hospital soon after delivery. Well, it's been a little over one week since Riley was born as the first child of our church Choir Director but, when I stopped by to see her for the first time today she was as fresh and new as the dew on a rose at the first light of morning!

I have never seen an ugly baby. Even those with "coneheads" from a long and difficult labor are beautiful beyond words.

It's this "beyond words" thought that always gives me "chicken skin" when I see a newborn baby. I feel like I have stepped back into the Garden of Eden on the morning of the Sixth Day of Creation. There is something "eternal" about the newness of a baby. It's almost as though the baby's "essence" has come from somewhere else only to emerge into our sight like a Spring Crocus pushing its way through the last remaining crust of the Winter's snow.

As a Christian I sense more "mystery beyond human understanding" in a baby than I do at any other time or on any other occasion. In the same way that a great painting draws us into its little world of artificial reality and somehow manages to open our eyes to some new understanding about the real world, a baby also seems to add up to more than the sum of its parts.

Little Riley is like a little link to something greater than herself. As the Psalmist says, God has made her just "a little lower than the angels."

Babies make me want to compose music or write poetry. Riley's father tells me he has already been creating songs to sing with her when he holds her at night while Mom gets to rest.

As we grow up we somehow seem to lose a bit of that mysterious "link" to something above and beyond, something greater than ourselves. Perhaps that is why Jesus loved children so much and declared that "to them belongs the Kingdom of Heaven."

There is spiritual power in a baby. I am always pleased when folks bring babies and young children to funerals. One squeal, one fit of crying, one snippit of unintelligible gurgling from a baby can transform the mourning of death into the celebration of life at a funeral.

I definitly want babies at my own funeral. Lots of them. If there is a shortage of them for some reason, please feel free to borrow or rent them. I want everyone to catch a glimpse of the Kingdom of Heaven at my funeral and babies will capture that eternal reality far more effectively than words alone.

Riley managed to "link" me to God this afternoon. I prayed a blessing on her but I was the one who received the greater blessing. From a baby. Imagine that!

FRIDAY, FEBRUARY 17, 2006

Italy Decides that Non-Virgin Teenagers May Be Molested With Lesser Legal Penalties

In Italy it is not such a big deal if the young girl you molest is not a virgin. That, at least, is the decision of the Italian Supreme Court in a case involving a man who forced his 14-year old step-daughter to have oral sex with him after she refused to have intercourse.

According to Reuters,

The (Italian) supreme court (ruled) that because of her previous sexual experiences, the victim's "personality, from a sexual point of view, is much more developed than what would be normally expected of a girl of her age".

"It is therefore fair to argue that (the damage for the victim) would be lower" if the abused girl was not a virgin, Italian news agencies quoted the court as saying.
Yep. That 14-year old is "damaged goods" all right. She's like a used car, not worth as much as it was when it was new.

The logic would seem to follow that stealing a used Mercedes would bring a car thief a lesser sentence than stealing a new Cooper Mini.

In Pakistan the girl's father would probably just slit her throat to preserve his sense of honor. In Italy, I'm sure the Supreme Court would be quite understanding of that, too.

A lot of folks in Italy are very upset by the decision. One commented that the ruling would have never been made if there had been a woman on the Court.

The same Court ruled some time ago that a man could not be held responsible for raping a woman because she had been wearing skin tight pants.

I suppose she should have been wearing a *burka*.

Don't Try Buying a "Danish Pastry" In Tehran These Days

Danish pastries are popular in Iran. But you can't buy them anymore . . . at least by that name.

Because of the continuing fall-out from the Muhammed cartoon caracatures the Iranian confectioner's union has renamed the pastries, "Roses of the Prophet Muhammed."

Yum!

"Waiter, I'll have one "Rose of the Prophet Muhammed and a side of Freedom Fries, please."

Stanford Prof Solves Social Security Crisis: Retire at 85

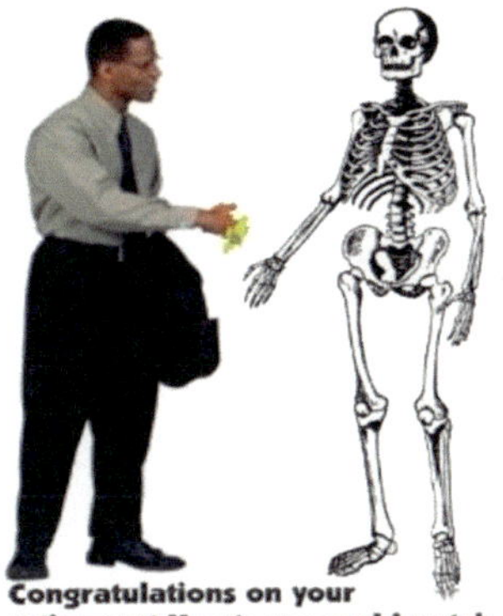

Shripad Tuljapurkar of Stanford University says that in the US by the year 2050, the cost of social security and medical care would almost double if people retired at 65. But an an increase in the retirement age to 85 would bring costs down to today's levels.

Tuljapurkar figures that folks will live a lot longer by then and that his scenario should be taken seriously as an economic proposal.

Sure.

SATURDAY, FEBRUARY 18, 2006

Muslims Riot In Nigeria Killing Christians & Burning Churches

If you think that the world-wide Muslim demonstrations have anything to do with Danish cartoon caracatures of Muhammed then you are sadly mistaken.

Consider Northern Nigeria today. Supposedly angry about the cartoons Nigerian Muslims rampaged through Maiduguri with machetes and iron bars today, beating and murdering Christian residents, looting Christian-owned businesses and burning churches. One reporter saw the crown force a car tire over one man, douse him with gasoline and set him on fire. At least ten people were killed, including three children and a priest.

What this has to do with Danish cartoons is beyond me. The cartoons have clearly become an excuse for violence against Christianity and Western Civilization. Those killed in Nigeria today were not Danes but Black Nigerians.

In Pakistan earlier this week, McDonalds and Kentucky Fried Chicken franchises were destroyed and future demonstrations (one is planned every other day) will be designed to weaken and eventually bring down the government of Musharrif. What does this have to do with cartoons?

Demonstrators in Pakistan held signs neatly caligraphied in English by a well-organized radical Islamist machine. One even carried a sign saying, "God bless Adolf Hitler." What does this have to do with cartoons?

In England, 15,000 Muslims marched in London but the demonstration was hardly spontaneous. Buses brought most of the participants from all over the country, a strategic deployment of radicalized Muslims coordinated by some centralized leadership organization.

The Nazis organized similar demonstrations in Germany during the 1930's claiming that they proved that the hatred of the Jews was a deep-set and widely-held belief among Germans. The German people were suckered into believing this propoganda so, when Jews began to be attacked, few said anything because they (wrongly) believed that everyone else hated the Jews.

Most Muslims are not supporting these demonstrations but there is no organized leadership to oppose them. We must not be suckered like pre-WW II Germany into believing that what we are seeing is a grass-roots groundswell of Islamic power.

The power is there but it is not in the crowds we are seeing on TV . . . it is in the Imams and members of radical Muslim groups (such as Muslim Brotherhood, al-Qaeda, etc.) who are brokering the power. Like the seeds of weeds buried in the garden soil, they cannot be seen until they sprout up and show themselves.

These radical instigators are keeping a very low profile and frequently working through local "small fry" to lead the public planning. They hope to remain invisible and anonymous as long as possible. When accused they will proclaim their innocence and bring forth charges of "anti-Muslim racism."

Jesus said that, at the end of history, at the time of "harvest," the weeds will be separated from the good grain.

In today's world, however, when the weeds are threatening to overwhelm the good grain it behooves us as nations responsible for the defense and welfare of a vulnerable citizenry, to begin the process of agressive weeding as quickly as possible. More than likely the weeds will seem like there will never be an end to them. But they must be contained. They are weeds. They are determined to supplant the harvest. Evil has sown a wind. We must respond with a whirlwind.

The whirlwind will not always need to be a violent response. But it must be decisive and clear in its objective. Christianity, the West and the world are under seige. Without countermeasures we will be overwhelmed and reduced to conversion to Islam, dhimitude or death.

Hamas Takes Power In Palestine

Today the newly elected representatives to the Palestinian Authority were seated in parliament. Hamas, of course, now holds the majority and will be forming a new government as soon as it can.

This means, of course, that Iran is no longer the world's only explicitly Islamist state. Countries such as Saudi Arabia are virtual Islamist states but places like Syria and Libya are simply totalitatian regimes as Iraq was until three years ago.

Hamas rejected an appeal to preserve and respect all legally signed treaties between Palestine and Israel. The Oslo Accords and the "Roadmap to Peace" have now been officially discarded into the ashheap of history.

As usual, Hamas is saying that, as the officially and democratically-elected government of Palestine it should continue to be recognized and supported by the very governments it spits on at every opportunity. They will even mouth words of "peace" and "cease fire" but always in the context of "I voted for peace BEFORE I slaughtered every Israeli Jew I could find."

The Palestinian people must learn that, to exist in the world of nations, they cannot have it both ways. They must either accept Israel's right to exist and cease their support for terror or be cut off completely from the civilized world.

Once again the Palestinians have chosen to self-destruct. Yassir Arafat is gone along with the PLO and the domination of Fatah. But Hamas will surely bring destruction and death and further deterioration of the Palestinian people whether they turn out to be corrup or not.

Bird Flu--Coming Soon to a Country Near You

Bird Flu is coming. Not if . . . but when. This past week it appeared in India, Iran, Nigeria, Austria, Egypt and France for the first time (click here for interactive chart showing how it has spread and here for "quick facts"). Birds have begun to die . . . especially domestic poultry. People are sick, too, although it has yet to be determined whether these latest illnesses are from this flu strain.

This spreading scourge will soon begin to take its toll on poultry products. Certain kinds of wildfowl are also at risk. Thus far, the only way to keep the virus from spreading is to kill the infected birds. This could mean millions of domestic fowl being killed in the next few weeks (France is Europe's largest producer of poultry) with heavy economic impact.

Even more worrisome is the potential for the flu to develop a strain that is easily transferable to humans. In humans the flu is fatal in at least one out of every two cases (90 deaths from 150 known cases so far). Almost all victims had been in close contact with infected birds but, because the disease is not food-borne, experts say it is still safe to eat poultry.

Should the flu begin to migrate freely between humans the outbreak could result in one of the world's worst pandemics since the great flu epidemic of 1918 that killed 40 million people.

Major metropolitan areas in the United States have already begun preparing for the worst. Morgues and mortuaries are being designated for the preparation and storage of bodies. There are even plans for dealing with a multitude of grieving family members and friends.

One strain of flu vaccine has already been found to be effective in innoculating poultry from the current strain. Human vaccines have not yet been manufactured because it is not yet clear what the human form of the virus might take if and when it should appear.

One way or another, whether through illegal transportation of uninspected poultry or simply from migrating wildfowl, the United States will soon discover that the Bird Flu has arrived.

We must pray that the Bird Flu comes and goes with relatively little harm to human beings. The odds are in our favor but, if the worst comes to past, we may experience death, suffering and grief on a scale not experienced since Germany, Poland and the Soviet Union in WWII .

May God have mercy on us all.

Olympic Games--All Muscle, Little Grace

I used to like the Winter Olympics because of the gracefulness of the ice skating and the sheer joy that the competitors radiated as they gave each event their best shot.

This year in Torino, the ice skating has become a test of who can do a quadruple jump without falling and who can throw their spinning female pairs partner the furthest without breaking her leg. The winner has often been the last skater standing. This has been boring, to say the least. There have been very few (among them men's single's champion Yevgeny Plushenko of Russia) who have been able to be both graceful and physical at the same time.

The dilemma is that if a man or woman does not attempt the most difficult (and sometimes nearly impossible) jumps they will have little or no hope for a medal. On the other hand, if they do not make the jump successfully they will not score high enough for a medal anyway.

So, some of the best skaters dare the impossible and lose while lesser skaters

get lucky and score the big points that make all the difference.

Some of the skaters concentrate so hard on preparing for the next jump that their routines have little coherence or artistry in them at all.

Fortunately, I have discovered the snowboard cross events . . . new to this year's Olympics. They have been exciting, unpredictable and "head to head." The snowboarders who are competing have not yet jaded into "professional money machines" with the heavy weight of sponsors and commercial pressure weighing them down. Even the cockeyness of World Champion Lindsey Jacobellis of the United States whose showboating caused her to fall on the home stretch of what would otherwise have been a sure and easy Gold Medal made me more happy for the *joie de vive* than sad for her disappointing second-place finish.

In fact, all the snowboarding events have been filled with the good spirit of both fun and competition. Traditional alpine skiing, even in the exhilaration of the downhill events, seems dull and wooden in comparison . . . with all the competitors taking themselves far too seriously.

In any case, the folks in Torino appear to have done a magnificent job and NBC's TV coverage has been far superior to past Winter Olympics . . . far less chit-chat and air-time for the big-name announcers and more of the real stuff we all want to watch.

My favorite quote of the Olympics so far was that of United States pairs skater Aliona Savchenko who, born and raised in Russia, is now an American citizen. When asked about his citizenship Savchenko said that he is happy and excited to be starting on the "American Dream."

I thought to myself, how many people, athletes or otherwise, immigrate to Russia to start on the "Russian Dream?" or to China to start on the "Chinese Dream?" People do not ordinarily immigrate to these countries at all. Rather, people emigrate away from these countries in pursuit of their "dreams" when given the opportunity.

I've got to say that Akiona Savchenko seemed to be a happy, smiling competitor even though he and partner Robin Szolkowy only came in seventh overall. Competing as an American was, apparently, the greatest thrill of all.

SUNDAY, FEBRUARY 19, 2006

Terror Wins Big In US Print Media

Someone in the US newspaper business finally had the courage to tell it like it is.

You might think this means that a newspaper had the courage to publish the Danish Muhammed cartoon caricatures but you would be wrong.

Instead, what we have is The Phoenix, a Boston alternative newspaper, printing the following editorial,

"Our primary reason," the editors confessed, is "fear of retaliation from . . . bloodthirsty Islamists who seek to impose their will on those who do not believe as they do . . . Simply stated, we are being terrorized, and . . . could not in good conscience place the men and women who work at the Phoenix and its related companies in physical jeopardy. As we feel forced, literally, to bend to maniacal pressure, this may be the darkest moment in our 40-year-publishing history."

Whatever happened to folks like Patrick Henry who were willing to declare, "Give me liberty or give me death!"?

Thus far only the Weekly Standard, the Philadelphia Enquirer and a handful of college and minor subsistence papers have shown the courage to publish the cartoons.

American newspapers ridicule and insult people and opinions every day. It appears that radical Islamists are the only exception. Those that say they are being "sensitive" to the feelings of Muslims are lying hypocrites.

The Phoenix, while choosing not to print the cartoons, at least had the "courage" to tell the truth.

While in its own way this honesty is commendable it is not enough.

When your neighbor tells you that he will burn your house down if you plant tomatoes in your back yard you get a restraining order on your neighbor and plant tomatoes in your back yard . . . even if you never had a garden before!

At the moment I feel like growing tomatoes just so I can throw them at the editors of our American newspapers. We either stand tall or bend over for those who threaten us. At the moment I see the American press bent over and bowing towards Mecca.

MONDAY, FEBRUARY 20, 2006

Jesus Cartoons Everywhere and Christians Are Not Rioting

I "Googled" and "Alta-Vista-ed" the phrase "Jesus Cartoon" this morning and found that there were quite a few to choose from. Most were from Christian sites, some from anti-Christian sites, many from European sites (mostly German with cartoon dialogues that defied translation by Babel Fish). There was even at least one political cartoon. I have posted eleven of them below. There were several that were so disgusting that I did not choose to post them.

When I was finished I checked for "Muhammed Cartoon" and found . . . nothing. Google and Alta Vista have apparently blocked access to the many Muhammed cartoon caractures that are everywhere on the internet these days. Even the newsworthy Danish cartoons that kicked off the current Islamist riots have been censured by these search engines.

I am sooooo glad that these internet gateways have no problems guiding me to all the pornography I (don't) want to find but are thoughtful enough (or scared of having their throats cut) to protect me from finding the images that have set off major international rioting.

A search for "Piss Christ", however, delivered over 45 "hits" (just of the image itself) on Google and 31 on Alta Vista. Go figure. Sure.

In any case, here are some of the drawings of Jesus that popped up. You decide if any of them are worth rioting, burning down an embassy, boycotting a nation or beheading somebody. (You can click on the pictures for their source)

Just water Mac...I'll make my own...

Jesus did come upon the church builders and said onto them, " Why have you built my father's house so that I may not enter ?"

Hello Katie
Hiya Christ
What should I do about my situation with Prevedel?
You should get back with him. He's a true pimp.
Damn this Cuban is good.

Run! It's Jesus and he's looking for MONEYCHANGERS!
Zuffaker
www.caglecartoons.com

JERUSALEM 3 K.
JESUS IS COMING
BB.

NOTHING IS FUNNY
EVERYDAY CARTOON
by TWood
Z
Z
Z
Z
JESUS WAS EXHAUSTED AFTER PLAYING THE BANJO FOR SO LONG. OF COURSE, THIS IS HIGHLY CONTESTED AMONG SCHOLARS.
©2005. Timothy Wood. EveryDayCartoon.com. nothingisfunny.com All Rights Reserved.
MIGHT NOT BE FUNNY TO ALL AUDIENCES
NOTHING IS FUNNY

World Council of Churches--US Churches Condemn the US and the War In Iraq

The AP summarizes the statement of the churches in this way:

PORTO ALEGRE, Brazil (AP) -- A coalition of American churches (particpating in the first meeting of the World Council of Churches since 1998) *sharply denounced the U.S.-led war in Iraq on Saturday, accusing Washington of "raining down terror" and apologizing to other nations for "the violence, degradation and poverty our nation has sown."*

I am not aware that this "coalition of American churches" has made any similar statement condemning the brutal and world-wide attacks and threats from Islamist terrorists (much of which has been explicitly targeting Christians).

What, I ask, is the United States to do in response to fatal attacks on its embassies, naval vessels, military, diplomatic and civilian personnel and, of course, the hijacking of US passenger airliners, devastating attacks on the World Trade Center (twice), the Pentagon and at least one other target foiled by the crash of United Flight #93?

What, you ask, did Iraq have to do with any of these attacks? Not much, apparently, except for providing moral support, financial support, training support, tactical support, medical care and the facilitation of travel for al-Qaeda and other terrorist groups through its territory.

Does this justify our attack on Iraq? Perhaps . . . perhaps not.

The universally held belief that Iraq still possessed WMD must also be taken into consideration as well as its continuing defiance and refusal to comply with the terms of the 1993 cease-fire agreement and all subsequent UN resolutions. (Not to mention the massive fraud involving the Oil for Food arrangement whereing Sadaam Hussein co-opted UN and national leaders in a corrupt scheme to siphon billions of dollars into their own private accounts and away from the Iraqi people). Oh . . . and, of course, the mass murders of hundreds of thousands of Iraqi citizens and the torture, disfigurement and rape of tens of thousands more.

A good argument could be made that it would have been immoral for the United States to NOT invade Iraq given the means and opportunity to do so.

Similar actions for similar reasons had previously been affirmed when the issue concerned the former Yugoslavia (when Bill Clinton was President).

Given the complex moral circumstances of the US invasion of Iraq it is nothing short of theological arrogance for one group of Christian leaders (known to be overwhelmingly liberal, who have repeatedly demonstrated their opposition to any policies enacted by Republican Administrations while remaining suspiciously quiet when it comes to policies lead by Democrats) to declare such sweeping and condemnative moral absolutes in the name of Christ.

In the face of the terrorist bombings of subways, trains, airports, hotels, nightclubs, airplanes, mosques, synagogues, Hindhu temples, Christian churches and the almost gleeful slaughter of women, children, humanitarian workers, journalists, United Nations personnel and the video-taping of the execution and beheadings of civilian hostages from many different nations, hearing these denominational representatives charge the United States with "raining down terror" on the people of Iraq and for "the violence, degradation and poverty our nation has sown" is nothing short of incomprehensible.

Just to show that the above quotes have not been taken out of context, here they are as written and signed by leaders of 34 US denominations:

We lament with special anguish the war in Iraq, launched in deception and violating global norms of justice and human rights. We mourn all who have died or been injured in this war. We acknowledge with shame abuses carried out in our name . . .

Our country responded (to the Sept. 11, 2001 attacks) by seeking to reclaim a privileged and secure place in the world, raining down terror on the truly vulnerable among our global neighbors ... entering into imperial projects that seek to dominate and control for the sake of national interests. Nations have been demonized and God has been enlisted in national agendas that are nothing short of idolatrous.

The statement also asks forgiveness for a world that's

grown weary from the violence, degradation and poverty our nation has sown.

The Rev. Sharon Watkins, president of the Christian Church (Disciples of Christ), worried that some may interpret the statement as undermining U.S. troops in Iraq.

We honor their courage and sense of duty, but ... we, as people of faith, have to say to our brothers and sisters, `We are so profoundly sorry,'" Watkins said.
Sorry for what? Sorry that the soldiers that they supposedly honor have been "raining down terror" on the people of Iraq and are participating in sowing the seeds of international "violence, degradation and poverty?" Oh, no. We wouldn't want anyone to think that this attitude was in any way undermining US troops in Iraq.

Also included in the two-page statement was a condemnation the current US government for ignoring critical international environmental needs (ie. global warming) and an assertion that, "Hurricane Katrina revealed to the world those left behind in our own nation by the rupture of our social contract."

In addition, the American churches issued a letter in support of the UN demand that the American prison facilities at Guantanamo Bay be closed, saying reports of alleged torture violated "the fundamental Christian belief in the dignity of the human person."

I have always supported those who bring their Christian conscience to bear against US policies both foreign and domestic. But I have little patience or empathy with church leaders such as these (who also represent the majority membership of the National Council of Churches) that will "speak truth to power" when condemning the United States but will not condemn the international Islamist movement and the terrorism that it has spawned as an explicit act of war against the United States, Western Civilization and the Christian Faith.

I can hardly wait to hear what they will have to say about Hamas as the new governing party in Palestine. I won't be holding my breath.

Correction: The good comment from Wesley Pattillo has identified a major error in my post. I had conflated the representatives of American churches attending the World Council of

Churches with the National Council of Churches. 34 US churches signed the statement and 35 churches are members of the NCC. This coincidence also added to my error. As requested I offer my apologies to the NCC and will attempt to make appropriate corrections to my posting. Given, however, the fact that the US/American churches attending the WCC are virtually identical to the churches that are members of the NCC the position adopted by them this past week obviously reflects the position of member churches in the NCC although not serving as an official position of the latter. An example of this can be found here, where the President of the NCC has initiated a letter (now signed by over 13,000 people) in support of the UNs call for the US to close the prison facility at Guantanamo. It would seem that the only difference between the American churches attending the WCC and the NCC itself is the letterhead.

Further Note: According to the WCC website there are 33 member churches from North America (including Canada). The NCC website shows 35 member churches.

TUESDAY, FEBRUARY 21, 2006

Palestinian Christians Suffer & Die Under Palestinian Authority

That is the title of an article printed in the January 16, 2006 issue of The Presbyterian Outlook. According to the author, Justus Reid Weiner, things are going from very, very bad to even worse for Palestinian Christians living in the West Bank and Gaza. The villain, in this case, is not Israel but the Islamist fundamentalists (ie. Hamas) who, by force of terror, have controlled most of the territory for some time. The article is chilling, especially since Hamas is now the controlling majority in the Palestinian Authority.

The article, while relatively short, is too long to reproduce here in it's entirety. You can read the first two paragraphs below but you will then need to click on the link to read the rest.

Palestinian Christians Suffer, Die
in Palestinian Authority Territory
by Justus Reid Weidner
c. 2005 Religion News Service

These are acutely trying times for the Christian remnant residing in areas governed by the Palestinian Authority. Tens of thousands have abandoned their holy sites and ancestral properties to move abroad, while those who remain do so as a beleaguered and dwindling minority Christians, who used to comprise the vast majority of the residents in the Bethlehem area, will fall past a critical point—and their community will no longer be viable.

Palestinian Christian leaders who should be protecting their co-religionists are instead abandoning them to the forces of radical Islam. Muslim religious law (Sharia) is an enormous influence on the inner workings of the Palestinian Authority. Indeed, the Palestinian Constitution states, "the Sharia will be the paramount source of legislation." By granting Islamic law primacy over every other legal source, including international human rights conventions, the minorities living in the Palestinian Authority are denied proper redress via the courts. (Click here to continue reading the whole article)

WEDNESDAY, FEBRUARY 22, 2006

Bombing of Shi'ite Shrine In Iraq Is BAD NEWS

Feb. 2, 2004

Feb. 22, 2006

One of the most sacred sites for Shi'ite Muslims was attacked and severely damaged today by well-trained bombers dressed as Iraqi police. The al-Askariya shrine, also known as the Golden Mosque, contains the tombs of two revered Shiite imams, who are considered by Shiites to be among the successors of the Prophet Muhammad. The shrine is located in Sunni dominated Samarra, 60 miles north of Baghdad.

The attack is believed to have been an attempt to force and Iraqi civil war between Shi'ite and Sunni Muslims. Although several of the attackers are reported to have been captured it is not yet publicly known who they represent.

This is, perhaps, the single most serious incident to have occurred in Iraq since the fall of Saddam Hussein and his ruling Baathist government. For Shi'ites it is nearly the equivalent of a Protestant terrorist bombing of the Roman Catholic St. Peter's Cathedral in Rome.

The shrine's association with the "hidden" 12th Imam (who will return as the Mahdi or Shi'ite Messiah at the end of history) has near-apocalyptic associations for many Muslims. Iran, which is overwhelmingly Shi'ite, has already condemned the bombing by holding the United States and Zionist plotters responsible. Since the currant Iranian President believes that these are, indeed, the "end times" this attack will only serve to fuel his missionary zeal to carry out his own form of Jihad against the non-Muslim world in general and Israel in particular. Would he use the nuclear bomb Iran is committed to produce? The fact that this question cannot be answered with a simple "yes" or "no" is ample evidence of the seriousness of today's bombing and its effect on radical Muslims of all flavors.

Whoever you are, please pray that this tragic event will somehow serve to unite the Iraqi people rather than divide them. Pray that both Sunni and Shi'ite will be so outraged that they will turn, not against each other, but against both the Iraqi "insurgents" and the "foreign" elements of al-Qaeda in Iraq headed up by Zarqawi

I have long said that the current Islamist crisis can ultimately only be cut off and subdued by more moderate Muslims holding both influence, respect and real power. I am praying that this vicious and evil act will return to those who ordered it as a curse leading to their destruction and eradication from Iraq.

The shrine will be rebuilt but today it is not certain that Iraq, as a unified nation, will remain standing.

Good insight on today's attack can be found at Iraq the Model, Bill Roggio and Andrew Sullivan (who has a tear-inducing link to a Time photo essay on the bombing)

FRIDAY, FEBRUARY 24, 2006

Life In Baghdad During Post-Mosque-Bombing Anarchy

Zeyad at Healing Iraq says that things are apparently calming down after two-days of anarchy, arson, murder and mayhem in response to Wednesday's bombing of the al-Askariya mosque in Samarra.

Early Friday Zeyad posted the following chilling account of what was going on in his own neighborhood:
Fierce streetfighting at my doorstep for the last 3 hours. Rumor in the neighbourhood is that men in black are trying to enter the area. Some armed kids defending the local mosque three blocks away are splattering bullets at everything that moves, and someone in the street was shouting for people to prepare for defending themselves.

There's supposed to be a curfew, but it doesn't look like it. My net connection is erratic, so I'll try to update again if possible. The news from other areas in Baghdad are horrible. I don't think it's being reported anywhere.

My father and uncle are agitatedly walking back and forth in the hallway, asking me what we should do if the mob or Interior ministry forces try to attack us in our homes? I have no answer for them.
In an earlier posting on Friday Zeyad expressed his feelings with heartfelt passion:
What kind of nation are we? What kind of nation kills its intellectuals and academics, its doctors and healers, its women and children, its clerics and preachers? What kind of nation blows up churches and mosques, hotels and schools, funerals and weddings? We have left nothing sacred. Yet we have the insolence to accuse others of offending us, of vilifying us. I announce today that we have proved ourselves worthy of that vilification. Ten years ago, I denounced religion and disavowed Islam. I do not want to be forced to disavow my country and nation today, but with every new day, I'm afraid I am getting closer to it.
Suddenly, here in my quiet corner of Hawaii, it seems strangely quiet and uncomofortably peaceful. I do not hear gunfire outside my home. I am not terrified and afraid that armed men might burst into my home at any moment, handcuff and blindfold me, drag me outside and put a bullet in my head.

There are tens of millions of Iraqis just like Zeyad tonight. They want peace. They want unity. They do not hate anybody (or would be happier if they didn't need to). Although I am remembering them in my prayers what I am actually asking is that God would answer theirs.

SATURDAY, FEBRUARY 25, 2006

Iran Says Tom & Jerry Zionist Plot

Following in the footsteps of Tele-Tubbies and Sponge Bob Square Pants, Tom & Jerry has now entered the hallowed pantheon of subversive "toons."

Hasan Bolkhari, Iranian "mass media expert" and cultural advisor to the Iranian Education Ministry has come to the conclusion that:
The Jewish Walt Disney Company gained international fame with this cartoon. It is still shown throughout the world. This cartoon maintains its status because of the cute antics of the cat and mouse – especially the mouse.

Some say that the main reason for making this very appealing cartoon was to erase a certain derogatory term that was prevalent in Europe . . .

(In Hitler's Germany the) Jews were degraded and termed "dirty mice." Tom and Jerry was made in order to change the Europeans' perception of mice. One of terms used was "dirty mice."

I'd like to tell you that... It should be noted that mice are very cunning...and dirty . . .

No ethnic group or people operates in such a clandestine manner as the Jews . . .
You can read the whole thing at MEMRI TV.

PS: T & J were, of course, an MGM production and not Disney.

ht:lgf

CNN Needs a New Story-Link Editor For Emerging Iraq Story

On the CNN main page today there is a link that reads, "Iraq curfew fails to stop fresh wave of bloodshed."

Fearing that the post-mosque bombing violence had begun to reappear I followed the link to a story headlined, "Iraqi leaders discuss unity government."

Now, which headline to believe? I suppose that would depend on the content of the story which begins,
BAGHDAD, Iraq (CNN) -- In a dramatic show of solidarity amid fears of escalating violence, Iraq's leaders from virtually all political factions met Saturday to discuss the formation of a national unity government.

The meeting included representatives of the Iraqi Accord Front, which had announced a boycott of national unity talks following violent reprisals against Sunnis.

The gathering, televised live on Iraqi TV, included Prime Minister Ibrahim al-Jaafari, President Jalal Talabani and former Prime Minister Ayad Allawi. Also attending was U.S. Ambassador to Iraq Zalmay Khalilzad.

Bolstering the show of unity were Shiite and Sunni religious and political leaders who met earlier in an effort to promote peace. They included representatives of Shiite cleric Muqtada al-Sadr, the Association of Muslim Scholars and the Iraqi Accord Front.
Further down the article adds,

Abdul Aziz al-Hakim, head of the Supreme Council for Islamic Revolution in Iraq . . . (and a) top Shiite political figure, joined the top Shiite cleric in Iraq, Grand Ayatollah Ali al-Sistani, in urging Iraqis to remain calm and unite against extremists.

I do not believe that this is the result the bombers of the Golden Mosque expected and hoped for.

I also do not expect that this is the result that one of the CNN editors expected or hoped for either.

Power Plays Being Made In Iraq

Update: *2/27 As soon as I had posted this I began to have second thoughts. Today, Omar at Iraq the Model has forced me to admit that the blame for the Samarra mosque bombing lies with the "Salafi/Wahabis" which could be either independent of or related to Zarqawi/al-Qaeda in Iraq (which traces its origins to Wahabbi-inspired bin Laden). With this caveat I am still comfortable with the rest of my analysis of the consequences (which are largely supported by what Omar has written today.)*

Whenever there is civil unrest there are power vacuums. This is especially true in Iraq since the new government has not yet been fully established.

The timing of the bombing of the al-Askariya Mosque was perfect for one of three scenarios:

1. The blast was planned by Sunni Baathists (ie. insurgent/terrorists) trying to destroy the formation of the Iraqi government and intitiate civil war between Shi'ite and Sunni so that they can step in and reclaim political power over the Sunni population.

2. The blast was planned by al-Qaeda (ie. Zarqawi) trying to destroy the formation of the Iraqi government and initiate civil war between Shi'ite and Sunni so that they can destroy the democratic movement and humiliate the United States, forcing them to withdraw in defeat.

3. The blast was planned by Muqtada al-Sadr (most likely in partnership with Abdul Aziz al-Hakim and in consultation with Iran) in order to: A. Cause civil war or unrest; B. Dethrone al-Sistani as Supreme leader of the Shi'ite Muslims in Iraq; and, C. Separate southern Iraq from the rest of the country and establish it as a Islamic Republic under *sharia* in alliance with Iran.

My personal guess is that the correct answer is hiding behind Door Number 3.

If true, then we have entered a new round of trouble with Iranian-allied Shi'ites being added to the Baathist insurgents and Zarqawi's al-Qaeda in Iraq in trying to bring the Iraqi experiment in democracy to an end.

These three groups are not working together. But they are each drawing upon the other to create an environment where they can attain their own particular goals.

Much of the Iraqi Security Forces have already been co-opted by former Baathist insurgents in central Iraq or the al-Sadr pro-Iranian Shi'ites in the south and in Shi'ite Baghdad. Under the cover of their status and uniforms they have been systematically adding to the terrorizing of personal enemies as well as leaders and supporters of their opposition.

The good news is that the vast majority of Shi'ites do not support al-Sadr; the vast majority of Sunni do not support the insurgents; and, the vast majority of everyone do not support al-Qaeda. What this means is that the vast majority of Iraqi's (although not, perhaps the Kurds who most likely would prefer semi- or complete autonomy from the rest of Iraq) really DO want to live together as one nation with a democratically-elected government operating under the legal boundaries set by a national constitution.

The corrupted government and Security Forces will need to be cleansed by an outraged population with the support of US forces in order for democracy and national unity to move forward.

Unfortunately, the passion, the organization and the power may well be shifting to minority militias like those operated by al-Sadr and, to a lesser degree, to the Baathist insurgents.

A worst case scenario would be the collapse of the new government, leaving Iraq in complete and total anarchy.

A more likely scenario would be a major setback in national security requiring government leaders to call on US military forces to join with those loyal to national unity in fighting and destroying al-Sadr and Hakim and their militias. This scenario would, in effect, be a proxy war with Iran, which has been supporting and arming these Shi'ite militias since the fall of Saddam.

I am quite sure that this Iranian/al-Sadr rebellion could be squelched but I am not sure that the United States congress and public opinion will be willing to join in taking sides in what will be characterized as a Iraqi civil war.

The truth will be, of course, that it is far less of a civil war and far more an attack upon Iraq by Iran.

It would be fatal if the United States did not hold its ground and stand in complete unity with those Iraqis who represent the majority of their people in preserving the unity of Iraq and driving out those who would steal the southern half of the country on behalf of Iran.

Dark days ahead. But days that will grow brighter should those who bombed the mosque be proven to have been associated with al-Sadr, Hakim and Iran. If this does prove to be true, they will have become completely discredited for having destroyed the second most holy shrine of the very Shi'a Islam that they pretend to be defending.

Best Sites To Find Out What Is Happening In Iraq RIGHT NOW

Amazing and thorough coverage of events unfolding in Iraq can be found at Healing Iraq (Zayed), Iraq the Model (Omar), Belmont Club & Mudville Gazette. Zayed has photos and, along with Omar, is the place to find the latest. Note that Zayed is a very brave man whose life could well be in danger. As always pray for him and for the people of Iraq, most all of whom want nothing more than peace.

Michelle Wie Defeats Her Critics With Class & Talent

Michelle Wie still hasn't won a professional tournament. As ESPN sports writer Eric Adelson put it today, "So what!"

On the last day of the LPGA Fields Open tournament played at Kapolei, Oahu(just 30 minutes from my home), Michelle came from ninth place to finish in third place after missing a putt on the final hole that would have put her into a first-place tie and three-way playoff. She finished alone in third place after leaving the gallery gasping for breath from the drama.

Michelle smiled the entire day, playing about as well as the best golfer her age in the world can play. She was a class act, gracious and poised far beyond her 16 years.

She definately stole the show from her playing partner and 17-year old rival Morgan Pressel, who finished tied for 11th place. By playing before her home-town gallery she even stole the show from Seon Hwa Lee and Meena Lee who tied for first (with Meena winning on the third playoff hole).

Michelle Wie is the real deal. Even if she never wins a tournament she has already helped reshaped the look of women's golf for the better. After today there is no doubt about it. Michelle Wie is a pro.

MONDAY, FEBRUARY 27, 2006

Rounding Up More Bad Guys In Iraq

According to AP,

Iraqi security forces announced the capture of a senior al-Qaida in Iraq figure . . .

The captured al-Qaida figure was identified as Abou al-Farouq, a Syrian who financed and coordinated groups working for Iraq's most wanted terrorist, Abu Musab al-Zarqawi, in the insurgent stronghold of Ramadi, according to an Interior Ministry officer who spoke on condition of anonymity because he was not authorized to address the media.

Acting on a tip from residents, members of the Interior Ministry's Wolf Brigade captured al-Farouq with five other followers of al-Zarqawi near Bakr, about 100 miles west of Baghdad, the ministry officer said.

The Defense Ministry said Iraqi security forces have killed 35 insurgents and arrested 487 in raids across the country since the bombing last Wednesday of the Samarra shrine.

It appears that the Iraqi people have finally "had it" with insurgents, militias, "security forces" who kill and kidnap them and, of course, al-Qaeda in Iraq.

They appear to be turning them in as fast as they can find them.

This is not a good sign for terrorists.

Consider this paragraph in the story,

Interior Ministry commandos fought a three-hour gunbattle with Sunni-led insurgents near Nahrawan, about 15 miles southeast of Baghdad, after about 15 Shiite families were driven from their homes in the nearby village of Saidat, police said. At least eight commandos and five insurgents were killed in the fighting, which also injured six commandos and four civilians, police said.

Four good things worth noting in this paragraph:

1. The Iraqi military is willing to fight and die to kill the insurgents. They have been well-trained by American and other coalition troops and are at least on an equal footing with even the most trained and sophisticated insurgents.

2. Insurgents are getting themselves killed.

3. Citizens are no longer keeping silent out of fear of reprisals. For the last several years insurgents, etc., have forced themselves into people's homes and living in them while threatening family members with death if anyone try to inform against them. This has worked quite well . . . until now. Families are now, apparently, willing to take the risk to flush these bums out and tell Iraqi military officials where to find them.

4. The Iraqi people have decided that it is safer to trust the Iraqi military and security forces than to give in to the insurgent/terrorists. Such trust can only be earned and it now appears that they have at last earned that trust.

All this is very good news. Coming off of a week of unrest that threatened to bring down the fledgling Iraqi democracy like a house of cards, the ongoing success against the "bad guys" certainly looks promising.

Folks like William F. Buckley, who have recently declared the United States' invasion and occupation of Iraq to be a failure may wind up eating their words if this trend continues.

Today, I think I saw, for the first time, light at the end of the tunnel.

Suspected Gunman Shoots and Kills Suspected Victim In Church

The AP story relating the tragic fatal shooting of a woman during morning worship in Detroit illustrates just how far the art of journalism has fallen.

The story begins with this paragraph,

*A **suspected gunman** who opened fire with a shotgun during a church service Sunday morning killed a woman and wounded two people before he shot himself a mile away, police said.*

A **suspected** gunman? You've got to be kidding!

Was the suspected victim shot and killed by a suspected gunman during what is suspected to have been a church worship service?

I guess until the legal system sorts all this out it wouldn't be fair to anyone, especially the suspected gunman, to prejudice the public with the obvious facts of the case.

I suspect that the suspected writer of this article, suspectly identified as Michael J. Feeney, suspected that the suspected gunman should be suspected of being innocent until proven guilty of actually being the suspected gunman suspected of shooting and murdering the suspected victim.

It all sounds suspicious to me.

Hillary Clinton & Karl Rove "Obsessed" With Each Other

At least that's the way that Hillary sees it.

She thinks that she scored points today by declaring that Rove "spends a lot of time obsessing about me."

"He spends more time thinking about my political future than I do."

This in response to Rove's new book which considers the likely possibility of Hillary becoming the Democratic Presidential nominee in 2008.

Personally, Hillary making a statement like this makes about as much sense to me as Field Marshal Rommel trying to sound tough by mocking Montgomery for "thinking about my military stategy more than I do."

Poor Hillary. She keeps kicking the ball into other people's goals and thinks she's scoring.

TUESDAY, FEBRUARY 28, 2006

Giant Squid In London Display Could Make Plenny Tako Poke

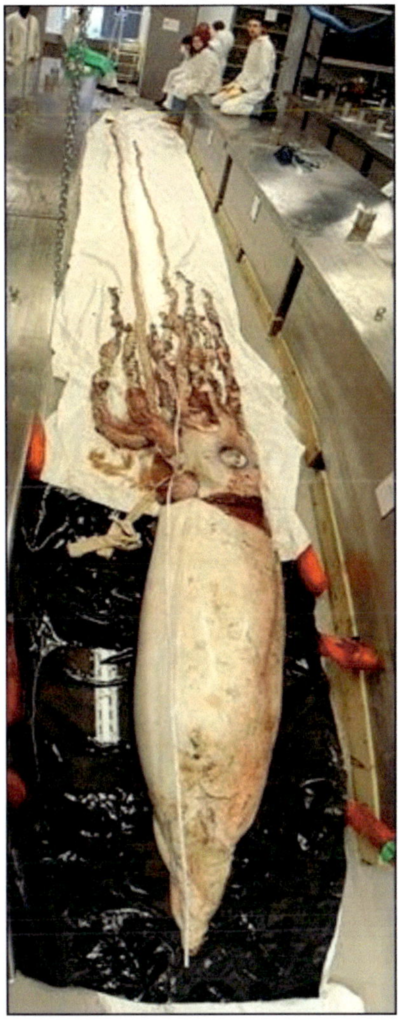

One of the largest intact giant squids ever preserved is now on display at the London Natural History Museum. The squid, caught in a trawler's net off of the Falkland Islands, measures 28 feet long. Wow!

WEDNESDAY, MARCH 01, 2006

Spinning Both Ways At Once: Two Timely Examples

It's sad yet funny the way spin comes flying back at you like a boomerang. It leaves you wondering if there was any point to it in the first place. Consider the following:

1. Hillary Clinton has fiercely denounced the Dubai Port World's purchase of administrative contracts for major US ports. Her web page proclaims, "**This sale will create an unacceptable risk to the security of our ports**" while adding that,"This issue transcends philosophical posturing and partisan bickering – it is about our nation's security."

Where's the twist? The twist is that Hillary's husband and former Commander-In-Chief of the United States, Bill Clinton, has been in Dubai consulting with the government and Port World and advising them on what they need to do to get the contract **approved** by the US Congress.

So, are we to assume that Hillary is right and her husband is busy helping to "create an unacceptable risk to the security of our ports?" Or are we to assume that Bill Clinton is convinced that there is no security risk while Hillary is simply bloviating, posturing and bickering about our nation's security?

Hmmm. Could the fact that Bill picked up $300,000 from making a speech at a Dubai conference back in 2002 have anything to do with his enthusistic support for Dubai Port World? (2002 was, by the way, the year the United States invaded Afghanistan in order to overthrow the Taliban regime that had been sheltering, protecting and supporting Osama bin Laden and al-Qaeda, a regime that was vocally and enthusiastically supported by the government of Dubai, a minor matter that did not deter Bill from claiming his paycheck from Dubai at the time).

Those Clintons! They have never let a few dollars ever get in the way of sucking up to our nation's enemies (remember China?) and, if they can play it both ways at the same time, all the better! What a crock!

2. Meanwhile, Texas Democrats are arguing before the US Supreme Court that the 2003 Republican majority Texas legislature had no business gerrymandering the state voting districts

because the 1991 Democratic-controlled Texas legislature had done a perfectly fair and impartial job of redistricting and gerrymandering the state themselves just 12 years earlier.

Democratic lawyers argued that the recent redistricting was racially motivated and has denied minorities their right to influence the outcome of elections.

The New York Times even published this graphic showing how the Republicans had effectively reduced Texas' minority representation in Congress by one.

What both the graphic and the New York Times article fail to tell you can be found in the **AP version** of the story: ie. that, at the moment,

(s)ix Hispanics and three blacks represent Texas in the House of Representatives — ***an increase of one more black congressman*** *from* ***before*** *the 2003 map was put in place.*

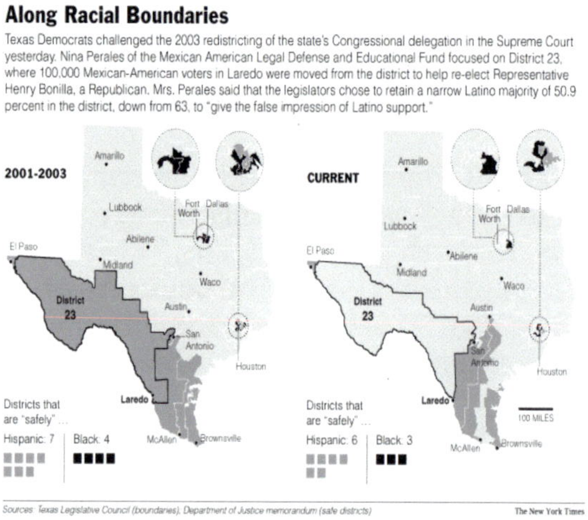

The AP story also takes time to mention that **Justice Ruth Bader Ginsburg fell asleep** before the two-hours of legal arguements were completed. Although the NY Times, Washington Post, Los Angeles Times stories of today's SCOTUS hearing did not mention Justice Ginsburg's nap, Captain Ed wonders if they would have been so polite, tactful and silent had the napping Justice been Scalia, Alito or Thomas? Any fair-minded person can make an educated guess on that question!

Spinning both ways at the same time in defiance of priciples of physics . . . and of reason!

THURSDAY, MARCH 02, 2006

Queen Mary 2 Visits Honolulu

The Queen Mary 2 is one very, very large ship . . . the largest passenger ship in history! This photograph, that graced the front page of today's Honolulu Advertiser, is one that I wish that I had taken myself. (click on photo to enlarge it)

One local measure of its size is that it is as long as six Aloha Towers (for many years the tallest building in the state) laid end to end.

It even has a planetarium for "heavens" sake! (pun intended).

Well, it didn't stay long, just overnight.

Only two years age the Queen Elizabeth 2 passed through Honolulu on her last cruise before returning to England.

Way back in 1966 I sailed into Southampton harbor after crossing the Atlantic on the SS Rotterdam, at that time the largest passenger liner engaged in world cruises.

There was a dock strike in England that week so shipping was all tied up (literally). As we passed through the harbor (or should I spell it "harbour?") it turned out that the original Queen Elizabeth (with two stacks) and Queen Mary (with three) were docked end to end. It seemed like it took forever for us to pass these two mammoth passenger liners, staring straight up from what we had thought was a large ship!

So, now I have personally seen all four of these great ships and I am content.

Big isn't always beautiful but, when it comes to a passenger ship that is 24-stories tall, it can be awesome!

SATURDAY, MARCH 04, 2006

Web Site Map Shows World-Wide Islamic Terror Attacks Sine 9/11/01

A site calling itself "The Bloody Border Project" has done a remarkable job of showing the dates, location and severity of Islamic terrorist attacks since 9/11. Particularly "striking" is the animation page with daily attacks flickering across the globe like firecrackers.

Guantanamo Detainees' Names Released--Sort-Of

Court hearing records for some terrorism detainees at Guantanamo have been released to Associated Press after the AP filed a "freedom of information" suit against the DOD.

We will be hearing many excerpts from these documents in the next several weeks and most of them will be used to cast more negative light on the Bush administration's handling of the situation.

This will all be somewhat deceptive and inconclusive for the following reasons:

1. The names of those still being held at Guantanamo are not necessarily the same as those in the documents. The documents involve only a partial list of those who have been detained over the past four years and does include some who have been released. Note we do not necessarily know the names of those released, either, making it near impossible to tell who, among those whose names have been released, are still being held or have been released.

2. Many of the statements made by detainees during their hearings contain very embarassing charges against the US military and government. What is not clear, of course, is whether those charges have any merit or have simply been made up out of thin air.

3. Apparently, the Washington Post has been keeping a list of Guantanamo detainees whose names have been recovered from news releases, attorneys, etc. The WaPo list currently contains 450 names. About 490 detainees are held at Guantanamo Bay. About 270 have been transferred or released. This would mean that there will probably be few new names discovered among the 5000 pages of documents released today.

Apparently the government polled the detainees at one point asking if they would mind having their names publically released or not. Most did not return the survey. Many did not answer the question. Most who answered said they would *like* their names released and 16 said they would *not* like their names released.

I should think that the records that have been released relate to those whose hearings have been completed. Otherwise the information contained in these hearing records could compromise their status in future hearings.

In the end I do not think that the information released today will make too much difference for those being held. It will just supply more data for the MSM to twist and misinterpret and increase their insatiable appetite to get even more information to enable them to make sense of it all.

In a strange footnote to the story, the AP reports that the court-ordered data was placed on a CD by the DOD and hand carried to AP. Before delivery, however, the CD was recalled because it contained copies of correspondance that was not supposed to have been included.

A correctly-formatted CD was eventually delivered, a little behind the court-ordered deadline but not late enough to make a stink.

How in the world could the DOD make such a mistake! The incompetence in mind-boggling! These are the people who are leading our military in the war against terror. These are the people entrusted with our military intelligence. These are the people entrusted with keeping classified material classified.

And they cannot even manage to hand deliver the right CD to AP.

Personally, I am not much comforted by this adolescent blunder.

Ilan Halimi--American News Blackout--Why?

Ilan Halimi was a 23-year old French Jew, an immigrant from Morocco . I say "was" because he is now dead. He was kidnapped and tortured to death over a three-week period by a gang of Muslims who held him for ransom. His screams could be heard by his parents during phone conversations with the kidnappers, along with shouted quotations from the Qu'ran and comments indicating that they were extinguishing their cigarettes by snuffing them out on Ilan's body.

Halimi was found naked, handcuffed with 80% of his body covered with cuts and burns (he had been set on fire at the end) on Feb. 13 near railroad tracks south of Paris. He died on his way to a hospital.

The story has been headline news throughout Europe. Somewhere between 10,000-100,000+ (estimates varied widely) people marched in Paris to protest his death and his funeral service was attended by French government officials including

President Jacques Chirac.

In the United States, however, the news media effectively buried the story. I doubt that, unless you read the news on-line or read blogs you will not have heard of this story at all.

For example, FoxNews on-line carried one story on the subject, a story that included the following mis-information:

It remains unclear whether anti-Semitism was the motive for the grisly killing, which may have been part of a suburban extortion racket. . . Interior Minister Nicolas Sarkozy said Tuesday that Halimi's attackers were primarily motivated by greed. "But they believed, and I quote, 'That Jews have money,'" he said. "That's called anti-Semitism." . . .

Anti-Semitic acts, as well as acts against Muslims, increased in France starting in 2000, reflecting the rise in Israeli-Palestinian violence. They've since fallen off their peak, but the Halimi case has revived fears anti-Semitism remains in French society.

Remarkably, no mention is made in the story that the kidnappers were Muslim . . . as if that fact was irrelevant to the story! No mention was made of the kidnapper's phone contacts with Ilan's family, either. But we are informed that there have been "acts against Muslims" as if to somehow negate the horror of Ilan's murder.

The French themselves are culpable in this matter. Ilan's dying body was found on February 13. Three days later,

Speaking on a Parisian Jewish radio on Thursday, the Paris public prosecutor said that "no element of the current investigation could link this murder to an anti-Semitic declaration or action."

Police even didn't mention the Jewish identity of the victim. "It is out of question to draw a line to the victim's membership of the community" Jean-Claude Marin told French Jewish radio Radio Shalom.

Talk about a nation in denial!

CNN on-line did somewhat better on the story, relating the anti-Semitic aspects of the case as details became known. But even CNN never identifies the kidnappers as being Muslim, instead repeating a report that they were of varying ethnicities yet reporting that pro-Palestinian (Hamas) propaganda was found in their apartment. In spite of not reporting that the kidnappers were Muslim CNN included this warning in their story:

(French Interior Minister) Sarkozy on Tuesday called the killers barbarian criminals and urged people not to draw racist conclusions -- a clear warning against blaming France's Muslim community, which was widely suspected in a wave of anti-Jewish attacks several years ago.

Why warn against a back-lash against Muslims if Muslims were not involved? Why is the US media so hesitant to tell the story the "way it is?"

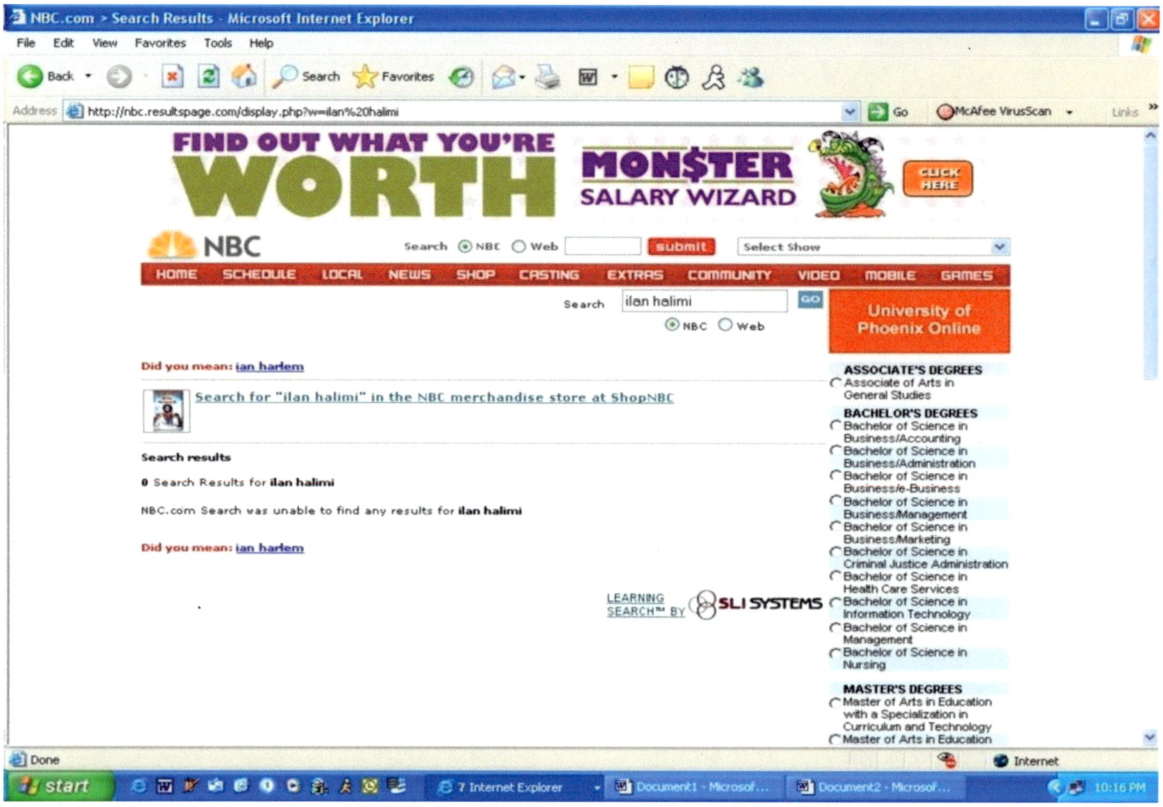

As far as CBS, NBC and ABC News, their web sites offer no video and only links to AP stories on the murder. Incredibly, in response to a NBC text search for "Ilan Halimi", nothing could be matched and I was given this suggestion, "Did you mean: ian harlem?" (Update: I found one CBS article here.)

National newspapers (notably the New York Times) did somewhat better, and even the LA Times carried at least two articles written by their own staff. A search of my own Honolulu Advertiser, however, could find no match for "Ilan Halimi."

So, was I right? Did you know about this story?

No wonder Americans are considered to be the most uninformed people in the world. Our TV News networks keep us that way.

SUNDAY, MARCH 05, 2006

An Incredible Shark Photograph--"Mind-Blowing"

British Director Sir David Attenborough narrates a new BBC project entitled, "Planet Earth." The project reportedly took four years to film. BBC has posted some photographs taken from the project including the one shown above. Attenborough himself describes this picture--of a Great White Shark leaping to catch a seal--"Mind blowing." I will not disagree.

The photo is so surreal and frightening that it could pass as an out-take from "Jaws!" I'm almost tempted to check with www.snopes.com to see if it's real or not!

Oscars For Everybody!

The Oscar Awards seemed to have been "hand picked" to give everybody something to go home feeling sort-of OK about.

Consider:

Best Picture went to "Crash" which, when announced, brought an audible gasp of shock from the audience of stars. No one expected Crash to win and, guessing from the surprise, most of the attendees appeared to have voted for and expected "Brokeback Mountain" to win. Why didn't it win? Hmmm.

Best Director went to Ang Lee for "Brokeback Mountain" which is almost as good a getting "Best Picture" except without the public numbness that would have ensued had it actually won that final award.

Best Actor went to Philip Seymour Hoffman for his title role in "Capote." This was, perhaps, the most competetive of the major awards this year and Hoffman's performance appears to have been worthy of being chosen as the "Best." It was one of the only awards to go to "Capote."

Best Actress went to Reese Witherspoon for her role as June Carter Cash in "Walk the Line." Reese was almost as much of a surprise winner as "Crash" was for Best Picture. Of all the major movies chosen for major categories "Walk the Line" was undoubtedly the most wholesome, family-oriented, morally-centered film to be nominated. Although Witherspoon was a worthy recipient of her award her role was totally overshadowed in the movie by the brilliant lead role of Johnny Cash played by Joaquin Phoenix (who did not win).

Best Supporting Actor went to George Clooney for his role in "Syriana." Clooney was nominated for four different Oscars and this was the only one he took home. "Good Night and Good Luck" was totally goose-egged.

Best Supporting Actress went to Rachel Weisz for her role in the much-touted "The Constant Gardner."

Spread the wealth. Something for everybody. Nothing too controversial. Nothing too wonderful. Nothing to write home about.

More than "Crash" winning the top award, this year's Oscars will be remembered for being the year the the Best Song award went to Three 6 Mafia for their inane number, "It's Hard Out Here For a Pimp." During the performace of the song at least one of the lyrics (such as they were) was "bleeped." When Jordan "Juicy J" Houston received his award one of his (or was it one of the other Three Mafiosis?) comments was also "bleeped."

Tonight Hip Hop replaced glamour as the Hollywood's cachet, and bling sparkled amidst the tattoos. One could almost hear the voice of Oscar crying out, "I've fallen and I can't get up!"

Jon Stewart can sleep well knowing that the "fizz" in this year's Oscar Awards program would have gone flat whether he had been there to help it along or not.

MONDAY, MARCH 06, 2006

Hawaii Revival--Micronesian Style

Some of the Pastors on Friday evening (I'm the one w/out a tie)

The Micronesian congregation that "nests" in our church facilities held a revival this past week. The congregation is mostly made up of new immigrants from the island of Nama, 40 miles or so from the famous atoll of Chuuk (formerly called "Truk").

Chuukese/Nama pastors flew in from Maui, Oregon, Chuuk and Nama to join the two pastors who serve the Nama community here in Central Oahu. For four nights they sang, praised, prayed and heard inspirational sermons delivered by the pastors.

On Friday evening I attended long enough to sing a few choruses (most were in English) and offer the folks (over 100 were present) a warm welcome from my congregation. Pastor Stanis Philips even gave me a "crash course" on how to say, "I'm glad you are all here this evening" in Chuukese. I spoke the words the way he told me but all I got from all the good people were puzzled looks!

Things really got rolling on Saturday evening with preaching and singing lasting until midnight.

It is good seeing folks so far from home enjoying a big get-together with friends and family and doing so in an atmosphere of joy and thanksgiving in the name of our Lord and Savior Jesus Christ. That sort of worship needs no translation!

Funeral Service at Punchbowl National Cemetery

Every so often I have the privilige of officiating at a memorial inurnment service at the National Cemetery of the Pacific (Punchbowl) in Honolulu, Hawaii. I have written of this before (**here**, **here**, **here** and **here**) but today the weather was especially wonderful and I thought I would include some photographs I took during and after the service.

Today's service was for Ernest Koichi Akiyoshi. Earnest passed away in San Diego over a year ago but I was asked to officiate because he and his wife, had been charter members of my congregation 35 years ago. Earnest had, in fact, been born in Central Oahu and grew up here so this was, for him, a sort of homecoming. His relatively short term of military service had begun in 1948 with the American occupation forces in Germany following the end of World War II.

In any case, the service went well and I enjoyed meeting so many wonderful members of his family. I hope you will enjoy the photos.

The site for the service

The unfolding of the flag

The display of the flag

The presentation of the flag

The inurnment site (click to enlarge). Apparently Ernie loved arare!

I then spent 30 minutes paying my respects to those who had given their lives in service to our country. As you look at each picture please say a prayer of gratitude for the one buried there.

Famed American news correspondant Ernie Pyle, killed in action on Okinawa shortly before the end of WW II

Ellison Onizuka, US astronaut who was born and raised in Hawaii and who died in the explosion of the Space Shuttle Challenger

This one speaks for itself

There are more than 100 of these markers adjacent to the gazebo where the memorial services are held. A deeply moving section of the cemetery.

I counted over 80 sailor "unknowns" from the USS Oklahoma in this one section of the cemetery.

If you have never visited the "Punchbowl Cemetery of the Pacific" be sure to do so . . . after you have visited the USS Arizona Memorial and the USS Missouri!

TUESDAY, MARCH 07, 2006

President Bush Tries His Hand At Cricket!

One under-reported story from President Bush's recent trip to Pakistan was his attempt at playing cricket with several of Pakistan's national team players.

Not only did he hit and bowl (pitch) but he even took one on the shoulder "for the team!" Whatever else "W" might be he is a good sport and coordinated and fit enough to not look like a fool doing it! See the rest of the photos here at BBC News.

Hollywood's Once Proud Record of Military Service

Some uncredited blogger sent Little Green Footballs the following insightful article. It is timely insofar as we just endured the Academy Awards just two nights ago. Read it and weep for what once was.

In contrast to the opinions and feelings of today's Hollywood, the real actors of yesteryear loved the United States.

They had both class and integrity. With the advent of World War II, many of our actors went to fight rather than stand and rant against this country we all love. They gave up their wealth, position, and fame to become service men and women, many as simple "enlisted men".

This group of only 18 men earned over 70 medals in honor of their valor, spanning from Bronze Stars, Silver Stars, Distinguish Service Crosses, Purple Hearts, to one Congressional Medal of Honor.

Most of these brave men have since passed on.

Real Hollywood Heroes

Alec Guinness (Star Wars) operated a British Royal Navy landing craft on D-Day.

James Doohan ("Scotty" on Star Trek) landed in Normandy with the U. S. Army on D-Day.

Donald Pleasance (The Great Escape) really was an R. A. F. pilot who was shot down, held prisoner and tortured by the Germans.

David Niven was a Sandhurst graduate and Lt. Colonel of the British Commandos in Normandy.

James Stewart entered the Army Air Force as a private and worked his way to the rank of Colonel. During World War II, Stewart served as a bomber pilot, his service record crediting him with leading more than 20 missions over Germany, and taking part in hundreds of air strikes during his tour of duty. Stewart earned the Air Medal, the Distinguished Flying Cross, France's Croix de Guerre, and 7 Battle Stars during World War II. In peace time, Stewart continued to be an active member of the Air Force as a reservist, reaching the rank of Brigadier General before retiring in the late 1950s.

Clark Gable (Mega-Movie Star when war broke out): Although he was beyond the draft age at the time the U.S. entered WW II, Clark Gable enlisted as a private in the AAF on Aug. 12, 1942, at Los Angeles. He attended the Officers' Candidate School at Miami Beach, Fla. and graduated as a second lieutenant on Oct. 28, 1942. He then attended aerial gunnery school, and in Feb. 1943 he was assigned to the 351st Bomb Group at Polebrook where he flew operational missions over Europe in B-17s. Capt. Gable returned to the U.S. in Oct. 1943 and was relieved from active duty as a major on Jun. 12, 1944, at his own request, since he was over-age for combat.

Charlton Heston was an Army Air Corps Sergeant in Kodiak.

Ernest Borgnine was a U. S. Navy Gunner's Mate 1935-1945.

Charles Durning was a U. S. Army Ranger at Normandy, earning a Silver Star and awarded the Purple Heart.

Charles Bronson was a tail gunner in the Army Air Corps, more specifically on B-29s in the 20th Air Force out of Guam, Tinian, and Saipan.

George C. Scott was a decorated U. S. Marine.

Eddie Albert (Green Acres, TV) was awarded a Bronze Star for his heroic action as a U. S. Naval officer aiding Marines at the horrific battle on the island of Tarawa in the Pacific, Nov. 1943.

Brian Keith served as a U.S. Marine rear gunner in several actions against the Japanese on Rabal in the Pacific.

Lee Marvin was a U.S. Marine on Saipan during the Marianas campaign when he was wounded, earning the Purple Heart.

John Russell: In 1942, he enlisted in the Marine Corps where he received a battlefield commission and was wounded and highly decorated for valor at Guadalcanal.

Robert Ryan was a U. S. Marine who served with the O.S.S. in Yugoslavia.

Tyrone Power (an established movie star when Pearl Harbor was bombed) joined the U.S. Marines, was a pilot flying supplies into, and wounded Marines out of, Iwo Jima and Okinawa.

Audie Murphy, little 5'5" tall 110-pound guy from Texas who played cowboy parts?

Most Decorated serviceman of WWII and earned: Medal of Honor, Distinguished Service Cross, 2 Silver Star Medals, Legion of Merit, 2 Bronze Star Medals with "V", 2 Purple Hearts, U.S. Army Outstanding Civilian Service Medal, Good Conduct Medal, 2 Distinguished Unit Emblems, American Campaign Medal, European-African-Middle Eastern Campaign Medal with One Silver Star, Four Bronze Service Stars (representing nine campaigns) and one Bronze Arrowhead (representing assault landing at Sicily and Southern France) World War II Victory Medal Army of Occupation Medal with Germany Clasp, Armed Forces Reserve Medal, Combat Infantry Badge, Marksman Badge with Rifle Bar, Expert Badge with Bayonet Bar, French Fourragere in Colors of the Croix de Guerre, French Legion of Honor, Grade of Chevalier, French Croix de Guerre With Silver Star, French Croix de Guerre with Palm, Medal of Liberated France, Belgian Croix de Guerre 1940 Palm.

Bonds Used Steroids? No Surprise Here!

So, it's news today that two sports writers for the San Francisco Chronicle have published a book, "Game of Shadows," that purports to reveal as fact that Bobby Bonds used undetectable "designer" steroids for five years, beginning during the 1998 season.

Color me unimpressed. I concluded this long, long ago and even posted my thoughts on the matter last September.

WEDNESDAY, MARCH 08, 2006

Salon.com Offers Abu Ghraib Photos In Exchange for Their Soul

Captain Ed reports that Salon.com is trying to entice paid subscribers with a solicitation letter that reveals that they are "planning to release hundreds more photos taken inside Abu Ghraib."

Editor Joan Walsh then goes on to write, "I'm contacting you and other former Salon Premium members to make sure these photos reach a large audience. Your expired Premium membership supported our ongoing mission to speak truth to power, but we need your help again now."

Gee, I wonder why they may have let their subscriptions lapse . . . could it be because they had grown tired of all the Abu Ghraib hype that the media used for self-promotion and anti-Bush/anti-war propaganda two years ago? What makes Salon think that even more photos will lure them back? The Bible declares that a "dog returns to its vomit." Perhaps that is what Salon.com has in mind?

In a remarkable demonstration of chutzpah, the letter's final paragraph begins, "We'll do our job with integrity and diligence."

Sure.

In any case, I have written Salon.com the following letter letting then know my thoughts on the matter:

I understand that you are attempting to woo subscribers by planning to publish more photographs of the Abu Ghraib prisoner abuse. Why would anyone want to rehash a news story that is over 2 years old and with all the players either convicted or charged with military crimes?

These photos are not newsworthy. They will in no way shed any more light on the misadventure nor will they inject any new information into the story than we already have.

It appears to me that your proposed project serves no other purpose than to effect emotion . . . all of it negative and pointless . . . except to effectively defame, tar and feather all American troops new serving in Iraq none of whom had anything to do with the photographs or the incident they represent.

On the other hand, the new images will be well received by the Islamist terrorists who will, without any doubt whatsoever, use them to stir up even more anger and hatred against the United States, encourage more volunteer recruits as suicide bombers, successfully prolong the conflict in Iraq and contribute to the death of many more American servicemen and women.

Jesus once asked, "What does it profit someone if they gain the world but lose their soul?"

Please do not "sell your soul" for a few subscriptions. Personally, I would be ashamed to have readers who would be enticed by what you are offering them.

Bipartisan US House Committee Proposes To Halt Dubai Port Deal

The House Appropriations Committee voted 62-2 today in support of legislation that would prohibit the Dubai-owned DP World from acquiring the Administrative contracts for 9 US ports.

President Bush has threatened to veto such legislation if it crosses his desk.

Personally, I hope he does. By doing so he gets the Executive Branch, the State and Commerce Departments off the hook, placing the full responsibility of the cancellation on the US Legislature.

I would guess that if the legislation passes the House and Senate once that there will likely be enough support to overide the veto.

Will this be enough to split the Republican party in Congress? No more than it already is! To be honest, this is one issue over which men and women of good will can differ without necessarily dividing along party lines. In light of the constant party-line divisions over Administration proposals during the past four years it may even be refreshing and helpful for Democrats and some Republicans to find something they can actually agree on.

Will this hurt President Bush politically? I doubt it. He is now a lame duck and his party faithful will only support him if an issue is core to their constituency or will otherwise help get them reelected this coming Fall.

Even so, some of the burbling gibberish usually associated with Democrats has begun to surface amongst the Republicans over this issue (Rep. Jerry Lewis R-CA offers a good example, *"This is a national security issue," said Rep. Jerry Lewis, the chairman of the panel. The California Republican said the legislation would "keep America's ports in American hands,"* a quote thoroughly trashed by both Cpt. Ed and Powerline's John Hinderocker).

There are, of course, legitimate issues of concern over this matter. But to obfuscate them with such uninformed clap-trap does not impress me much at all.

SATURDAY, MARCH 11, 2006

Masterpiece Side-walk Chalk Drawings--2-Dimensional Illusion

Julian Beever is an English sidewalk chalk drawing artist. He is better than good. Check out these photographs of some examples of his work. But be careful you don't trip over the Coca-Cola bottle!

And keep in mind that these drawings disappear very quickly, via rain or simply underfoot!

ht:Michelle Malkin

SUNDAY, MARCH 12, 2006

"Islamic Calvinism" Appears In Turkey and "Calvin" Responds

BBC has an interesting article describing a burst of entrapeneurial success in central Turkey.
A new form of Turkish Islam is emerging here, one which is pro-business and pro-free market, and it's being called Islamic Calvinism.

One of the first to use this description was the former mayor of Kayseri, Sukru Karatepe.

A softly-spoken man who taught sociology before entering politics, Karatape noticed striking similarities between the changes in Kayseri and the famous thesis of the German economist Max Weber, who argued that the strong work ethic of the Protestant movement gave birth to modern capitalism.

"I had read Weber, who'd written about how Calvinists work hard, save money and then reinvest it into business," he says.

"To me, it seemed very similar to what was happening in Kayseri.

"People in Kayseri also don't spend money unnecessarily. They work hard, they pride themselves on saving money. Then they invest it and make more money.

"In fact, in Kayseri, working hard is a form of worship. For them, religion is all about the here and now, not the next life. Making money is a sign of God's approval, and this is also similar to what Weber said about the Calvinists."
On the one hand I am pleased to see my Presbyterian/Calvinist heritage getting such good press withing Turkey these days.

On the other hand I wish that Muslim countries would be more tolerant of the Christians whose work-ethic they are now emulating!

The article does comment that some Muslims are not particularly happy with the phrase "Islamic Calivinism."

The label of Islamic Calvinism, however, has caused a furore in the Turkish press.

Critics say it's a Western conspiracy to Christianise Islam, but others have passionately argued in its favour, holding it up as a model for how Islam and modernity can co-exist.

This, of course, is not surprising. After all, would Christians readily accept a description of something they are doing as (for example) "Christian Iqtisadunaism?" Probably not.

As for the high-profile publicity surrounding the "Islamic Calivinism" in Turkey, I suspect that it has much to do with government "PR" in support of their desire to join the European Economic Union.

The BBC article supports this view with its closing paragraphs:

One of its most prominent defenders has been Turkey's Deputy Prime Minister, Abdullah Gul, himself a native of Kayseri and the son of an entrepreneur.

He sees no contradiction in the term and argues that Turkey can provide a lasting template for a new kind of modern Islam . . .

"This is what modernism means to me, and this is why this new Turkey will ultimately be an asset to the European Union."

I wonder what Calvin hismelf would think of this?

Actually, during Calvin's life, the Muslim Turks had conquered Hungary and had entered Poland, Roumania and even had sent ships to attack Nice, in southern France. There was a genuine threat to what remained of the Holy Roman Empire and "Christendom." It should not surprise us then, that Calvin was concerned over the political situation as well as the spiritual corruption of the religion of Muhammed. As Calvin put it, "As Mahomet says that his Al-Coran is the sovereign wisdom, so says the Pope of his own decrees. For they be the two horns of Antichrist..."

"Calvin," says Australia's Rev. Prof. Dr. Francis Nigel Lee in a paper entitled 'Calvin On Islam,' "was not discouraged to see Islam more and more challenging th4e claims of Christ, and ultimately drawing closer to the the Standarad-bearer of Antichrist's abominable kingomd. For Calvin knew . . . that Christ's Kingdom would nonetheless increase and unltimately triumph over Islam . . .

On the other hand, based on the Old Testament command for Israel to be kind to Egyptians (because some had been hospitable to them), Calvin "argues further, that although the unbaptized Moslem is not (yet) our brother--just as the uncircumcised Egyptian was back then not (yet) the brother of the Israelite--we may never-theless not abhor the Moslem . . . That, then is how Christians should treat Moslems . . . to reciprocate (their) hospitatlity--and, indeed, even to show them precisely spiritual hospitality."

This is, of course, for the purpose of leading those who are God's elect out of the Muslim faith and into faith in the saving Lordship of Jesus Christ and the true worship of the triune God.

Calvin personally did not spend much time worrying about economics . . . at least not of the monetary kind. He was more concerned about the economics of God and of the spiritual nature of humanity.

"Let the Moslem call himself what he chooses," Calvin might say. "Such titles are of no consequence to God or to eternity unless that choice should entail calling himself a baptized disciple of Jesus Christ. That, of course, would matter a great deal!"

Milosevic's Death Surrounded in Mystery

The recent death of former Serbian President Slobodan Milosevic seems destined to provide grist for the rumor mill for many years to come.

According to patholocists involved in his autopsy, the dictator, who was found dead in his "cell" yesterday, was found to have had a combination of drugs in his body that were contraindicated (ie. they were working against each other).

24-hours before he died, Milosevic sent a six-page letter to Russia accusing his captors of "poisoning" him and giving him medications that were harmful to his health.

The UN Tribunal has already "ruled" that the man who they had on trial for 4 years did not die from poisoning. This is surprising since the enquiry has not yet been completed.

There appear to be four scenarios rising to the top of the speculation ladder today:

1. That Milosevic died of natural causes specifically related to his serious heart condition.

2. That he was systematically given inappropriate medications with the intent to cause his death.

3. That he was, of his own choice, refusing to take the prescribed medications as intended and was taking alternative medications instead (or in addition) prescribed by other doctors or medical advisors. The unintended consquences of this self-chosen and defiant medication mess contributed to his death.

4. That the mismanaged medical treatments were intentionally self-inflicted with the intent to commit suicide.

Personally, I feel confident in eliminating #2 from this list. After all, Milosevic and his interminable trial by an international tribunal, had become a dependable cash-cow for the judges, prosecutors, defencers and many, many other personnel involved in the case. His death effectively puts most of them "out of work."

No, for once I think I can let the UN off the hook. If there was any corruption or deceit in this matter it wasn't that these people wanted Milosevic dead, but that they wanted to keep him alive and on trial for their own personal gain.

The man has died. He has already been found guilty by the court of world opinion. The tribunal would have added little or nothing more to this matter.

For the best interest of history, I suggest that the tribunal sentence his dead body to be cremated and the ashes scattered somewhere over the North Sea. This is one person who is not worthy of either a memorial to his life or even a final "resting place."

WEDNESDAY, MARCH 15, 2006

How to Talk Politics and Lead an Adult Sunday School Class At the Same Time

One of our Sunday morning adult small groups has decided to make a list of the most challenging topics they can find and then discuss one of them each week. As pastor, my job will be to provide relevent Biblical truths and, if possible, applicable statements in our PCUSA Book of Confessions and Book of Order. If our General Assembly has taken a position or made a statement on the subject I will try to provide that as well.

The group leader will be responsible for sharing this information and then leading a wide-open discussion on it for the rest of the hour each week. The subjects could result in disagreements and differing conclusions so I was considering how to prepare the group leader for moderating the conversation.

Fortuitously, Hugh Hewitt provided a link to The Dinner Book where I came across a wonderful outline for how to have a productive and civilized political conversation between polarized opposites.

It struck me that this particular approach would work well in any situation, whether political, religious, etc., where disagreement could arise.

The writer, Terry L Paulson, PhD, has this to say,
Free and open political discussions have always helped make America strong. There is a value in facing differences. Good political dialogue becomes the fire that tests the metal of your convictions and the depth of your understanding. You can't truly grasp a truth until you have explained and contested it. Constructive debates that involve strong opinions and heartfelt convictions are not then to be avoided; they are to be harnessed in a way that risks influence without demonizing our adversaries.
I couldn't agree with him more. My prayer is that this Sunday morning small group will generate some of that sort of light and respect instead of the smoke and frustration that can sometimes arise.

In any case, I am copying the article and sending it to the small group's leader to peruse as he prepares for their first hot-topic this coming Sunday.

Take a moment to read the entire article. It is short. Like me, you will wish that the members of the Congress (and Muslims and Christians and other religious leaders) would also read it and take it to heart. One can always dream . . . . !

THURSDAY, MARCH 16, 2006

Battling the Bees

Our church preschool has been under assault by bees for the past three weeks. The honeybees especially seem to like the lanai area behind Room 2. Only one child has gotten stung so far but the bees seem intent on hanging around until they find another "victim."

Today I went out and searched high and low (and even in the park across the street) for either a nest or some other source for the bees. I could not find a thing.

So, as an experiment, I picked up a child's sand strainer and spent 15 minutes swatting bees. I wound up with "confirmed kills" of 51 bees ("confirmed" means I swatted them, found where they fell and stepped on them). There were also 10-15 others that I "hit" but couldn't find afterwards.

In any case, by the time I finished there were more bees buzzing around than before I started swatting them. My guess is that there is a nest somewhere close by (possibly in the ground) that is "swarming" (meaning it has gotten too large and is releasing bees to start another nest). Hopefully the bees will find a better welcome at St. John's Roman Catholic Church down the street and make their new home there. If not, we'll have to hire the bee-seeking equivilent of Sherlock Holmes to track down the source of the bees and eradicate them.

All in all I learned a thing or two about bees today. One thing I learned is that it is not a good idea to wear shorts when swatting bees. I swatted one right onto my leg where he must have landed tail side first. I did manage to pull the stinger out but I have a large red area on my right shin (that still hurts a little) to show for it.

Is a New Al-Qaeda Attack On It's Way?

"Chatter" is up concerning the possibility of one or more al-Qaeda attacks on the United States in the next few days or weeks.

Internet speculation, compiled by the Anchoress here, here and here, is looking at the Sear's Tower in Chicago and this weekend's NASCAR race on March 19 in Atlanta where up to 125,000 people are expected to attend. March 19 would be doubly symbolic, being one day short of the third anniversary of the invasion of Iraq.

Too many Americans have become fat, sassy and deluded into thinking that we are not really vulnerable to a terrorist attack. Small-scale attacks causing light damage and relatively few casualties could be brought off fairly easily, along the lines of Hamas suicide bombers in Israel.

But in the past, al-Qaeda has scorned such amateurish attacks, preferring to go for the massive, well-planned, spectacular assault such as the African embassy bombings, the USS Cole, Bali and 9/11.

If they do manage to pull off another attack it will be a big one. But, if they think it will recreate the panic and crushing emotional devastation of 9/11, they will be very mistaken.

My guess is that the media and Democrats will immediately blame the Bush administration for incompetence in implementing an effective Homeland Security program.

The American people, however, will instinctively be drawn to the stability and single-minded purpose of President Bush.

In the aftermath of another attack the Democrats will shrink and shrivel in size as the public recalls their constant nay-saying and negative criticisms of everyone about everything. This negativity will come back to haunt them and label them as the party that says "No" to every Republican idea without offering even one single positive idea of their own.

When the going gets tough, Americans can be trusted to gravitate towards a rock and away from a waffle.

Al-Qaeda . . . be warned. Another attack will not be good for your health.

Pray, along with me, that these master-minds of terror will falter and their plans come to nothing.

FRIDAY, MARCH 17, 2006

Florida Teachers Caught Cheating Are Fired--But Just Barely

According to AP,

The Miami-Dade County School Board voted 5-4 on Wednesday to fire six teachers and accept resignations from 26 others.

The teachers had all purchased continuing education credits from a former teacher who operated a transcript scam. That teacher has plead guilty and has been sentenced to two years in prison.

Florida requires credentialed teachers to complete 6 credit units of continuing education every five years. These units sustain their credentialed status and, in some cases, qualify their for pay increases.

Ohio's Oberlin College has voided 10,000 credits received 657 teachers who supposedly earned them through the scam program that had contracted with the College.

The biggest surprise in this story is that the Dade County School Board's vote was not unanimous. The decision to fire the teachers only passed by a vote of 5-4.

The strongest argument against the firings came from parents and educators who said that the terminations would cause discontinuity in the student's education. I suspect that a likely difficulty in finding qualified replacements for them was also a factor.

Personally, I support the firings. What message does it send to young students if teachers caught cheating on their own education were allowed to continue teaching and being paid for it?

Perhaps those teachers who gained financially by receiving pay raises for their fake credits should be forced to pay that money back to the school district and be fined for contractual fraud in addition!

The best teachers are not only good teachers but good role models for their students. A teacher who teaches Social Science well but also tells her students that it's OK to smoke pot has disqualified themselves from the privilege of working with young students in the classroom.

Teachers who cheat on their own education have committed an even greater crime: They have undermined the integrity of the very vocation that they were hired to represent.

Hopefully these teachers' students will learn a valuable lesson from all of this. Perhaps they will learn that "cheaters never prosper." Perhaps they will also be reminded that the very purpose of education is to actually learn something.

The four Dade County Board Members who voted "No" should be required to write, "Cheaters never prosper" on the blackboard 100 times each.

SATURDAY, MARCH 18, 2006

Two Reasons Why Palestine Should Be Left For the Wolves

In reference to this posting's title, I'm not suggesting that the world should turn their back on the West Bank and Gaza Palestinians . . . at least not completely. But there are many reasons to do so.

Lately, the fact that Hamas has won the recent election and has taken over governing the Palestinian Authority has provided the best reason. Why should the democratic West provide financial support for a government (and its people) who have perpetuated and engaged in suicide bombings of civilians in Israel and who have publicly sworn that their first *raison d'etre* is to kill Jews, destroy Israel as a nation and reclaim that land for the Palestinian people?

Aside from having pity on the much abused and manipulated Palestinian people in the West Bank and Gaza (and I do not necessarily mean "abused and manipulated" by the Israelis) there is no rational reason whatsoever for giving this government even one American tax dollar of support.

But I am writing about a different reason for leaving Palestine to the wolves. And this reason begins with the premise that the wolves have already taken the would-be-country over.

As I have written many times before (see here, here, here, here, here, here, here, here, here, here and here) the Palestinian people and those who govern them have spent hundreds of millions of dollars behaving in ways that have brought themselves into utter ruin. Had money been invested in creating a functional nation of Palestine we would have such a nation today. It would be a prosperous nation. A nation that would have taken advantage of its greatest resource: the Palestinian people.

If people had been taught to build rather than to destroy; to live rather than to die; to work hard rather than to complain about everyone else; to accept both blame and responsibility rather than to blame Israel and the rest of the world for their troubles; Palestine would be a place where people would want to live. A place where people would want to immigrate to rather than emigrate from. A place where people would want to invest money instead of siphoning it off into Swiss bank accounts.

There would be industry. There would be vast areas under cultivation with sophisticated irrigation systems. There would be abundant and profitable trade with Israel and with Jordan, with Syria, Iraq, Egypt, Lebanon and Saudi Arabia. There would be a thriving tourist industry with hotels and beautifully restored treasures from antiquity, including precious sites of pilgrimage for Jews, Christians and Muslims. There would be paved roads, electricity and sanitation facilities.

Quality education for children would be mandatory as it is in Jordan and Israel. The education system would prepare children for lives of responsibility and service to others. The historic colleges and universities would be revived into places of open dialogue and discussion of all sides of all issues. Scholars and statesmen/women would come from around that world to speak to international issues which would involve Palestine. Issues such as economics and trade, medical care, politics, religion and the basic rights of all people would be openly and fairly covered in a free and uncensored press.

Treaties and other agreements with a recognized Israel would provide land access from the West Bank to Gaza and world nations would either loan or give money for the construction of a world class seaport along the Gaza Coast as well as a free and open international airport.

BUT . . . instead of this, the people of Palestine have been duped and betrayed by their so-called "leaders" into trading all of this away for poverty, conflict, bloodshed, corruption, lawlessness, hopelessness, constant grieving and a culture of death.

It appears that the people of the Palestinian territories have decided that anything that has any positive benefit for them must be destroyed.

Take, for example, the photograph featured at the beginning of this post. It is from msnbc's photos of the week, March 9-16. It shows a Palestinian youth helping to burn down a British council office in Gaza on March 14. Why would driving out the Americans, the British and other foreign representatives be a good thing for the Palestinians? The answer is, of course, that driving them out by behavior such as this is a very bad thing for the Palestinians. So, of course, that is exactly what they do . . . over and over again *ad nauseum*.

Two phrases come to mind that seem to capture the deranged behavior of these unfortunate people:

Cutting off your nose to spite your face;

and

Shooting yourself in the foot and boasting that you hit your target.
There are other, less complimentary images that could also represent this self-destructive mentality but I will leave these to your own imagination.

Is there any sense of justice in their complaint over the existence of Israel? Yes, of course there is. It is an issue worthy of discussion and debate. It is worthy of pursuing a solution and a resolution, a compromise and a settlement.

But for the Palestinian people, the issue is "all or nothing." Either Israel goes away for good or . . . or . . . the Palestinian people will suffer increasing hardships and social/cultural degeneration for themselves and their posterity.

It is the Palestinian people who have decided on this "all or nothing" scenario. They appear to be willing to lose everything rather than to accept the existence of Israel as a neighbor nation.

With Hamas now in control it seems to me to be politically reasonable to let them reap what they have sown. They have freely chosen a destiny filled with despair, grief, bitterness, and hopelessness.

It is their choice. Perhaps we should let them live with the consequences of that choice.

It deeply grieves my own heart to see how far these honorable and naturally hospitable people have fallen.

In the end it will up to the Palestinian people to decide whether they will forever blame Israel for their problems or whether they will let Israel exist and turn their energy towards creating a prosperous and glorious nation for themselves.

Sadly, and ironically, their desire to destroy Israel has manifested itself in the destruction of themselves.

And the wolves seem to be quite happy with the arrangement.

SUNDAY, MARCH 19, 2006

Afghanistan--Where Becoming a Christian Can Be (Very) Bad For Your Health

The AP story is neatly summed up in the first paragraph:

An Afghan man who allegedly converted from Islam to Christianity is being prosecuted in a Kabul court and could be sentenced to death, a judge said Sunday.

Abdul Rahman was turned in by his family last month. He has confessed to have become a Christian while working in Pakistan 16 years ago and says he has no intention of returning to the Muslim faith (read my earlier post on this subject here).

The end of the story carries an interesting statistic, noting that 99% of Afghanistan's population is Muslim with a small percentage of Hindus mixed in.

The charges against Rahman seem to offer some explanation as to why virtually everyone in Afghanistan is Muslim. You see, if one of them became something else, they would be killed and, as a result, would not show up in the statistics.

Pray for Abdul Rahman. Pray that his trial judge will be lenient in his sentencing and spare him the death penalty.

And, by the way, someone should write to the Afghani legislature and remind them that Article 18 of the International Declaration of Human Rights (adopted by the United Nations on December 10, 1948) reads as follows:

Article 18

Everyone has the right to freedom of thought, conscience and religion; this right includes freedom to change his religion or belief, and freedom, either alone or in community with others and in public or private, to manifest his religion or belief in teaching, practice, worship and observance.

Note as well that Rahman did not publicly reveal himself to be a Christian. One can only wonder how many thousands, ten thousands or even hundreds of thousands of similar "Muslims" are secretly Christian converts, living double lives out of fear for themselves and their families.

We may not know . . . but God does.

Pray for them, too.

Iran Has Back-Up Plans In Case Nuclear Option Fails

If Iran fails in its quest to acquire nuclear weaponry they have at least two back-up plans in their hip pocket.

The first is, of course, the tens of thousands of volunteer suicide bombers that have been recruited and trained to spread terror around the world should that ever be deemed necessary.

Less known, perhaps, are the members of Iran's women's paramilitary units.

The photo above, gleaned from this week's BBC photo gallery, shows chador-clad paramilitary women in Tehran boning up on their rifle skills.

I should think that there must be some religious concession that permits them to remove the veil before taking aim. Killing infidels as part of jihad, apparently, seems to be one of the allowed exceptions.

This photo from 1986 shows Iranian women practicing for the police force.

Here are some recent graduates from the Tehran Police Academy via AP (March 11, 2006).

2004 women paramilitary trainees do everything the men do (including rappelling down buildings) but with more challenging clothing.

Lastly, just in case you are not concerned, consider the fact that the only Iranian woman to participate in the Athens Olympics was Nassin Hassan Pour, entered in the pistol-shooting events!

MONDAY, MARCH 20, 2006

My Reply to One Who Has Called Me "Racist" and "Odious"

If you read the comment I received in the previous post you will find the words of someone who has taken deep offense from what I have written concerning the Palestinian Authority, the Palestinian people and the ongoing conflict over the existance of Israel.

This person, who goes by the name Umkahlil, has written an emotional and angry response to another recent post of mine which I entitled, "Why Palestine Should Be Left To the Wolves."

In response to her posting I have written and posted a comment of my own.

By following the link to her blogsite you can read what she wrote about me.

What follows is the comment by which I responded to her.

As always, read all that you can and make up your own mind.

Umkahlil, I am the "debased Zionist schill" the "so-called 'man of God'" and "hack preacher" who posted the "Why Palestine Should Be Left For the Wolves." I am the one who wrote,

"In reference to this posting's title, I'M NOT SUGGESTING THAT THE WORLD SHOULD TURN THEIR BACK ON THE WEST BANK AND GAZA PALESTINIANS . . . at least not completely. But there are many reasons to do so."

I am the one who wrote,

"Is there any sense of justice in (the Palestinian's) complaint over the existence of Israel? Yes, of course there is. It is an issue worthy of discussion and debate. It is worthy of pursuing a solution and a resolution, a compromise and a settlement."

I am the one who wrote,

"It deeply grieves my own heart to see how far these honorable and naturally hospitable people have fallen.

In the end it will up to the Palestinian people to decide whether they will forever blame Israel for their problems or whether they will let Israel exist and turn their energy towards creating a prosperous and glorious nation for themselves.

"Sadly, and ironically, their desire to destroy Israel has manifested itself in the destruction of themselves."

I am the one who believes that the 1948 Palestinian-Israeli War still continues today.

I am the one who believes that Israel's original desire was to live peaceably with her neighbors.

I am the one who believes that, after declaring its independence and establishing itself as a recognized nation, Israel made no effort to expand its borders beyond those proposed by the United Nations.

I am the one who believes that, although it coveted Jerusalem and desired to establish that city as its capital, Israel made no attempt to do so and cooperated with the international divisions and administrations of that city for 20 years.

I am the one who believes that, in an expanded continuation of the 1948 war, Israel was attacked in 1968 and 1973 by combined military forces representing the countries of Egypt, Syria and Jordan, supported by the active participation of many Palestinians, many of whom had been displaced from the land now occupied by the nation of Israel.

I am the one who believes that these two wars were initiated with the clear aim of defeating and destroying the nation of Israel and replacing it with a non-Jewish state dominated by Palestinian Arab Muslims (and a smaller share of Palestinian Christians); a state that would have been allied with the same Middle East Arab nations that attacked Israel.

I am the one who believes that Israel expanded and enlarged its borders (including Jerusalem) in response to these attacks upon its national existance.

I am the one who believes that Israel occupied the "West Bank" and Gaza as a defensive measure to protect itself from those nations and peoples who wished to see it destroyed.

I am the one who believes that Jordan was then attacked by Palestinians under the guidance and leadership of the PLO and Yassir Arafat with the intention of overthrowing the monarchy and establishing a national identity for the Palestinian people.

I am the one who believes that after being defeated by Jordan the more militant Palestinians fled into Lebanon where, with the tacit support of Syria, they shared in fomenting the civil war that destroyed Lebanon as an independent nation.

I am the one who believes that, with northern Lebanon and the Bekaa Valley under the firm control of Syria, the displaced militant Palestinians, forced out of Jordan and the West Bank by both Jordan and Israel, used that location to continue to attack Israel along its northern border.

I am the one who believes that, once again in a defensive response to these attacks, Israel entered southern Lebanon and attempted to occupy, control and destroy those who were seeking its annihilation.

I am the one who believes that there was once a time when Israel would have been content to return to its original borders in exchange for an international guarantee of peace and security.

I am the one who believes that Israel no longer believes that, in the forseeable future, there is any real likelihood of either Fatah or Hamas (as elected representatives of the Palistinian Authority) pursuing a negotiated peace settlement that would affirm, accept and recognize Israel as a sovereign nation.

I am the one who believes that a state of war exists between Israel and the recognized leaders of the Palestinian Authority and that those under their authority must also be counted as citizens of a "nation" at war.

I am the one who believes that the casualties and suffering you have ennumerated so graphically in your own posting are casualties of war . . . as are those Israelis who have also suffered and died in the ongoing exchange of violence.

I am the one who believes that Israel has not always acted wisely or well in its response to the incessant attacks which have been directed against it; including its decision to build "permanent" settlements in Gaza, the West Bank and in East Jerusalem.

I am the one who believes that the Palestinian people in the West Bank and Gaza have suffered terribly as a result of this ongoing conflict.

I am the one who believes that this suffering is a direct result of the conscious and intentional decision of Palestinian leaders to refuse to recognize the state of Israel and to perpetuate the state of war with the expressed aim of destroying Israel.

I am the one who does not believe that a nation should be condemned for failing to extend friendship, medical services, economic trade and financial support to a neighbor nation which has openly declared and continues to wage war against it.

I am the one who believes that a nation should not be condemned for building a "security fence/wall" in an effort to protect itself against those who are seeking to destroy it...even if that barrier is built on land claimed, but not controlled, by its enemy.

I sm the one who believes that "peace" will only come when either Israel is destroyed and swept away as a nation or when Israel is accepted as a nation by a Palestinian people who will build their own nation alongside in peaceful cooperation and coexistance with Israel.

With the second scenario I can envision a bright and prosperous future for the Palestinian people.

With the first scenario I can envision only continued suffering, despair, destruction and death for the people of Palestine.

Both scenarios embrace some measure of injustice. Neither scenario is completely satisfying from the perspecive of history, religion, international law or personal and national aspiration.

Yet one path has the potential to lead towards life and hope for both nations.

The other path will bring only more suffering and death.

I am the one who wishes that there was another, better, more just and satisfactory option for peace. But I, along with the rest of a concerned world, has yet to find it.

In light of this unsolvable dilemma, I am the one who believes that the suffering of the Palestinian people remains a direct result of their choice, their decision, to continue their war against Israel.

I am the one who seeks neither the destruction of Israel nor the suffering of the Palestinian people.

I am the one who believes that, at the present moment in history, to support the Palestinian Authority and Palestinian people who elected them is to support them in their efforts to destroy the nation of Israel.

My heart is broken. I am torn. I yearn for peace and justice for all sides in this conflict.

If this makes me a "racist" in your eyes then I will not attempt to argue that point with you.

If this makes me "odious" in your eyes then I will not attempt to argue that point with you either.

In the biblical book of Ezekiel 18:32 I read, "I take no pleasure in the death of anyone, declares the Sovereign LORD."

With this I agree.

With the Christian writer, John Donne, I affirm that "every man's death diminishes me." Whether the one who suffers or dies is Jewish, Muslim or Christian; Palestinian or Israeli, it is all one and the same to me. I say this because I agree with John Donne's conclusion, "Do not ask for whom the bell tolls; it tolls for thee."

Call me what you will. I wish you no ill will. I shall not label you or call you any name that you do not wish to be called. And yet I stand by my use of the word "wolves;" acknowledging that there are wolves in Palestine, in Israel, in Germany and in the United States as well.

On occasion, Israel has elected "wolves" to represent them in their government. It is my belief that, in the last election, the people of Palestine did so as well.

While I respect the right of the Palestinian people to choose who they wish to rule over them, it does not logically follow that I must endorse and support their choice.

Our actions have consequences for which we must learn to take responsibility.

WEDNESDAY, MARCH 22, 2006

Palestinian Christians Fleeing What? Israeli Occupation or Muslim Persecution?

This post's title asks a question that I cannot answer with any confidence. I have read many different versions of this but always written by someone who was Pro-Palestinian Authority or Pro-Israel.

I finally found an on-line article that, while biased, does make an interesting comparison between two Palestinian Christian cousins who take polar-opposite positions on this subject.

You can read it here. It will be well worth your while.

By the way, if you are a Palestinian Christian still living in the Middle East or have emigrated to another region of the world, please leave a comment stating your own personal experience or opinion.

The ideological fog is almost too thick for me to see where the reality is!

While I am confident that Israel's initial displacement of Palestinians in the 1948 "catastrophy" and their subsequent (beginning in 1967) occupation of the West Bank and Gaza has caused great despair and suffering among the Palestinian Christians, my own bias is inclined towards the opinion that the rising power and influence of Islamist fundamentalism has, in recent years, made life almost unbearable for those Palestinian Christians who remain and have not yet been converted to Islam. (I have previously linked to an article that supports my bias. You can find it here).

I am open to any non-ideological information on this subject. Thank you.

Kauai's Case of the Missing Spillway

Today's Honolulu Advertiser carried another follow-up story about last week's disaster on the neighbor island of Kauai when heavy rains caused a collapse of a 100-year old irrigation reservoir. The ensuing flood swept away seven known people. So far only four bodies have been recovered.

Today's story is headlined, "Dam safety fixture disputed--Inspectors can't find spillway but owners say it's still there."

Well, a spillway is a spillway . . . and either it is there or it isn't and in either case it is not exactly a "safety fixture" but a necessary part of any dam. (A dam without a spillway is like a car without brakes).

In any case, the owners say the spillway is buried under the collapsed earthen dam.

Older neighborhood residents say they remember seeing the spillway back in the 1980's and '90's. Other folks say that the spillway had been backfilled by the owners and was no longer functional.

As you can see the "case of the missing spillway" could involve a whole lot of liability.

The owner's lawyer is quoted as saying, "Our inspection shows that the spillway is still there and intact."

According to the Advertiser story,
Numerous state and federal officials said they have carefully inspected the site and found no spillway. The Hawaii state adujant general said, "We couldn't find a spillway." Ray Kong, and engineer with the Army Corps of Engineers said, We were surprised not to find (a spillway). We looked."
I have heard that "justice is blind" but I had never taken that phrase literally before now.

I guess in the end it will be a "he-said-she-said" case and a jury will have to decide which story they actually believe!

Then again, I suppose the owner's lawyer could simply be asked to point out the spillway to somebody without a vested interest in the case.

Sure.

Military Deaths Under "G. W." Lower Than Under. . . JIMMY CARTER!

Sometimes statistics don't lie!

Consider this little gem from Proud Kiffer:

On the third anniversary of the Iraq war, the MSM keeps bombarding us with stories and statistics trying to compare this war to the carnage in Vietnam, trying to make us think that US soldiers are dying at an alarming number due to Bush's failures.

While every lost serviceman and servicewoman is certainly tragic and should be mourned, the actual statistics tell quite a different tale from the MSM and Democratic doom-and-gloom outlook. Comparing the numbers of lost US military personnel to past years, and past presidential terms, may even be a shock to supporters of the war.

Take a look at the actual US Military Casualty figures since 1980. If you do the math, you will find quite a few surprises. First of all, let's compare numbers of US Military personnel that died during the first term of the last four presidents.

George W. Bush 5187 (2001-2004)
Bill Clinton 4302 (1993-1996)
George H.W. Bush 6223 (1989-1992)
Ronald Reagan 9163 (1981-1984)

Even during the (per MSM) utopic peacetime of Bill Clinton's term, we lost 4302 service personnel. H.W. Bush and Reagan actually lost significantly more personnel while never fighting an extensive war, much less a simultaneous war in two theaters (Iraq and Afghanistan). Even the dovish Carter lost more people during his last year in office, in 1980 lost 2392, than W. has lost in any single year of his presidency. (2005 figures are not available but I would wager the numbers would be slightly higher than 2004.)

In 2004, more soldiers died outside of Iraq and Afghanistan than died inside these two war zones (900 in these zones, 987 outside these zones). The reason is that there are usually a fair number that die every year in training accidents, as well as a small number of illness and suicide. Yet the MSM would make you think that US soldiers are dying at a high number in these zones, and at a significantly higher number than in past years or under past presidents. This is all simply outright lies and distortion.
ht:lgf

SUNDAY, MARCH 26, 2006

Dueling Church Signs

My only regret in this Baptist/Catholic church sign pseudo-dialogue is that the Presbyterians didn't even get a mention!

Visit the clever exchange at wuzzadem.

PS. If you are left wondering what PWN3D means, according to the comments section, *"Pwn3d" is 733t haXXor, excuse me, elite hacker-speak. It means "owned", as in "you got owned", meaning, "you lost the argument and looked like a fool".*

TUESDAY, MARCH 28, 2006

Candles In the Night

Last night, around 9:00 pm, the electricity went out in most of Mililani. My wonderful wife, Daughter #3 and I grabbed some flashlights, found some candles and lit them. Our living room looked like a religious shrine with candles, large and small, flickering in the darkness.

Although the power was out for over three hours I still managed to take a hot shower and finish a Sudoku puzzle before falling asleep for the night. The last one up blew out the candles.

No harm was done. We were not inconvenienced in any real way. And the candlelight was beautiful.

For a short time we were transported back into a time before electricity; a time without light bulbs, television, computers and DVDs. Things may not have been simpler back then but time was not as rushed and the world was quieter, calmer and the stars could be seen in their full night-time glory.

And, as I said, the candles were beautiful.

WEDNESDAY, MARCH 29, 2006

Hugh Hewitt & Michael Ware: A Great Interview

There is little doubt that Hugh Hewitt is one of the best interviewers around. There are times when he talks far more than the one being interviewed. There are times when he acts more like a prosecuting attorney on a cross-examination than an interviewer. But his recent interview with Australian/Time magazine journalist Michael Ware was one of the best I have ever heard broadcast on his "Hugh Hewitt Show."

Ware, who has covered every angle on the Iraqi war during the past three years, was articulate and, for the most part, clear and straightforward in his response to Hugh's questions.

During the interview Hugh raised legitimate concerns about Ware's repeated close contacts with insurgents and jihadis. Does the threat of reprisal compromise Ware's reporting?
"(O)ne has to be careful that, as the Islamic army of Iraq reminded just last week on Al Jazeera, the insurgent groups study very closely everything that we hear, say and write. And given that we're within their grasp, one always must be diplomatic..."

"I mean," he added, "one has to be careful about how you couch things, but it doesn't stop you reporting the facts."
The interview made it clear that Ware's reporting must, of necessity, be shaped (if not actually compromised) by matters of personal safety as he decides what he will say and how he will say it. This is particularly true in his coverage of the insurgents who, as he admits, would have no hesitation in killing him if he overstepped that fine line of "diplomacy" in his reporting.

Ware did, on occasion, give questionable responses to reasonable questions.

He would not, for example, say one way or the other whether the Soviet Union was better off under Stalin or Khrushchev. Given that Hugh was trying to make a parallel between Iraq under Saddam Hussein and Iraq today it is not surprising that Ware would try to avoid getting mixed up the in the generalities and assumptions involved in embracing that parallel outright. Still, Ware could have condemned Stalin while declining to endorse the particular parallel that Hugh was trying to make.

Despite a few dodgy responses such as this, it is virtually impossible, given Ware's coverage of all sides of the war in Iraq, not to admire and respect him as both an individual and a journalist. He is clearly not one of the "balcony watcher" journalists we have heard so much about lately.

If Hugh set out to discredit Ware he was not successful, at least not in this interview.

If, on the other hand, Hugh's intention was to provide insight into the life, work and thoughts of a complex and influential journalist while raising important questions concerning the moral complexities and compromises involved in Ware's style of war-zone journalism, then this may have been the most successful interview Hugh has ever done.

In the end, the big question of the interview was never clearly settled one way or the other. The following statement by Hugh sums up that question:

I'm really fascinated by the question of whether or not it's ever good journalism to consort with the enemy in search of interesting stories. And there's not denying, Michael, where you

get scoops. It's fascinating to read. You've got a great deal of courage, of physical courage, in doing this. So no one's denying that. I'm just wondering whether or not there's a line that you have in your mind reconciled yourself to crossing not once, but scores and scores of times, to report on the enemy, and whether or not that's a good thing.
Hopefully this subject will be revisited again and again in future interviews with Michael Ware and others who have chosen to cross back and forth enemy lines in pursuit of information, insight and a "good" story.

FRIDAY, MARCH 31, 2006

You Just Gotta Watch This!

Juggling as you have never seen juggling before! A *tour de force* without sound. *With* sound this video is breath-taking, heart-stopping and reality-suspending. I've watched this video three times and still can't believe that Chris Bliss actually did this on stage in front of a live audience with spotlights shining in his eyes. Wow. Wow. And . . . Wow!

SATURDAY, APRIL 01, 2006

My Solution to the Illegal Immigration Crisis

I've already advocated a border wall ("Call it a 'Welcome Wall'")between Mexico and the United States. Not a solid wall, mind you, but one with open doors for those who are willing to go through them legally.

But what about the 11-12 million folks who are already here illegally?

Here is what I would suggest for legislation.

1. First, before anything here suggested becomes law, secure the border.

2. Require every person in the United States illegally to register with the Immigration Service within two years.

3. Registering would involve applying for either a visa or "green card" depending on the person's circumstances.

4. Upon registering/application each person would receive a "Temporary US Guest Visitor" card authorizing them to remain in the United States until their application is processed.

5. Those with legal papers providing proof of identity, permanent address in the United States, references from US. citizens and a legal birth certificate will be eligible to receive a "green card" or a visa, giving them legal residency in the the United States that can lead to citizenship.

6. Those without such identifying papers will be eligible to receive a "Guest Worker" card good for two years. At the end of two years the person can either reapply for a "green card" or revert to an illegal status. If the application is rejected the individual must leave the United States for a period of six months after which they can reapply for either a visa, "green card" or a new "Guest Worker" card (good for two years) and re-enter the United States.

7. Two years after this program begins, all unregistered persons remaining in the United Stated illegally will be guilty of a Class 1 misdemeanor and subject to imprisonment and/or deportation.

8. Anyone, whether registered or unregistered, found in possession of either forged or fraudulent legal documents will be guilty of a felony and subject to imprisonment and/or deportation with no right of return.

9. Any crime committed by an unregistered person will be subject to prosecution for the crime at a level one step higher than someone who is in this country legally. (ie. a Class 2 misdemeanors offense would be prosecuted as a Class 1 misdemeanor and a Class 1 misdemeanor offense would be prosecuted as a Class 6 felony, etc.)

10. Children must show proof of legal residency before being enrolled in public schools as must everyone seeking medical care in hospital emergency rooms. Medical services will be provided to all regardless but those without proper identification must be reported to law enforcement officials.

11. Children born to unregistered parents in the United States would NOT qualify as natural-born citizens of the United States (this might require tinkering with the 14th Amendment to the US Constitution).

*11. Employers hiring unregistered persons must pay them 20% *more* than what they pay legally resident employees. (This would lead them to hire legal workers before hiring illegal ones). Employers found in violation of this rule would be liable to a minimum fine of either one year's full-time pay per employee or $15,000 whichever is higher. (*optional suggestion)

The entire point of this would be to turn these folks into legal residents of the United States, giving them every chance to become full citizens through the usual, legal means given to every other immigrant.

Those willing to register would be welcomed as contributing members of American society.

Those unwilling to legally register for whatever reason would be *persona non grata* by their own choice. Those with criminal records (Class 1 misdemeanors and above) while living in this country illegally would be ineligible for being approved for either a "green card" or a "Guest Worker" card.

Is this a form of amnesty? Yes. But with a positive purpose and an incentive to register.

Is this manageable? Not without a great investment in our Immigration budget and staff. Fully-staffed regional registration offices would need to be set up throughout the United States so as to be accessible for those registering.

Powerful new computer technology would be needed for fast-tracking these applications and for cross-checking criminal records, credit violations and terrorist connections.

This program would be offered only for two years, beginning not less than three months or more than six months *after* the Mexican-American border has been declared "secure." Only those who can prove residency in the United States *prior* to the securing of the Mexican-American border (whenever that takes place) would be eligible for the registration program.

Comments that point out any large matters overlooked will be welcomed.

THURSDAY, APRIL 06, 2006

The Gospel of Judas--What's All the Hype & Fuss About?

My daughter in LA sent me a news link concerning a translation of the ancient Gnostic Christian writing called the "Gospel of Judas" that was rediscovered in 1970. Here is what I emailed back to her:

April 6, 2006
Re: The Gospel of Judas

(Daughter #1), thanks for forwarding the link to the article regarding the "Gospel of Judas." I first heard it referred to on the radio this afternoon but I guess the story was widely reported on Tuesday. There are many, many early Christian writings that we know once existed but have disappeared (sometimes literally) into the sands of time. Not all were "burned" as heretical books although many manuscript copies undoubtedly were destroyed by zealous believers. One of the earliest post-scriptural Christian documents from the 2nd Century, The Shepherd of Hermas, was only rediscovered early in the last century (I have the text in my office). If even well-known orthodox documents have disappeared and been lost over the centuries it should not be surprising that "heretical" texts, such as the gnostic Gospel of Judas also disappeared. I do not expect to be surprised by anything in this document. I suspect that its contents will be very predicable, reflecting a Greco-Roman "Mystery Cult" "Gnostic" revision of the four historic Gospels that were written by or directly linked to those who actually knew Jesus as his disciples.

This "new" (actually simply recovered) gospel will shed light on the complex diversity of early Christianity and, perhaps, answer some long unanswered questions concerning the actual contents of this document. It is doubtful that very many people will be "inspired" by what it says and be lead away from the truth of the Gospel that has been affirmed as canon by the Christian Church for over 2,000 years.

People like Elaine Pagels actually make their living off of writing and publishing and sensationalizing these things (like the Gospel of Thomas). There is nothing new. Only a new shred of history that arrives at a perfect time to hype and fan even more interest in the upcoming release of "The DaVinci Code" in a theater near you!

In many ways the early Church was much as it is today, filled with diverse opinions about the meaning of scripture and doctrine and splintered into competing cultic factions not unlike today's Mormons, Christian Science, Jehovah's Witnesses, Unification Church, Jim Jones, David Koresh and, of course, Benny Hinn!

No one would consider any of these to be threatening the integrity of the Christian faith as we know it. And writings such as the Gospel of Judas did not really threaten the ancient church either.

The major points of disagreement in the first centuries of the Christian faith were not over such fringe beliefs as represented by the Judas or Thomas gospels. The disagreements mostly concerned interpretation of the books that are firmly fixed as our New Testament today; in particular "In what way do we understand the nature of a triune God, Father, Son and Holy Spirit" and "In what way do we understand the nature of the incarnate Son of God, Jesus Christ."

After nearly 100 years of debate the final conclusions on these matters were incorporated into the "Nicene Creed" which has, for some 1600 years, been considered the true measure of the Christian orthodox faith for Roman Catholics, Protestants and Eastern Orthodox believers.

My only concern over the Judas gospel is that there are far too many vulnerable folks who may be led astray by all the hype. This very situation was described in I Timothy 4:3,

For the time will come when men will not put up with sound doctrine. Instead, to suit their own desires, they will gather around them a great number of teachers to say what their itching ears want to hear.

And also described by I Peter 2:1-3,

But there were also false prophets among the people, just as there will be false teachers among you. They will secretly introduce destructive heresies, even denying the sovereign Lord who bought them—bringing swift destruction on themselves. Many will follow their shameful ways and will bring the way of truth into disrepute. In their greed these teachers will exploit you with stories they have made up. Their condemnation has long been hanging over them, and their destruction has not been sleeping.

And by Ephesians 4:14,

. . . we will no longer be infants, tossed back and forth by the waves, and blown here and there by every wind of teaching and by the cunning and craftiness of men in their deceitful scheming.

Although these canonical New Testament letters were written nearly 100 to 200 years before the so-called "Gnostic" writings we are seeing being "resurrected" today, the New Testament writers had these very teachings in mind. For Greek "Gnosticism" existed long before the Christian faith arrived. It is not, therefore, that the early Christians were "Gnostic," it was that the "Gnostics" took the outline of the Christian faith and reshaped it according to their own pre-Christian spirituality!

Where "Gnostic" spirituality claimed that the flesh was corrupt and only "spirit" is pure, the Christian gospel affirms the goodness of the physical world, reflecting and revealing the goodness and love of God the Creator of all things.

Where "Gnostic" spirituality claimed to have "hidden" and "secret" knowledge (the word "knowledge" is derived from the Greek word "gnosis" by the way) the Christian gospel held nothing back, revealing everything that could be recalled about Jesus, his miracles, teachings, crucifixion, death, resurrection and ascension.

A safe rule of thumb is that, if there are secrets, then it isn't Christian. (In fact the only time the New Testament talks about "mysteries" is when the writers are discussing *former* mysteries that have now been revealed to us, not by spiritual revelation, but through the historical person of Jesus Christ.

I John 1:1-4 addresses all of these concerns when we read

That which was from the beginning, which we have heard, which we have seen with our eyes, which we have looked at and our hands have touched—this we proclaim concerning the Word of life. The life appeared; we have seen it and testify to it, and we proclaim to you the eternal life, which was with the Father and has appeared to us. We proclaim to you what we have seen and heard, so that you also may have fellowship with us. And our fellowship is with the Father and with his Son, Jesus Christ. We write this to make our joy complete.

As Ecclesiastes 1:9 tells us,

What has been will be again, what has been done will be done again; there is nothing new under the sun.

While it may be a curious and valuable historic relic from the past, the Gospel of Judas is, in the end, just the "same old, same old." Been there. Done that. "Nothing new."

In any case, thanks for the link.

Love and Aloha, Dad

Update: For more thorough commentary on "The Gospel of Judas" by Christians who have taken a bit more time to articulate their thoughts I urge you to click on some of the following links, beginning with the one by Mark Roberts. You will note that we are all saying more or less the same thing in different ways:

http://markdaniels.blogspot.com/2006/04/what-about-gospel-of-judas-first-brief.html

http://www.donaldsensing.com/index.php/2006/04/07/gospel-of-judas-a-yawner.html

http://martinmusings.blogspot.com/2006/04/gnostic-gospel-of-judas-resurfaces.html

SATURDAY, APRIL 08, 2006

Quote of the Week: "Whack-a-Mole" Ham

In an *April 5 post* at Hugh Hewitt's site, Mary Katherine Ham spoke about political campaign reform proposals moving through the Congress. Without any apparent embarrassment whatsoever, she faced the fickle-metaphor-of-Fate face-on and came up with the following sentence:

The money will just pop up again through some other loophole and both Dems and Republicans will be stuck playing a perpetual game of "Loophole Whack-A-Mole" at the Chucky Cheese of Failed Campaign Finance Reforms.

For her remarkable accomplishment we award Ms. Ham the B of P "Quote of the Week."

MONDAY, APRIL 10, 2006

Donating Blood With a CMV-Negative Sub-Factor

I have donated blood since I was in college. Since moving to Hawaii 13 years ago, however, I have often received a phone call from the Honolulu Blood Bank asking me to come in to make a donation. Sometimes they have told me that my blood was desparetely needed. Until this past week, however, they never told me why!

Since I have O+ Blood (which is the most common blood type in North America and Europe) I never felt as though my blood was particularly in demand. Yes, it is sometimes (mistakenly) referred to as the "universal donor" but what was it about my blood that seemed to merit special phone calls.

Well, it seems that my blood has a sub-category that marks it as CMV-Negative. According to the on-line Dr. Judith Feinberg,

"CMV negative" means you have never been infected with cytomegalovirus. For most people with healthy immune systems, infection with CMV or not is usually of little consequence, but people with damaged or immature (like newborns) immune systems are susceptible to life-threatening CMV infection. You are lucky.

According to the Puget Sound Blood Center, CMV-Negative blood is indicated for

-Premature Infants

-Infants Under 4-Weeks of Age and;

-Patients Requiring Intrauterine Transfusions.

CMV-Negative Blood is also indicated for CMV-Negative patients in the following categories:

-Bone marrow or organ transplant recipients (if the marrow or organ donor is also CMV negative)

-Potential candidates for transplant

-AIDS or HIV infected patients

-Patients who have congenital immune deficiency

-Patients undergoing splenectomy, and

-Pregnant women

Today there was a need for 27 pints of blood for two people (one an infant?) undergoing open heart surgery and another who was having an amputation. Two of these three patients were, I was told, "bleeders." The need for CMV-Negative blood, in combination with my O+ status, made me a Very Important Donor on their list. So, of course, since I haven't given since January, I made a 2:00 pm appointment, took some church work along with me, drove downtown and give them a pint.

Afterwards, the donut they gave me tasted good, but not anywhere near as good as I felt from contributing my small but vital share of the "gift of life."

For a blow-by-blow description (complete with photos) of what it's like to donate a pint of blood you can check out a previous post here.

Afterwards, be sure to schedule an appointment to make a donation yourself. Who knows, your blood may be the exact kind that someone needs in your neighborhood right now!

FRIDAY, APRIL 14, 2006

South Park, Comedy Central, Jesus & Muhammad

On Wednesday evening's episode of South Park, host network Comedy Central censored a depiction of the Muslim Prophet Muhammad but allowed a segment showing Jesus Christ defecating on President Bush and the American flag.

Several conclusions can be reached. I will allow you to choose which one(s) you believe to be true. The answer, of course, could be "all of the above."

1. Comedy Central loves Muhammad and Muslims and hates Jesus Christ and Christians.

2. Comedy Central is scared out of their wits that radical Muslims will kill them if they show an image of Muhammad but know that tolerant and wimpy generally non-violent Christians ("turn the other cheek") will give them a pass.

3. Comedy Central is lead by hypocrites who endorse blatant double-standards when it comes to supporting "free speech" on their network.

4. Many Muslims assert the validity of their faith by responding to their enemies by threatening to kill them while most Christians assert the validity of their faith by responding to their enemies by loving and praying for them.

5. South Park is taking a brave, commendable and controversial stand in defense of free speech

at the expense and embarrassment of their network, Comedy Central.

6. South Park is taking a contemptible and self-righteous stand so as to generate controversy, increase their fan-base, spit in the face of everyone, gain tons of free publicity, make lots of money and fool everyone into thinking that they have done something noble.

As a Christian pastor I must say that I am offended by the depiction of Jesus in this latest episode. I am saddened to think that Christians, our faith, our Lord and our God are considered "fair game" for ridicule on public television.

On the other hand, I am content in the thought that my brothers and sisters in Christ are faithful to our Lord in responding to such insults with non-violence and reasoned debate--even when those who insult us do not show us any respect in retiurn.

Psalm 2:2,4 says,
The kings of the earth take their stand and the rulers gather together against the LORD and against his Anointed One...
The One enthroned in heaven laughs; the Lord scoffs at them.
and Psalm 37:10-13 adds,
A little while, and the wicked will be no more; though you look for them, they will not be found. But the meek will inherit the land and enjoy great peace. The wicked plot against the righteous and gnash their teeth at them; but the Lord laughs at the wicked, for he knows their day is coming.
My God is big enough and grown up enough to take care of himself. I am bound to defend him in both word and in deed but always in a manner consistent with the life and teachings of Christ. In the end, it is God who will judge the earth and take care of the details.

It does not really matter how you or I rate the six points I listed above. The only thing that matters is how God will rate them. He is, after all, the Lord of South Park and Comedy Central as well as Muhammad and his followers.

Oh . . . and you and me, too!

UPDATE: lgf has a copy of the form letter released by Comedy Central in response the flood of complaints they have received over their decision to "censor" the image of Muhammad. The letter proves that threats, intimidation and fear work wonderfully in limiting the freedom of speech. The letter is also a cruel indictment of virtually the entire US media industry. It appears that radical Islamists are dictating what we can and cannot say in the United States. I, for one, am not willing to accept this situation as it stands. The letter includes this statement:
Comedy Central will continue to produce and provide the best comedy available and we will continue to push it right to the edge.
That is to say that, after consultation with their radical Islamist advisors, they will do whatever they are told they can and cannot do.

Is it just me or do you feel a chill?

SATURDAY, APRIL 15, 2006

Easter 2006

A crescent moon illumes the star-struck dome
Of heaven's inverted bowl. Upon a hill
There stands a bloodied cross. The night-air's chill
Embraces all; and Darkness bids Death, "Come!"

While shadows fill the earth with black and grey
The moon has reached her zenith and descends;
A slivered orb whose stolen glory ends
As night withdraws before the coming day.

God's "greater light" has risen from restless sleep;
And Death and Darkness fall beneath the cross
That marks their grave, their final resting place.

'Tis Life that rises with the sun! As deep
Cries out to deep a tomb reveals its loss.
The Son has risen indeed! God's gift of grace!

SUNDAY, APRIL 16, 2006

The Rev. Jesse Jackson One-Ups Jesus

After saving the life a woman about to be stoned for adultery, Jesus commanded her to, "**Go and sin no more**."

In contrast, the Rev. Jesse Jackson apparently does not feel that either truth, sin or repentence ought to get in the way of a good deed.

On the day before Easter Sunday Jackson announced that his PUSH Coalition would be offering the 27-year old unnamed black woman who has accused members of the Duke University Lacrosse Team of raping her (following her performance as a stripper at a off-campus party) a full-tuition scholarship to assist her in completing her studies at North Carolina Central University.

Although Jackson admitted that ***he had not yet spoken to the woman*** he did affirm that his group had pledged to pay for her tuition ***even if her story proves false***.

According to an article by **Associated Press**, Jackson said that the woman should be able to support her two children and pay her tuition without having "to sacrifice her body to make money."

I must say that I can agree with that last sentiment. No woman should "have" to sacrifice her body to make money.

On the other hand I'm not exactly sure why this woman "has" to do this. Nor am I sure who is forcing her to take her clothes off in front of young, rowdy, intoxicated college men in private homes and other unchaperoned locations.

I imagine that the woman "caught in adultery" in John 8:1-11 also had her reasons for doing what she did. Why she "had" to do what she did, however, was not the issue that Jesus confronted her with.

First of all, Jesus accepted that she had committed the sin she had been accused of. He then refused to condemn her for it, effectively forgiving her. He then held her accountable for her future behavior, making a clear distinction between right and wrong.

Jackson, on the other hand, does not appear to consider the matter of "right and wrong" to have any bearing on this case at all. It does not seem to matter to him that, unlike the "woman in adultery" who was charged with a crime, the woman he wants to help is the one who has brought a charge against others.

Jackson says that it does not matter if what she has said is true or not.

Does this mean that, if the charges she has made are false and that the slander and accusations against the Duke University lacrosse team players, the public demonstrations and loss of job prospects, the cancellation of the entire team's lacrosse season, the resignation of their coach and the malicious defamation of Duke University's reputation were all caused by misdirected, mistaken or manufactured purjoritive statements, she is still worthy of being rewarded by a full college scholarship?

If what the woman has said proves to be true, then give her the scholarship.

But, if what she has said proves to have been concocted out of thin air, then let her at the very least confess her sin, accept the responsibility of making some measure of atonement or apology and face the possibility that criminal charges may, in fact, be brought against her instead.

There is no doubt in my mind that at least some members of the Duke University lacrosse team behaved badly. Those guilty of misbehavior other than the charge of rape should be subject to either severe reprimand and/or dismissal from either the lacrosse team (with loss of scholarships, if any) or the university itself. If found guilty of rape then they should be subject to appropriate criminal sentencing according to the law of North Carolina

There is also no doubt in my mind that this 27-year old woman has suffered from physical abuse. Even so, it remains to be seen whether or not she experienced any such abuse from the accused lacrosse players. According to the student's lawyers, the woman arrived at the party already drunk and already showing signs of physical abuse. According to the police records, she was found intoxicated and unconcious in a car following her alleged appearance at the party.

This, in no small way, at the very least calls into question her competency to provide a safe, protective and nurturing environment for her children. Where were her children that night? Is not this a question worthy of investigation by the local child protective services agency?

Don't get me wrong. I want only the best for this woman. It is clear that she needs more help than a college scholarship can provide for her. As a Christian minister, the Rev. Jackson should be the first to understand that her needs are not only physical, but moral and spiritual as well.

Giving her a scholarship without also requiring a supportive confrontation with her concerning the effects of her substance abuse and other self-destructive behaviors that put both herself and her children at risk will miss the point of her primary needs completely.

Jesus knew that the woman he forgave needed to change herself from the inside out.

Jackson apparently believes that he can change his personal "Eliza Doolittle" from the outside in.

Jesus desired the woman to change her behavior.

Jackson, however, appears to have offered her a reward instead.

Jackson's interests clearly revolve around race, economics and political power.

It is worth noting that Jesus renounced all three.

Scripture tells us that Jesus knew what was in the hearts of all he met.

Jackson, on the other hand, would have us believe that he knows the needs and the heart of a young mother in North Carolina without ever having met her or spoken to her.

Personally, given a choice between Jesus and Jackson I would take Jesus every time.

If the young woman caught up in this scandal in North Carolina knows what is good for *her* (and, unfortunately, there is no clear evidence that she does) she will do the same.

TUESDAY, APRIL 18, 2006

Western Civilization's Last Stand In Europe

A new, prophetic, troubling and convincing analysis of the growing confrontation between Muslim immigrants (including Islamist radicalism) and the "indigenous" representatives of Western European culture (by which I mean those we have commonly referred to as "the Danes" or "the French" or "the Germans" or "the British" etc.). The post, entitled "The Fall of France and the Multicultural World War" was written by the Norwegian blogger Fjordman and posted at The Gates of Vienna.

Like my previous posts from last January (Mark Steyn Predicts the Collapse of "The West"--Sadly, I Agree) and April of last year (Is Europe As We Have Known It Beginning To Disintegrate?) Fjordman provides several likely scenarios that may emerge from the "Clash of Civilizations" in Europe.

These scenarios range from "Eurabia" wherein Europe slowly capitulates to Muslim domination, "Global War" wherein violent civil war erupts like falling dominoes in one nation after another against Islamist forces, beginning in Europe and spreading across the globe (with millions of deaths and the fragmentation of the world into Muslim-held and non-Muslim held territory . . . Potentially leading to the mass expulsion of Muslims from non-Muslim areas and vice-versa) or "Western Resurgence" wherein the majority population of Europe takes the lead in reclaiming their cultural heritage and takes a bold stand against the growing Islamist threats from within and without.

Personally, I believe that the liberal/socialist European dream (or should I say, "religion") is so deeply ingrained that it will be virtually impossible for any current Continental political party to have either the historical insight, the philosophical/moral foundation or the political fortitude to take the radical actions that would be necessary to mitigate the looming catastrophe.

The "common sense" philosophy of the United States (with its strong Judeo/Christian moral foundation) and Canada (with its liberal leadership but still reasonable majority population) will be far more likely to take strong and prudent positions to forestall such a crisis in North America. North America has the additional advantage of having our largest immigrant labor force comprised of Latin Americans who carry at least some form of Roman Catholic or Protestant Christian faith and world view along with them. (Unlike Europe whose immigrant

Please take the time to read Fjordman's post and, if you have not done so already, follow the links to my previous posts as well as Mark Steyn's. Current events seem to be supportive of our fears and warnings.

And don't forget to fall on your knees and to pray for peace . . . the kind that only the one true God, the Lord of history, can provide.

Easter Lily

The beauty of Easter and celebration of the Resurrection of Jesus Christ continues at my home with the help of the Easter Lily that we shared during Sunday's worship service. My wife and I actually donated two lilies, one in memory of her mother and one in memory of my father. We only brought one lily home afterwards but it is a beauty and serves as a good reminder of the hope we share with our parents in the good news of God's saving love in Jesus Christ.

In any case, I hope you enjoy the photo while I still get to enjoy the real thing!

Christ is risen! Christ is risen indeed! Alleluia!

Easter Sermons

Each year I preach two different sermons on Easter Sunday morning, one for the Sunrise service and the other at our normal worship hour at 9:00 am. If you would like to read them you can by clicking on the links below.

"Very Early In the Morning"
and
"Peter, John & the Great Easter Race"

If you would like to listen to the second one you can find it in an MP3 file at our church web page http://mpc-hi.org/mpc-online